D0485990

Blank
Darkness

Christopher L. Miller

Blank Darkness

Africanist Discourse in French

The University of Chicago Press
Chicago and London

CHRISTOPHER L. MILLER is assistant
professor of French and of Afro-American
Studies at Yale University.

The University of Chicago Press, Chicago 60637
The University of Chicago Press, Ltd., London

© 1985 by The University of Chicago
All rights reserved. Published 1985
Printed in the United States of America

94 93 92 91 90 89 88 87 86 85   5 4 3 2 1

Library of Congress Cataloging in Publication Data
Miller, Christopher, L., 1953–
   Blank darkness.

   Bibliography: p.
   Includes index.
   1.   French literature—History and criticism.
2.   Africa in literature.   I.   Title.
PQ145.7.A35M55   1985   840′.9′96   85-1157

ISBN 0-226-52621-6 (cloth)
ISBN 0-226-52622-4 (paper)

To my parents

Contents

List of Illustrations

Preface

The idea that Europe is an idea is one whose time has come. But to reach back to the point of its origin is not an easy task. A more feasible project is to observe Europe in the act of reaching back or out toward an idea of what Europe is not: the "primitive," the "Orient," "Africa." These too are concepts whose dependence on ideology rather than pure fact needs to be exposed. Since the dawn of Western literature in Homer, there has been the constant, ambivalent profile of a certain non-Western object, variously called "Ethiopia," "Libya," or "Africa." The role of that profile in French literature is the object of this study.

Most scholars have defined the problem as that of an "image"; I have chosen the term "discourse," to place more emphasis on the linguistic than the visual, although there are problems with the term, which I will discuss. My treatment of the subject will be literary, aimed at a linguistic rather than a natural object; but it will necessarily be involved, like the discourse it describes, in the "zone of interferences" between strict literary theory and proper history, for I believe that a mutual contamination between the two is more interesting than a strict adherence to either. This may prove dissatisfying to partisans of both camps. In fact, this study is framed by an unresolvable tension between a pseudo-object projected onto the void and a real object that bears the same name: Africa.

It will be evident that the conception of this study follows on the work of Edward Said and his *Orientalism,* which I will discuss presently. Léon-François Hoffmann's *Le Nègre romantique,* with its excellent bibliography, formed the basis of my research. Roger Mercier's *L'Afrique noire dans la littérature française,* Léon Fanoudh-Siefer's *Le Mythe du nègre,* and William Cohen's *The French Encounter with Africans* all provided useful information. I also profited from works on adjacent topics whose intellectual caliber enhanced their relevance: David Brion Davis' *The Problem of Slavery in Western Culture,* Winthrop Jordan's *White over Black,* and Philip D. Curtin's *The Image of Africa.* All translations are my own, except where otherwise noted.

I am indebted to Barbara Johnson, who encouraged this project from its inception. I am grateful to Henry Louis Gates, who directed the "Idea of Blackness" research project in which I participated, and to the Menil Foundation, which funded the project; without their support the materials for this study would have been much poorer. Ladislas Bugner, of the Menil Foundation, was helpful during my year in Paris, as were Jean Devisse and Michèle Duchet. Barbara McCorkle, of the Sterling Library, helped me find geographical sources. I was aided by advice from José Piedra, Elizabeth Archibald, Peter Brooks, Jacques Derrida, and Paul de Man. The manuscript benefited from readings by Ross Chambers and James Olney, who provided welcome support and guidance. David Civali patiently helped with the proofreading. My friends Jeff Humphries, Mary Rice, and Michèle Cone-Chang provided both intellectual support and relief from it.

I gratefully acknowledge the following permissions: from the Sterling Memorial Library, Yale University, for the engravings from Eugène Roger, François Levaillant, and for the D'Anville map; from the Beinecke Rare Book and Manuscript Library, Yale University, for quotations from the manuscript of Conrad's *Heart of Darkness;* from the University of Michigan Library for the engraving from Hugo's *Bug-Jargal;* from Nico Israel for the reproduction of a map from Münster's *Geographia.*

Chapter 7, on "Dis-Figuring Narrative," appeared in an earlier version in the Winter 1983 issue of *L'Esprit créateur;* I am grateful for permission to reprint.

The following works (or portions of works) by Baudelaire are reproduced by permission of Editions Gallimard, Paris: from *Les Fleurs du mal,* "Obsession," "A une dame créole," "Sed non satiata," and portions of "Le Cygne." From *Le Spleen de Paris,* "La Belle Dorothée." All are published in the Bibliothèque de la Pléiade edition of Baudelaire's *Oeuvres complètes.* Copyright © 1975 Editions Gallimard, Paris.

The following works (or portions of works) by Rimbaud are reproduced by permission of Editions Gallimard, Paris: "Démocratie," from *Illuminations;* "Mauvais sang," from *Une saison en enfer;* and a letter from Isabelle Rimbaud to Paterne Berrichon, from *Correspondance,* all published in the Bibliothèque de la Pléiade edition of Rimbaud's *Oeuvres complètes.* Copyright © 1972 Editions Gallimard, Paris.

Part One

Introduction

Une première pensée apparaît. L'idée de culture, d'intelligence,
d'oeuvres magistrales est pour nous dans une relation très
ancienne,—tellement ancienne que nous remontons rarement
jusqu'à elle,—avec l'idée d'Europe. . . .
    Tout est venu à l'Europe et tout en est venu. Ou presque tout.
                —Paul Valéry, "La Crise de l'esprit" (1919)

On n'est pas obligé de rendre raison d'une chose où il n'y en a
point.
        —Charles de Brosses, *Du Culte des dieux fétiches* (1760)

Curiously enough, it seems to be only in describing a mode of
language which does not mean what it says that one can
actually say what one means.
        —Paul de Man, "The Rhetoric of Temporality" (1969)

1

"Telle figure que l'on veut":
Deriving a Discourse

L'Africain paroît être une machine qui se monte & se démonte
par ressorts, semblable à une cire molle, à qui l'on fait prendre
telle figure que l'on veut.

—Abbé Demanet,
Nouvelle Histoire de l'Afrique françoise (1767)

A Discourse with Tails

Ex Africa semper aliquid novi.

—Pliny

In the middle of the nineteenth century a book about Africa was published
in France. It purported to contain "information" and was written in a style
of scientistic precision. The title was *Renseignements sur l'Afrique centrale
et sur une nation de Niam-Niam ou "hommes à queues" qui s'y trouverait,
d'après les nègres du Soudan.*[1] Many centuries after Herodotus had reported
that Africa was filled with "dog-eared men, and the headless that have eyes
in their chests," when a discourse of purified realism called science had
supposedly distinguished itself from fable, how was this possible?

The Niam-Niam question was hotly debated in the scientific community of
Paris. The Société de Géographie de Paris published an article by the same
author, Francis de Castelnau, "Sur les Niam-Niam ou hommes à queues,"[2]
and the Académie des Sciences and the Société Orientale were also caught
up in the controversy.[3] This singular error was, however, not new: a Dutchman
"named Struys reported in 1677 having seen a black man with a tail one foot
long."[4] Castelnau himself makes no claim to direct experience, yet he musters

1. Francis de Castelnau, *Renseignements sur l'Afrique centrale . . .* (Paris: P. Bertrand,
1851). The full title, translated, reads: "Information on Central Africa, and on a nation of Niam-
Niams or 'men with tails' who are said to live there, according to the Negroes of the Sudan."
2. *Bulletin de la Société de Géographie* 4th ser. 2 (1851).
3. William B. Cohen, *The French Encounter with Africans* (Bloomington: Indiana University
Press, 1980), p. 242.
4. Larousse, *Grand Dictionnaire Encyclopédique du XIXe siècle*, article "Niam-Niam."

a great semblance of exactitude in "information that I have been able to obtain from Negro slaves from Bahia . . . on sections of this vast continent that remain entirely unknown" (p. 5). The reporter is a slave named Manuel, who had participated in a raid of Hausas into the country of the "Niam-Niams":

> Ils avaient tous des queues d'environ quarante centimètres de long et qui pouvaient en avoir de deux à trois de diamètre; cet organe est lisse; parmi les cadavres se trouvaient ceux de plusieurs femmes qui étaient conformées de la même manière; du reste ces gens étaient semblables aux autres nègres; ils étaient absolument nus. . . . Manuel faisait partie de l'avant-garde et a vu tuer beaucoup de ces gens; il a examiné les cadavres, mesuré les queues, et il ne peut concevoir aucun doute relativement à leur existence. [P. 15]

> They all had tails, about forty centimeters long and perhaps two or three in diameter; this organ is smooth; among the cadavers there were those of many women who were formed in the same fashion; aside from this, they were the same as the other Negroes; they were absolutely naked . . . . Manuel was in the advance party and saw many of these people killed; he examined the cadavers, measured the tails, and he can conceive of no doubt concerning their existence.

Obviously, there were no such men with tails, only men who used "leather ornaments" *representative* of tails.[5] The error, and its literalistic acceptance in Europe, reveal underlying assumptions about Africa, which, as we shall see, reach back to Antiquity: Africa produces monsters. But the adage says "always something new," and, not long before Castelnau's Niam-Niams appeared, Charles-Antoine Pigault-Lebrun had written "Le Blanc et le noir," with a preface that has a very different idea of what Africans might be like:

> Sur les bords du Niger, les femmes sont presque toutes belles par la justesse des proportions. Modestes, tendres et fidèles, un air d'innocence règne dans leurs regards, et annonce leur timidité. Leur accent est extrèmement doux; leurs noms seuls en indiquent le charme: Zélia, Calipso, Fanni, Zamé. Les hommes ont la taille avantageuse, la peau d'un noir d'ébène, les traits et la physionomie agréables. L'habitude de faire la guerre aux bêtes féroces leur donne une contenance noble.[6]

5. See ibid. See also A. J. N. Tremearne, *The Tailed Head-Hunters of Nigeria* (London: Seeley, Service, 1912), where the tails are described as ornaments worn on the back, and a photograph of them is provided (p. 92).
6. *Oeuvres complètes* (Paris: J. N. Barba, 1822), 11:7.

On the banks of the Niger, the women are almost all beautiful in the exactness of their proportions. Modest, tender, and faithful, an air of innocence rules their glance and reveals their timidity. Their accent is extremely sweet; their names alone indicate the charm: Zélia, Calipso, Fanni, Zamé. The men are advantageously built, with ebony-black skin and pleasant features and aspect. The habit of making war against wild beasts gives them a noble countenance.

The difference in attitudes cannot be explained by a separation of thirty years or by the fact that this passage was taken from the Abbé Raynal's *Histoire des deux Indes* of 1770.[7] Throughout the history of Africanist writing there is a striking tendency toward dual, polarized evaluations, which are often too hastily ascribed to this or that historical trend. Africa has been made to bear a double burden, of monstrousness *and* nobility, all imposed by a deeper condition of difference and instability (Pliny's "newness").

The result is a European discourse at odds with itself. Castelnau's claim to science brings him, with each argument he advances, farther and farther beyond anything he can demonstrate, and, as fable and realism melt together, the reading process becomes more difficult. The gesture of reaching out to the most unknown part of the world and bringing it back as language—the process we will be analyzing in this study—ultimately brings Europe face to face with nothing but itself, with the problems its own discourse imposes. Thus Pigault-Lebrun takes us to the banks of the Niger to introduce us to women named "Calipso" or "Fanni," creatures of European origin, fulfilling European desires.

This is not an African problem but an "Africanist" one, born and nurtured in Europe of European ideas and concerns. The paper reality of Africanist objects must be sharply distinguished from the reality, paper or not, of Africa itself. Since any Western attempt to understand the latter must come to grips

7. Abbé G. T. Raynal, *Histoire philosophique et politique des établissements et du commerce des Européens dans les Deux Indes* (Paris: Amable Costes, 1820), 6:32–33: "Sur les bords du Niger, les femmes sont presque toutes belles, si ce n'est pas la couleur, c'est la justesse des proportions qui fait la beauté: modestes, tendres et fidèles, un air d'innocence règne dans leurs regards, et leur langage se sent de leur timidité. Les noms de Zilia, de Calipso, de Fanni, de Zamé, qui semblent des noms de volupté, se prononcent avec une inflexion de voix dont nos organes ne sauraient rendre la mollesse et la douceur. Les hommes ont la taille avantageuse, la peau d'un noir d'ébène, les traits et la physionomie agréables. L'habitude de dompter les chevaux et de faire la guerre aux bêtes féroces leur donne une contenance noble." Piguault-Lebrun begins his preface by saying, "J'ai lu Raynal, et j'ai écrit cet ouvrage," and he offers "quelques détails, extraits de cette histoire"; but one is surprised to find that those "details" are Raynal's words themselves, without quotation marks. Repetition, quotation, and plagiarism, as we shall see, are all part of the Africanist tradition in European writing. See Cohen, *The French Encounter,* pp. 17–18. Cf. Michèle Duchet, *Anthropologie et histoire au siècle des lumières* (Paris: Maspéro, 1971), p. 81: "les fables les plus absurdes . . . des faiseurs de recueils, qui les colportaient sans vergogne, en se copiant les uns les autres."

with the ways in which European discourse ineluctably inscribes and blocks such an understanding, I have chosen to focus on the former. The question I will ask is not what is different about Africa to make it appear in a certain fashion but what is different about a certain European discourse when it produces an object aberrant to the system that created it. The pages that follow are thus a study not of Africa but of the conditions within certain French and other European utterances that give rise to that peculiar empty profile called "Africa." But one must not assume that one knows those contours, that the object preexists analysis. For this reason I find it necessary to start as if from zero, with the most basic of terms, to see how it all comes to pass.

Names for a Distance

Toute la terre est couverte de nations dont nous ne connaissons que les *noms*.
—Rousseau

Beside [Asia], Africa looks like a shapeless, uncouth giant. A flat cake without a form, vast and amorphous.
—Leo Frobenius

Utterances on Africa tend to be hints rather than statements, hearsay rather than direct evidence, allegory rather than realism. Millennia before Conrad's "unreadable report" in *Heart of Darkness,* a tradition without a beginning had been established and perpetuated. Texts on Africa were severely limited in number until the nineteenth century and tended to repeat each other in a sort of cannibalistic, plagiarizing intertextuality. Pliny repeats Herodotus, who repeats Homer, just as later French and English writers will copy each other and even copy the Ancients. Thus the status of these utterances: ideas received from always anterior sources, which cannot be located; hearsay from "one who has witnessed" but remains absent; hints, rumors, and reports, which frustrate the reading process. Names for Africa and parts of Africa—those that come from Europe—tend to follow this pattern and to have a peculiarly tenuous relationship both with the thing they describe and with their own etymologies.

It was relatively recently that "Africa" came to be the sole representative of a single continent, differentiated and circumscribed. Although it has been claimed that the Ancients circumnavigated Africa,[8] the contours of the continent remained unknown to literate geography. Some versions of Ptolemy's geography ended in the south with the frank label "terra incognita"; others, such as Sebastian Münster's *Geographia* of 1540, chose to fill in the blank unknown with myths and speculations (see figure 1). As late as 1508 the land

8. Catherine Coquery, *La Découverte de l'Afrique* (Paris: R. Juilliard, 1965), passim.

Figure 1. Sebastian Münster's map of Africa, from his *Geographia* of 1540 (Amsterdam: Theatrum Orbis Terrarum, 1966). Reproduced by permission of Nico Israel. This map shows multiple uses of the word "Africa." Note "Africa" in the northern littoral as opposed to its use in the title as well as in the labeling of the southern tip of the continent as "Africae extremitas." "Africa" is both the part and the whole, and the whole is connected to "Seylam" in the East.

mass to the south bore no label "Africa."[9] A single name for the continent
as a whole was problematical, and names for its parts floated inconsistently
for ages. Names such as Ethiopia, Africa, Niger, Sudan, Nigritia, Libya,
Guinea, etc., have had a slippery history of application to places, and interpreters of these names tend to see in them thematic content that is unexpected
in place-names.

   Ethiopia would appear to be the oldest Western name for Africa; by tradition, "Ethiopia" and "Libya" are Greek terms, "Africa" is Roman. The
applicability of "Ethiopia" to the whole of the continent and its parts is a
question that has been dealt with elsewhere;[10] the role of the word in signification is relevant here. "Ethiopia," according to the *Shorter Oxford English
Dictionary*, is commonly believed to be from αἴθειν, "to burn" + ὤψ,
"face," and to mean primarily "burnt-face." The place is thus defined by
its people and by the single characteristic that sets them off from the Greek
speaker, the darkness of their skin. For everyone, "Aethiops" seemed to refer
exclusively to Black Africans (Devisse, *L'Image du noir*, p. 53). Fitzgerald
translates "Ethiopians" as "the sun-burnt races,"[11] and the addition of the
sun is not gratuitous, for it is understood as that which can burn a face black.
Man, Ethiopian man, is the locus where the light of the sun becomes darkness.
From the moment "Ethiopia" is spoken, darkness and its cause, light, are
posited together. I will return to the "idea" of darkness in discussing Homer;
for the moment it suffices to note the coincidental positing of darkness *with*
light in this etymology: the two are given at once and are counterparts to each
other.

   Place-names, anyone who has read Proust knows, are as charged with
significance as any words can be; yet their absence from dictionaries and
relegation to encyclopedias (when the two genres separated) shows the purely
referential status they are given. A map is all that is needed to "define" a
place-name. But if the world "is filled," as Rousseau wrote, "with countries
of which we know only the names," what kind of knowledge is that? Is a
name that which one "calls oneself," as in French *(je m'appelle . . .)* or
that which one is named by the outside world (my name is . . . ; I am
called . . .)? Names such as Ethiopia and Sudan are evidently the inventions
of outsiders, of lighter complexion, who named the place in relation to them-

   9. On Ptolemy and the status of "Africa," see R. V. Tooley et al., *History of Cartography*
(London: Thames & Hudson, 1968), p. 51.
   10. "Ethiopia" had late applications to the entire continent. Editions of Ptolemy as late as
1540 labeled the whole continent as "Aethiopia," whereas "Africa" was only the region around
Carthage. A chart of 1689 shows the South Atlantic as the *Océan Ethiopien* (Tooley, *History of
Cartography*, p. 51). On applications of "Ethiopian" to real peoples, see Frank Snowden, *Blacks
in Antiquity* (Cambridge, Mass.: Belknap Press of Harvard University, 1970), preface. See also
Jean Devisse, "De la menace démoniaque à l'incarnation de la sainteté," in *L'Image du noir
dans l'art occidental* (Paris: Bibliothèque des Arts, 1979), 2:47–49 (henceforth cited as *L'Image
du noir)*.
   11. *The Odyssey*, trans. Robert Fitzgerald (New York: Doubleday, 1963), p. 2.

selves. By doing so, they attached a kind of significance to that which would normally have none.

We have already seen that, when etymologies are proposed, significance is spun around the referential core of the word. Thus "Ethiopia" already bespeaks a white subjectivity manipulating tropes, opening the door to significance. Such is also the case with "Niger." Recent scholarship claims that this name was originally *Nigeir,* a wholly unrelated word coming from a number of possible African languages.[12] *Nigeir* means "river": the simplest possible of designations between word and thing. It was only through a misreading of this word by Latin-based Europeans that "darkness" entered. The phonological resemblance of *nigeir* to *niger* replaced "river" with "black" in such a way that Europe can say, "The natives call it Black." The role of the name thus moves away from a simple, immanent river/river to a "significant" river/idea-of-blackness: difference and signification intervene by the arrival of this gap between word and thing. The scene depicted here between the lines is a familiar one in colonial mythology: the colonizer asks the colonized, "What is this?" and misinterprets the reply. In the case of the Niger River and the Zaïre as well, the answer was simply "Water!" which was then construed as a proper noun. In reply to "Who are you?"— "Bantu," i.e., "people."

The replies would at first appear to be a primally innocent sort of utterance, free of the difference between common and proper nouns, as if this were a lost paradise where word and thing coexisted harmoniously, water being only and everywhere water. But this simplicity is a differential, bicultural phenomenon, imposed by the colonizer's question. For the elicited response does not tell all that the colonized knows, of other rivers, other peoples. The moment of innocent, immanent naming occurs only through the prism of European perception. The difference between the discourse of the European and that of the "native" *projects* an innocence onto the latter, a world where there is no difference between common and proper nouns.

The word "Sudan" has been used since well before the eighth century A.D. in application to everything south of the Mediterranean littoral and north of the Congo Basin. One who says "Sudan"—which means "the blacks" in Arabic, just as "Ethiopia," in Greek, includes blackness in its meaning— implies a "white" point of view. The Moslem traveler-writer Ibn Battuta (1307–77), one of the very first reporters on the "Sudan," cast the problem

12. C. K. Meek, "The Niger and the Classics: The History of a Name," *Journal of African History* 1, no. 1 (1960): "Ptolemy's use of the words Geir and Nigeir suggest that these are not native titles for particular rivers, but generic words for river . . . . Dr. Barth seems to have been of this opinion when he records that east of Timbuktu the Niger was called Eghirreu. This is merely the Temashight (or Tuareg) term for any river. Duvéyrier . . . declared some years later that Gir, Ger, Niger and Nigris of the ancient geographers were all identical words representing the Berber or Libyan ger, guir and djir = running stream . . . ; I have found the same root among a number of other Nigerian tribes" (p. 14).

clearly in terms of white and black, self and other, civilized and savage. He observes, "The pagans hadn't eaten him [a Moslem] solely because of his white color. They say that eating a White man is unsafe because he isn't ripe; according to them, only the Black man is ripe."[13]

The etymologies of Africanist names would thus seem to be drawn toward meanings of darkness and otherness. This is evident with words whose etymologies and language of origin are established—Ethiopia in Greek, Sudan in Arabic—but it is far more complicated with the word "Africa" itself.

By convention, the word is Latin. But the search for its origin beyond the Romans leads to a group of divergent hypotheses. Many sources agree that the Romans acquired the word from the Carthaginians. Again the colonial interrogation ("What is this?"—"Africa"), but this time the original meaning is lacking. "Africa" originally applied only to the region around Carthage, but by synecdoche it came to represent the entire continent. The progress of the word in Western languages is that of a movement from Africa "proper" to Africa as a whole, inserting a difference where before there was none. Diderot's *Encyclopédie* distinguishes between "Africa *proper* or Little Africa" surrounding Carthage, and Africa in general.[14] The movement away from the proper coincided with the insertion of the word in European language and discourse. From this moment on "Africa" will be a trope—a part for a whole or a whole for a part—recounting a colonial history, designating a difference.

The answer to this would be an adjournment back to an authentic source, a simple designation within the confines of a local language, on the model of "nigeir." But the Carthaginians may have handed the Romans a purely insignificant place-name, devoid of meaning in any language, "Africa" meaning only "that place called 'Africa.'" This, however, cannot prevent etymologies from being produced, among which I have found ten different hypotheses:

—"Africa" may have been "derived from the ethnic designation of some tribe in the neighborhood of Carthage whose name signified 'The Wanderers'"; the word is "probably Punic, at all events Semitic" (Isaac Taylor).[15]

—It may mean the "South Land" (Taylor).

—"Its name is a mystery; it is supposed to be derived from Afrigah, which word, in the ancient Phoenician, is said to have meant colony;

13. Ibn Battuta, *Textes et documents relatifs à l'histoire de l'Afrique*, trans. R. Mauny et al. (Dakar, 1966), p. 68.

14. Diderot et al., *Encyclopédie* (Geneva: J. L. Pellet, 1778), 1:596.

15. Isaac Taylor, *Words and Places* (London: Macmillan, 1864), p. 84.

the name given by the founders of Carthage to their territory, having spread to the whole continent" *(New American Cyclopaedia)*.[16]

—*Aphar* in Hebrew, meaning "dust" (Diderot, *Encyclopédie*).

—The grandson of Abraham and Keturah, about whom almost nothing is written, was named "Ophres" or "Epher" (Genesis 25:1–4) (Diderot).

—"Ou bien l'Afrique a esté nommée de ceste particule α et φρίκη qui signifie froid, comme estant sans aucune froidure" ("Or else Africa was named from the particle α and φρίκη, which means cold, as being without any cold" [Thévet].)[17] Others cite this possibility of the Greek *"aphrike* (without cold)" *(Encyclopedia Britannica).*[18]

—"De Afer, lequel comme nous lisons ès histoires Grecques et Latines, pour l'avoir subiugée, y a regné, et faict appeller de son nom: car auparauant elle s'appelloit Libye" ("From Afer, who as we read in Greek and Latin histories, subjugated and reigned over it, and had it named after himself" [Thévet]). Similarly: "Lybie was so named of *Lybia,* the daughter of Epaphus, and Affrick of *Afer* the Sonne of *Hercules* the Lybian" (Gaius Julius Solinus).[19]

—"Perhaps from the Latin *aprica* (sunny)" *(Encyclopedia Britannica).*

—The Arabic word for ear of corn, *phérick* (Diderot).

—*Faraca* in Arabic means "it has separated," and has been cited as the root of "Ifrichia" or Africa (Leo Africanus).[20]

The diversity of meanings should tell us something about the nature of this etymology: it appears to mean whatever one wants, in the language one wants. European researchers find that the Arabic place-name *Ifriqiyah* is apparently a "transliteration of Africa" *(Encyclopedia Britannica),* a Roman word; those of Islamic schooling find the original meaning of the word in Arabic, from which the Latin would be only a derivative.[21]

16. *New American Cyclopaedia* (New York: Appleton, 1858), 1:169.

17. André Thévet, *Les Singularitez de la France Antarctique* (Paris: Maisonneuve, 1878), p. 11.

18. *New Encyclopedia Britannica* (Chicago: Encyclopedia Britannica, 1974), 1:177.

19. Julius Solinus Polyhistor, *The Excellent and pleasant worke of Iulius Solinus Polyhistor,* trans. A. Golding (London: Th. Hacket, 1587), chap. 36.

20. Leo Africanus, *Description de l'Afrique,* trans. A. Epaulard (Paris: Librairie d'Amérique et d'Orient, 1956), p. 3.

21. "L'Afrique est appelée en arabe Ifrichia, du mot faraca qui a le sens du mot latin *separavit"* (ibid.).

There appear to be three steps in the construction of these etymologies. First a purely phonological link is made to a word *(phérick, faraca, aphrika, aprica)* in the language that the writer sees as most authentic. By this choice of word and language, restrictions are imposed: the political background is set for the story of a conquest of Africa (by the Romans, by Afer, etc.). The second step, common to all these etymologies, is the oppositional function of language. By calling the place "dusty, sunny, without cold, southern," a comparison is inevitably made to places that are colder, more northern, etc. Thereby another subjectivity is at work, capable of comparing the two and dominating. The name contains and circumscribes Africa as a distinct whole, and this is possible only from the outside. The outside in effect calls the inside into being by naming it. Thus to compare Africa's shape to an ear of corn, the usual understanding of this root, is to perceive it as a whole from the outside and inscribe it in a misinformed geography. This second step is the intervention of the outside, of alterity, between the word and the thing, in the very process by which the thing becomes a thing. This step is not exclusively Africanist: the etymologies of America, of Asia ("land of the rising sun," "bright land"),[22] and even of Europe itself remain at this level.

The third step, common to only some of the etymologies of "Africa," takes this negative, differentiating function of the word and allegorizes it in stories of exile and subjugation. "Colony," "Afer," and "It has separated" are attached to significant events in the mind of the etymologist, who reads into the word "Africa" the story of a separation. Meanings such as *sunny* or *dusty* impose a difference; but "colony" goes beyond this by thematizing difference itself. "Colony" as an etymology is a political allegory of the word's imposition on a passive territory. The "founders of Carthage" allegorize the role of any speaker of the word "Africa": in both cases there is containment, subjugation, and negation of the object at the same moment that the object is brought into being. The role of Afer is the same. But the most interesting etymology, with the most far-reaching consequences, is that of Leo Africanus.

The importance of the *Description of Africa* is that is is located precisely on the cusp between Europe and Islam: El-Hasan ben Mohammed el-Wazzān ez-Zayyāti, as he was first named, was born in a Grenada newly captured by Ferdinand and Isabel, and he spent his young life traveling the Moslem world, even into the "Land of the Blacks" to Timbuktoo.[23] Taken prisoner on the high seas by an Italian corsair, he was presented to Pope Leo X, was catechized and baptized by the pope's own hand with the name Johannis Leo de Medici, and became known to posterity as Leo Africanus. His *Description of Africa* appeared in 1550 and effectively disseminated throughout Europe the knowl-

22. J. J. Egli, *Nomina geographica* (Leipzig: F. Brandstetter, 1892), p. 36.
23. A. Epaulard, introduction to Leo, *Description de l'Afrique,* pp. v–xii.

edge of Black Africa that Muslim traders had possessed for centuries. It was immediately translated from Italian into French and English.[24] His text is a voice out of the "Orient" and the Occident at the same time, and in Leo's opening paragraph some idea comes through of what Africa is for both worlds:

> Africa is called in Arabic Ifrichia, from the word *faraca,* which has the meaning of the Latin word *separavit* ["it has separated"]. There are two opinions on the origin of this label. The first is based on the fact that this part of the world is separated from Europe and from a part of Asia by the Mediterranean. The second is that this name derives from Ifricos, king of Yemen [Arabia Felix], who was the *first to come and inhabit it.* This king, defeated in battle and driven out by the kings of Assyria, *could not return to his kingdom;* he quickly crossed the Nile and, pursuing a westward course, he did not stop until he had reached the area around Carthage. This is why the Arabs consider as Africa almost nothing but that area around Carthage, and give to Africa as a whole the name of Occident *[Maghreb].* [Emphasis mine]

This may be the most allegorical of all the etymologies: the first phonological step back to the Arabic *faraca,* while "wrong" according to every other source, hastily imposes a meaning that consists of pure otherness. The second and third steps I described are thus accomplished at once. "Africa" has no native source and so did not exist before its definition as an other in relation to Europe and Asia. Leo's *faraca* posits a primal sundering as the origin of "Africa" and at the same time reads and thematizes that difference. "Africa," in the stories in which it is made to tell about "its own" past as a word, recounting conquest and subjugation, is created as an allegory of inauthenticity, a tale of primordial colonialism, "bound to violence."

In the first "opinion" the separation remains geographical; there is only to note that the separation is tripartite, with Africa as distinct from the Islamic East as it is from Europe. But in the second "opinion" a sort of real history is proposed, in which it becomes evident that the status of Africa was that of a void and a nothingness until the arrival of an outsider. King Ifricos, an exile from the East, "was the first to come and inhabit" Africa. Africa was a blank slate on which the name of the firstcomer would be forever inscribed. This is in the nature of a nullity, which will become familiar in readings to follow: Africa is conceived of as void and unformed prior to its investment with shape and being by the Christian or Islamic outside. In the story of Ifricos, the Nile River becomes the boundary betwen named and nameless, home and exile, constituted whole and nullity. We will continue the reading of Leo in the next section.

24. English translation, 1600; French translation, by Jean Temporal, c. 1550.

All words are merely representations of something that is missing, and all etymologies impose a temporal difference. But with "dusty," "sunny," or "land of the rising sun," it is the reader who must realize the differential logic at work and see that an outside point of view is implied. With etymologies such as "colony" or "it has separated," however, difference is thematized, made explicit, and recounted as a real, a historical, phenomenon: these etymologies I would call allegorical. The conjunction of realism and allegory—a subject to which I shall return—is a peculiarly Africanist form of discourse.

Orientalism and Africa

Les Africains sont chrétiens, mahométans ou idolâtres.
—*Larousse du XIXe siècle*

Il n'y a pas d'Autre de l'Autre.

—Jacques Lacan

"Africanism" does not have the function in English that would be convenient for this study: that of denoting things said about Africa, or denoting the image of Africa, in European writing. The dictionaries say that an "Africanism" is a retention of African speech patterns, style, or performance by Latin authors and, currently, by Afro-Americans or other emigrant descendants or that it represents political advocacy of African independence. The science of the study of Africa has no name as such in English, although *Africanisme* in French is recognized as the "group of human sciences applied to the study of Africa" *(Trésor de la langue française)* and is therefore somewhat opposable to a term such as "Orientalism." The study of Africa is a poor relation, lexically and institutionally, to the long-prestigious and well-endowed study of the "Orient."

The comparison of these two discourses as discourses thus begins, appropriately, with a certain disharmony. Orientalism was recognized by its authors, in its heyday in the nineteenth century, as a category of thought and a principle of organization—this in spite of, or perhaps due to, the fact that the "Orient" was a purely artificial construct, based rhetorically more on *direction* than location: "East," but how far East? Its relativism is explicit, whereas that of "Africa" has been forgotten. Africa is "real," the "Orient" was made up. But I hope to have demonstrated, by analyzing the etymologies of "Africa," that this seemingly referential term is as loaded with rhetorical agendas as the obviously fictive "Orient." It will be my aim to collapse the distinction between geography and willful myth and to prove that a discourse has always surrounded the "real" term Africa. Africanist discourse—which I should not call "Africanism"—consists of a series of repeated rhetorical moves, remarkably similar through the ages, which set it apart from Orientalism. Of course there is considerable overlapping in these two points of view on the "Other," but I believe the distinction to be deeply influential.

First, what is "Orientalism"? Edward Said's important recent study, *Orientalism*, analyzed the way in which such a term, conceived as a description of the world, generates concepts and categorizes thought until it becomes a massive screen between subject and object. From that moment on, perception is determined by Orientalism rather than Orientalism's being determined by perception. Said's book is part of a crucial reappraisal of European knowledge, possible only when the categories of thought—all "isms" and their attendant classifications—are recognized as arbitrary judgments made by discourse rather than real distinctions in the world. Said writes, "It is enough for 'us' to set up these arbitrary boundaries in our minds; 'they' become 'they' accordingly, and both their territory and their mentality are designated as different from 'ours.' "[25]

But within that general project of reappraisal, there is more than one "they" to be analyzed, more than one discourse of otherness to be extricated from its elaborate guise of realism. According to Said's work, what is the determining mode of Orientalism? The Orient is a negative for Europe, conforming to the profile of what Europe thinks Europe is *not;* the opposition is therefore diametrical, producing a single, symmetrical Other. That Other always has a separate identity of its own, an "inferior" culture but a culture nonetheless—namely, Islam. The negativity of Orientalism is that of a fully constituted nonself. To explore Arabia, the European can try to adopt that other identity, "becoming an Oriental," "perhaps disguised as an Indian Muslim doctor," as did Sir Richard Burton. Said sees Burton as the most successful of Orientalists because "he knew that the Orient in general and Islam in particular were systems of information, behavior and belief, that to be an Oriental or a Muslim was to know certain things in a certain way" (p. 195). Said describes Orientalism as "all aggression, activity, judgment, will-to-truth and knowledge" (p. 204), as a discourse of acquisition and domestication. The vocabulary is that of grammars, dictionaries, maps, museums, codes, and classifications, within which "the Orient is all absence, whereas one feels the Orientalist and what he says as presence" (p. 208). The archetypal Orientalist was Ernest Renan, a philologist whose "exact science of the objects of the mind" (p. 132) enabled him to create, command, and marshal his own Orient in a *tour de force* of knowledge as power. Said's readings bring out the happy ability of thinkers such as Renan to live in a world of their own design, to both precede and follow an object: to make a distinction that "could be applied to any complex of historical and political events in order to pare them down to a nucleus both antecedent to and inherent in them" (p. 231). The Orient is the Other that is produced when this kind of thinking "succeeds," when

25. Edward Said, *Orientalism* (New York: Vintage, 1978), p. 54.

the European will-to-truth satisfies its own demands. That success and satisfaction must be understood as a purely rhetorical stance.

The two interlocking profiles of Europe and the Orient leave no room for
a third element, endowed with a positive shape of its own; as on a sheet of
paper, both of whose sides have been claimed, the third entry tends to be
associated with one side or the other or to be nullified by the lack of an
available slot in our intellectual apparatus. It is Africa that was always labeled
the "third part of the world," and Africanist discourse reads as a struggle
with the problems inherent in that figure. Driven by the same will-to-truth as
Orientalism, Africanist writing projects out from itself an object that refuses
to conform to the demands placed upon it. In the following pages I will offer
a series of brief examples from various periods in literature to illustrate the
difference between Orientalist and Africanist discourses, beginning with a
return to the etymology of "Africa" according to Leo Africanus.

The last sentence of Leo's etymology reads: "This is why the Arabs consider
as Africa almost nothing but that area around Carthage and give to Africa as
a whole the name of Occident." The speaker conceives of two nonselves:
"the Arabs" and "Africa." On the biographical level, it is known that Leo
came from non-Arab Muslims, who felt themselves to be superior;[26] add to
that his conversion to Catholicism and his adoption of a European viewpoint,
and it becomes clear that this "Orient," the "Arabs," is a negative to him,
defining the profile of what he is not. But Leo first brackets the Arabs as
other, then tells how the Arabs themselves bracket Africa: they "give to
Africa as a whole the name of Occident." Both steps are certainly, in Said's
words, "constraints upon and limitations of thought" (p. 42), acts of discursive power, first of the European over the Arab, but then of the Arab
over . . . what? There *is no Africa* here, prior to the arrival of an outsider,
King Ifrichos, to a land that has no shape or identity of its own. The first
"African" was an Oriental according to this legend, and primal Africa is a
nullity. Africa is the Other's other, the Orient's orient, which happens to be
called "Occident," and which is nothing. The etymologies of "colony" and
"Afer" tell exactly the same story of an empty slate, written on by outsiders.
Africa often occurs as the third part in cultural hierarchies, but, from the
moment it is spoken, "Africa" is subsumed by one of the other two. In the
relationship between the self and the other, the third is null.

When that self is Joseph de Gobineau (1816–82), the self-styled ethnologist
of mid-nineteenth-century France, the difference between the Other and the
Other's other becomes an elaborately scientistic slander. Gobineau, dubbed
by Sartre as "the father of racism," has the distinction of being offensive to
all the most basic of our contemporary assumptions on language, race, and
difference in general. He produced the master text of nineteenth-century racial

26. Epaulard, introduction to Leo, *Description*, p. X.

thinking (although its influence is said to have been slight before the twentieth century), the *Essai sur l'inégalité des races humaines* (1853–55), to which we will have reason to refer later in this study. The *Essai* divided humanity into "three great races," and the distinction between the two nonwhite ones is pertinent here. Of the "black, the yellow, and the white,"

> La variété mélanienne est la plus humble et gît au bas de l'échelle. Le caractère d'animalité empreint dans son bassin lui impose sa destinée, dès l'instant de la conception. Elle ne sortira jamais du cercle intellectuel le plus restreint. Ce n'est cependant pas une brute pure et simple, que ce nègre à front étroit et fuyant, qui porte, dans la partie moyenne de son crâne, les indices de certaines énergies grossièrement puissantes. Si ces facultés pensantes sont médiocres *ou même nulles,* il possède *dans le désir* et par suite dans la volonté, une intensité souvent terrible. . . .
>
> La race jaune se présente comme l'antithèse de ce type. Le crâne, au lieu d'être rejeté en arrière, se porte précisément en avant. . . . Peu de vigueur physique, des dispositions à l'antipathie. Au moral, aucun de ces excès étranges, si commune chez les Mélaniens. [Emphasis mine][27]

The Melanian variety is the humblest and lives at the bottom of the scale. The animalistic character etched in his loins imposes his destiny from the minute of conception. His fate holds him within the most limited intellectual scope. However, he is not a pure and simple brute, this Negro with a narrow and sloped forehead, who bears in the middle section of his brain the signs of certain grossly powerful energies. If these thinking faculties are poor *or even null,* he is possessed, *by his desire* and also by his will, of an often terrible intensity. . . .

The yellow race presents itself as the antithesis of this type. The skull, instead of sloping backward, is inclined precisely forward. . . . Little physical vigor, dispositions to antipathy. As for character, none of the strange excesses so common among the Melanians. [Emphasis mine]

It is only the black race (one assumes he is referring to Africans, but his category of "Mélaniens" is appropriately vague and fictive) that inspires Gobineau to the project of a *nullity,* a human being who may actually not think. The notion of a nullity is a key to understanding European conceptions of Black Africa; it will crop up many times in this study, usually in phrases as ambiguous as Gobineau's *"or even* null." This is because the burden of

27. Joseph de Gobineau, *Essai sur l'inégalité des races humaines* (Paris: Pierre Belfond, 1967), pp. 205–6.

proving a nullity, and of maintaining it in a logical discourse, is crushing, and the overextension of discourse in relation to this object of its own design is most typical of Africanist utterances. It is only the black African that Gobineau and other writers seek to depict as a pure "human machine," stripped of reasoning faculties and moved only by a blind sensorial *desire*. The meaning and consequences of these terms are at the heart of the Africanist problem.

But it is later in the *Essai,* while trying to explain away the fact that the dark-skinned Ethiopians produced a civilization, that Gobineau produces his most fertile metaphor for the black race:

> Pour la première fois, nos recherches viennent de trouver dans l'Ethiopie un de ces pays annexes d'une grande civilisation étrangère, ne la possédant que d'une manière incomplète et absolument comme le disque lunaire fait pour la clarté du soleil. [P. 297]

> For the first time, our research has now found in Ethiopia one of those countries adjacent to a great foreign civilization, possessing that civilization only in an incomplete fashion, absolutely as the moon does with the light of the sun.

Black African civilization is for Gobineau a contradiction in terms; any accomplishment in Ethiopia ("Abyssinia" to Rimbaud) is directly attributable to white blood in the veins of the population, blood "infinitely subdivided" but sufficient to make the Ethiopians the "first of the black peoples." Black Africa, like the moon, exists for Gobineau only insofar as it reflects *something white*. His choice of the word *disk* is revealing in that it describes a perception in only two dimensions, although of course Gobineau knew the moon to be three-dimensional. The lunar sphere is reduced to a mere reflecting disk; the absence of innate light dictates this stripping-away of knowledge; darkness does not "exist" in this image, darkness is nothing. By the same token, Black Africa is reduced to a noncivilization, receiving life only from the outside:

> La population égyptienne avait à combiner les éléments que voici: des noirs à cheveux plats, des nègres à tête laineuse, plus une immigration blanche, *qui donnait la vie à tout ce mélange*. [P. 276; emphasis mine]

> The Egyptian population was composed of the following elements: blacks with flat hair, Negroes with woolly heads, plus a white immigration, *which gave life to the whole mix*.

The most interesting aspect of the lunar metaphor is the breach in Gobineau's own knowledge that it represents: the question of the moon's negated third dimension, which Gobineau did not "intend" but which his discourse imposes, raises a similar question concerning Black Africa. What happens to the fullness of an object within a discourse that takes that fullness away? How can one read a text that all but denies the existence of the thing it has created? How can negativity be read? This last is a question that Gobineau "answers" to his own satisfaction in the following passage from the *Essai*, with a different truth from the one he sees:

> Mais de dire quand la barbarie a commencé, voilà ce qui dépasse les forces de la science. Par sa nature même elle est *négative*, parce qu'elle reste sans action. Elle végète inaperçue, et *l'on ne peut constater son existence que le jour où une force de nature contraire se présente pour la battre en brèche.* Ce jour fut celui de l'apparition de la race blanche au milieu des noirs. [P. 217; emphasis mine]

> But to say when barbarism began is a question that is beyond the forces of science. By its very nature it is *negative,* because it remains without action. It vegetates unperceived, and *its existence can be noticed only on the day when a force of opposite nature presents itself and barbarism is breached.* This day was that of the appearance of the white race among the blacks.

Knowledge *(science)* is light. But the miraculous appearance of the white race among the blacks here, inaugurating history and knowledge (see *Essai*, pp. 445 ff.), must destroy what it "knows." Darkness can be known only by shedding light on it; that is, it cannot be "known" as such. The writer who persists in detailing that kind of knowledge is working on Africanist ground.

Restoring the lost dimension to the Africanist object, reconstituting the plenitude of the African past, is the work of historians, and it is finally being accomplished. The literary task as I conceive it consists of interpreting the process by which the initial distortion took place and of trying to understand the conditions that made that distortion possible, even inevitable.

Knowledge about Africa, as opposed to the "Orient," has tended to be proffered with caveats; Africanist authors frequently call their own authority and mastery of the subject into question. Thinking back to the perfection of Renan's method for producing and describing the discrete "essence" of the Orient, consider this passage from the *New American Cyclopaedia,* published in 1858, ten years after Renan's *Pensées:*

> Its name is a mystery. . . . Its size is unknown. . . . Its population is an unsolved problem: geographers have set it down at various figures, of which the lowest is 60,000,000, the highest 110,000,000.

Its configuration is a matter of guess-work . . . with lakes believed
to be of large extent, with rivers which are sanguinely expected to
prove navigable. . . . But it will be borne in mind that much of this
presumed configuration rests upon conjecture. In regard to the ethnology and languages of Africa, we know hardly any thing. . . . Of
the people of the centre of the continent we have as yet no satisfactory
account. . . . Each tribe has a language of its own, and many have
two—a dead and a living tongue. . . . None of the native African
languages are thoroughly understood by foreigners.—It is generally
understood that the shape of the continent bears a rude resemblance
to a palm leaf; but we are far from knowing the exact outline. [1:169]

In contrast to Renan's perfect control, the encyclopedist feels himself confronted with an intractable object. Access to any "essence" or to "things of
the mind" is denied to the outsider in a continent where "the people of the
islands of Lake Chad . . . speak a language which is not understood by the
residents of the lake shores." But the distinction between Africanist and
Orientalist discourses is most definitely not based on any characteristics of
either Africa or the "Orient." Nor is it based on any real difference in
European knowledge of the two places. In 1858 a great deal *was* known about
Africa, certainly more than this article would indicate. Heinrich Barth's *Travels and Discoveries in North and Central Africa*, which, according to Philip
Curtin, "still remains the greatest single contribution to European knowledge
of West Africa,"[28] was published in 1857–58, and the outline of the continent
had certainly been charted for centuries. Even in the presence of empirical
knowledge, Africa and things African are a privileged locus of lags, breaches,
delays, and failures in understanding and knowledge. The perception of
the continent remains "dark." In spite of Barth's accomplishments, the
American Cyclopaedia and Castelnau's Niam-Niams remain typical utterances.

Jacques Berque describes the exchange between Africa and Europe during
its Industrial Revolution as a complicated "zone of interferences" between
"unequal partners":

This "heart of darkness" responds not only with silence or inertia.
It defends itself, first with its distances, its difficult voyages, the
strangeness of its ways. Against the guile of outsiders, Africa presents
a screen of unintelligibility.[29]

That screen, reducing European knowledge to "a matter of guess-work,"
does not represent a renunciation of the desire to know, but it throws doubt

28. Philip D. Curtin, *The Image of Africa* (Madison: University of Wisconsin Press, 1964),
p. 311.
29. Jacques Berque, preface to René Caillié, *Voyage à Tombouctou* (Paris: Maspéro, 1982),
p. 17.

on the capacity of the discourse to create an object that will strictly obey the rules of knowledge: to have an identity of its own, or to so appear. That identity must in turn appear to shape information about itself rather than be shaped by the inquiry, creating the illusion of a "preexisting essence."

A typical Africanist problem in which no such essence can be found and in which the discourse is forced to call itself into question is that of the cause of the African's skin color: this has been a source of frustration for European knowledge since Herodotus. From an "initial environmental approach" in Antiquity,[30] through the theory of the curse of Ham, to present-day science, the question why blacks are black has persisted unanswered. Empirical evidence, readily available and highly valued in eighteenth-century England, somehow conformed to Edward Long's claim that "Europeans and Negroes did not belong to the same species" and that therefore "mulattoes were unfertile hybrids."[31] Long was a resident of Jamaica, living in the midst of a slave population. The Abbé Demanet, of whom we will be reading more later, claimed in his "Dissertation physique et historique" that "Negroes are born white" and "become white at death and regain their color after death" because "blackness [is] so extrinsic and accidental to the Negroes that it erases itself in many fashions."[32]

The most interesting series of texts on the subject in French are the result of a competition organized by the Académie of Bordeaux in 1741 on the question, "Quelle est la cause phisique de la couleur des Négres, de la qualité de leurs cheveux, et de la dégéneration de l'une et de l'autre?" ("What is the physical cause of the color of Negroes, of the quality of their hair, and of the degeneration of both?"). Underneath the title in the archives it is noted: "Le Prix ne fut point adjugé; et ce Sujet fut abandonné." ("The Prize was not attributed; and the Subject was abandoned.") Perhaps this was due to passages like the following, from the fourth manuscript in the group:

> Il reste encore bien des phénomènes dont on ne sauroit rendre raison, & une grande partie de la Nature n'est encore pour nous qu'un paÿs de conjecture, c'est à dire une espèce de paÿs perdu. Le Sujet que

---

30. Frank M. Snowden, *Blacks in Antiquity* (Cambridge: Harvard University Press, 1970), p. 178.

31. Curtin, *Image of Africa*, pp. 43–44. Cf. David Brion Davis, *The Problem of Slavery in Western Culture* (Ithaca: Cornell University Press, 1966), p. 459: "Few eighteenth-century writers could equal Edward Long in gross racial prejudice, and because Long's most outrageous slanders have often been quoted, it is easy to overlook the fact that he assumed the mantle of the scientific philosopher, and expressed opinions . . . which were . . . apparently acceptable to an influential minority in Europe."

32. Abbé Demanet, "Dissertation physique et historique sur l'origine des négres et de la cause physique de leur couleur," in *Nouvelle Histoire de l'Afrique françoise* (Paris, 1767), p. 241: "Les Négres naissent blancs . . . deviennent blancs à la mort & reprennent leur couleur après la mort . . . . La noirceur tellement extrinsèque & accidentelle aux Négres, qu'elle s'efface en plusieurs manières."

vous proposez aujourd'huy au public est une bonne preuve de ce que
je viens de dire; Sujet sur lequel il est bien plus aisé de réfuter ce
que d'autres ont dit que d'établir soy-même quelque chose de
solide.

There still remain many phenomena that cannot be rationalized, and
a great part of Nature is still but a land of conjecture for us, that is,
a lost land. The Subject that you are proposing to the public today
is a good proof of what I have just said, being a Subject about which
it is much easier to refute what others have said than to establish
something solid oneself.[33]

Pruneau de Pommegorge, author of *Description de la Nigritie* (1789), described the problem with ingenuous puzzlement: the cause must be the heat
of the sun, yet removal of the African to a cool climate fails to change his
color. Environment is the manifest cause, yet the evidence remains latent,
invisible. The problem reduces itself to an impossible, visible invisibility,
and Pruneau concludes that it is "a secret of nature."[34]
     Winthrop D. Jordan's recent and highly rigorous treatment of the subject
in *White over Black* concludes on a note of similar "surprise":

It is . . . surprising that the facts concerning skin color remain in
doubt. . . . It is far from certain whether dark skin as such affords
important protection against the sun. . . . Certainly, the precise
adaptive value of the Negro's skin is not as yet known. It is ironic
that a scientific problem which has been acknowledged for several
millenniums still remains unsolved.[35]

That *irony* is the epitome of Africanist discourse in the West.

From earliest times, Black Africa was experienced as the literal end of European knowledge: on the earliest maps of Ptolemy's *Geography,* "Libia
Interior" and "Ethiopia Interior" are the last namable places before the map

33. Archives Départmentales de la Gironde, Bibliothèque Municipale, Bordeaux, No. 828/
65, 1741: MS 4, p. 1.
34. While it was recognized that a European would darken under the sun's rays, this immediate
cause, once removed, would not lighten the black man's skin. Pruneau writes, "Ce n'est ni à
la chaleur du climat, ni à la nourriture qu'il faut attribuer la noirceur de cette espèce d'hommes."
In Martinique, for example, "les blancs créoles y sont cependant établis depuis près de cent
cinquante ans; ils n'ont pas dégénéré, puisqu'ils ont le même teint que les européens." He
concludes: "C'est un secret de la nature" *(Description de la Nigritie* [Amsterdam: Maradan,
1789], pp. 58–61).
35. Winthrop D. Jordan, *White over Black* (New York: Norton, 1968), p. 585. Discussions
of the question of skin color and its attributed causes throughout history can be found in the
following: Jordan, *White over Black,* pp. 11–20; Davis, *The Problem of Slavery,* pp. 450–59;
Cohen, *The French Encounter,* pp. 9–13, 80–84; Curtin, *The Image of Africa,* passim; Wylie
Sypher, *Guinea's Captive Kings* (New York: Octagon, 1969), pp. 50–55.

is cut off with the label "Terra Incognita," and such was the case well into the fifteenth century.[36] The unknown could be labeled as such or projected onto with a "mixture of thinly disguised hearsay and barely rehashed fable."[37] Still, the most modern Michelin map of Africa bears this caveat: "En Afrique, les indications de distance ne peuvent avoir qu'une valeur relative." (Their English translation reads: "In Africa distances can rarely be given with absolute accuracy.") The same problem will face the navigator in *Heart of Darkness:* the lack of an all-determining principle, a *point de repère.*[38]

These brief examples of Africanist discourse share the same will-to-knowledge seen in Orientalism but find their will and desire pitted against an otherness that appears to have no "actual identity," that refuses to be acquired and domesticated. The "rigidly binomial opposition of 'ours' and 'theirs'" is thus undone, and all "aggression, activity, judgment, will-to-truth, and knowledge" fail. Africanist discourse is at the least an *unhappy* Orientalism, a discourse of desire unfulfilled and unfulfillable. More ambitiously, it represents a radical confounding of European discourse in its production of objects, for the object "Africa" (or 'blackness," or "idolatry," or "irreflection") will call into question the terms and conditions of the discourse that created it.

Ambivalence in Antiquity

Negra sed [sic] formosa sum.

—Song of Songs

Blameless Ones and Headless Ones

The problem begins at the beginning of Western literature, in Homer's *Odyssey,* where an object called Ethiopia is established, one that will become embedded in all classical literature. Frank Snowden, author of the recent study *Blacks in Antiquity* (which I will discuss presently), paraphrases the passage literally in this fashion: "Homer's Ethiopians are remote peoples, sundered in twain, the farthermost men, some dwelling where the sun rises and others where it sets."[39] Homer, as interpreted throughout European translations,

---

36. Tooley et al., *History of Cartography,* map of 1447, p. 51.
37. Jehan Desanges, "L'Afrique noire et le monde méditérranéen dans l'Antiquité (Ethiopiens et Gréco-Romains)," *Revue française d'histoire d'outre-mer* 62 (1975): 407, where he says of Ptolemy's geography that it "se contente . . . de mêler les duplications de toponymies et les données plus ou moins mythiques, de projeter dans le vide de l'inconnu, un mélange de déjà-dit à peine fardé et de fable à peine rajeunie."
38. Joseph Conrad, *Heart of Darkness* (New York: Signet Classics, 1910), p. 109: "Sometimes I would pick out a tree a little way ahead to measure our progress towards Kurtz by, but I lost it invariably before we got abreast."
39. *Blacks in Antiquity* (Cambridge, Mass.: Harvard University Press, 1970), p. 101.

defines Ethiopia's first condition of possibility as distance, difference: Ethiopia
is "farre,"[40] "the farthermost,"[41] "the uttermost,"[42] "far off."[43] So begins
the tradition of two Ethiopias, one in Africa, one in Asia; the literal interpretation of Homer will become geography and will last well into the Middle
Ages. Here is the root of the general tendency to confuse things Oriental and
things African.

But the distance of the object in relation to the subject is not the extent of
the problem. Homer describes Ethiopia as a vast distance *in relation to itself,*
a single nation divided against itself: the Ethiopians are "sundered in twain,"[44]
"farre disundered in their seat, (in two parts parted . . .)," "In two parts
parted, at the Sunne's descent / and underneath his golden Orient / The first
and last of men" (Chapman). By locating the Ethiopians at opposite extremes
of the universe at the same time, Homer creates Ethiopia as a paradox. The
geography (literally, "earth-writing") is of an object that can never be fully
present to itself, for its other self will always be at the farthest possible remove.
Other references in the *Odyssey* show Ethiopia as almost a catchall for remoteness, being both beyond Egypt ("Egypt and still farther / among the
sun-burnt races" [Fitzgerald's translation, p. 55]) and in Asia ("over the
mountains of Asia from the Sunburned land" [ibid., p. 89]).

The other important aspect of Homer's Ethiopia is the "delight" it provides.
This same passage in the *Odyssey* is taken as the beginning of a tradition of
Ethiopians perfect in religion, beloved of the gods, and "given over to Delight" (Chapman). After describing the sundering of Ethiopia, the passage
goes on to tell Poseidon's purpose in going there, which is "to be regaled
by smoke of thighbones burning, / haunches of rams and bulls a hundred
fold. / He lingered delighted at the banquet side" (Fitzgerald), "given over
to Delight." There are two passages in the *Iliad:* one where Zeus has gone
"to the blameless Aithiopians . . . to feast, and the rest of the gods went
with him"[45] for a twelve-day stay; the other where it is reported that the
Ethiopians "are making grand sacrifice to the immortals" (Lattimore, p. 455).
On these three passages a tradition is founded of "godlike and blameless"
Ethiopians, "the justest men," whom "the gods leave their abode frequently
to visit" (Snowden, p. 148, quoting Lactantius Placidus).

The prospect of "delight" is one that the ancient view of Ethiopia seems
to hold today. I believe that Frank Snowden, in his important study *Blacks
in Antiquity,* succumbs to a one-sided temptation by which the misty nobility

40. *Chapman's Homer* (Princeton: Princeton University Press, 1967), p. 12.

41. Homer, *The Odyssey,* trans. A. T. Murray (London: Heinemann, 1930), p. 5.

42. *The Complete Works of Homer,* trans. S. H. Butcher and A. Lang (New York: Modern
Library, 1935), p. 2.

43. *The Odyssey,* trans. Robert Fitzgerald (New York: Doubleday, 1963), p. 2.

44. This phrase is used by Butcher, Murray, and Snowden in their translations.

45. *"The Iliad"* of Homer, trans. Richmond Lattimore (Chicago: University of Chicago
Press, 1951), p. 70.

of Homer's Ethiopians is taken for real. An ancient relationship with Black Africa based on admiration and respect has an obvious appeal in our times as a corrective to racism, especially if the interaction between black and white could be grounded in real referential "reports," not just "an idealization of dark-skinned" people (p. 150). Snowden's conclusion is that "Color was inconsequential": "The Greeks and Romans attached no special stigma to color, regarding yellow hair or blue eyes a mere geographical accident, and developed no special racial theory about the inferiority of darker peoples qua darker peoples" (p. 176). This is the "initial environmental approach" (p. 178). Snowden marshals a great deal of evidence to the effect that racial and color prejudice did not exist in Antiquity. Herodotus expresses no surprise at the Ethiopian conquest of Egypt, and he speaks of them as the equals, the counterparts, of their enemies.[46] Diodorus describes them as "pioneers in religion," and Augustine will report that it was the Ethiopians who first brought writing to Egypt.[47] There is clearly a whole tradition of literature that runs counter to the more familiar—negative—representations of Africa.

The significance of Snowden's accomplishment lies in showing the degree to which real-life black people were exempt from racial discrimination *de jure* and *de facto* in Antiquity. But based on readings of the same passages that Snowden quotes, I would hesitate to call the trope of color "inconsequential"; for there was always the other Ethiopia: of virtueless slaves, of speechless savages with illicit desires, sunk below the level of humanity, squeaking of heresy and sin. Many ancient writers repeated the Homeric tradition of the blameless Ethiopian while producing, through a process of constant binary distinctions, another object quite unlike the first: in addition to an Other-as-dream, an Other-as-nightmare. Criticism designed to uplift our current point of view takes the former as its object and represses the latter. Snowden makes passing reference to Greek "knowledge" of "primitive Ethiopians . . . resembling wild beasts in their way of living and cultivating none of the practices of life as found among the rest of mankind," but this "did not cause the Greeks to overlook more developed Ethiopians or to generalize and to classify all Ethiopians as primitive because some were savage" (p. 180). Diodorus Siculus, for example, made a distinction between two kinds of Ethiopians, but only one, the favorable side, is given space in Snowden's *Blacks in Antiquity,* in an attempt to found the positive tradition in "reports" and to forget the negative tradition. Diodorus' important contribution, according to Snowden, was to observe that "a) the Ethiopians were the first to

46. The fifty-year reign of Ethiopia is described in Herodotus 2. 137, trans. A. D. Godley, Loeb Classical Library, 4 vols. (London: Heinemann, 1921), 1:441.
47. *Diodorus of Sicily,* trans. C. H. Oldfather, Loeb Classical Library, 12 vols. (Cambridge, Mass.: Harvard University Press, 1935), 2:109; Augustine, *City of God* 18. 3, trans. E. M. Sanford and W. McA. Green, Loeb Classical Library, 7 vols. (London: Heinemann, 1965), 5:377: "Other writers say that she [Io or Isis] came to Egypt from Ethiopia as queen . . . and instituted many useful customs for them, including the art of writing."

be taught to honor the gods and to perform religious rites in their honor, b)
by reason of their piety the Ethiopians enjoyed divine goodwill and, as a
result of this favor, were blessed with internal security and freedom from
invasion" (p. 146). The desirability of such a state is obvious; it represents
a rêverie du repos even more fulfilled than Homer's.

But the very next chapter of Diodorus begins:

> But there are also a great many other tribes of the Ethiopians, some
> of them dwelling in the land lying on both banks of the
> Nile . . . others residing in the interior of Libya. The majority of
> them, and especially those who dwell along the river, are black in
> color and have flat noses and woolly hair. As for their spirit they
> are entirely savage and display the nature of a wild beast . . . and
> are as far removed as possible from human kindness to one another;
> and speaking as they do with a shrill voice and cultivating none of
> the practices of civilized life as these are found among the rest of
> mankind, they present a striking contrast when considered in the
> light of our own customs. [Pp. 103–5]

Aristotle "knew not of any [slaves] who were so utterly devoid of any semblance of virtue as are the Africans."[48] In Herodotus, both points of view are
readily expressed. His Africa consists of Libya, Ethiopia, and the great unknown to the south of everything, and any attempt to attach his Troglodytes
to this or that real location would be misguided.[49] A radically unhuman human
appears only through a series of oppositional removals that carries the text
ever further from familiarity. The Ethiopians, when Herodotus discusses them
alone, appear as another civilization, ruling over Egypt for fifty years, and
black only "by reason of the heat" (p. 301). Yet in opposition to the more
northerly Garamantes of Libya, the burnt-faces show another potential:

> these Garamantes go in their four-horse chariots chasing the cave-
> dwelling Troglodyte Ethiopians: for the Ethiopian cave-dwellers are
> swifter of foot than any men of whom tales are brought us. They
> live on snakes and lizards and such-like creeping things. Their speech
> is like none other in the world; it is like the squeaking of bats.
> [P. 387]

The land to the south and west (as the Nile was supposed to divide the
earth) was not exclusively monstrous, but it was the only place in the Ancient
cosmography that was capable of producing "dog-eared men, and the headless
that have their eyes in their breasts, as the Libyans say, and the wild men

48. David Brion Davis, The Problem of Slavery in Western Culture, p. 440.
49. For a discussion of this problem, in relation to Snowden's conclusions, see Desanges,
"L'Afrique noire," p. 408.

and women, besides many other creatures *not fabulous."* But in the nomad's country to the north, "there are none of these." Herodotus' distinction is clear.

But this is mild compared to Pliny's version of the same story. He reports that the Cave-dwellers

> have no articulate voice, but only utter a kind of squeaking noise, and thus they are utterly destitute of all means of communication by language. The Garamantes have no institution of marriage among them, and live in promiscuous concubinage with their women. The Augylae worship no deities but the gods of the infernal regions. The Gamphasantes . . . go naked and are unacquainted with war. . . . The Atlantes, if we believe what is said, have lost all characteristics of humanity; for there is no mode of distinguishing each other by names . . . *nor are they visited with dreams like the rest of mortals.*[50]

The privilege of the voice is to represent consciousness as present to itself, prerequisite to the "intercourse of speech" and therefore to the *ritus,* the ways of civilization. Consciousness is "utterly" denied to these specific groups; for them a complete nullity is reserved, and they represent a total refutation of the notion of civilization as based on consciousness and inter-subjectivity. They do not wear exotic costumes; they "go naked." The Blemmyae "have no heads, their mouths and their eyes being seated in their breasts." No voice, no dreams, no heads, no clothes: European discourse projects an object onto the unknown, an object of impossible nullity. Each category (marriage, clothing, speech, religion) is filled, but with an object (promiscuous concubinage, nakedness, squeaking, worship of the infernal regions) that is a negation of the category itself.

Africanist discourse in the West is one in which the head, the voice—the logos, if you will—is missing. Later, Medieval writers will represent this as an absence, among the Ethiopians, of the Godhead—the all-determining principle that holds phenomena in their proper relations. In Julius Solinus "Polyhistor" (translated by Golding in 1587), family relationships, symbolic of the relationship between God the Father and man, are reduced to a chaotic mishmash in which "the name of Father hath no reverance at all . . . . For who is able to knowe hys Father, where such incestuous lecherie runneth at large . . . ; they [the Ethiopians] have infringed the discipline of chastitie, and by a wicked culture destroyed the knowledge of their succession."[51] The logical succession is annihilated by an absence of *knowledge,* a missing head.

50. Pliny, quoted and translated in C. K. Meek, "The Niger and the Classics: The History of a Name," *Journal of African History* 1, no. 1 (1960): 11; emphasis mine.

51. Solinus, Chap. 42 (see note 19, above).

From this flow the other predicates: sin, earthly pleasure, "evaporation of the spirit,"[52] the deformation of vice. It becomes possible for Saint Jerome to interpret Chusi (which in Hebrew means Ethiopian) in Psalm 7, "this Ethiopian," to be "no other than the devil" and to add, incredibly, that he "is Ethiopian by reason of his vice." In the same homily, Jerome says that the devil is a snake *because* "every part of him is completely on the ground; his head and the rest of his body are all on the same level . . . . The other animals may rest on the ground but *long* to rise up from it, but the devil cleaves to it with head, tail, and the middle part of him."[53]

This discourse can thus produce monstrous, nonhuman objects in which no part of the body transcends the others; the head has no priority; control is missing. Such utterances and visual images constitute a whole tradition, passed on from the Ancients through the age of discovery and still alive in the Niam-Niam question of the 1850s. The contrast between this and the first tradition of "blameless Ethiopians, beloved of the gods," could not be stronger. How could they possibly be objects with the same name?

The horror of monstrousness and the delight of fulfillment are counterparts in a single discourse, sharing the same conditions of possibility: distance and difference. Dream and nightmare are both agencies of sleep; the two sides of Africanist discourse are made possible by a critical gap that ruptures the principles of identity and noncontradiction. It would be wrong to ask which Ethiopia was the "real" one, for the extremeness of the object's positive and negative susceptibilities show that another logic is at work.

Homer's Ethiopia had two characteristics, remoteness and delight, the latter being made possible by the former. Ethiopia was located at the farthest edge of the earth—in fact at both edges—and this distance radicalizes the potential of the object. The fact that Ethiopia was in two places at the same time is representative of this contradictory discourse. Homer's Ethiopia presents the story of the fulfillment of a desire: a "grand sacrifice," "given over to Delight," where Poseidon "lingered delighted at the banquet side": this has come to represent, along with the whole tradition it spawned, the fulfillment of a desire on the part of modern interpretation for a world without racial prejudice. But in the other tradition, desire returns travestied, and dream turns to nightmare. Agriophages, Troglodytes, and Garamantes prance across the stage with the same alacrity as the Blameless Ones because they are products

52. Albertus Magnus, "De Natura Loci" 2. 3, In *Opera Omnia* (Aschendorff, Germany: Monasterii Westfalorum, 1980), 5:26–27.

53. *The Homilies of Saint Jerome,* trans. Marie Liguori Ewald (Washington, D.C.: Catholic University of America Press, 1964), 1:33. Jerome's Latin text reads: "Coluber dicitur, quoniam totus terrae haeret. Cetera animalia licet ambulent in terra, tamen non omne corpus in terra iacens habent . . . aliam partem corporis sursum habent . . . . Quoniam cetera animalia (preduns lector intellege) licet terrae haereant, tamen a terra *cupiunt* recedere: ceterum diabolus et caput et caudam et mediam partem totam in terra haerentem habet" *(Sancti Hieronymi Presbyteri,* ed. D. Germanus Morim [Maredsoli: J. Parker, 1895], p. 24; my emphasis).

of the same agency. The void across which they are projected permits both a desire and a loathing to be fulfilled. They have everything in common that black has with white, and it is this paradox we turn to now.

The "Idea" of Blackness

Blanche couleur, couleur des anges,
Mon âme était digne de toi . . .
—U. Guttinger, "Ourika" (1824)

Discourse on color moves between a reef and a maelstrom. Blackness would appear to be a rock of negativity: from Sanskrit and ancient Greek to modern European languages, black is associated with dirt, degradation, and impurity,[54] as if it were the perfect representation of an idea. In texts from the Ancients on, whether the speaker's attitude is positive or negative in regard to black *people*, blackness remains a powerful negative element. If black people are deemed blameless, it is usually in spite of their blackness. By actively forgiving and overlooking the color of their skin, one perceives an "inner whiteness." Snowden quotes a Greek epitaph from the third century A.D. where a black slave says, "Among the living I was very black, darkened by the rays of the sun, but my soul, ever blooming with white flowers, won my prudent master's good will," and Snowden concurs with a modern comment that this is "a remarkable example of the lack of race feeling based upon distinctions of color" (p. 178). Yet, plainly, "color" is more than a neutral term in that utterance. Snowden construes this repression of blackness as a positive moment:

Remarkable though the sentiment [of the above epitaph] may be for certain later ideologies, it is not surprising from the Greco-Roman point of view but is, rather, just what would be expected in light of the classical outlook—the initial environmental approach to racial differences. [P. 178]

The "environmental approach" is one in which black skin is seen as purely a quirk of nature, an effect of the sun. But the blackness still needs to be explained away in these utterances and interpreted in terms of *light:* the sun did it. The "sundered" nature of the word "Ethiopia" is at work. Once the reversal is effected, it is possible to see blackness in positive terms, but only at the price of undoing "the idea of blackness." Discourse moves from the

54. Cf. Cohen, *The French Encounter,* p. 14: "In Indo-European languages black seems to have had consistently negative connotations. Thus in Sanskrit, white symbolizes Brahmans . . . black typifies outcasts. In Greek black is associated with dirt in both the physical and the moral sense." Cf. Jordan, *White over Black,* p. 7: "No other colors so clearly implied opposition . . . ; no others were so frequently used to denote polarization."

rock of a secure idea to a maelström of reversals: white inside/black outside, white soul/black body, etc.

Blackness is a stumbling block; one must make excuses for it. Although the Song of Songs was read by early commentators, "I am black *and* beautiful" instead of the more familiar "black *but* beautiful" of King James and the Vulgate (Snowden, p. 198), the speaker goes on to implore, "Stare not at me that I am swart / That the sun has darkened me."[55] The interpretations of this passage, even those based on "black and beautiful," are drawn toward an inner whiteness, a latent redemption, for "Christ came into the world to make blacks radiantly bright" (Snowden, p. 200). Outward blackness and inner whiteness become commonplaces in references to Ethiopians; the point reiterated is that *"even* the Ethiopians, the remotest and blackest of men" (Snowden, p. 205), can be redeemed, made white.[56] This active flight from the meaning of color (a meaning the discourse itself put there) is hardly the same as not perceiving it in the first place; thus the "rejection of color as a criterion for evaluating men" (p. 216) is highly paradoxical. It is based on a highly charged inside/outside distinction, a fall into constant reversals of black and white. Blackness does not exist on its own terms as an idea, but that is not to say that "color was inconsequential."

In fact the reduction to polar opposites of black and white represents a fall out of color. Colors occur on a spectrum, with infinite possibilities of variation. As tropes they are taken to represent infinite varieties of meaning; they are "symbols." But black and white are not part of this system; they are invariable negatives of color. For example, blackness is said to have definite negative meanings. Yet in the writings we have seen, from the moment blackness is uttered its meaning is altered by intercourse with whiteness. Pure darkness is felt as a force so powerful that is must be repressed as a "criterion for evaluating men." The consequence of this, however, is that meaning itself will fall out of a secure grounding in symbolism and be forced always to point elsewhere. Black and white designate each other before they designate any meaning, and their meanings follow suit by reversing constantly.

The history of Africanist writing is the history of the collapsing-together of black and white—of their inability to remain as meaningful opposites— and of the frustrations of meanings attached to them. The *Oxford English Dictionary* calls "black" a "word of difficult history"; "in Old English . . . confused with blàc, shining, white . . . ; in Middle English the two words are often distinguishable only by the context, and sometimes not by that." The "literal" definition given is this: black is "the proper word for a certain quality practically classed among the colors, but consisting

55. The Song of Songs, in *The Anchor Bible*, trans. Marvin Pope (Garden City, N.Y.: Doubleday, 1977).

56. For a general discussion, see Jean-Marie Courtès, "Traitement patristique de la thématique 'éthiopienne,'" in *L'Image du noir*, 2, pt. 1:9 ff.

optically in the *total absence of color,* due to the absence or total *absorption* of light, as its opposite white arises from the *reflection* of all the rays of light" (emphasis mine). "White" is "fully luminous and *devoid* of any distinctive hues." That *void* is the point where white and black meet and reverse; for if white is an empty fullness (fully luminous but *void*), then black is a full emptiness (*total* absence). Both are *blank,* absent, the null set of color.

Black and white are to color what promiscuous concubinage, squeaking, and nakedness were to marriage, speech, and clothing: they negate the category they occupy. Thus the *Grand Robert* defines the French *noir* as "reflecting no visible radiation," but it adds: "If black, properly speaking, does not designate a color, everyday speech, as well as the language of art, admits perfectly well the *color black.*" Black and white must be "practically classed among the colors" for lack of a better term; by the same token, "blackness" persists in passing itself off as an idea. For lack of such better terms our own critical discourse finds itself faced with the same problem as the Africanist writers we are interpreting: how to write about a nullity. We are forced into utterances on the paradoxical order of "the color black."

The question of the relationship between colors and meanings is one we will take up in reading Baudelaire. There is, of course, a relationship, put there by certain authors, often with disastrous results. Consider in passing the definition of black in French as that which "does not reflect" *(ne réfléchit pas),* as the potential for a horrendous pun. "Le noir ne réfléchit pas" means both "Black does not reflect" and "The black man does not think." In a text such as Gobineau's *Essai,* that play on words is the very foundation of an entire world view, the starting point for an elaborate "description" of humanity, of which the "nullified civilization" *[la nullité civilisatrice]* of the blacks is the zero point.[57]

Africanist utterances, by hitching themselves to blackness and whiteness, become involved in polarizations and reversals. Thus it can be said in the same breath that "Color was inconsequential" and that the Ancients in fact "regarded as black all men who had not been illumined by God's light," thus reconfirming the consequences of color, light, and blackness. Black and white are counterparts that alter meanings and remove discourse from the categories it sets for itself. The two radically opposed traditions about Ethiopia coexist only as functions of one blankness. Homer's lost paradise and He-

57. Gobineau, *Essai,* p. 311: "Partout où l'on étudie les effets des mélanges, on s'aperçoit qu'un *fond noir* . . . crée les similitudes entre les sociétés en ne leur fournissant que ces aptitudes négatives bien évidemment étrangères aux facultés de l'espèce blanche. Force est donc d'admettre, devant la *nullité civilisatrice* des noirs, que la source des différences réside dans la race blanche." Cf. p. 318: "Le nègre, dont l'esprit est obtus, incapable de s'élever au-dessus du plus humble niveau, du moment qu'il faut *réfléchir* . . ." (emphasis mine).

rodotus' nightmare, the "white" and the "black" traditions of Africanist writing, are founded on the same void and constitute different ways of writing on the void.

The ambivalence present in the Ancients has been carried down through the centuries and received by us; regardless of the historical determinations that channel and flavor it, ambivalence persists.

In the section that follows I will leap forward to seventeenth-century France to describe a clear case in which the double valency of things Africanist comes into play.

Aniaba and Zaga-Christ

At this point, although chronology will be frustrated, I would like to open parentheses and illustrate the problem of a discourse "in two parts parted," attached to opposites and fraught with ambivalence. Our object is a highly symbolic sequence of texts from the seventeenth and eighteenth centuries, a small and unified corpus concerning certain African visitors to the France of the Ancien Régime.

"A" is for Aniaba. On the occasion of the visit of this African "prince" (who may or may not have been an impostor, a slave bought by Dominican priests, who dreamed up the whole charade), Louis XIV is reported to have said laughingly, "Prince Aniaba, il n'y a donc plus de différence entre vous et moi que du noir au blanc." (There is thus no more difference between you and me than from black to white.") But read the statement over. There is no difference but a total difference: the difference is only a matter of color, but the colors are complete opposites. Black and white as tools for effacing difference cannot help but reconfirm it. The utterance, by its involvement with the problem of color (or, more precisely, with the noncolors black and white), reads two perfectly opposite ways, and with the king's chuckle the prospect of a happy harmony becomes irony.

The little speech of the Sun King to the "sun-burnt" prince may be the most condensed Africanist utterance in French: the contrast between the legitimate light of the king and the dubious darkness of the slave-prince could not be more pronounced. For Aniaba was a prince or a slave depending on your point of view, and his story is one among several that unfolded curiously when Black Africa visited seventeenth- and eighteenth-century Europe. We will look briefly at two groups of texts: the first dealing with Aniaba, the second with a character named Zaga-Christ.

Aniaba was apparently a real visitor to the court of Louis XIV. Beyond that fact, all accounts differ. Some say he was the son of the king of Issiny (in the present Ivory Coast) but that this did not make him a prince and heir.[58]

---

58. Abbé Jean-Baptiste Labat, *Voyage du Chevalier des Marchais* . . . (Paris: Chez Saugrain, 1730), 1:230–47.

Others maintain that Dominican priests, having bought Aniaba as a slave in Issiny, sent him to France with a letter that presented him as a prince.[59] His real birthright came to have little importance compared to the effective roles he would play in French court life and literary phantasm. Received as a legitimate prince, Aniaba was presented to Louis XIV and taken in like a lost brother. Baptized by none other than Bossuet, Aniaba was instructed in religion by Cardinal de Noailles and was confirmed as "Louis Aniaba," with Louis XIV as his godfather. In 1700, on the death in Africa of the real king of Issiny, Aniaba was prepared by the French to return ascendant, first being invested by Noailles with "l'Ordre de l'Etoile de Notre Dame." (A painting of this event was commissioned by Aniaba, but it has been lost.) This is the point at which the Abbé Godefroy Loyer picks up the story in his *Relation du voyage d'Issiny* (1714):

> Je trouvai le Prince Loüis Aniaba que le Roy renvoyait dans son Païs d'Issyny. Monsieur le Marquis de Férolle . . . me présenta à ce Prince, auquel ayant communiqué mon dessein [d'aller à Issiny], il me dit en m'embrassant qu'il en étoit ravi, et que sa joye étoit parfaite, puisqu'un Religieux de l'Ordre de Saint Dominique l'ayant conduit idolâtre en France, il en voyait un autre s'offrir de le reconduire Chrétien en son Païs.[60]

> I found Prince Aniaba, whom the king was sending back to his country of Issiny. The Marquis de Férolle introduced me to this prince, to whom I told my plan [to go to Issiny]; he embraced me and told me that he was delighted and that his joy was perfect, in that a clergyman of the order of Saint Dominic had brought him, as an idolater, to France, and now another comes to bring him home as a Christian.

But his arrival in Issiny, in a warship donated by Louis XIV, was less auspicious. Loyer describes him as being fined for adultery (p. 176) and as disappearing just before a battle, only to show up afterward to congratulate the victorious French. Labat describes Aniaba as stripping off his French clothes ("il se mit tout nud comme les autres Nègres") and with them his thin veneer of civilization, "taking five or six idolatrous wives, with whom he abondoned himself to the most shameful excesses."[61] With dizzying ra-

59. Shelby T. McCloy, "Negroes and Mulattoes in Eighteenth-Century France," *Journal of Negro History* 30 (1945): 281; Charles Woolsey Cole, *French Mercantilism* (New York: Columbia University Press, 1943), p. 104. On Aniaba, see also Léon-François Hoffmann, *Le Nègre Romantique* (Paris: Payot, 1973), pp. 30, 37; Paul Roussier, *L'Etablissement d'Issiny* (Paris: Comité d'Etudes historiques et scientifiques de l'Afrique occidentale française, 1935), pp. i–xxxv; biobibliography in Hans W. Debrunner, *Presence and Prestige: Africans in Europe* (Basel: Basler Afrika Bibliographien, 1979), pp. 70–71.
60. Reprinted in Roussier, *L'Etablissement d'Issiny*, p. 122.
61. Labat, *Nouveau voyage*, quoted in Hoffmann, *Le Nègre romantique*, p. 30.

pidity, Aniaba passes from the exalted state of princehood to what Léon-François Hoffmann calls a debased "état de nègre." Between the magnificent prince and the virtueless slave we find all the ambiguity latent in Louis XIV's phrasing. Aniaba was both perfectly "white" (assimilated to Frenchness, all traces of difference being effaced) and perfectly "black" (repugnantly different, irredeemably other).

The literary sequence is curious. The first text to relate the story of Aniaba was Loyer's *Relation de Voyage* of 1714, written fourteen years after Aniaba's departure from France. Labat seems almost to have plagiarized Loyer in his *Nouveau voyage* of 1722; but these negative first versions did not prevent a completely "white" rendition of the tale from appearing in 1740. The anonymous novel *Histoire de Louis Aniaba* presents a perfectly positive view of the African visitor. This means that Black Africa is portrayed as a mirror image of Ancien Régime France: with "the King and all his Court" in a "magnificent castle," where slaves are versed in Italian and French and where the religion is Islam. Issiny and France thus worship "the same Infinite Being,"[62] and their difference becomes a simple question of counterparts.

Histoire de Louis Aniaba is probably the only Africanist novel written in the first person from the African point of view before the advent of the antislavery movement later in the eighteenth century, and this is no surprise. The narrator Aniaba is completely interchangeable with Europeans in both his inner subjectivity and his outer appearance. Once he arrives in Europe, he must have himself "introduced as a foreigner" (p. 65) so as not to be taken for French; some take him for an "Italian gentleman" (p. 97). The cost of the positive portrayal is thus the suppression of Aniaba's constitutive difference, his Africanism, his blackness. Nowhere in *Histoire de Louis Aniaba* is blackness mentioned, except in the repetition of clichés that can be found in Racine or Corneille, such as "la plus noire de toutes les ingratitudes" (pp. 44, 113) or "un noir chagrin" (pp. 39, 45, 68). Placed before the noun, blackness is a metaphorical, moral quality; physical blackness is repressed in spite of the references to Issiny, a known location in Black Africa.

The whole story unfolds as a legitimist dream: Louis XIV picks Aniaba out of a parade, recognizing his princely countenance. He holds his hand out to Aniaba: "not wanting to permit me to kiss it, . . . he had me advance to his right side" (2:5). The baptism has five cardinals and thirty bishops. Aniaba's return to Issiny involves overthrowing a usurper and converting the kingdom to Christianity, an accomplishment for which Pope Innocent XI accords him the title "Restorer of the Faith" (2:111). The novel ends with

62. *Histoire de Louis Aniaba, roi d'Essenie en Afrique* . . . (Paris: Aux Dépens de la Société, 1740), pp. 9, 8, 31, 78.

a "happy and profound peace." The repression of all otherness in this text
represents one way of reading Louis XIV's remark: there is no difference
between Europe and Black Africa that a simple flight from color does not
erase. Africa is a perfect ally because it is perfectly malleable.

"Z" is for Zaga-Christ, a figure who emerged in the middle of the seventeenth century as a personification of legitimacy usurped. He was supposed
to be the son of Emperor Jacob of Ethiopia, rightful heir to the throne, and
"one of the greatest and most unfortunate Princes in the world."[63] The emperors of Ethiopia had been the objects of European myths and speculation
for centuries, long before "Ethiopia" was the single place on the map of
Africa we now know. In the earliest myths, that emperor, known as Prester
John, was located in Asia, but an Asia undifferentiated from Africa. Prester
John was regarded as a real, contemporary individual for centuries; from the
twelfth to the fourteenth centuries various "letters" from Prester John cir-
culated in Europe and caused great excitement; his kingdom migrated in
European thought until it became identified with Ethiopia. Sebastian Münster's
map of Africa of 1540 shows "Hamarich, Sedes Pręte Iohan," located vaguely
in what we now call Ethiopia (see figure 1). In the period we will look at,
the emperors of Ethiopia were referred to as "Emperor X, also known as
Prester John."[64]

Prester John's *raison d'être* in European mythology was of course his
Christian faith. He represented the possibility of encircling and transcending
Islam, for he was a pure projection of the European self onto the unknown:
instead of the other as complete alien, the other as double of yourself. This
is the baggage with which "Zaga-Christ of Ethiopia, son of the Emperor
Jacob, commonly called Prester John," arrived in France.

The two seventeenth-century texts on Zaga-Christ tell a story much like
that of *Histoire de Louis Aniaba*—of peregrinations and adventures in search
of a birthright. *Les Estranges evenemens du voyage de son altesse, le serenissime Prince Zaga-Christ d'Ethiopie . . . fils de l'Empereur Iacob, com-
munément appellé Preste Ian* (1635), by Jean de Giffre de Rechac, begins in
"the most flourishing and powerful" kingdom of Africa (Ethiopia), in a state
of "total goodness where nothing is lacking" (p. 2). An evil cousin, Susneos,
defeats the emperor in battle and seizes the throne. Prince Zaga-Christ, with
three hundred attendants, goes into exile and begins his search for allies to

63. Jean de Giffre de Rechac, *Les Estranges evenemens du voyage de son altesse le Serenissime Prince Zaga-Christ d'Ethiopie* . . . (Paris: Chez Louis Sevestre, 1635), p. iv.

64. On Prester John, see Henri Baudet, *Paradise on Earth: Some Thoughts on European
Images of Non-European Man* (New Haven: Yale University Press, 1965), pp. 14 ff.; Charles
de la La Roncière, *La Découverte de l'Afrique au Moyen Age* (Cairo: Société Royale de Géographie d'Egypte, 1925), 2:112 and passim; and Pierre Bontiers, *Le Canarien*, ed. Gabriel Gravier
(Rouen: Société de l'Histoire de Normandie, 1874), p. 91n. A fifteenth-century letter of Prester
John is found in *Oeuvres complètes de Rutebeuf*, ed. Achille Jubinal (Paris: Daffis, 1875), 3:
355–75.

help regain the kingdom. His eventual arrival in Europe is celebrated by the pope, "who received him benignly." Having fallen sick, Zaga-Christ rises, "aspiring after France to throw himself completely between the arms of his Very Christian Majesty: He left from Savoy and came at last to Paris, where he is at the moment: waiting for the chance to make himself known to His Majesty." The account thus ends with narration and history coincident in the publication date of 1635, with the mythical foreigner represented as fully present and real.

Eugène Roger's *La Terre sainte* (1664) contains one chapter on Zaga-Christ, "Une Relation veritable de Zaga-Christ Prince d'Ethiopie, qui mourut à Ruel prez Paris l'an 1638." Much the same story is related and for much the same motivation: "to make known to all those who have seen this Prince the truth of his extraction, and that he was a Prince and legitimate son." Zaga-Christ's stay in France and his death are related with extreme sketchiness:

> Monsieur de Crequi estoit alors à Rome Ambassadeur, où voyant souvent Zaga-Christ, il luy persuada de voir la France, & de venir à Paris. Ce qu'il fit, & a demeuré en cette ville de Paris environ trois ans: apres lequel temps Dieu l'appella de ce monde en l'autre, mourant d'une pleuresie à Ruël; où son corps fut inhumé auprés du Prince de Portugal, l'an 1638.[65]

> Monsieur de Crequi was then ambassador to Rome, where, often seeing Zaga-Christ, he persuaded [the prince] to see France and to come to Paris. He did so and stayed in that city for about three years, after which time God called him from this world to the other one, Zaga-Christ dying of a pleurisy at Rueil, where his body was buried near the prince of Portugal in the year 1638.

The engraving of Zaga-Christ in *La Terre sainte* (see figure 2) leaves nothing to be desired in an alter ego for Europe: black "but" beautiful, Zaga-Christ has real Negroid features, but between the neck and the feet the illustration could be that of a Roman cardinal. His pensive dignity suits a consciousness fully assimilated to Europe.

But, as with Aniaba, Zaga-Christ's other incarnation is radically opposed. In Jean Dubois-Fontanelle's *Anecdotes africaines* (1775), Zaga-Christ becomes the usurper instead of the usurped:

> On vit encore sous ce regne un autre imposteur qui se dit fils de Jacob, & qui prit le nom de Zaga Christos. Après avoir essayé vainement d'exiter une révolution en Abyssinie, il quitta ce pays pour passer en Europe; il en imposa au cardinal de Richelieu & à

65. Eugène Roger, *La Terre sainte, ou Description topographique très-particulière des saints Lieux . . .* (Paris: Antoine Bertier, 1664), pp. 412–13.

Figure 2. Zaga-Christ, from Eugène Roger's *La Terre sainte . . . et une Relation de Zaga-Christ . . .* (Paris: A. Bertier, 1664). Reproduced by permission of the Sterling Memorial Library, Yale University.

toute la cour. Il obtint une pension considérable. Son séjour en France
offre quelques particularités singulieres; il avoit, selon Ludolf, un
penchant violent pour les femmes. Avec ce tempérament excessif,
il avoit la force d'Hercule. On prétend qu'il enleva la femme d'un
magistrat, & qu'il fut arrêté & obligé de comparoître à l'interrogatoire
du lieutenant criminel au Châtelet. Il refusa de répondre, en disant
qu'un homme tel que lui n'avoit de compte à rendre de ses actions
qu'à Dieu seul. Peut-être auroit-il subi un jugement sévere, si la
mort ne l'avoit pas prévenu: quelques personnes prétendent qu'il
s'étoit empoisonné; d'autres jugent que sa maniere de vivre étoit
bien suffisante pour abréger ses jours. Il fut enterré à Ruelle, en
1638; on lui fit cette épitaphe:

> Ci gît le roi d'Ethiopie
> L'original ou la copie.[66]

There was another impostor seen in this reign, who called himself
the son of Jacob, and who took the name of Zaga-Christos. After
trying in vain to foment a revolution in Abyssinia, he left that country
to come to Europe; he fooled Cardinal Richelieu and the whole court.
He obtained a considerable pension. His stay in France offers some
singular particularities; he had, according to Ludolf, a violent penchant for women. With this excessive temperament, he had the
strength of Hercules. It is claimed that he abducted the wife of a
magistrate and that he was arrested and made to appear for examination before the magistrate of the Châtelet. He refused to respond,
saying that a man such as himself had to account for his actions only
to God. He might perhaps have received a severe judgement if death
had not prevented it. Some persons claim that he poisoned himself;
others judge that his manner of living was sufficient to shorten his
days. He was buried at Rueil in 1638; this epitaph was made for
him:

> Here lies the king of Ethiopia
> The original or the copy.

The ''original or copy'' question runs through European reactions to African
visitors with the force of a terrible ambivalence. The noble prince and the
virtueless slave were like one personality divided against itself, being never
more bizarre than when they were fully domesticated. The problem is not
fully explained by a historical shift from positive to negative views of Africans,

66. Jean Dubois-Fontanelle, *Anecdotes africaines* (Paris: Vincent, 1775), pp. 41–42. On
Zaga-Christ, see also Hoffman, *Le Nègre romantique*, pp. 28–29; Debrunner, *Presence and
Prestige*, pp. 52–53; René Pintard, *Le Libertinage érudit dans la première moitié du XVIIᵉ siècle*
(Paris: Boivin, 1943), p. 259: ''Une autre fois, c'était Zaga-Christ qu'on comblait d'honneurs,
Zaga-Christ, neveu ou supposé tel du roi d'Ethiopie: et il profitait des faveurs du Pape pour
courtiser les dames romaines et s'aventurer jusque dans les couvents où, prétendait l'impertinent
chroniqueur [Gabriel Naudé], il mêlait à sa façon la couleur noire à la couleur blanche.''

for *Histoire de Louis Aniaba* comes too late. Underlying the extreme bivalency of these personalities is a single irony, a removal from definitive meaning. Aniaba and Zaga-Christ were anything Europe wanted to make of them, like soft wax with no character of its own. Douglas Grant, describing in *The Fortunate Slave* a British version of the same phenomenon, offers this conclusion: that the enslaved prince Job-ben-Solomon (and Louis Aniaba and Zaga-Christ) "had 'no character at all.' He existed only insofar as he had been interpreted according to current notions of Africa."[67]

From Homer to Louis XIV we have not come very far. Ethiopians are still "the farthermost men," living "farre disundered in their seat (In two parts parted)," "the first and last of men." Aniaba and Zaga-Christ, as creatures of French discourse, exist divided against themselves, first as princes, last as slaves or debauched impostors. These texts demand a kind of reading that is neither willfully positive nor willfully negative but that understands the irony between the two poles. For Louis XIV's little remark is emblematic of Africanist discourse in general, which, by its involvement with the noncolors black and white, is susceptible to a peculiar instability of meaning.

Nigri Idolatrae

Le Fétichisme a été antérieur à toute loi positive.
—Benjamin Constant

A citer ce fils de la Sainte mère l'Eglise, un dominicain, dont la soeur . . . rapportait . . . que, du sol, tête levée pour cracher en l'air, de toutes ses forces, de tout son héroïsme, sans crainte que ça lui retombe dessus, il baptisait les idolâtres grimpeurs que le spectacle de sa personne décolorée ne décidait pas à descendre de leurs cocotiers, avec ces mots: *Je vous baptise si toutefois vous avez une âme.*
—René Crevel, "Le Patriotisme de l'inconscient," *Le Surréalisme au service de la révolution*

A key part of Europe's understanding of Black Africa was the notion of idolatry. Marvin Pope finds a link between blackness and idolatry in ancient Hebrew texts ("Do not despise me because I am darker than you. . . . They taught me to worship idols.").[68] The sequence of meanings of εἴδωλα in Greek, according to the *OED*, is "appearance, phantom, unsubstantial form, image in water or a mirror, mental image, fancy, material image or form," but in Jewish and Christian usage *idol* refers more specifically and pejoratively to "image of a false god." What comes through in texts from the thirteenth

67. *The Fortunate Slave: An Illustration of African Slavery in the Early Eighteenth Century* (London: Oxford University Press, 1968), p. ix.
68. Song of Songs, trans. Pope, p. 327.

to the nineteenth century is an insistence that the idol is "nothing in the world" (1 Cor. 8:4), that the similitude it bears is an empty one, and that the process of idolatry is the negative of religion. I would define "idolatry" in Africanist discourse as a nullity and an immanence in the religious realm, a violation of the transcendent nature of divinity, characterized as a reign of the pure present, of the senses over the mind, desire over repression. While "idolatry" can no longer be thought of as a real entity in the world, it has at times been applied to Islam, Catholicism, and animism; it is always the outcast in any religious hierarchy. Europe consistently perceived Africa as the capital of idolatry.

A text of 1283, purporting to tell of the first European to penetrate the Sudan, reports, "The people there are all idolatrous Negroes, living in delight. . . . [There was] a dragon honored with sacrifices by the people of this land and worshiped like a God. . . . There are numerous idolater kings and princes there who worship the sun, the stars, the birds and the beasts. . . . They are Negroes; *they observe no law.*"[69] The absence of Godhead and law reflects the general absence of constitution as any fixed entity. Being "nothing in the world," the idol, idolatry, and the idolater are all outside the bounds of reason. A schematic rendering of maps from 1375, 1413, and 1447 shows legitimately constituted ethnic groups to the north of the Senegal and Niger rivers (Touaregs, Toucouleurs, etc.), in the area of Islamic influence; to the south lies nothing but "Nigri idolatrae" (La Roncière, *La Découverte,* p. 137). Recalling Said's statement that "the Orient in general and Islam in particular were systems of information, behavior and belief," no contrast could be greater than that between perceived Islam and perceived "idolatry" or "fetishism," its next of kin. The latter pair alone can be described in this fashion: "Fetishism cannot be a systematic, coherent, and strictly identical concept."[70]

The perception of idolatry perpetuates itself in European literature on Africa, unchanged by the advent of supposed eyewitness accounts. The first of these in French, the *Voyages auantureux* of Jean Alfonce de Sainctongeois (1559), while largely a practical guide to navigation, includes among its "facts" remarks on "Mohamétistes" and "Idolâtres." Some are yellowish *(jaunâtres)* and "part Mohametist, part Idolatrous" *(partie Mahométistes, partie Idolâtres),* others are "very black" *(forts noirs)* and "almost all idolaters" *(quasi tous Idolâtres).* Alfonce describes another group:

69. Ramon Lull, *Blanquerna* (first published in 1283), quoted in Charles de la Roncière, *La Découverte de l'Afrique au Moyen Age* (Cairo: Société Royale de Géographie d'Egypte, 1925), 1:111: "E aquelles gents son totes negres, e adoren ydoles, e son homens alegres . . . ." La Roncière does not give the original of this passage: "Là il y a de nombreux rois et princes idolâtres qui rendent un culte au soleil, aux étoiles, aux oiseaux et aux bêtes. Les habitants de ce territoire sont nombreux; de haute stature, ils sont nègres; ils n'observent aucune loi" (p. 112).

70. *Dictionnaire apologétique de la foi catholique* (Paris: Beauchesne, 1925), 1:1904.

Si y ha de belles gens noirs, qui n'ont point le nez large comme ceux de la Guynee. Ilz font leur Dieu de la premiere beste qu'ils peuuent auoir le mesme iour, ainsi chacun iour ilz font vn Dieu: touteffois ilz adorent le Soleil & la Lune côme les autres.[71]

Here are fine black people, who have not the wide nose like those of Guinea. They make their God of the first beast they can find that day; thus every day they make a God. However, they worship the Sun and the Moon like the others.

The "native's" idolatry is a fact among others, made in sequence with remarks on diet and geography. The blackness of idolatry and its fickleness are repeated by the notoriously unreliable cosmographer André Thévet in his *Singularitez de la France Antarctique* (1570). Passing by Africa, he finds "very strange people, for their dark and ignorant idolatry and superstition" ("peuple fort estrange, pour leur idolâtrie et superstition tenebreuse et ignorante" [p. 79]). He states categorically that between the Senegal River and the Cape of Good Hope, the people

sont tous idolâtres sans cognoissance de Dieu, ne de sa loy. Et tant est aueugle ce pauure peuple, que la première chose qui se rencontre au matin, soit oyseau, serpent, ou autre animal domestique ou sauuage, ils le prennent pour tout le iour, le portans auec soy à leurs negoces, comme un Dieu protecteur de leur entreprise. [Ibid.]

are all idolaters without knowledge of God or of His law. And this poor nation is so blind that the first thing encountered in the morning, be it bird, serpent, or other animal, domestic or wild, they take it for the whole day, carrying it with them on their errands, like a patron God of their enterprise.

These sixteenth-century value judgments remain unchanged into the seventeenth and eighteenth centuries: it is the exceptional text on Africa that does not mention idolatry in relation to the black peoples south of the Senegal River. It is commonplace to observe that idolatry and "fetishism" are "neither cult nor religion,"[72] that idolaters "serve their fetishes [which] not one of them was able to explain clearly. . . . Not one of them knows his religion" (Loyer, *Relation*, p. 213). But there is more to the European perception of idolatry than the blackness and nullity seen so far; it takes on a wider philosophical burden in the seventeenth and eighteenth centuries.

71. Jean Alfonce de Sainctongeois, *Voyages auentureux* (Poitiers: [1559]), p. 57.
72. Paule Brasseur, "Le mot 'nègre' dans les dictionnaires encyclopédiques français du XIXe siècle," *Cultures et développement* 8, no. 4 (1976): 591: "D'autres, notamment, et on pouvait s'en étonner, Virey, Bory de Saint-Vincent, reprochaient à l'Africain de manquer de croyances religieuses et de cultes, 'car le fétichisme n'est ni l'un ni l'autre.'"

Bossuet, an important thinker for black history because of his doctrine that slavery was the model of all political relationships,[73] begins to reveal the underlying problem in the following epistle *(Lettres diverses,* no. 257), where St. Athanasius is paraphrased:

> Il enseigne donc que la cause de l'idolâtrie, c'est que l'homme ayant quitté par le péché la *contemplation* de la nature divine invisible et intellectuelle, s'est plongé entièrement dans les sens; en sorte qu'il est incapable d'être frappé d'autres objets, que des objets sensibles: d'où il est venu à l'*oubli* de Dieu, à adorer le soleil, les astres, les éléments, les animaux, les images même, les passions et les vices, et enfin toute autre chose que Dieu. [*Oeuvres,* 11:264; emphasis mine]

> He therefore teaches that the cause of idolatry is that man, through sin, left behind the *contemplation* of divine, invisible, and intellectual nature and sank wholly into the senses, with the result that he is incapable of being touched by other objects than the objects of the senses; hence he has come to the *forgetfulness* of God and worships stars, elements, animals, even images, passions, and vices, and, finally, everything other than God.

The choice of modes is between "contemplation" (specular, binary, transcendental) and "forgetfulness" (immanent, monodic, self-contained); the choice of objects is between "a divine nature invisible and intellectual" and "the senses." The idolater has "forgotten" the intellectual, contemplative head and dwells in the confines of the body. Thévet described idolatry as blindness ("tant est aueugle ce pauure peuple"); by contrast, in Bossuet sight is the machine of sin, receiving only things present and visible, blind to the transcendent and invisible Divinity:

> Le sens humain abruti ne pouvait plus s'élever aux choses intellectuelles; et les hommes ne voulant plus adorer que ce qu'ils voyaient, l'idolâtrie se répandoit par tout l'univers. [*Oeuvres,* 10:194]

> Besotted human sense could no longer raise itself to intellectual objects; and, men no longer desiring to worship anything but what they saw, idolatry spread throughout the universe.

God is mediate; sin is immediate: the idolater can see only the latter. Worship of things visible means not only cows, the sun, and the stars but also "passions

73. Cf. Bossuet, "Cinquième avertissement," in *Oeuvres* (Paris: Lefèvre, 1836), 6:302: "L'origine de la servitude vient des lois d'une juste guerre . . . *servi,* qui devenu odieux dans sa suite, a été dans son origine un terme de bienfait et de clémence. . . . Toutes les autres servitudes . . . sont formées et définies sur celle-là . . . [L'esclave] n'a point d'état, point de tête."

and vices.'' In general, Europeans will agree that the African is given over to the flesh,[74] for "they are lazy, and laziness is the nursemaid of carnal pleasures."[75]

But the lubriciousness is only a figure of Europe's deepest objection to its perception of Africa: the crime of immanence. Sexual abandon and idolatry are both functions of a perceived failure to transcend and dominate the lower regions. The characterization of the third element in this paragraph of Diderot's *Encyclopédie* is typical:

> La religion n'y est pas la même par-tout: il y a des Chrétiens en Egypte & dans l'Abyssinie; le Mahométisme regne en plusieurs endroits; une autre partie est plongée dans l'idolâtrie; on prétend même qu'il y a dans la Cafrérie & dans le royaume d'Ardra des peuples qui n'ont *aucune idée de religion & dont toutes les vues se bornent à la vie présente, sans aucun soupçon d'un état futur.* [Emphasis mine]

> Religion is not everywhere the same [in Africa]: there are Christians in Egypt and in Abyssinia; Mohammedanism rules in many places; another part is sunk in idolatry; it has even been claimed that in Cafreria and in the kingdom of Ardra there are peoples who have *no idea of religion and whose entire view is limited to present life, with no inkling of a future state.* [Emphasis mine]

An unmediated present, untroubled by past memories or worries of the future—this is the existence of the idolater. He "thinks neither of the past nor of the future" (Dubois-Fontanelle, *Anecdotes africaines,* p. 2); his sleep will never be troubled by concerns of signifier and signified, image and reality, contemplation and divinity.

A turning point in European thought on idolatry was reached with the publication in 1760 of *Du Culte des dieux fétiches* by Charles de Brosses, first president of the Dijon parliament, man of letters, traveler, and erstwhile friend of Voltaire's (they fought over land ownership). Our current dictionaries attribute to de Brosses the etymology of the term "fetish" (in both French and English), although he seems only to have made its use more widespread by taking what was a strictly Africanist term, inherited from the Portuguese, and applying it to all primitive cultures.[76] *Du Culte des dieux fétiches ou*

---

74. This part of Europe's opinion of Africa has been well documented by Frantz Fanon in *Black Skin, White Masks,* trans. C. L. Markmann (New York: Grove, 1967), and by William Cohen in *The French Encounter,* among others.

75. Joseph-Romain Joly, *Les Aventures de Mathurin Bonice . . .* (Paris: 1783–87), 3:151: "Les Nègres sont doux, traitables, hospitaliers mais . . . ils sont paresseux, et la paresse est la nourrice des voluptés charnelles."

76. Thus, when de Brosses introduces the term for the first time, he explains: "quoique dans sa signification propre, elle [cette expression] se rapporte en particulier à la croyance des Négres de l'Afrique, j'avertis d'avance que je compte en faire également usage en parlant de toute autre

parallèle de l'ancienne Religion de l'Egypte avec la Religion actuelle de Nigritie was based on the premise that civilizations and religions all follow the same evolutionary path, once they get started, but that some are "stuck" at the zero point, outside of progress, for, "their customs not changing at all, two thousand years bring no alteration in practices" (*Culte*, p. 224). Black Africa provides de Brosses with a happy crossing of the temporal with the spatial, for in its perpetually arrested state it presents (makes present) a condition identical to that of ancient Egypt; to go to Africa, spatially, is to travel backward in time to a point of "pure anteriority." This conflation of space and time is so much a part of our current assumptions about non-European cultures that we may not even recognize its metaphorical basis; reading de Brosses, one of the first to think this way—a "primitive primitivist"—may help us to understand the problem better.

The "state of savagery from which many nations have slowly emerged": this is the beginning of things, which ancient Egypt and contemporary Black Africa represent. No nation, "excepting the chosen race," has been exempt from the "puerile cult" of idolatry, but it is maintained "especially in Africa." Black Africa has no monopoly on this "brutish stupidity," but it is the capital locus (*Culte*, pp. 14–15). De Brosses uses the term *fétichisme,* but his definition conforms to that of idolatry as "worship of a created thing":

> Ces Fétiches divins ne sont autre chose que le premier objet matériel qu'il plaît à chaque nation ou à chaque particulier de choisir & de faire consacrer en cérémonie par ses Prêtres: c'est un arbre, une montagne, la mer. . . . Ce sont autant de Dieux, de choses sacrées & aussi de talismans pour les Négres, qui leur rendent un culte exact & respectueux, leur adressant leurs voeux. . . . Ils jurent par eux; & c'est le seul serment que n'osent violer ces peuples perfides. [*Culte,* pp. 18–19]

> These divine Fetishes are nothing other than the first material object that it pleases each nation or each individual to choose and to have dedicated in a ceremony by their Priests: a tree, a mountain, the sea. . . . They are so many Gods, sacred objects, and talismans as

---

nation quelconque, chez qui les objets du culte sont des animaux, ou des êtres inanimés que l'on divinise" (*Du Culte des dieux fétiches* [Paris: n.p., 1760], p. 10). The real point at which "fétiche" was imported into French would be difficult to determine. It is used by Godefroy Loyer in his *Relation . . . d'Issyny,* p. 138: "Les idolâtres servent leurs Fétiches comme le reste des Négres de la Cote." De Brosses quotes Loyer at length in *Culte,* pp. 22 ff. It is also used by the Abbé Antoine Banier in his *Histoire générale des cérémonies, moeurs et coutumes* (Paris: Chez Rollin fils, 1741), in the feminine gender, and clearly defined: "Les Fétiches sont les Divinités particulières des Nègres" (p. 211). Banier relies heavily in his notes on Villault de Bellefond, a seventeenth-century writer I will discuss later. A discussion of de Brosses' role in the idea of the fetish is to be found in David Simpson's *Fetishism and Imagination* (Baltimore: Johns Hopkins University Press, 1982), pp. 9–22.

well for the Negroes, who offer them an exact and respectful devotion, asking them for favors. . . . They swear by them; and this is the only oath that these perfidious peoples dare not violate.

De Brosses proceeds to document at length the absurd practices of "the Negroes, today the most superstitious nation in the universe" ("les Nègres, aujourd'hui la plus superstitieuse nation de l'univers"; p. 25), cataloguing their *slavish*[77] devotion to creatures and objects, their "thousands of senseless actions" ("mille actions denuées de sens"; p. 185): marrying virgins to snakes (p. 40), spending huge sums on the comfort of a beast, before whom the fetishists prostrate themselves (pp. 86–87). But it is in section 3, "Examen des causes auxquelles on attribue le Fétichisme" ("Examination of the causes to which Fetishism is attributed"), that the profoundest objections of Europe emerge. The fetishism perceived in Africa is offensive because it is

> ce *culte direct rendu sans figure* aux productions animales et végétales . . . . On n'est pas obligé de rendre raison d'une chose où il n'y en a point, & ce seroit, je pense, assez inutilement qu'on en chercheroit d'autre que la crainte & la folie. . . . L'homme est ainsi fait, que laissé dans son état naturel brut & sauvage, non encore formé par aucune *idée réfléchie* ou par aucune *imitation,* il est le même pour les moeurs primitives & pour les façons de faire en Egypte comme aux Antilles. [Pp. 182–84; emphasis mine]

> This direct worship, offered without figures to animal and vegetable objects . . . . One is not obliged to see reason where there is none, and I believe it would be quite futile to look for any other than fear and madness. . . . Man is constituted such that, left in his raw and savage natural state, not yet shaped by any *reflexive idea* or by any *imitation,* he is the same in his primitive customs and his ways of doing things in Egypt as in the West Indies.

Fetishism is an affront to the representational nature of religion: bypassing figuration ("sans figure"), reflexive ideas, and imitation, this "direct cult" is a travesty of worship. Its thought processes are null and immanent (like Bossuet's "forgetfulness"), so that a discursive impasse is reached and the object becomes impossible to describe. Thus de Brosses speaks of "animals whose divinity was only local" ("des animaux dont la divinité n'étoit que locale" [p. 103]), having just written that "it was a question of an animal taken for itself and not considered as an arbitrarily chosen emblem of the real

77. This "slavish"-ness of idolatry is put in full perspective by David B. Davis' *Problem of Slavery,* which works from a starting model sentence, "Sin is slavery," to evolve toward the eventual abolitionist thought, "Slavery is sin." De Brosses' text is a perfect illustration of Western discourse laboring the first of these ideas.

Divinity" ("il s'agissoit de l'animal pris en lui-même & non pas consideré comme un emblême arbitrairement choisi de la Divinité réelle" [p. 94]). On the one hand, it is a "pure Zoolâtrie directe"; on the other, there is this persistent paradox, a "local divinity" whose lowercase initial d cannot prevent it from designating a transcendental object, necessarily opposed to a purely animal condition. The animal, taken only for itself, nevertheless contains this unholy divinity, which cannot be described in de Brosses' discourse. It is a nontranscendental, nonfigurative figure, an impossible immanence.

But what, then, is new about "fetishism" compared to "idolatry"? Since *Du Culte des dieux fétiches,* "fetishism" has taken the place of "idolatry" as the Other of religion, the most primitive of religions, and "idolatry" has slipped on the scale of meanings and come to be seen as the insertion of figuration within a purely immanent fetishism, as the recourse to representation. Thus the *OED,* crediting de Brosses with expanding the term, states: "A fetish differs from an idol in that it is worshipped in its own character, not as the image, symbol or occasional residence of a deity."[78] It will become commonplace in the nineteenth century to refer to a "pure and simple fetish-religion" (Gobineau, *Essai,* p. 312). But maintaining that purity poses problems, for the truly nontranscendent, nonrepresentational fetish is a discursive product doomed from its creation. In his description of the pure fetish, de Brosses is obliged to use phrases such as "l'animal *dont* la divinité" ("the animal *whose* divinity"), which necessarily describe a figure alongside, and incongruent with, its object (literally, as two words), one always pointing to the absence of the other. The experience is that of a continually rocking either/or, as seen in the *OED*'s actual definition of fetish, after de Brosses, as "An inanimate object worshipped by savages on account of its *supposed* inherent magical powers, *or* as being animated by a spirit" (emphasis mine). Is the object God or the house of God? Is it fetish or idol? By holding the topic at arm's length (the writer of the *OED* shows that *he* isn't a savage by inserting the word "supposed"!), the Western writer cannot allow fetishism to exist in tranquillity, for it is an affront to the workings of his or her language. The "animal taken for itself" and the "divinity" cannot coincide placidly; one must designate and thus negate the immediate presence of the other from the moment that discourse poses the problem. The discourse of fetishism and idolatry specializes in asking a question to which there is no answer and then reacting indignantly to the impasse it has itself created.

De Brosses' whole project—a description of "fetishism"—is thus more problematical than it seemed at first, being the phenomenology of a pure noumenon, the formulation of something that has no form. "Fetishism" and "idolatry" will always remain somewhat outside the power of Western dis-

---

78. Cf. "l'Idolâtrie (culte rendu à une image visant à la *représentation* d'un dieu: ce qui n'est pas le cas du fétiche)," *Dictionnaire apologétique de la foi catholique.*

course, and this overextension is characteristic of the specific discourse that gathers around the figure of Africa. The real contours of African religion have little importance to the functioning of this discourse, which proceeds through the centuries to project onto Africa a monstrous impossibility whose only existence is on paper. What is essential here is less African religion than European desire.[79]

Certain European interpretations of African religion allegorize this desire, depicting all strictures as fallen away in a free reign of the "id." With de Brosses, the Godhead is completely forgotten; with the Abbé Loyer, monotheism exists for the African only in a travestied form, where God has abdicated all authority, gone fishing:

> Ils ne croient pas qu'il [Dieu] puisse leur faire jamais de mal, persuadez qu'il est naturellement si bon, qu'il ne sçauroit leur en faire; parce qu'il a donné son pouvoir aux fétiches et ne s'est presque rien réservé pour lui. [Godefroy R. Loyer, *Relation . . . d'Issyny*, p. 213]

> They do not believe that He can do them harm, being persuaded that He is of such a kindly nature that He would not know how; for He has given His power to the fetishes and kept almost nothing for Himself.

Instead of a God of authority, repression, and all-defining constancy there is a god of released tension, wish-fulfillment, and malleability. While the desire may be all in the psychology of the European speaker, it is depicted as realized in Africa, which conforms perfectly and reflects it back.

A remarkable text of 1767 illustrates this projection and shows how an analysis such as de Brosses' or Loyer's becomes possible. Written within seven years of *Du Culte des dieux fétiches*, the Abbé Demanet's *Nouvelle Histoire de l'Afrique françoise* is more typical of seventeenth- and eighteenth-century works on Africa in its combination of travel, geography, botany, zoology, and what we would now call anthropology. In the section "Moeurs et Religion des Africains," Demanet's description of idolatry reaches the same stumbling block as did de Brosses', the "difficulty of knowing where [the idol] is, where it comes from, and what it does . . . . Trees consecrated

---

79. The true contours of African religion are, of course, well buried beneath this purposeful European discourse. Cf. John M. Jantzen and Wyatt MacGaffey, *Anthology of Kongo Religion: Primary Texts from Lower Zaire*, University of Kansas Publications in Anthropology no. 5 (Lawrence: University of Kansas, 1974), p. 2: "The BaKongo employ a stock of French expressions because, in practice, they have been found to leave European curiosity satisfied. Usually these conventions, of which fetish is a notorious example, correspond more closely to European expectations of African religion than to the original concepts, functions of an entirely different cognitive structure." Cf. Dominique Zahan, *Religion, spiritualité et pensées africaines* (Paris: Payot, 1970), p. 87: "L'Afrique interrogée sur ses croyances ne répond qu'au pied de la lettre."

in this fashion are either the Gods or the dwelling-places of the Gods."[80] The Abbé Raynal repeats this notion that the fetish "has no determinate form" (*Histoire*, 6:26). The indeterminacy between god and dwelling-place or figure of god, between fetish and idol, makes Africa a protean, perverse, and nonsensical other of religion. Says Demanet, "The idolaters . . . are the easiest to convert, for with a little persuasion they are easily brought about, because they have no established and regulated religion" (*Nouvelle Histoire*, p. 48).

But now Demanet goes beyond the others, in the following passage, where he *reads* the very condition of possibility of such an object as idolatry and, I dare say, of Africanist discourse in its entirety:

> L'Africain paroît être une machine qui se monte & se démonte par ressorts, semblable à une cire molle, à qui l'on fait prendre telle figure que l'on veut . . . ; avide d'être instruit, il saisit avec ardeur ce qu'on lui propose . . . ; il n'a rien qui le fixe. [Ibid., p. 1]

> The African appears to be a machine, wound and unwound by springs, similar to soft wax, which can be made to take on any figure one wishes . . . ; eager to be instructed, he fervently grabs on to whatever is given him . . . ; he has nothing to hold him in place.

Raynal almost seems to have plagiarized Demanet:

> Ce sont des espèces de machines qu'il faut comme remonter toutes les fois qu'on veut les mettre en mouvement. [*Histoire*, 6:128][81]

> It is as if they were machines, as if they had to be wound up every time you wanted to make them move.

It will be a long time before man as a "desiring machine," to be plugged into other "desiring" systems, having no fixed totality of his own, can be seen in anything but the most pejorative terms.[82] The importance of this

80. Abbé Demanet, *Nouvelle Histoire de l'Afrique françoise* (Paris: 1767), pp. 46–47: "La difficulté est de savoir où elle est, d'où elle vient, & ce qu'elle fait . . . . Les arbres consacrés en leur manière son ou les Dieux ou les demeures des Dieux."

81. Both Raynal and Demanet may have found the idea in Charlevoix' *Histoire de l'île espagnole de Saint-Domingue* (Paris, 1730–31), 2:499: "Les Noirs ne sont que des machines dont il faut remonter les ressorts à chaque fois, car ils n'ont ni mémoire, ni prévoyance, de faibles lumières."

82. Cf. Gilles Deleuze and Felix Guattari, *L'Anti-Oedipe* (Paris: Minuit, 1975), p. 43: "Toute machine, en premier lieu, est en rapport avec un flux matériel continu *(hylè)* dans lequel elle tranche"; p. 50: ". . . des fragments qui aient pour rapports entre eux leur propre différence en tant que telle, sans référence à une totalité originelle même perdue. . . . La production désirante est multiplicité pure, c'est-à-dire affirmation irréductible à l'unité. . . . Nous ne croyons plus à une totalité originelle ni à une totalité de destination." Deleuze and Guattari also insist, along with Demanet, that the machine is not a representation but rather an escape from representationality: "En quoi les machines désirantes sont-elles vraiment des machines, *indépendamment de toute métaphor?* [emphasis mine.] Une machine se définit comme un *système de coupures*" (p. 43; emphasis mine).

passage is that Demanet is reading and thematizing the underlying condition of Africa as an object in Western discourse: a protean machine, "soft wax." Soft wax is to form what black is to color, what idolatry is to religion, what nakedness is to clothing: a nullity. Each of these Africanist creations must be called by a name that is thereby negated: form is undone by soft wax, religion by idolatry, etc. But to be left with a "real" nullity is to fall silent, to cease reading and writing, to die. So the nullity takes a concrete form, or rather any form that you wish, so that it reflects any desire. Demanet's reading of the "soft wax" differs from other utterances in that it allegorizes the most profound condition of blankness, going beyond the usual observations of black and white.

Two centuries after Demanet, when Marcel Mauss issues the death certificate for "fetish" as a valid anthropological term, he will use familiar terms to describe it: the fetish "corresponds to nothing definite," "only to an immense misunderstanding between two civilizations, African and European."[83] Whether seen as a false term in discourse or as a real object in the world, the fetish defies form, frustrates intellection, and is ever a word for "nothing in the world."

French Priority and French Desire

Toute la Guinée . . . ne respire que les François.
—Villault de Bellefond

With a view toward the nineteenth century, when masses of new information on Africa reached Europe, one might wonder if this "soft wax" were merely an early consequence of misinformation. For the blank space at work in Africanist writing is certainly related to European ignorance. To reverse a piece of imperialist rhetoric, "There is no difference between the Black and the White except that which is produced by superior opportunities of receiving information."[84] It is evidently the White who lacks information about the Black here, and, as real contacts begin and increase, one would expect the measure of blankness to diminish. The opposed caricatures in Homer and Herodotus should become irrelevant and lapse into oblivion; positive characteristics of Africa and Africans should replace empty myths and myths of emptiness. This, however, is not the case, and I think that the discourse of the first French "discovery" of Guinea will help to illustrate how, if not why, myth was not wholly displaced.

We are dealing with the traces of an alleged event of the fourteenth or fifteenth century and with the story of French writers on the subject into this century. While there appears to be a consensus among most French historians

83. *Oeuvres* (Paris: Minuit, 1969), p. 144.

84. Thomas Fowell Buxton, expressing a belief in racial *equality* in the British House of Commons, 1830. Quoted in Curtin, *Image of Africa*, p. 242.

that it was the Portuguese who first reached Black Africa by sea, there are
still discordant voices; my interest is not in settling the question but in examining what has kept it going for so long. The theory of French priority
states that French-Norman mariners first discovered "Guinea" (that part of
Black Africa from Senegal to the Congo) either *(a)* in 1364, under the lead-
ership of Jehan le Roannois, or *(b)* in 1402, under Jean de Bethencourt, either
eighty-one or forty-three years before the generally accredited Portuguese
discovery. In 1434, there is no doubt, mariners sent out by Henry the Navigator
finally became the first to round Cape Bojador and make their way south to
the "Land of the Blacks," which they reached in 1445. The French claim to
priority has persisted controversially for three hundred years. It apparently
began at some point in the sixteenth century, as hearsay rather than history;
it was restated seriously as recently as 1972. The mercantilist, missionary,
and imperialist motivations behind this claim are a necessary part of the
explanation, but the politics, lies, and outright forgeries involved in the story
unfortunately only enhance its relevance to the general problem. The Africa
created in this apocryphal story is a dream come true for France.

The text that should lie closest to any real contact between the French and
Black Africa in the fourteenth century exists only as the publication of a
second-hand transcription of a manuscript that a scholar claimed to have seen
but that had since disappeared. It has been (almost) "unanimously declared
to be a forgery."[85] In 1867, Pierre Margry claimed to have a transcription of
the manuscript that one Lucien de Rosny had been shown by its owner, a
Britisher named William Carter; it presented "the solution to a problem for
the honor of our country."[86] The text is called "Briev estoire del navigaige
Mounsire Jehan Prunaut, Roenois, en la tiere des noirs homes et isles à nous
incogneus avec les estranges façons de vivre des dits noirs et une colloque
en lor language" ("Brief history of the navigations of M. Jehan Prunaut of
Rouen to the land of the blacks and to islands unknown to us, with the strange
ways of living of said blacks and a colloquy in their language"). The veracity
of the text would be easier to determine if the last two items—on the life and
language—were present in the manuscript, but they are conspicuously absent.

The story is of a benign and profitable encounter with the "noirs homes,"
who, while slightly frightened at first, develop a healthy appetite for trade
and quite a fondness for the Normans:

> Li Gilofs (ainsi sont apielés les gents cel partie, qui tot noir sont de
> visaige et de pel et tot nus, sinon là o côvient de mucer), onc n'avoient
> vu homs blancs, si que ceus qui virent la nes furent espoven-

85. Prince Yusuf Kamal, *Monumenta Cartographica Africae et Aegypti* (Cairo: n.p., 1926),
p. 1271.
86. Pierre Margry, *Les Navigations françaises et la révolution maritime du XIVᵉ et XVIᵉ siècle*
(Paris: Tross, 1867), p. 55: "je trouvais la solution d'un problème en l'honneur de notre pays."

tez . . . jusques ils furent asseurtez que cil Normans ne voloient mi les le dangier o les navrer. Les boun navoirs, qui tos estoient de grant cuer, lor dounèrent a fuson petits juiaus et présouns, et les firent boire boun vin vermail. . . . Adoncques les gents noirs de céans lor douèrent morphi, piaus de bestes sauvages et autre coses de lor pais fort estranges à veoir. Quât lur not fut plein d'aveirs precios et autre belle rien que ce estoit mervelle, Mesire Jehan . . . [fit] entendre cel homes noirs qu'ils rétorneroient enkoires là l'an ensuyvant et qu'ils se approvisionassent de cel marchâdises, cô que il li asseurerent. . . . Les seingnors cel partie moult desiroient l'alliance messire Jehan, et de ce tems comença li fait de marchandise avoec li naviors de Normandie et cils homs noirs. [Ibid., pp. 57–58]

The Gilofs [Wolofs] (thus are called the people of these parts, who are all black of face and of skin, and all naked, except for that which must be covered) had never seen white men, so that those who saw the ship were terrified . . . until they were assured that these Normans wanted neither to attack nor to harm them. The good sailors, who were all open-hearted, gave them enormous amounts of little trinkets and presents and had them drink good red wine. . . . Then the black people thereabouts gave them morphi [ivory], skins of wild beasts, and other things of their country, very strange to behold. When their ship was so full of precious goods and other fine things that it was a marvel, Monsieur Jean . . . made these men understand that they would return there again the next year, and that they should supply themselves with this merchandise, so that it be assured them. . . . The lords of these parts greatly desired the alliance with M. Jean, and from then began the fact of trade between the ships of Normandy and these black men.

The text is a mercantilist dream, with blackness, nudity, fear, and difference in general offset by the presence of ''precious commodities'' and the formation of an alliance *by the desire of the natives*.[87] It is the wish of the blacks to have Jehan as their lord; so the text would have it.

Philology has proved the text to be a forgery,[88] which makes it easier to conclude that the banality of the encounter is a pure fantasy. It reflects a mendaciously benign impression, a repression of difference; for example, no

87. Such alliances, in which the African accepts and even requests an unequal relationship in return for favors and trinkets, are, according to Curtin, ''an ancient aspect of European action and thought in West Africa'' (*Image of Africa*, p. 301).

88. Ch.-André Julien, *Les Voyages de Découverte et les premiers établissements* (Paris: PUF, 1948), p. 11n: ''Le nom de Jehan Prunaut (le preux nautonnier) a été créé pour les besoins de la cause, les expressions 'amirax' pour 'admiral,' 'ambedin' pour 'tous deux' n'avaient plus cours au XIVᵉ siècle; le roi n'était pas à Dieppe à la date indiquée; les 'Gilofs' ou Ouolofs sénégalais n'ont jamais habité le cap Bojador.'' See also La Roncière, *Découverte*, 1:14.

mention is made of idolatry, which would be a remarkable anachronism at best. But the inauthenticity of the text only increases its relevance to the Africanist tradition by reducing the referent to a pure fiction, to nothing but the projection of a European desire. As the discourse of French priority moves into the age of real physical contact, nothing will change. The desire will continue to be represented as the desire of the Africans, who "moult desiroient" ("greatly desired") precisely what the European would like.

The French encounter with Africa thus begins with a false event in 1364. The propagation of the myth is largely the work of Villault de Bellefond's *Relation des Costes d'Afrique* (1669), which is the first text to narrate fully the nonevents of 1364. For this reason the whole story has been called a pure invention of Villault's, a function of his desire to please Colbert (to whom the book is dedicated) by expanding French claims in Africa.[89] But Villault was evidently repeating and elaborating a tradition, for references of 1548, 1605, and 1643 indicate a French belief in a long-standing claim over Guinea.[90] Its original source is nowhere to be found.

The boldest function of this legend, which is repeated in most seventeenth- and eighteenth-century accounts, is the assimilation of "Guinea" to French subjectivity. This occurs through name and language. A Dutch description of 1602 reports on a place in Africa called Paris, so named by the French. G. Fournier's *Hydrographie* of 1643 states, "Before the Portuguese had taken La Mine [a French settlement on the coast] from us, all Guinea was filled with our colonies, which bore the names of the cities of France." Cartography from this period designates "Petit Paris," "Grand Setre," and again "Petit Paris." Villault cites the presence of these *names* as proof of French priority (Yusuf Kamal, *Monumenta Cartographica*, pp. 1272–73). The chevalier des

89. Vicomte de Santarem, *Recherches sur la priorité de la découverte des pays situés sur la côte occidentale d'Afrique* (Paris: Dondey-Dupré, 1842), pp. 53–54: "Cet ouvrage [*Voyage en Afrique* by Moquet] est une nouvelle preuve qu'avant Villault personne en France n'avait entendu parler des prétendues découvertes des Dieppois sur la côte de la Guinée dans le XIVᵉ siècle." It should be noted that the viscount is hardly a disinterested party; he has a claim of his own, that "les relations des Portugais avec l'Afrique n'ont jamais éprouvé d'interruption depuis l'antiquité la plus reculée jusqu'aux expéditions de l'infant D. Henri" (p. 6). See also R. Hennig, quoted in Th. Monod, "Un Vieux problème: Les navigations dieppoises sur la côte occidentale d'Afrique au XIVᵉ siècle," *Bulletin de l'Institut français d'Afrique noire* 25, no. 2 (1963):428: ". . . d'autres raisons, depuis [Santarem], sont apparus, obligeant à reconnaître impartialement que les récits correspondants de son [Villault's] ouvrage sont entièrement inventés, et ne sont rien de plus que d'imprudents mensonges de propagande"; Ramond Mauny, "Les prétendues navigations dieppoises à la côte occidentale d'Afrique au XIVᵉ siècle," *Bulletin de l'Institut français d'Afrique noire* 12 (1950):131: "Villault de Bellefond était justement un agent de Colbert . . . : il n'est pas question le moins du monde de faire acte d'historien—sauf lorsque l'histoire vient étayer sa thèse."

90. Yusuf Kamal, *Monumenta Cartographica*, p. 1271: "Ensuyt le lengaige de Guynée par le francoys" (Bibliothèque nationale, no. 24269); "les Franchois, qui y ont nauigué long tamps y a" (P. de Marees, 1605); "Avant que les Portugais nous eussent enlevé la Mine, toute la Guinée étoit remplie de nos colonies, qui portoient le nom des villes de France dont elles étoient sorties" (Fournier, 1643).

Marchais wrote in 1730, "The Negroes of the country have kept the name of Petit Dieppe for this Island, and the English, Dutch, and other Europeans who traffic on the coast have continued to name the place Petit Dieppe . . . , unquestionable proof that the French Normans were established at this place well before those who habitually call themselves the first."[91] The use of the name, the European utterance, by both Europeans and natives is the work of European discourse, but it is taken as referential proof.

This is more clearly thematized in Villault's text in his chapter entitled "Remarques sur les costes d'Afrique & notamment sur la Coste d'Or pour justifier que les François y ont esté longtemps avant les autres Nations." He relates a story so similar to that in the Prunaut text that one is tempted to see the latter as a translation of Villault into pseudo–Old French.[92] The natives put forth a "great welcome." Villault's thesis is not only that the French were there first but that they have a natural affinity with the Africans: "the humor of the Moors [blacks] is in better agreement with that of the French than with any other." A double optic is created by the author's technique of relating his own voyage to Africa in conjuction with that of the merchants of Rouen in 1364.

> Dans le mesme temps que l'Escrivain alloit à terre, il aborda un Canos que l'Alcair avoit envoyé avec des gens qui me surprirent. Ils sont noirs, la mine un peu moindre que nos gueux de France, tous nuds hors un petit linge qui les couvre par-devant.
>
> Ils demandèrent qui nous estions, nous leur dismes que nous estions François. Ils dirent: Estes vous venus pour demeurer ou seulement pour avoir des rafraichissements? Nous leur dismes que nous retournerions pour demeurer, à quoy *ils répondirent en François, Bonbon, les François valent mieux que les autres.* [Ibid.; emphasis mine]

91. Chevalier des Marchais, *Voyage en Guinée,* 1:146, quoted by Yusul Kamal, p. 1275: "Les Nègres ont toujours conservé le nom de petit Dieppe à cette Isle, et les Anglois, Hollandois, et autres Européens qui trafiquent à la côte, ont continué de nommer ce lieu le petit Dieppe, et le marquent ainsi sur leur Cartes, preuve sans réplique que les Normans François étoient établis en ce lieu bien avant ceux qui affectent de se dire les premiers qui ont découvert et établis le commerce en Afrique."

92. Villault de Bellefond, *Relation des costes d'Afrique, appellées Guinée* (Paris, 1669), quoted in Yusuf Kamal, *Monumenta Cartographica,* p. 1273. The passages similar to the Prunaut text are these: "De là ils passerent devant le Cap de Moulé, d'où les Habitans de ces deux places et de toute la coste furent fort étonnez, croyant que tous les hommes estoient Noirs. . . . Là ils acheverent de prendre leurs charges de morphi et de ce poivre appellé malaguette. . . . Le grand accueil, et la douceur, avec la quelle les Habitans de ce lieu les receurent, joints à la riviere et à la richesse de ce poivre, firent qu'ils appellerent ce lieu Paris. . . . Ce vaisseau arriva vers la fin de Décembre [1380] à la rade des lieux, où seize ans auparavant ils avoient esté. Les Habitans qui avoient reconnu, que dans les terres plus avancées, ils recherchoient les marchandises qu'ils avoient acheptées de nous, et que nous les traitions doucement, apporterent quantité d'or, et le vaisseau, neuf mois apprés, retourna à Dieppe richement chargé. Ce fut ce qui commença de faire fleurir le commerce à Roüen."

At the same time that the scribe went ashore, he met a canoe that
the Alcair had sent with people who surprised me. They are black,
of somewhat lesser demeanor than our beggars of France, all naked
excepting a small cloth, which covers them in the front.

They asked who we were; we told them we were French. They
said: Have you come to stay or only to have refreshment? We told
them that we would return to stay, to which *they replied in French,
Good-Good, the French are better than the others.* [Emphasis mine]

It is a curious element in the legend of French priority that the "native" is
made to support the French claim ("The French, *according to what the natives
say,* were established in this place before the Portuguese arrival");[93] curiouser
still is the demise of the African from the moment he appears in European
discourse. The sentence italicized above is to my knowledge the earliest
utterance in French literature attributed to a Black African on native ground,
and the fact that he is cast as speaking French to welcome the French should
indicate the extent of wish-fulfillment at work in this discourse. The African
first opens his mouth to deny his own otherness, to invite colonization, to
invoke a manifest destiny that the French will merely fulfill.

Those who maintain the theory of French priority will often refer to the
fact that in their own time (the seventeenth and eighteenth centuries), African
natives speak a French that they apparently inherited from their primal contacts
with the Normans.[94] But when Villault tells the story, an even more radical
possibility arises.

Le quatriéme vaisseau passa la Coste des Dents et poussa jusques à
celle de l'or, d'où il en rapporta quelque peu, mais quantité d'yvoire.
Comme ces peuples ne leur avoient pas fait si grand accueil que les
autres, sur tout ceux de la Coste des Dents; qui sont tres-mechans,
les Marchans sur le rapport de leurs Commis, se bornèrent au Petit-
Dieppe, et au grand Sestre ou Paris, ou ils continuerent d'y envoyer
les années suivantes, et mesmes une colonie. D'où vient qu'encore
aujourd'huy le peu de langage que l'on entend de *ces peuples, est
François.* [*Relation des costes d'Afrique,* in Yusuf Kamal, *Monumenta Cartographica,* p. 1273; emphasis mine]

The fourth vessel passed the Ivory Coast and pushed on to the Gold
Coast, from which they brought out some [gold], but a quantity of
ivory. As these peoples had not welcomed them as much as the
others, especially those of the Ivory Coast, who are very mean, the

93. O. Dapper, 1668, quoted in *Monumenta Cartographica,* p. 1272.
94. See quotations from Corneille's *Dictionnaire universel* and from Barbot, in Yusuf Kamal.
Cf. Abbé A. Anthiaume, *Cartes marines, constructions navales, voyages de découverte* (Paris:
Dumont, 1916), p. 375: "A la fin du XVᵉ siècle, les Français fréquentaient la côte occidentale
de l'Afrique jusqu'à la Guinée, et les Sénégalais parlaient notre langue" (emphasis mine).

Merchants, on the report of their Clerk, held themselves to Petit-Dieppe and to Grand Sestre, or Paris, where they continued to send in the following years, and even a colony. Whence the fact that still today *the little bit of language that one hears [understands] from these people is French.* [Emphasis mine]

And elsewhere:

> . . . outre mesme que le grand Sestre conserve ce nom de Paris; c'est que *le peu de langage que l'on peut entendre est François.* . . . Aprés le salut ils crient, Malaguette tout plein, tout plein, tant à terre, de Malaguette, qui est le peu de langage qu'ils ont retenu de nous. [Ibid.; emphasis mine]

> . . . besides that Grand Sestre has kept this name of Paris, there is the fact that *the little bit of language that one can hear [understand] is French.* . . . After the greeting, they shout "Malaguette [pepper] plenty, plenty, so much Malaguette on shore," which is the little of our language that they have retained. [Emphasis mine]

The reader may be struck by an ambiguity in the first italicized sentence. The verb *entendre* means both "to hear" and "to understand," the former being the more modern usage. The logical interpretation of the sentence would be, "The little bit of their language that one understands is French." This is already a daring claim, for it means that the Africans have preserved some intelligible traces of their contact with the Normans, which had supposedly occurred *three hundred years earlier.* But if *entendre* were to mean "hear," then the only speech these people possess is French; perhaps the rest of the noise they make is like "the squeaking of bats." In both cases the African achieves signification only through French, but in the second case all possibility of another subjectivity, beyond the reach of Europe, has been forgotten. If French is the only language that can be "heard," then the African has become a pure projection of French desire, with no identity or language of his own. If French is the only language that can be "understood," then the hallucination is considerably diminished, for the European recognizes himself as a limited subjectivity in the presence of an Other with a language of his own. I am told that in the sixteenth century the meaning would have been clearly "understand," in the eighteenth century clearly "hear"; but, in the seventeenth, the sense is purely indeterminate. I will return to this problem by way of conclusion, as a model for the interpretation of "discourse."

If that cheap version of French subjectivity, *le petit nègre,* is born in Villault's text ("Bonbon . . ."), it is for good reason. The African is putty in the European's hands; even when all French monuments had disappeared from Africa, there remained "the name and the desire of the inhabitants to

see them [the French] again'' (Villault); for the language and the desire are
those given by France. The Portuguese historian who debunked the French
claim to priority in Guinea, the viscount de Santarem, wrote in 1842: ''We
know from experience that the Negroes in their answers [i.e., the answers
we write for them] always affirm what we want them to say'' (*Recherches
sur la priorité,* p. 32).

Attempts to prove the French claim all depend on evidence that is somehow
missing. The forces at work are a litany of negativity: the disappearance of
the Prunaut manuscript; the fire that destroyed the Dieppe hall of records in
1694; the erasure and altering of dates; misreadings of manuscripts willfully
or innocently; and, above all, the ''profoundest silence,'' ''resting on no
historical fact'' (Santarem, pp. 27–44). The negativity was apparently at work
on an object that never existed—the fire destroyed the records of a dream.
The fact that the claim cannot be proved is even cited as proof in itself, for
the Normans would have been anxious to avoid foreign competition and thus
could have ''jealously kept the secret of all their itineraries'' (Anthiaume,
Cartes maritimes, p. 372). Yet the theory of French priority was passionately
restated, in 1972, by someone who promised a photocopy of a corroborating
document.[95] The current Michelin Guide to Normandy cites 1364 as a red-
letter date in Norman history, when ''the Dieppois disembark on the coasts
of Guinea.''

Although this claim has been relegated by most historians to the realm of
the ''apocryphal,'' of ''myth'' (Mauny, ''Les prétendues navigations,'' p.
130), and although the fourteenth-century voyages ''never had any reality
except on paper'' (Monod, ''Un vieux problème,'' p. 432), that paper reality
persists. Thus the process of moving beyond the ancient legends, of increasing
real information about Africa, begins with another legend. The inscription of
''Africa'' within French discourse begins as this ''cruel enigma,'' neither
provable nor refutable. While the chauvinism, plagiarism, and mendacity of
this whole tradition might appear to make it irrelevant to true history and
authentic literature, it must be remembered that this legend was at the root
of France's understanding of its relations with Black Africa for at least two
hundred years and that the manipulation of ''Africa'' as soft wax is the same
in the (probably) forged Prunaut text as in travel accounts based on real
observation.

A fifteenth-century chronicle, whose veracity is accepted for the most part,
contains passages on Africa that have been largely ignored. *Le Canarien,
livre de la conquête et conversion des Canaries,* was revived by G. Gravier
in 1874 in the interest of preserving some French claim after the Prunault

---

95. Leonard Sainville, *Histoire du Sénégal depuis l'arrivée des Européens jusqu'à 1850*
(Saint-Louis du Sénégal: C.R.D.S., 1972), p. 6.

tradition had been discredited.[96] Jean de Bethencourt was a Norman nobleman
born in 1360, known for the conquest and conversion of the Canary Islands
between 1402 and 1406. The chronicle ("this precious relic both to the glory
of the house and the glory of the nation"; Gravier, p. lxxiii) was written by
two monks, Pierre Bontier and Jehan Le Verrier, in the service of the
Bethencourt house, and its pedigree is scrupulously documented. In contrast
to the Prunault "mystification," this chronicle "is of an incontestable authenticity" (Anthiaume, p. 373). This means that its basic claims—the conquest of the Canaries and the first doubling of Cape Bojador—are accepted
by modern historians as fact.

To better define our problem here, we can begin by discerning two types of
discourse in this text. The first purports to be an eyewitness account told by
the two author-monks who accompanied Bethencourt. It is characterized by a
language of events reported directly, perceived without the means of perception
being called into question: "Et mons.^{r} de Bethencourt et sa compagnie prin-
drent leur chemin, et quant ils eurent doublé la cap de Finiterre, ils suiuirent
la cotiere de Portugal" (p. 7). I would tentatively call this *perceptual discourse*,
for it depicts phenomena as being realized before the senses.

With the conquest accomplished, the narrative shifts its focus from events
to intentions and desires within the mind of Bethencourt, and the discourse
changes from direct perception to the filtering of the outside world through
thought. The vocabulary that appears deals with doubt, desire, sight, reason,
fear, astonishment, and information:

> Et Bethencourt, qui toutes les ysles canariennes a veues et visi-
> tées . . . dit ainssi que se aucuns nobles princes du royaulme de
> France ou d'ailleurs vouloient entreprendre aucune grant conqueste
> par dessà, qu'il seroit vne chose bien fesable et bien resonable. [*Le
> Canarien*, p. 83]

> And Bethencourt, who saw and visited all the Canary Is-
> lands . . . said that if any noble princes of the kingdom of France
> or elsewhere wanted to undertake a great conquest there, that it would
> be a feasible and a reasonable thing.

The narrative moves from accomplished facts to schemes and speculations
and, finally, to legend. For the moment I will call this *thought discourse*,
since it occurs within the understood brackets of a specular mode.

The object of all this intentionality is the vast unknown continent beyond
Cape Bojador, which marked the end of the earth for Europe at this time.

---

96. Santarem's *Recherches* had discredited the 1364 hypothesis in 1842. Gravier him-
self calls the Prunault manuscript a "mystification" (*Le Canarien*, ed. Gabriel Gravier [Rouen:
Méterie, 1874], p. xxii). The authors of the chronicle were Pierre Bontier and Jehan Le
Verrier.

Mariners knew no way to return against the wind, and Bojador is here referred to as "the tip of terra firma" ("la point de la terre ferme"). Bethencourt's mind is filled with a "great will" ("grant voulenté," p. 87), and an *intention* ("intencion," p. 86) to penetrate, conquer, and convert Africa. Intentionality depends on a binary opposition between two constituted selves and on their ability to maintain this constitutive difference. Such is the case with the main object of Bethencourt's thought discourse, the "Saracen miscreants," a constituted enemy about whom Bethencourt has "a great will to know the truth" ("a grant voulenté de sauoir la verité, l'estat et gouuernement"; p. 87). So, as the text projects itself beyond the realm of immediate perception, its first object is cast as a question of information, truth, and conquest. The first object of thought discourse is thus Orientalist.

The second is Africanist and "sundered in twain." Africa consists of "Sarazins," "crestiens," and "paiens." The relationship of the discourse to the first object is different from that to the second and third; in relation to the latter two, intentionality will fail. The pagans will be called "idolaters," and almost nothing about them will be reported. Yet their presence in opposition to apocryphal "Christian kingdoms" makes clear the double valency of the totally unknown. Thus within Bethencourt's thought discourse three objects appear: the known Saracen enemy, the Christian other, and the idolatrous other.

The Christian appears in a passing reference to Prester John, with more importance than length, in the midst of the plans for dealing with the Saracens:

> car on ne peult estre si fort armé come l'on seroit en France pour la longeur du chemin, et aussi pour le pais qui est vng pou plus chaut. *Et pourroit on auoir legierement des nouuelles de prestre Iehan.* Et qui seroit entré au pays on l'en trouueroit assés près de là vne maniere de gens qui s'apellent Farfus, qui sont crestiens, pouroient adresser de moult de choses qui seroient grandement proufitables, car ils sceuent les pais et les contrées, et parlent les langagez. [Ibid., p. 85; emphasis mine]

> For one cannot be as well armed as one would be in France, due to the great distance and to the country, which is a little hotter. *And news could be easily had of Prester John.* And one who entered the country would find near there a kind of people called Farfus, who are Christian, and could discuss many things that would be greatly profitable, because they [the Farfus] know the country and the landscape and speak the languages. [Emphasis mine]

There has been controversy concerning the importance of the Prester John figure as an impetus for voyages of discovery. Although one historian finds it absurd to attribute such religious motivations to the fifteenth-century Portuguese, those same Portuguese, in the court of Prince Henry the Navigator, listed the finding of a Christian ally among their explicit reasons for troubling with exploration.[97] In this way they echo the Bethencourt chronicle. The desire for Prester John is the desire for an Other who is a perfect reflection or fulfillment of yourself, a prince who at the farthest reaches of the earth will make you whole and allow you to encircle your enemy, these "Saracen miscreants." Like Villault's Africans greeting the French in French, Bethencourt's Prester John represents the fulfillment of a desire.

The leap into the void—the blankness of "Africa"—is marked by a movement from fact to hearsay, history to legend, positive to conditional mood, direct narration to a book within a book. In chapter 55 of *Le Canarien* a bridge is made between the two monks' narrative and a book that they cite:

> . . . auons si endroit mis aucunes choses, touchans ses marches, extraites d'un liure que fit vng frere mandeant, qui auironna iceluy pais, et fut à tous les pors de mer, lesquelz il diuise et nomme, et ala par tout les roy^mes cretiens et des paiens, et des Sarazins qui sont de ceste bende, et les nome tous, ... Et pour ce qu'il parle si au vray des contrées et des pais dont nous auons vraie congnoissance, il nous semble que ainssi doit il faire de tous les autres pais. Et pour ce auons nous si apprès mis aucunes choses qui sont en son liure, dont nous auons mestier. [P. 88]

> . . . we have put here things concerning his marches, taken from a book by a mendicant friar, who went around this country and was at all the seaports, which he distinguishes and names, and went through all the kingdoms, Christian and pagan and that of the Sarazins, who are of this area, and he names them all. . . . And because he speaks so truly of the landscapes and countries of which we have true knowledge, it appears to us that he must do so for all the other countries. And for this reason we have used things here which are in his book, from which we have benefited.

The title of chapter 56 is "Coment vng frere mandeant deuise des choses qu'il a veues par vng liure qu'il en fit" ("How a mendicant friar recounts things he has seen in a book he wrote about them"), and it is known to be "the story of an *imaginary* voyage (in reality a simple description of a fourteenth-century portulan)."[98] But this shift from history to legend, from the direct knowledge of the monks to pure received tradition, is denied as such, passed off as a continuation of "real knowledge." And within the confines

---

97. See Catherine Coquery, *La Découverte de l'Afrique* (Paris: René Juilliard, 1965), pp. 83 ff.; Gomes Eanes de Zurara, *Conquests and Discoveries of Henry the Navigator*, trans. B. Miall (London: Allen & Unwin, 1936), p. 133.

98. Mauny, "Les prétendues navigations," p. 128. A portulan or portolano is a book of sailing directions.

of this chapter, the discourse is as factual and direct as any perceptual discourse can be.

> Et se partit le Frere d'eulx, et s'en ala contre orient par maintez contrées iusquez à vng roy^{me} qui s'apelle Dongala, qui est en la prouynce de Nubye, habitté de cretiens, et s'appelle prestre Iehan, en vng de ses tiltres, patriarche de Nubye, qui marchist d'un des costés aux dezers de Egypte, et de l'autre costé à la riuiere de Nylle, qui vient des marches de prestre Iehan. [Pp. 90–92]

> And the brother left them and went into the east, through many countries, into a kingdom called Dongala, which is in the province of Nubia, inhabited by Christians, and called Prester John, in one of his titles, patriarch of Nubia, who marched from one of the coasts to the deserts of Egypt and, from the other coast, to the Nile River, which comes from the outposts of Prester John.

Passing south to the "land of the Blacks," the friar mentions termites that "bring up gold ore from under the earth" ("qui tiroient grauelle d'or de desous la terre"). Following a river, he comes to an island and mentions the only people he finds anywhere who are neither Moslems nor Christians: "Là sont les gens ydolatres." In 1350, long before any actual European contact with Black Africa, this text projected onto its blackness a nullity of religion, with a specific name and valorization. Yet idolatry and Prester John ride in tandem, both spoken of as real, both *visited* by the friar:

> Et de la s'en ala le Frere touiours aduant . . . par maint pais et par maintes diuersses contrées iusquez à la cité de Melée, là où demouroit prestre Iehan, et la demoura moult de iours. [Pp. 97–98]

> And from there the brother went still forward . . . through many countries and through many different terrains, to the city of Melée, where Prester John lived, and there he stayed many days.

"He lingered, delighted, at the banquet side." The desire is depicted as realized, literally made real before the eyes: "Pour ce qu'il y veoit assés de choses meruilleusez, desquelles nous ne faisons nulle mencion" ("For he saw there many wonderful things, of which we shall not make mention").

It would be wrong to infer that the passage to legend here is merely a function of indirect speech or of the lack of real contact. It so happens that *Le Canarien* maintains its place as a historical document only so long as it remains with the places the monks saw. But the delight and the horror of the friar's tale are both recounted in the same discourse of direct perception, only inside the occasional brackets of "according to the Friar's book." Direct contact with Black Africa will not put an end to the play of delight and horror, of black and white, of idolatry and natives "beloved of the gods." These will merely find "real" objects and change names. When Prester John reaches identification with the real Christian kings of the real Ethiopia, the discourse has found its happiest moment: the object projected into the void returns perceptually as reality itself.[99]

The importance of the whole French-priority question lies in the return of desire (and loathing) from an apocryphal reality. The natives' cry of "Bonbon," their mercantile lusts, Prester John, and the idolaters all depend on the unresolved difference between the two meanings of *entendre* in Villault's *Relation*. What sort of identity can be granted to the object? Was it actually heard or merely understood? And what are the implications of the two sorts of discourse that ride on that difference?

"Africa," Dream and Discourse

Zita: Apprends à moi, bon ami,
　　Discours si joli,
　　Discours tant joli;
Moi veux dire de même à toi
　　Toi comme moi
　　Moi comme toi. . . .
　　　　　　　—J.-B. Radet and P. Barré, *La Négresse*
　　　　　　　ou le pouvoir de la reconnaissance (1787)

This study began as an equation containing two unknowns, "Africanist" and "discourse." I would hope that the general profile of the adjective has now become clear. The term "discourse," however, may appear persistently ambiguous: appropriately so, for its polymorphousness is necessary for a phenomenon such as the figure of Africa. "Discourse" is not a category equal or opposable to "language," "speech," "writing," "thought," or "idea." It participates in all of these but is not reducible to any of them. There is no "discourse" in the sense that there is a classical system of tropes known as "rhetoric"; there are only *discourses,* forming themselves according to the shape of their objects. To speak of a discourse is thus to express a critical attitude, a bias toward reducing utterances to their "paper reality," understanding them as contingent and overdetermined rather than necessary and immutable.

The term can hardly be used without reference to Michel Foucault, whose *Archéologie du savoir* justifies a methodology such as the one I have used in this chapter, with its readings of conditions of possibility rather than intended meanings. From the analysis of the word "Africa," for example, it should be evident that the object "does not preexist itself" but is constituted by every utterance of the word. Foucault says that a discourse cannot be "a

99. See La Roncière, *La Découverte de l'Afrique*, 2:112.

majestically unfolding manifestation of a thinking, knowing, speaking subject" but rather is an act of the speaking subject's "discontinuity with itself."
That discontinuity and that rupture of Western knowledge have been seen
here in the scientific fantasy of the Niam-Niams, the godless religion of
idolatry, the headless ones, and the "real-life" descriptions of Prester John.

But Foucault makes the task appear too easy by positing a discourse-
criticism divorced from thought-criticism. The former would only "determine
the condition of existence of an utterance," its limits and its differences from
other utterances, with no desire to penetrate "from outside to inside, from
text to thought, from surface to depth."[100] This is the alternative to thought-
criticism, which, according to Foucault, is "always allegorical in relation to
its subject," asking, "Qu'est-ce qui se disait dans ce qui était dit," chasing
after the intentions of the speaking subject. At stake in the choice of meth-
odologies is the status, the "identity," of the literary object. A pure *analysis*
of discourse would trade among differential noumena divorced from intentions, desires, and emotions. A pure *interpretation* of voices in "thought-
criticism" would grant the object (Africa) reality as a phenomenon on which
"thoughts" are molded; these thoughts would therefore be acts of perception
instead of projection. I have tried to follow neither doctrine absolutely, but
I believe that any discourse, and any criticism of discourses, finds itself caught
between the two. A similar problem faced Freud in the *Interpretation of
Dreams,* and his answer serves to reorient one's understanding of discourse
in general, away from a simplistic real / unreal dichotomy.

Africanist discourse resembles dream in Freud's description. Both are made
possible by a condition of blankness—of distance and ignorance, of sleep.
Within that frame, a discourse unfolds having the singular capacity to appear
real, to break the frame and fill the universe: a dream is not a dream unless
the dreamer cannot distinguish it from reality. Similarly, Africanist fantasies
come armed with measurements in centimeters, eyewitness accounts, and
every appearance of accurate perception. But like the figure of "Africa,"
dream is felt to be "something alien, arising from another world and contrasting with the remaining contents of the mind," "extraneous to our
minds."[101] Yet, paradoxically, dreams can only be a result of "the arbitrary
decision of the mind." They are the closest object to the mind and the furthest
from it. The central question of the *Interpretation of Dreams* is the assignment
of an etiology and a status to this uncanny discourse, for Freud's predecessors
tended to "leave a great gap when it comes to assigning an origin for the
ideational images which constitute the most characteristic material of dreams"
(p. 74). This "riddle of the sources of dreams" runs parallel to our concern
here with the status of the Africanist object.

    100. Michel Foucault, *L'Archéologie du savoir* (Paris: Gallimard, 1969), pp. 61, 40, 85.
    101. Sigmund Freud, *The Interpretation of Dreams* [1900], trans. James Strachey (New York:
Basic Books, 1965), pp. 39, 80.

It is well known that Freud's main thesis is that "a dream is the fulfillment of a wish." But the nature of that fulfillment is called into question by Freud's positing two identities or types of fulfillment. Perceptual identity *(Wahrneh-mungsidentität)* occurs when "a psychical impulse . . . seeks to re-cathect the mnemic image of the perception and to *re-evoke the perception itself,* that is to say, to re-establish the situation of the original satisfaction" (p. 605; my emphasis). This is the "regressive" path of the unbridled primary process, the unsubdued preconscious, and this identity is founded in an illusionary Realism that consists of a "taking-for-real" *(Wahrnehmung)* of its object. The coincidence of the object and the investment is defined as wish-fulfillment: "An impulse of this kind is what we call a wish; the reappearance of the perception is the fulfillment of the wish" (ibid.).

The relevance of Freud's dream theory to Africanist discourse should become clear in his next sentence: *"Nothing prevents us from assuming that there was a primitive state of the psychical apparatus in which this path was actually traversed, that is, in which wishing ended in hallucinating"* (my emphasis). That "primitive state" of wish-fulfillment is how Europe conceives of African thought: as a free reign of fulfilled desire, a place to "linger delighted" with the gods, where dualities of representation have been abolished in a single "fetish-religion," where ornamentation and physique coincide, where the alien native cries welcome in your own language, where the people are nothing but a "soft wax," and where "any figure that you wish" can be realized. Freud's projection of such a "primitive state" constitutes yet another *rêverie du repos;* it parallels Homer, Herodotus, de Brosses, Demanet, and the others by dreaming, in effect, of a world without dreams. Pliny wrote that the Ethiopians "are not visited with dreams like the rest of mortals" (see p. 26, above): no dreams or nothing but dreams, this "primitive state" is in either case the end of the distinction between dream and reality.[102]

The opposite of perceptual identity is described by Freud as "thought identity," which is "nothing but a substitute for a hallucinatory wish" but "has abandoned this intention [of coinciding *perceptually* with a prior experience of satisfaction] and taken on another in its place—the establishment of a *thought* identity [with that experience]" (p. 641). Because dreams are caught within the confines of thought, "no matter what impulses from the normally uninhibited Unconscious may prance upon the stage, we feel no concern; they remain harmless" (p. 607). The thought identity is what Europe attributes to itself in relation to the African's "null" mode: Christianity with

---

102. It is interesting to note in passing that a perceptual identity *avant la lettre* is precisely what Marx, in *Capital,* described as a *fetish.* Such is his contempt for the notion of the *commodity* that he "must take recourse to the mist-enveloped regions of the religious world. In that world the productions of the human brain *appear as independent beings endowed with life.* This I call the Fetishism which attaches itself to the products of labour, so soon as they are produced as commodities" (*Capital: A Critique of Political Economy,* trans. Samuel Moore and Edward Aveling [New York: International Publishers, 1970], p. 72; emphasis mine).

its symbols, opposed to idolatry with its fetishes, "contemplation" instead
of *oubli* ("forgetfulness"; Bossuet), "reflexive ideas" and "imitation" instead of a "direct cult without figures" (de Brosses). Thus, in Africanist
discourse it is always the European subject who represents *thought* (sane
contemplation of an object recognized as other) as opposed to *hallucination*
(illusory identification with the nonself, desire fulfilled and canceled out).
Europe conceives of Africa as the direct, immanent, unself-conscious an-
nulment of its (Europe's) own binary modes of thought.

The exact place of dream between perceptual and thought identity is the
central question of the *Interpretation of Dreams*. If dreams were limited to
a pure thought identity, they would not be swayed by the "darker regions,"
and, having renounced any desire or intention to fulfill a wish, their force
and energy would no longer exist: they could not take themselves for reality.
But if dreams were total perceptual identities, we would have taken "a step
beyond what can be demonstrated" (p. 645), for the primary process of the
Unconscious is purely sensorial and alien to representation. Freud's answer
is magnificently evasive: "I have intentionally left gaps in the treatment of
my theme because to fill them would on the one hand require too great an
effort and on the other would involve my basing myself on material that is
alien to the subject of dreams." Those gaps, if filled, would falsify the nature
of dream, which is constituted by its free play between perception and thought.
In this section of sublime difficulty ("The Psychology of the Dream-Processes:
The Primary and Secondary Processes"), Freud makes his own theory infinitely more complex than simple wish-fulfillment. To end that complexity by
defining dream as one or the other identity would be to cure the system of a
disease without which the system would not be.

The difficulty of maintaining an identity in discourse is the central Africanist
problem. Fetish-religion was projected by de Brosses as the annihilation of
dualistic religion, "imitation," and "reflexive ideas" by an "animal taken
for itself "; yet that animal was inexorably contaminated by a transcendent
"real Divinity" not congruent with the animal itself. This means that a purely
perceptual identity (the animal being "taken for real" as a sensorial god) was
reduced to a thought identity (only representational) by de Brosses' discourse.
The impossibility of maintaining an immanence is what constitutes Africanist
discourse: de Brosses' arrival at an immanent transcendence, a nonfigurative
figure, emblematizes the incompatibility of the discourse with its own aims,
an incompatibility that constitutes the rigor of the discourse rather than undermines it.

To return to Foucault's terminology (which uses the word "thought" in a
way exactly opposed to Freud's use: for Foucault, "thought" is the hallucinatory "taking-for-real"), discourse-criticism can no more free itself of
regressive, hallucinatory "thought" than dream can free itself of the drive
toward wish-fulfillment. To take our most basic example: it would be falla-

cious to assign either a purely perceptual or a pure thought identity to the verb *entendre* in Villault's sentence "Le peu de langage que l'on peut entendre est François." If the verb were used solely in its perceptual sense, as meaning that French is all one can hear because it is all they speak, then referential, linguistic proof would exist that the French had priority over Guinea, and a whole hallucination of a Europeanized Africa, robbed of its identity and fulfilling Europe's wishes, would be taken for real. This would be the pitfall of a pure "thought-criticism," in Foucault's sense. If, on the other hand, a pure thought identity (in the Freudian sense) were assigned to the object, *entendre* would apply only to the Frenchman's intellectual understanding, and Africa, remaining on its own as a constituted subjectivity (with its own language, but speaking a few words of French, which are thus "understood"), would hold no "delight" for the European. A pure discourse-criticism, in Foucault's sense, using only the "thought identity" of *The Interpretation of Dreams,* could not account for the force of a desire that depicts itself as fulfilled before the senses, for the *perceived reality* of utterances such as "Bonbon, les François valent mieux que les autres."

The Africanist object takes life from its inability to remain on one side or the other. This "discours si joli" offers the possibility of both "delight" and reality, of thought and perception, of dream and wakefulness. Such a discourse must be taken seriously and examined in depth, for, from the point of view of its practitioners, its fantasies are real.

Part Two

Africanist Poetics

2

Baudelaire in the Nineteenth Century: Black and White in Color

Introduction

The problematics of distance, difference, and absence that we have seen thus far are not the exclusive property of any single literary or nonliterary form of writing. In fact, the study of a discourse cannot properly respect the confines of that distinction. But since the largest part of this study will be devoted to texts that are categorized as "literary," it must be kept in mind that their relevance here is as participants in a discourse whose roots and fundamental workings are not limited to any particular genre.

My reasons for turning to Charles Baudelaire are perhaps not those one would expect: Jeanne Duval, the poet's half-black mistress of many years, is of little importance here, as is the accepted notion that a certain number of his works are addressed to her. The so-called "Jeanne Duval Cycle" is a constraint on interpretation produced by biographical information, requiring that Baudelaire the man who lived and breathed be identified with the narrator of his poems. As such, the Cycle produces a limitation on reading that the poems themselves do not demand.[1] The "element of blackness" is not unique to the Jeanne Duval poems.

1. "The satisfactions afforded by poetry are at times rooted in cultural and psychological realities which we may be reluctant to confront. Such is the poetry of Baudelaire associated with his mulatto mistress, Jeanne Duval. . . . The impact of the Jeanne Duval poems is inescapably related to interactions involving self and other, male and female, black and white. In this case at least, the esthetic fulfillment of poetry is revelatory of interpersonal and racial themes which remain at issue in our culture" (Edward Ahearn, "Black Woman, White Poet: Exile and Exploitation in the Jeanne Duval Poems," *French Review* 51 [December, 1977]: 212).

"When we take poems XX–XXXV (first edition) of the *Fleurs du mal* as the Jeanne Duval group, as is often done, we do not claim an interest in biographical study. On the contrary, when we accept Baudelaire's own ordering of the book and we isolate an area in it, our assumption is that ordering did not occur at a documentary level (as a man would order his journal for purposes of record) but at the level where the poet has already invented himself into character. He is the 'speaker of the poem,' and knows it" (P. M. Pasinetti, "The 'Jeanne Duval' Poems in *Les Fleurs du mal*," in *Baudelaire: A Collection of Critical Essays*, ed. Henri Peyre [Englewood Cliffs, N.J.: Prentice-Hall, 1962], p. 86).

"A composite picture would produce a tall, young woman with large, dark eyes, a nose neither characteristically Caucasian nor Negroid, and full lips. Her crowning glory was her thick, curly hair that fell in waves and curls over her shoulders. Her skin color has been described in varying shades of brown to yellowish. Biographers seem to attach much importance to the question

I would like to reopen and redefine the question of Baudelaire's relationship with "blackness," and with geographical, political, and racial concerns, from within various parts of his opus. I propose to be both more literal—reading blackness wherever it occurs—and less documentary—not limiting my reading to the Jeanne Duval Cycle. To do this properly we must start, almost from scratch, to trace the genealogy of a negative. We have seen that, since the ancient Greeks, blackness has in some way been a resistant element within the system of colors. Black is "devoid of reflection," which is the sine qua non of color, yet black can be classed only among the colors. At the same time, the notion of blackness was consistently involved in European evaluations of Africa and Africans, and it still is. Baudelaire, being an art critic with important observations on the theory of color as well as a pundit and a poet, presents an opus with an almost unique opportunity to explore the discourse of color both in a pure state and in its unwonted cooperative relationship with the discourses of race and geography.

Our agenda thus calls for abandoning, momentarily, Africanist thematics to concentrate on a single underlying problem, that of color as seen in the art criticism of *Les Curiosités esthétiques*. But it will quickly become evident that color and geography were closely associated in Baudelaire's mind as parts of a political puzzle. "Africa" is of course not a major theme in his works—it does not compete with the landscape of Paris for a central role; but it is embedded in an extensive series of reflections on the very notion of centrality and periphery, on France and the outside world, white and black, redeemed and primitive. Race was an important category for Baudelaire, and in the geography of his mind the "other" race in the world was something called "the black race of Eastern shores."[2] Baudelaire's "Africa" is primarily a place of *islands,* scattered and lost at sea, signs of cultural crossing more than cultural identity, places where denaturalized Europeans meet pseudo-Africans in an atmosphere of sweet alienation: it is a place of seduction. As we move into the poems of *Les Fleurs du mal* and the prose poems of *Le Spleen de Paris,* with a general purpose of analyzing blackness and negativity, the profile of that "black race" will take various shapes. Readings of "A

---

of her being quadroon, octoroon or mulatto. . . . These poems [of the Jeanne Duval Cycle] remain apart from the others because they interpret and crystallize, not only the emotions of the poet, but his poetic theory through an element unique to the subject—the element of blackness. For Baudelaire, . . . this was the essence of the exotic. This *differentness* we shall term 'black exoticism'" (Beatrice Smith Clark, "Elements of Black Exoticism in the 'Jeanne Duval' Poems of *Les Fleurs du mal*," *CLA Journal* 14, no. 1 [September, 1970]: 63–65.)

2. In reference to a change in the text of "La Belle Dorothée" made by the editor of *La Revue nationale,* Baudelaire protested: "Croyez-vous réellement que *'les formes de son corps',* ce soit là une expression équivalente à *'son dos creux et sa gorge pointue'?*—Surtout quand il est question de la race noire des côtes orientales" (p. 1333). (References to the poetry of Baudelaire, including the prose poetry, are to the Pléiade edition of *Oeuvres complètes* [Paris: Gallimard, 1975], volume 1.)

une dame créole," "Sed non satiata," "La Belle Dorothée," and "Le Cygne" will reveal a complex series of power relations in which equality is the constant tease.

Les Curiosités esthétiques

The *Salon* of 1845

Our first question is thus, leaving everything else aside, What is "color" on its own terms in Baudelaire's art criticism? Baudelaire's thoughts on color should perhaps not be called a "theory," yet the current of feelings and observations is so strong, and seems to have such importance for the author, that it deserves considerable attention. It begins as a strong if undeveloped series of opinions in the *Salon* of 1845, reviews of that year's crop of accepted paintings, writings by which the young Baudelaire hoped to make a mark and enter the métier of art criticism. Particularly in the section on Delacroix there is a concern with the opposition of color to drawing, the opposition of the school of Delacroix to the school of Ingres. I am less interested in the real history of that quarrel than in Baudelaire's uses of color or, more precisely, his use of the *idea* of color. There is little concern for *les couleurs* in these essays, but *la couleur* is made to play a very important role. Baudelaire's admiration for Delacroix stems from the fact that he draws *with* color, thereby breaking down the barrier between the two schools: Delacroix subsumes drawing into the art of color. On Delacroix's "Dernières paroles de Marc-Aurèle," Baudelaire writes:

> Enfin, disons-le, car personne ne le dit, ce tableau est parfaitement bien dessiné, parfaitement bien modelé.—Le public se fait-il bien une idée de la difficulté qu'il y a à modeler avec de la couleur? La difficulté est double,—modeler avec un seul ton, c'est modeler avec une estompe, *la difficulté est simple* [emphasis mine];—modeler avec de la couleur, c'est dans un travail subit, spontané, compliqué, trouver d'abord la logique des ombres et de la lumière, ensuite la justesse et l'harmonie du ton; autrement dit, c'est, si l'ombre est verte et une lumière rouge, trouver du premier coup une harmonie de vert et de rouge, l'un obscur, l'autre lumineux, qui rendent l'effet d'un objet monochrome et *tournant*. [Pp. 11–12; emphasis mine][3]

> Finally, let us say it, for no one does: this painting is perfectly well drawn, perfectly well modeled.—Does the public have any idea how difficult it is to model with color? The difficulty is double,—to model

---

3. The page numbers here and in later quotations refer to this edition of Baudelaire's essays: *Curiosités esthétiques, L'Art romantique* (Paris: Garnier, 1962). In translating, I have generally adhered to the idiosyncratic syntax of the original.

with a single tone is to model with a stump, *the difficulty is simple* [single]; modeling with color is, in a sudden, spontaneous, complicated stroke, to find first of all the logic of the shadow and the light, next the correctness and the harmony of the tone; in other words, it is, if the shadow is green and a light red, to find immediately a harmony of green and of red, one obscure, the other luminous, which make the effect of an object monochromatic and *turning*. [Emphasis mine]

The simplicity of single-tone drawing is a sign of its inferiority: "drawing with a stump" is impoverished compared to color-drawing ("the enormous paradox," the "impudent blasphemy"). Color associates itself with a higher register of harmony and logic, with music and ideas. Single-tone drawing appears to be excluded from the complex specular mental processes that color-drawing includes. Single-tone drawing is the "other," the object that Baudelaire chooses to disdain and almost ignore; but in this short shrift, the object that is foreign to "logic" is dismissed with a far more interesting phrase: "la difficulté est simple." Baudelaire of course meant for "difficulté" to refer to "the task of drawing," but the word "simple," in conjunction with "difficulté," tends to complicate the issue. "Simple" in French has two meanings in English: as "single," the opposition with the phrase "la difficulté [of color-drawing] est double" makes perfect sense, but as "simple" the phrase becomes paradoxical. "The difficulty is simple" makes a kind of sense in the context, but it would be the "incorrect" English translation. The original phrase contains both meanings and thereby undermines the simplicity it seeks to describe.

From the moment that color is posited, "noncolor" takes shape negatively, and it seems to have two principal characteristics. Line drawing is strictly limited to *materiality* in Baudelaire's description; it is monodimensional, performed with a "stump," and, most importantly, leads to nothing of interest for Baudelaire. But this description of simplicity produces a rhetorical paradox where the referent (drawing) was supposed to hold none. Although it is color-drawing that is labeled "the enormous paradox," this is only an argument *ex concessis,* and it is the opposite whose terms are actually paradoxical. *Logique* and *justesse* pose no real problems and generate no real incompatibilities; it is the material world and the "material minds" captivated by it that are hard to accommodate in discourse.[4]

The word "color" never appears in the *Salon* of 1845 (or of 1846) without the immediate expression of a value judgment. Color in painting can be

4. Raphael is Baudelaire's example of what good drawing might be for someone else but not for him: "Donc, quand nous disons que ce tableau est bien dessiné, nous ne voulons pas faire entendre qu'il est dessiné comme un Raphael; nous voulons dire qu'il est dessiné d'une manière impromptue et spirituelle" (p. 13). Later, in the *Salon* of 1846, that ambiguous reference is cleared up: Raphael, "quelque pur qu'il soit, n'est qu'un *esprit matériel* sans cesse à la recherche du solide" (p. 104; emphasis mine).

anything from "distinguished" to "magic" to just plain "bad," but it is never neutral.

> La couleur est d'une crudité terrible, impitoyable, téméraire même, si l'auteur était un homme moins fort; mais . . . elle est *distinguée,* mérite si couru par MM. de l'école d'Ingres. [P. 18]

> The color is of a terrible, pitiless, even reckless crudity, if the author was a less strong man; but . . . it is *distinguished,* a quality so sought after by the gentlemen of the school of Ingres.

> Nous voyons dans cette oeuvre toutes sortes d'excellentes choses;— une belle couleur, la recherche sincère de la vérité, et la facilité hardie de composition qui fait les peintres d'histoire. [P. 30]

> We see in this work all sorts of excellent things: fine color, the sincere pursuit of the truth, and the bold facility of composition that makes painters of history.

> . . . Tableaux qui visent à la couleur, et malheureusement n'arrivent qu'au coloriage de cafés, ou tout au plus d'opéra. [P. 32]

> . . . paintings that aim for color and unfortunately achieve coloring only as in a café or, at most, an opera.

> . . . la couleur un peu crue . . . [P. 39]

> . . . the color a bit raw . . .

> La couleur est une science mélodieuse dont la triture du marbre n'enseigne pas les secrets. [P. 40]

> Color is a melodious science of which marble-grinding does not teach the secrets.

Although Baudelaire's vocabulary of science, music, truth, and logic might lead one to believe that he sees meanings in individual colors, such is not the case. "Les couleurs" occurs rarely compared with "la couleur"; there is no symbolics of color here of the kind that explicates colors on a one-to-one basis with meanings. Color for Baudelaire is not a vulgar access to meaning or a system of coded emotions any more than it is simple immanent form. The fact that colors and value judgments both are seen to occur on spectrums does not inspire any direct linkage in Baudelaire, except in passing examples. ("Certain other parts are unfortunately of a brown and reddish color, which gives the painting a rather obscure aspect—but all the light or rich tones are very successful" [p. 70].) Color is the only concrete, physical aspect of painting that is put on an equal footing with "the sincere search for the truth"; color is the only technical characteristic capable of occurring in a chain with the high qualities of modern art: "intimité, spiritualité, couleur, aspiration vers l'infini'' (p. 103). There is not so much a critique of colors in the *Salon* of 1845 as a reading of color as the worth of a painting. Color is judgment itself, synonymous with the value of a painting in Baudelaire's discourse; but ''color'' in Baudelaire's usage is therefore somewhat removed from its object, the painting. It becomes a trope of a trope, made to bear ''logic'' but denied actual meaning; color takes on significance without signification. So we are still left to wonder what that significance is attached to in Baudelaire's mind, a question that is given something like an answer in his *Salon* criticism of the following year.

The *Salon* of 1846

> Comment le désir de présence se laisserait-il détruire? C'est le désir même.
>
> —J. Derrida

Baudelaire was having some success as an art critic; the publication of his second little *Salon* book was already seen as a literary event. Where the *Salon* of 1845 only implied a theory of color, that of 1846 becomes explicit and goes on to give color geographical and political ramifications. Baudelaire continues the practice of mentioning color only in connection with a certain merit or quality of a painting (''Color was its finest aspect, its great and sole occupation'' [p. 139]; ''Its color is dull and vulgar'' [p. 143]; ''This unhappy imitation of color saddens me'' [p. 155]), but this time a treatise ''On Color'' precedes and clarifies the practice. In the second and third sections of the *Salon* of 1846 (''Qu'est-ce que le romantisme?'' and ''De la couleur''), color is defined in two different vocabularies, that of geography and that of music.

Toward the end of ''Qu'est-ce que le romantisme?'' Baudelaire proposes a geographical correlation:

> Que la couleur joue un rôle très important dans l'art moderne, quoi d'étonnant? Le romantisme est fils du Nord, et le Nord est coloriste; les rêves et les féeries sont enfants de la brume. . . .
>
> En revanche le Midi est naturaliste, car la nature y est si belle et si claire que l'homme, n'ayant rien à désirer, ne trouve rien de plus beau à inventer que ce qu'il voit: ici, l'art en plein air, et, quelques centaines de lieues plus haut, les rêves profonds de l'atelier et les regards de la fantaisie noyés dans les horizons gris.
>
> Le Midi est brutal et positif comme un sculpteur dans ses compositions les plus délicates; le Nord souffrant et inquiet se console avec l'imagination. [P. 104]

Why should it be surprising that color plays a very important role in modern art? Romanticism is a son of the North, and the North is coloristic; dreams and fairy-pageants are children of the fog. . . .

However, the South is naturalistic, for nature is so beautiful there, and so clear, that man, having nothing to desire, finds nothing more beautiful to invent than that which he sees: hence, art in the out-of-doors and, a few hundred leagues above, deep dreams in the studio and the glance of fantasy drowned in the gray horizons.

The South is brutal and positive like a sculptor in his most delicate compositions; the ailing and disquieted North consoles itself with the imagination.

Addressed only on a European scale ("le Midi" refers mainly to Italy and to Raphael), these paragraphs hark back to an ancient variety of North/South thinking that we have already seen applied to Africa. The mode of the North is dualistic, specular and idealistic: Colorism, as seen in 1845, is a "double difficulty," characteristic of indirect, highly evolved modes, such as "rêve" and "féerie." It depends on transcending the fog of the immediate sensorial world in favor of something imagined. In the North, thought must serve as a supplement to inadequate nature. Color is necessarily the art of the North for Baudelaire, for color is complex and evolved; it is associated with Romanticism and modernity: one might even say, with modernization and industrialization. The South, on the other hand, is depicted as "natural" and thus raw, unreworked, null. Its art is described as two nothings: "nothing to desire" and "nothing more beautiful to invent than what is seen." The primacy of nature is a negation of the artist's task, which depends on the world of dream: "deep dreams in the studio and the glance of fantasy drowned in the grey horizons." Most simply, this means that sensorial vision can suffice and satisfy man with its unreworked beauty, excluding any desire to transcend and see what is not there. Within Baudelaire's discourse, the North arrogates to itself alone the ability to go beyond *perception* of raw materials into *thought* about them. The comparison below is intended as nothing more (or less) than a series of literary *echoes*.[5]

5. John Hollander proposes echo as a figure of nontotalizing intertextuality: "In contrast with literary allusion, *echo* is a metaphor of, and for, alluding, and does not depend on conscious intention" *(The Figure of Echo* [Berkeley: University of California Press, 1981], p. 64). The implications of this theory are brilliantly brought out by Jefferson Humphries' review "Haunted Words, or Deconstruction Echoed" *(Diacritics* 13, no. 2 [Summer, 1983]: 29–38): "Echo points to a loss of the Logos, a deferment of origin through the ever repeated, always provisional postulation of a primal anteriority" (p. 30). That postulation is, of course, both the theme and the operative theory of Africanist discourse, whereby a topos of eternal origin is *addressed* and made to "echo." A description of "discourse" as an accumulation of such empty echoes would be a possible elaboration.

The most obvious "echo" of this Baudelaire passage is Madame de Staël's *De l'Allemagne* (Paris: Hachette, 1958), 2:xi, "De la poésie classique et de la poésie romantique," in which "Romanticism," a neologism in 1810, is linked both to the Germanic North and to Christianity, as opposed to the pagan South (including France) and its Classicism. Classicism is qualified by a direct relationship with nature: "L'homme, réfléchissant peu [the definition of blackness], portait toujours l'action de son âme au dehors; la conscience elle-même était figurée par des objets extérieurs" (p. 131). With Christianity came the mode of self-reflection, Baudelaire's

Baudelaire	*Precursors*

les rêves et les féeries sont les enfants [du Nord] . . . les rêves profonds de l'atelier . . . [sont] quelque centaines de lieues plus haut.

The Atlantes [the South] . . . are not visited by dreams like the rest of mortals.—Pliny.

le Nord se console avec l'imagination. . . .

L'homme ayant quitté par le péché la contemplation de la nature divine invisible et intellectuelle . . .

. . . l'homme [du Midi] . . . ne trouve rien de plus beau à inventer que *ce qu'il voit.*

. . . les hommes ne voulaient plus adorer que *ce qu'ils voyaient*[;] l'idolâtrie se répandait par tout l'univers.—Bossuet, *Oeuvres,* 10:194

l'homme [du Midi], n'ayant *rien à désirer.* . . .

The people there are all idolatrous Negroes living in *delight.*—Ramon Lull

Enfants de la nature et comme
      elle innocents,
Soumis aux seuls besoins im
      posés par les sens,
Riches de peu de biens, *sans
      désirs,* sans envie,
Occupés à jouir d'une trop
      courte vie.

—Ange-Benjamin Marie du Mesnil, *L'Esclavage* (1823) [Emphasis mine]

Children of nature and innocent like her, / Subject only to those

---

"rêves" and "féeries": "Les anciens avaient pour ainsi dire une âme corporelle, dont tous les mouvements étaient forts, directs et conséquents, il n'en est pas de même du coeur humain developpé par le christianisme: les modernes ont puisé, dans le repentir chrétien, l'habitude de se replier continuellement sur eux-mêmes" (p. 133). Mme de Staël outlines the same risk we will see elaborated by Baudelaire, that of the North becoming purely "academic," or cut off from materiality; she writes: "La simplicité de l'art, chez les modernes, tournerait facilement à la froideur et à l'abstraction, tandis que celle des anciens était pleine de vie." But the echo is at its strongest when Mme de Staël names *color* as the quality that keeps modern (Romantic, Christian) poetry alive: "La poésie païenne doit être simple et saillante comme les objets extérieurs; la poésie chrétienne a besoin des *mille couleurs de l'arc-en-ciel pour ne pas se perdre dans les nuages*" (p. 134; emphasis mine).

needs imposed by the senses, /
Rich on few worldly goods,
without desire, without envy, /
Busy enjoying a too-short life.
[Emphasis mine]

le Midi est *naturaliste* . . . , brutal et positif . . . [c'est] l'art en plein air.	Ces Fétiches divins . . . c'est un arbre, une montagne, la mer. . . . [Ce] culte puéril . . . doit sa naissance aux tems où les peuples ont été de purs sauvages plongés dans l'ignorance & dans la barbarie.—Charles de Brosses, *Du Culte des dieux fétiches* [See above, p. 44]

The appearance of a southern European object similar to the African one—exempt from dualistic thinking, representing desire as fulfilled, and negating the transcendental nature of art/religion—serves only to show that geographical distinctions are arbitrary figures like any others. The theory of climates was centuries old in Baudelaire's time. In 1606 the English translation of Jean Bodin's *Six Bookes of a Commonweale* related: "even so it fares with people that inhabit the Northerne parts, which have the inward heat more vehement than those of the Southerne regions: which heat causeth the forces and naturall powers to be greater in the one than in the other."[6] Bodin's North and South continually alternate in superiority: "Wisdome . . . is proper to the people of the North, but they of the South being lesse capable of goverment, give themselves wholly to the contemplation of naturall and divine sciences, and to discerne truth from falshood" (p. 561). The distinction rests on the definition of a "wisdom" independent of "truth"; the terms are as arbitrary in the analysis as in their geographical referents. The play of this constantly oppositional thinking over "a few hundred leagues" of Europe in Baudelaire's passage, instead of several thousand in de Brosses, Pliny, or Marie du Mesnil, emphasizes the discursive nature of geographical judgments. They are produced by the discourse that perceives them. The other can be the idolatrous Negro, but he can also be Raphael, Rome, and Italy.

Resituating the Baudelairean South in its context will of course reveal differences in "intention": the column on the left cannot be understood to represent a totally debased form of alterity. The referent is Raphael, the "popular king of draughtsmen" (p. 152) and therefore inferior to a colorist like the Northerner Rembrandt, but, together with the colorists, infused with "artistic vitality" (p. 221). The North/South opposition is necessarily sym-

6. Jean Bodin, *The Six Bookes of a Commonweale*, English trans. of 1606, edited by Kenneth Douglas McRae (Cambridge: Harvard University Press, 1962), p. 549.

metrical in that it constantly opposes one figure to another, yet it seems that
the nature of that other is not restricted to symmetry.

The turning of the question from civilization and barbarism to the effete
quarrel between color and drawing is shocking: the connection cannot be
"justified," yet it must be followed as it occurs in Baudelaire's essay.
"Qu'est-ce que le romantisme?" ends with the opposition of North and South,
Rembrandt and Raphael, then leaps into the question of color. The nature of
that leap remains to be seen.

The third section of the *Salon* of 1846, "De la couleur," begins with a series
of longish paragraphs written in a (literally) florid style, leading toward several
important definitions and increasingly short, aphoristic utterances. The incipit
"Let us suppose" posits a universe out of nothing, effecting a movement
from the blankness of the page to the presence of a natural world known to
all: "a beautiful space of nature." Since this universe is taken as nature, it
is presumed to be "that which . . . is produced spontaneously, without man's
intervention" *(Robert)*. We know that this "nature" was produced by the
tracing of black lines on paper, yet the intervention of the mind through
writing effaces itself, and all the suppositions that follow take on an air of
necessity. The discourse then becomes scientific, with "nature" developed
in a series of interlocking imperatives: "color" (sensorial perception thereof)
is grounded in "molecular constitution" (an invisible imperative). The first
sentence thus posits two universes at once and as one—"nature" known to
the eyes, contingent, and "nature" unseen and determinant.

> Supposons un bel espace de nature où tout verdoie, rougeoie, pou-
> droie et chatoie en pleine liberté, où toutes choses, diversement
> colorées suivant leur constitution moléculaire, changées de seconde
> en seconde par le déplacement de l'ombre et de la lumière, et agitées
> par le travail intérieur du calorique, se trouvent en perpétuelle vi-
> bration, laquelle fait trembler les lignes et complète la loi du mouve-
> ment éternel et universel. [P. 105]

> Let us suppose a beautiful space of nature where everything turns
> green, turns red, rises in the dust, and glimmers in full freedom,
> where all things, diversely colored according to their molecular con-
> stitution, changing from second to second with the movement of
> shadow and light and stimulated by the interior workings of heat,
> find themselves in perpetual vibration, which makes the delineations
> tremble and completes the law of eternal and universal movement.

The arbitrary perception of color (arbitrary in that different languages do not
recognize the same number of basic tones in the spectrum) is thus tied by
Baudelaire to the totality of a necessary, natural world, and the spectrum is
anchored, with one color in particular privileged as basic to nature:

Les arbres sont verts, les gazons verts, les mousses vertes; le vert serpente dans les troncs, les tiges non mûres sont vertes; *le vert est le fond de la nature,* parce que le vert se marie facilement à tous les autres tons. [Emphasis mine]

The trees are green, the grasses green, the mosses green; green slithers among the trunks; the young shoots are green; *green is the basis of nature,* because green is easily married to all the other tones. [Emphasis mine]

If green represents full polyvalency linked to nature, its opposite is quick to follow but more difficult to understand:

Ce qui me frappe d'abord, c'est que partout,—coquelicots dans les gazons, pavots, perroquets, etc.,—le rouge chante la gloire du vert; *le noir,*—quand il y en a,—*zéro solitaire et insignifiant,* intercède le secours du bleu ou du rouge. [Emphasis mine]

What strikes me first is that everywhere—the poppies in the grass, the flowers, the parrots, etc.—red sings the glory of green; *black*— when there is some—*the solitary and insignificant zero,* intercedes the help of blue and red. [Emphasis mine]

Zero is the nullity of numbers—it occupies the category "number" but leaves it empty. The other numbers are infinite; there is only "one" zero. Similarly, Baudelaire implies, there is only one insignificance in relation to the infinite possibilities of meaning. Black comes as the representative of that zero and that absence of signification. The link between color and signification is thus made negatively, by showing where it is *not,* and the grounding of the color green that preceded becomes clearly a trope of meaning. With black isolated as the sole zero of color (white does not enter the question here), all other colors are attributed the security of a positive "number," the possibility of meaning.

The relation is that of nothing to something, and it is defined as an intercession. The verb "intercéder" is used in a bizarre transitive sense to show the role of black in relation to all the other colors: black "intercedes the help" of other shades; while itself standing aside, black throws the others into relief. Later in the *Salon* of 1846 Baudelaire writes of "La Mort de Cléopatre" by Lassale-Bordes: "L'ajustement vert et rose de la négresse tranche heureusement avec la couleur de sa peau" (p. 132; "The Negress's green and pink attire contrasts happily with the color of her skin"). The happy participation of black in the system of colors is defined as an exclusion that throws the other tones into relief.

Gray rather than black is the color that condenses all colors, according to Baudelaire: "La nature ressemble à un toton qui, mû par une vitesse accélérée, nous apparaît gris, bien qu'il résume en lui toutes les couleurs" ("Nature resembles a top which, spinning at an accelerated rate, appears gray although it is the sum of all the colors").

Black is to color as zero is to infinity. The next paragraph describes the fecund conjugation of colors with each other, dependent on the medium of light and excluding all mention of blackness. Flowing from the periphrastic cliché of the sun ("l'astre du jour"), light ("lumière") repeats itself three times and engenders a musical vocabulary of "melody" and "harmony." The final hypothesis is this:

> Cette grande symphonie du jour, qui est l'éternelle variation de la symphonie d'hier, cette succession de mélodies, où la variété sort toujours de l'infini, cet hymne compliqué s'appelle la couleur. [P. 109]

> This great symphony of the day, which is the eternal variation of the symphony of yesterday, this succession of melodies, where variety always comes from infinity, this complicated hymn is called color.

Baudelaire goes on to remark that he does not know "if some analogist has established a complete scale of colors and feelings."

Frédéric Portal had done precisely that nine years earlier in his *Des couleurs symboliques dans l'antiquité, le moyen âge, et les temps modernes,* a work of some influence, reissued in the twentieth century, which tends to provide a useful contrast to Baudelaire's theories. Each color is there interpreted as a "symbol," bearing a synecdochal relationship to meaning ("Le blanc est le symbole de la vérité absolue, le noir devait être celui de l'erreur, du néant, de ce qui n'est pas" ["White is the symbol of absolute truth; black must be that of error, of nothingness, of that which is not"]).[7] Portal is worth mentioning because his project is a naive version of thoughts that seem to be implied by Baudelaire: the *Salon* never goes so far as to place a color and a meaning in direct one-to-one relations, yet that project is a logical extension of Baudelaire's assumptions about color. If color is a "complicated hymn," filled with "infinite variations," and *if black alone is insignificant,* then the colors might as well be explicated, interpreted. The interesting thing is that Baudelaire never makes that logical extension, that jump.

In summary, the assumptions about color in Baudelaire's "De la couleur" contain both an important although undeveloped analogy between color and meaning and a characterization of color as linked to the infinity of numbers. It is my continuing aim here to follow the geographical and political ramifications of the act of giving meaning, or of giving "color," to the world.

7. Frédéric Portal, *Des Couleurs symboliques* (Paris: Niclaus, 1938), p. 103.

A theory of drawing in its pure form is not really developed in *Les Curiosités esthétiques*. In opposition to ''De la couleur,'' there is only ''De quelques dessinateurs,'' an unequal match between theory and practice. Since our object here is not the historical division between Delacroix and Ingres but rather the theoretical distinction between color and blackness, the following is the passage that most concerns us:

> Les purs dessinateurs, s'ils voulaient être logiques et fidèles à leur profession de foi, se contenteraient du crayon noir. Néanmoins ils s'appliquent à la couleur avec une ardeur inconcevable, et ils ne s'aperçoivent point de leurs contradictions. Ils commencent par délimiter les formes d'une manière cruelle et absolue, et veulent ensuite remplir ces espaces. Cette méthode double contrarie sans cesse leurs efforts, et donne à toutes leurs productions je ne sais quoi d'amer, de pénible et de contentieux. Elles sont un procès éternel, une dualité fatigante. Un dessinateur est un coloriste manqué. [P. 151]

> Pure draughtsmen, if they wanted to be logical and faithful to their credo, would be content with a black pencil. Nonetheless, they apply themselves to color with an inconceivable ardor, and they are unaware of their contradictions. They begin by delimiting shapes in a cruel and absolute manner and want to fill in these spaces afterwards. This double method constantly thwarts their efforts and gives to all their productions a certain bitter, painful, and contentious quality. They [the productions] are an eternal process, a tiring duality. A draughtsman is a colorist *manqué*.

The ''single'' or ''simple'' difficulty of pure drawing (which no one practices) would consist of manipulating a black line on a blank background. Black was defined as ''the solitary and meaningless zero''; pure drawing adds a zero to a void. Drawing, and certainly *writing,* would consist of the play between two negativities, that of the ''cruel and absolute'' black line, and that of the empty (white) spaces. Drawing is an escape from mediation, symbolism, signification, and their representative: color. Therefore it does not exist— draughtsmen do not remain loyal to negativity and seek to break into the infinitude of color. The empty spaces that, according to Baudelaire, characterize noncolorist painters[8] are obliterated by the force of a desire (''une ardeur inconcevable''). Pure drawing remains as a null hypothesis in this essay because the nostalgia of the draughtsmen brings their unmediated play of negativity back to a lame version of color, like Orpheus toward the light. While the drawing that they then proceed to do is the ostensible problem for

---

8. ''Dans presque tous les peintres qui ne sont pas coloristes, on remarque toujours des vides, c'est-à-dire de grands trous produits par des tons qui ne sont pas de niveau, pour ainsi dire; la peinture de Delacroix est comme la nature, elle a horreur du vide'' (pp. 126–27).

Baudelaire, the problem of pure drawing remains the more perplexing one. Baudelaire accuses the draughtsmen of playing a double game, of contradicting their own logic; yet the project that he defines for them is the very problematical "simple difficulty" of unmediated negativity. At this point in Baudelaire's discourse, that project cannot be allowed a serene position.

The flight from nullity, seen in the technical example of drawing, and the movement of desire toward a spectrum of positive, infinite meaning produce a play of value judgments (rather than a fully constituted "theory") in the *Salon*s of 1845 and 1846—judgments that always favor the full over the empty, color over blackness or blankness, infinity over nothingness. Colors are anchored to the world of light and meaning; the elements that fall out of that realm (the South, line-drawing, empty spaces) are brought into the discourse as exiles. Desire in these essays defines itself as a movement away from these objects. By this reading, one might conclude that Baudelaire in his art criticism was a rather mediocre logocentrist. I have also hinted that there is an analogy between the desire for meaning as presence and certain political realities of the nineteenth century. But before following that analogy through Baudelaire's works, I do not wish to assume a simplified understanding of presence and absence, of meaning itself, in Baudelaire's writings. For alongside the texts we have already seen, there is a rather different sort of Baudelairean discourse that actively "seeks the void and the black and the naked" ("Car je cherche le vide et le noir et le nu" ["Obsession"]). Although this will again take us away from the "image of Africa" momentarily, a detour through certain poetic concepts of negativity is essential to reconsidering the larger questions.

We return, therefore, to the question at hand: can one desire absence? And what is absence, once desired?

Writing on the Void

Peut-on illuminer un ciel bourbeux et noir?
   Peut-on déchirer les ténèbres
Plus denses que la poix, sans matin et sans soir?
   Sans astres, sans éclairs funèbres?
Peut-on illuminer un ciel bourbeux et noir?
                              —"L'Irréparable," p. 55

Can one light up a muddy and black sky? / Can one tear apart the darkness / Denser than pitch, without morning, without night? / Without stars, without funereal lightning? / Can one light up a muddy and black sky?

Je suis comme un peintre qu'un Dieu moqueur
Condamne à peindre, hélas! sur les ténèbres.
                              —"Un Fantôme—Les Ténèbres," p. 38

> I am like a painter whom a derisive God / Condemns to painting
> Alas! on the darkness.

> Les enfants sont, en général, doués de la singulière faculté
> d'apercevoir, ou plutôt de créer, sur la toile féconde des ténèbres
> tout un monde de visions bizarres.
> —"Un Mangeur d'opium," p. 480

> Children are, in general, endowed with the singular faculty of
> perceiving, or rather of creating, on the fertile canvas of the
> darkness, a whole world of bizarre visions.

> Mais les ténèbres sont elles-mêmes des toiles
> Où vivent, jaillissant de mon oeil par milliers,
> Des êtres disparus aux regards familiers.
> —"Obsession," p. 76

> But the darkness is itself a canvas / Where live, spurting from my
> eye by the thousands / Disappeared beings with familiar glances.

In the quotations above, a fundamental trope on the "idea" of blackness is
repeated and modified: that of painting on darkness, on the multiple "ténèbres" ("Obscurité cachant totalement à la vue le milieu environnant et
pouvant provoquer la crainte, la peur, l'angoisse" ["Darkness hiding totally
the surrounding medium from sight and able to provoke fright, fear, anguish."]; *Grand Larousse*). But the nature of the darkness, and of the subject's
encounter with it, is completely different between, for example, "Les Ténèbres" and "Obsession." In "Les Ténèbres" (the first section of "Un
Fantôme"—one of the "Jeanne Duval" poems), the project is a condemnation
to futility, a mockery perpetrated by God. "To paint on the darkness" here
means to be forced by the total authority of God to do something that is totally
impossible. The setting is a cavern, in a complete absence of light:

> Dans les caveaux d'insondable tristesse
> Où le Destin m'a déjà relégué;
> Où jamais n'entre un rayon rose et gai;
> Où, seul avec la Nuit, maussade hôtesse . . .

> In the caves of unfathomable sadness / Where Fate has already
> relegated me; / Where never enters a pink and gay ray of light; /
> Where, alone with the Night, a sullen hostess . . .

Without a single ray of light, the light-dependent project of painting is impossible; the speaker's state is "like" (he says) that self-destructive ("Je fais
bouillir" ["I boil"]) *and* self-nourishing ("et je mange mon coeur" ["and
I eat my heart"]) activity of painting in the dark. It both consumes and creates;
yet its creation is empty. Darkness here is not a virgin surface but the void

of space on which nothing can be imprinted, where any painting or writing would be reduced to an empty *gesture*. The double bind is perfect in that the subject is condemned and forced to consume himself in a task that cannot be performed.

In "Obsession," darkness would seem to have associated itself with an Other, transcendental light, unmentioned as such but implied by the vocabulary of sight, painting, "beings," and "glances." Darkness is recuperated as a blank canvas, no longer the all-consuming void of space but the possibility of creation on a virgin surface. One could play with the verse and read "Les ténèbres sont elles-mêmes d'étoile"—made of star material, that is, of *light* perceived within the blackness of space. It would thus appear that in this last tercet a happy version of painting on darkness had been achieved: in place of the condemnation to a nullified labor there is an effortless creation of "beings" "by the thousands."

Onto the surface of the canvas, the self projects itself or, rather, lets itself be projected by the involuntary ejaculation from the eye of beings that had disappeared. The most striking verb in the stanza, "live" *(vivent),* stands in contrast to "disappeared" *(disparus)*: the living beings are nonetheless "disappeared" at the same time. Their "familiar glance" confirms a plausible explanation for this: projection onto darkness, the transformation of darkness into a canvas, is the work of subjectivity rather than intersubjectivity. The "living beings" are projected facets of the self, creatures of its desire and therefore *familiar*.[9]

But they are not only familiar; they are simultaneously alien, disappeared: like Villault de Bellefond's Africans speaking French, they are *uncanny,* both homelike and foreign. The tension of their existence is between, on one hand, the speaker's eye, the "home" or focal point from which everything emanates (and which is mimicked by the glance of the beings), and, on the other hand, the darkness, alterity, defining anything that comes to life as always already "disappeared." Darkness is the frame and the canvas itself: nothing can be cast out of the eye onto this screen without being at the same time relegated to disappearance; any gain of appearance on the screen of darkness is always already a moment of loss. Discourse tends to re-present, make present again (or at least try to do so); a discourse that represents itself as darkness, as a canvas on which images disappear rather than appear, is manifesting a mode of *desire* we have not yet encountered.

The subjectivity represented by the eye of the last tercet is determined in the preceding tercet, where a clear language of desire is linked to the problem of painting on darkness.

9. *Robert* lists as antonyms of *familier: académique*—a word that Baudelaire uses, as we will see, in his "Exposition universelle" article—and *noble,* a word of capital importance in "A une dame créole."

Comme tu me plairais, ô nuit! sans ces étoiles
Dont la lumière parle un langage connu!
Car je cherche le vide, et le noir, et le nu!

How you would please me, O night! without these stars / Whose
light speaks a known language! / For I seek the void and the
black and the naked!

The light speaks. Light is the prerequisite to "language" as it was to the
spectrum of colors and all differential sign systems. The darkness that is
desired here is the real and absolute kind, with no stars, and the object of
desire is a litany of negativity: "the void and the black and the naked."
Baudelaire's speaker takes figures familiar to us in this study—figures that,
because they are null and empty, are susceptible to becoming "any figure
that you wish," of fulfilling any desire—and makes them his explicit object.
He is thus seeking the annihilation of his object and his desire, for his objects
are the canceling-out of objectivity itself. Black was defined by Baudelaire
in the *Salon* of 1846 as the "meaningless and solitary zero," whereas color
was synonymous with relative, positive value. The search of subjectivity for
the fulfillment of its valorizations becomes quite different when the valorized
object is the defeat of any differential value. In the *Salons*, desire was for
color, desire was color, and black was zero and null; now the wish is to
escape from the spectrum, from light, and from language ("sans ces étoiles, /
Dont la lumière parle un langage connu!"). The valorized project in "Obsession" is the end of valorization; the desire is for the end of desire. The
tautology is truly obsessive. There remains only the escape into the world of
the last tercet, where darkness determines everything.

It would be tempting to say that that world encapsulates and reorients the
whole Africanist tradition of writing "on" nullities, but in fact it is the avatar
of only one extreme, of a discourse that diminishes the realism of perception
in favor of a pure tautology of projection. This is a discourse that recognizes
itself as projective, thereby ceasing to project in the true sense: the circuit is
broken once subjectivity no longer perceives its projections as real, which is
the case in "Obsession."

The last stanza of "Obsession" reduces the Other ("des êtres disparus")
to a pure figment of the self ("mon oeil"); the subject alone produces the
world he perceives, "understanding" *(entendre)* rather than "hearing" *(entendre)* any figure that he likes. This tercet is thus an allegory of projection
within a poem about the gradual withering-away of intersubjectivity. It is only
the last stanza that does not contain a direct address or apostrophe to some
other subject. Reading the whole sonnet now—"backwards"—from the ori-
entation of the last stanza, one can see a progressive disintegration of the

intended object, from multiple to singular, from *vous* to *tu,* from "woods" to "Ocean" to "night" until, finally, there is no Other left:

> Grands bois, vous m'effrayez comme des cathédrales;
> Vous hurlez comme l'orgue; et dans nos coeurs maudits,
> Chambres d'éternel deuil où vibrent de vieux râles,
> Répondent les échos de vos *De profondis.*
>
> Je te hais, Océan! tes bonds et tes tumultes,
> Mon esprit les retrouve en lui; ce rire amer
> De l'homme vaincu, plein de sanglots et d'insultes,
> Je l'entends dans le rire énorme de la mer.
>
> Comme tu me plairais, ô nuit sans ces étoiles
> Dont la lumière parle un langage connu!
> Car je cherche le vide, et le noir, et le nu!
>
> Mais les ténèbres sont elles-mêmes des toiles
> Où vivent, jaillissant de mon oeil par milliers,
> Des êtres disparus aux regards familiers.

Great woods, you terrify me like cathedrals; / You bellow like the organ; and in our condemned hearts, / Chambers of eternal mourning where old death-rattles reverberate / The echoes of your *De Profundis* answer. // I loathe you, Ocean! your leaps and uproars / Are repeated within my mind; the bitter laughter / Of the vanquished man, full of sobs and insults. // How you would please me, O night! without these stars / Whose light speaks a known language! / For I seek the void and the black and the naked! // But the darkness is itself a canvas / Where live, spurting from my eye by the thousands / Disappeared beings with familiar glances.

The first two stanzas are oriented toward hearing ("hurler, orgue, vibrent, râles, échos, rire . . . Je l'entends"), and are animated by a cacophony of cries and roars, whereas the last two stanzas will be silent except for the "language" of the stars, which is absorbed into the void. The sensorial world could not be more aggressive than in the first eight verses, and the whole effect is a tour de force of *perception*. The subject is acted upon by the outside world and reacts in his turn to the stimuli ("dans nos coeurs . . . *répondent*": or "Tes bonds et tes tumultes, / Mon esprit les *retrouve* en lui"). Yet already the distinction between active outside and passive inside is less clear than in the first stanza. The subject's mind has started to act alone, and it finds the outside world "again" within itself ("en lui"). The last purely perceptual utterance ("Je l'entends dans le rire énorme de la mer") is a hinge that moves the poem toward the negation of the Other, away from external objects emitting noises toward the eye, which perceives only what it projects. The first line of the first tercet marks the change, making the last direct address ("ô nuit!") to an object that at the end will be absorbed into the tautology of projection.

If the Other is thus effaced, it is not in favor of a fully constituted self coinciding with itself. We have seen that the eye and its counterpart, darkness, do not produce between them any specular exchange; they mimic the specular mode while confounding appearance and disappearance, life and death, darkness and the blank (white) canvas. So when the mode shifts to "pure" projection, projection is revealed to be *a primal perception where there is nothing to perceive,* and the subject that engages in it, having no other subject but itself, creates itself in the void.

My insistence on this "deconstruction" even before any major "construction" has taken place will perhaps seem perverse. But in preparing a comparison between the poetic subject and the role of France in relation to the primitive world, between the "academic" and the "barbarous," I felt it essential to outline the complexities of desire, presence, and subjectivity in Baudelaire's writing lest a vulgar oversimplification be inferred. For Baudelaire cannot be so easily pinned down.

Baudelaire and Gobineau

Black Irreflection

Tout peuple est académique en jugeant les autres,
tout peuple est barbare quand il est jugé.
  —"L'Exposition universelle de 1855," p. 212

All peoples are academic when judging others; all peoples are
barbaric when they are judged.

The poetic subject of "Obsession" projects itself into the darkness of an unsubstantial and nonreferential space. My intention now is to situate that subject in Baudelaire's conceptualization of the real world, beginning with the maxim above. To paraphrase: all peoples take themselves for the norm, which is dualistic, hierarchical, "academic" thought, when contrasting themselves to others. The Academy is that which thinks and that which abrogates the right of others to think for themselves. To be "académique" is, first, "to belong to an academy, a learned society" *(Grand Larousse),* that is, a nobility of the mind. But this produces two meanings, by extension, that undermine the privilege of thought: "Conforming to the norm, to habitual custom," and "lacking originality, strength; conventional." The "academic" is both endowed with thought and deprived of the spark of real, original thinking. "Academic" is also listed as an antonym of "familiar" and is thus to be distinguished from the overclose uncanniness of those "beings with familiar

glance" in "Obsession." A people that is academic in relation to another
must be unfamiliar and removed, making the other "barbarous."

The academic subject, charged with bringing objects to the light through
thought, may be accused of merely exercising in emptiness: thought can be
either a means of retrieval or a barrier between subject and object. When
thought is codified and approved by academies, it is elevated and canceled
out; it has lost its originality. At that point, the role of the object changes.
The barbarian, to whom thought is denied, is nonetheless the cause of
"thought" in others, the foil against which one can cast oneself as academic,
superior. But, by extension, the academic has substituted normality for originality and has let creative thought shift over to the barbarian. It is by this
mechanism that a strange reversal can take place: the academic nobility becomes mere convention, dull and lifeless, therefore losing its superiority. The
power of a certain kind of thought is reattributed to one whose thought
previously held no interest.

This occurs only because of a differential definition of what is interesting:
original thought or art worthy of the name must surprise, break away from
the norm. In a discourse of modern criticism such as *Les Curiosités esthétiques*
the prime value will not be academic normality (Baudelaire refers to one
painter as "un talent froid et académique") but creative originality. This is
surely part of Baudelaire's "modernity." But what does it do to the object
that obliges by being "different?" What price does the barbarian pay for his
or her participation in esthetics? The laurels of artistic superiority and imagination do not necessarily bring with them any true intellectual attributes.

On this point of the barbarian's superiority in the arts, a comparison between
Baudelaire and Gobineau is necessary. The pseudo-count's *Essai sur l'inégalité des races humaines* is at the origin of a notion that gained wide
acceptance: that blacks are endowed with greater "imagination" than whites
and are thus the source of the arts. From the *Essai,* through Guillaume
Apollinaire's theories on "fetish-art,"[10] to Sartre's "Orphée noir," this assumption continually endows the black with a type of thinking that simultaneously robs him of the ability to think as a fully reflexive intellect. The
Essai often reads as a caricature of other, subtler texts, such as Baudelaire's.
Gobineau wrote:

> Nous avons vu que, pour les deux civilisations primitives [de l'Eu-
> phrate et du Nil], ce qui organisa, disciplina, inventa des lois, gou-

10. Guillaume Apollinaire, preface to *Sculptures d'Afrique, d'Amérique, d'Océanie* (New
York: Hacker Art Books, 1972), p. 2: "L'évolution de la sculpture fétichiste des noirs, d'après
des probabilités qu'il est permis d'envisager, s'est effectuée selon des rythmes infiniment plus
étendus que ceux qui ont présidé à l'évolution de l'art européen et de l'art chinois par exemple."
Cf. J. C. Blachère, "Apollinaire et l'évolution de l'art nègre," *Afrique littéraire et artistique*
43 (1977): 67: "Apollinaire lui-même se reconnaît une certaine dette à l'égard de l'auteur de
l'*Essai sur l'inégalité des races humaines,* dans la mesure même où il le cite. . . . Gobineau a
bien pu mettre Apollinaire sur la voie à propos de la paternité des arts."

verna à l'aide de ces lois, en un mot, fit *oeuvre de raison,* ce fut l'élément blanc, chamite, arien et sémite. Dès lors se présente cette conclusion toute rigoureuse, que *la source d'où les arts ont jailli est étrangère aux instincts civilisateurs. Elle est cachée dans le sang des noirs.* Cette universelle puissance de l'imagination . . . n'a pas d'autre cause que l'influence toujours croissante du principe mélanien. . . . La puissance des arts sur les masses se trouvera être toujours en raison directe de la quantité de sang noir que celles-ci pourront contenir. [Emphasis mine][11]

We have seen that, for the two primitive civilizations [of the Euphrates and the Nile], that which organized, disciplined, invented laws, governed with those laws—in a word, made things rational—was the white, Hamitic, Aryan, and Semitic element. From this point a highly rigorous conclusion presents itself: that *the source from which the arts sprang forth is foreign to civilizing instincts. It is hidden in the blood of the blacks.* This universal power of the imagination . . . has no other cause than the always-growing influence of the Melanian principle. . . . The power of the arts over the masses will always be directly proportional to the quantity of black blood that those masses possess. [Emphasis mine]

No sooner is the crown placed on the African's head, however, than Gobineau derides it:

C'est, dira-t-on une bien belle couronne que je pose sur la tête difforme du nègre, et un bien grand honneur à lui faire que de grouper autour de lui le choeur harmonieux des Muses. L'honneur n'est pas si grand . . . que faut-il pour construire une lyre? un fragment d'écaille et des morceaux de bois. . . . Certainement l'élément noir est indispensable pour développer le génie artistique dans une race, parce que nous avons vu quelle profusion de feu, de flammes, d'étincelles, d'entraînement, d'*irréflexion* réside dans son essence, combien *l'imagination, ce reflet de la sensualité,* et toutes les *appétitions vers la matière* le rendent propre à subir les impressions que produisent les arts. [P. 317; emphasis mine]

It's a fine crown, they will say, that I am placing on the misshapen head of the Negro, and quite a grand honor, to group around him the harmonious choir of the Muses. The honor is not so great. . . . What does it take to build a lyre? A fragment of shell and some pieces of wood. . . . Certainly the black element is indispensable for developing the artistic genius of a race, because we have seen what a profusion of fire, of flames, of sparks, of impulse, of *irreflection* dwells in his essence, how the *imagination, that reflection*

11. Joseph Arthur de Gobineau, *Essai sur l'inégalité des races humaines* (Paris: Pierre Belfond, 1967), p. 317.

of sensuality, and all the *concupiscence toward matter* make him proper to receive the impressions that the arts produce.

The mode necessary to art is "imagination, which is the work of matter," and a "reflection of sensuality": it is a type of reflection based on "irreflection,"[12] a nullification of thought. "Null" *(nul)* is one of Gobineau's favorite words, and he uses it almost exclusively in reference to the black races: "la nullité civilisatrice des noirs"; "la tête, le visage, sont nuls"; "l'idéalisation morale est nulle."[13] The imagination is alien to civilization; civilization is alien to blacks; and the arts, proper to blacks, are therefore a special, nullified category of thought, extrinsic to civilization. Gobineau, faced with the problem of accounting for a type of thought that is immanent and purely material yet still somehow manages to *create,* follows a course similar to that of Charles de Brosses in *Du Culte des dieux fétiches.* Having labeled the barbarian's mode of thought or religion as absolutely material and therefore immanent and null, both writers insert a new category into their language, one that permits them to describe an impossible object. De Brosses used a neologism, "fétiche," to describe an animal "taken for itself" yet "divine." Now Gobineau sees fit to combine "artistic genius" and null "irreflection"; he does so by manipulating the word "imagination." The *Larousse du XIX*ᵉ *siècle* makes clear that this faculty of "representing to oneself objects by thought" is dependent on three "facts": "memory, abstraction, and judgment."[14] For Gobineau, however, the imagination is a much baser tool. Being excluded from "the work of reason," the imagination is still full of the "fire, flames, and sparks" of *genius.* The *Larousse* and common sense would indicate that this genius is an intellectual phenomenon, based on the *reflection* of matter and objects, but Gobineau insists that it is *irreflexive.* Gobineau *refuses to read the reflection of matter as anything but a material process,* and his version of the imagination winds up as precisely a "reflexive irreflection." Nearly a century after *Du Culte des dieux fétiches,* Gobineau has transposed the Africanist object into a new context and a new language, finding a new version of de Brosses' transcendental immanence.

---

12. "Irreflection" is a word that passed from French into English only in 1835, according to the *OED.*

13. "The nullified civilization of the blacks"; "The head, the face are null"; "The moral idealization is null" (*Essai,* p. 357). For Gobineau, blackness is headlessness, as in this description of an African status: "Dans le buste, dans les jambes, dans les bras, le désir qui animait l'artiste, de peindre le mouvement de la vie, est poussé au delà de toutes mesures. Mais la tête? la tête, que dit-elle? que dit le visage, ce champ de la beauté, de la conception idéale, de l'élévation de la pensée, de la divinisation de l'esprit? La tête, le visage sont nuls, sont glacés. . . . C'est que là . . . il ne s'agissait que du corps" (ibid., p. 315).

14. "Imagination . . . : Faculté d'imaginer, de se représenter des objets par la pensée . . . . Il y a trois faits à considérer dans l'imagination: 1 le souvenir, qui apporte ce que l'on pourrait appeler les matériaux; 2 l'abstraction, qui étudie et compare ces éléments divers; 3 le jugement, qui les admet ou les rejette."

The denial of the other's capacity to think—the ultimate "academic" gesture—works by contradiction, by positing a category that cannot be filled, then remarking on its emptiness.

Baudelaire's remark about the academic and the barbarous comes from an essential essay called "Méthode de critique—De l'idée moderne du progrès appliquée aux beaux-arts—Déplacement de la vitalité." His point is that creativity gets its spark from displacement (travel, distance, difference), that the French poet may well need a primitive world to inspire him. Within the conformism of the academic world, if no outside element were to enter, "beauty itself would disappear from the earth, since all types, all ideas, and all sensations would be confounded in one vast unity, monotonous and impersonal, immense like boredom and nothingness" (p. 215). The present world needs the outside world to disturb its complacency and make it see things anew: "If I take a man of the world, an intelligent man, and if I transport him to a faraway land . . . it will create in him a new world of ideas." The outside world is full of "uncanny phenomena" *(phénomènes insolites)*, with "these forms of buildings which at first baffle the academic eye . . . this vegetation, disturbing to his memory, full of native recollections, these men and women whose muscles do not move according to the classical gait of his country." These indications of trouble and shock in the idea of beauty then culminate in the famous formula "The beautiful is always bizarre":

> *Le beau est toujours bizarre.* Je ne veux pas dire qu'il soit volontairement, froidement bizarre, car dans ce cas il serait un monstre sorti des rails de la vie. Je dis qu'il contient toujours un peu de bizarrerie, de bizarrerie naïve, non voulue, inconsciente, et que c'est cette bizarrerie qui le fait être particulièrement le Beau . . . . Renversez la proposition, et tâchez de concevoir un *beau banal!* Or, comment cette bizarrerie, nécessaire, incompressible, variée à l'infini, dépendante des milieux, des *climats,* des *moeurs,* de la *race* [emphasis mine], de la religion et du tempérament de l'artiste, pourrait-elle jamais être gouvernée, amendée, redressée, par les règles utopiques conçues dans un petit temple scientifique . . . ? [P. 215]

> *The beautiful is always bizarre.* I do not mean willfully, coldly bizarre, for in that case it would be a monster gone off the deep end. I am saying that it always contains a bit of bizarreness, of naive, involuntary, unconscious bizarreness, and that it is this bizarreness that particularly makes it the Beautiful. . . . Reverse the proposal and try to imagine a *dull beauty!* Moreover, how could this bizarre quality, which is necessary, incompressible, infinitely varied, dependent on the surroundings, on *climates, habits,* and *race* [emphasis

mine], on the religion and the temperament of the artist, how could
this ever be governed, amended, rectified by the utopian rules conceived in some little temple of science?

Baudelaire's contention is that the idea of *progress*, of infinite perfectibility,
has been grossly misapplied to the fine arts: that artists "have no precursors";
that "any flowering *[floraison]* is spontaneous, individual." He is referring
specifically to the decadent state of Italian painting in the nineteenth century
as opposed to its Renaissance glory. But if progress has no validity except
after the fact, as an observation of difference, difference is nonetheless capital.
While one cannot with justification establish a sequence of differences between
individuals over time and then label it "progress," at any point in time
prosperity, light, imagination, and *poetry* are not equally distributed over the
globe. At this point Baudelaire establishes the vital connection between individuals and nations: "One must never forget that nations, *vast collective
beings,* are subject to the same laws as individuals" (emphasis mine). Some
poets are better than other poets; some nations are in a more privileged position
than others, are more capable of manufacturing beauty. Of France he says,
for example:

> La prospérité actuelle n'est garantie que pour un temps, hélas! bien
> court. L'aurore fut jadis à l'orient, la lumière a marché vers le sud,
> et maintenant elle jaillit de l'occident. La France, il est vrai, par sa
> situation centrale dans le monde civilisé, semble être appelée à re-
> cueillir toutes les notions et toutes les poésies environnantes, et à
> les rendre aux autres peuples merveilleusement ouvrées et façonnées.
> [P. 220]

> The current prosperity is guaranteed, alas! for only a very short time.
> The promise was formerly in the East; the light marched toward the
> South and now springs from the West. France, it is true, by her
> central location in the civilized world, seems to be called to gather
> all the notions and all the poetries from around her and to return
> them to other peoples marvelously worked and fashioned.

This is poetic mercantilism, if not colonialism. In the express object of the
essay, "the comparison of nations and of their respective products," Baudelaire claims that he "does not wish to assert the supremacy of one nation
over another" ("I want only to affirm their *equal* usefulness in the eyes of
HIM who is undefinable"). But it seems that the metaphor of *centrality* con-
ceals a structure of control and domination: in the quotation above, raw
materials come from other countries, that is, the shock of the new emanates
from faraway lands. But in order to be "worked and fashioned" into art,
these materials must be shipped back to France: the French poet alone sits at

the center of the world, in a superior position for the perception of raw materials and the production of beauty.

The barbarian is thus explicitly seen as raw material in the economy of beauty. It follows that the attentions of the "well-educated, intelligent" Frenchman will "work and fashion" the primitive into something else—an esthetic commodity. But Baudelaire's problem with the other peoples of the earth is that they lack the differential perspective necessary to create anything worthwhile themselves. America (the United States), for example, represents the idolatry of progress, "this grotesque idea," "this perfidious beacon." The average Frenchman is being "Americanized" by the love of material progress—gas, steam, and electricity—and is losing "the notion of the *differences* that characterize the phenomena of the physical and the moral worlds, of the natural and the supernatural." To be Americanized is to have lost the ability to discern that difference and therefore to work and fashion the material into the beautiful. Such is the decadent state of what Baudelaire describes in 1857 as "the noble country of Franklin, inventor of the morality of the counting house, the hero of a century devoted to materiality" ("Notes nouvelles sur Edgar Poe," p. 628). So even if it is grotesque to translate the notion of progress into the esthetic realm, Baudelaire describes a hierarchy among nations, which are, after all, "vast collective beings" following a sort of progress or life: "Like childhood, they wail, stutter, get fat, grow up."

Creole Creativity

Je crois que je reviens avec la sagesse en poche.
—Baudelaire, on his return from La Réunion island

A Frenchman who has visited the primitive world, as Baudelaire himself did, has seen the "bizarre" and can best produce the "beautiful." It might therefore seem to follow that a Frenchman living in the tropics would be credited with poetic privileges. But, as we shall see in reading Baudelaire on the *créole*, such is not the case: in fact the Creole becomes a figure of almost racial weight. By straddling the line between a discourse of pure geographical distance and one of race or "blood," Baudelaire's Creole reveals much about nineteenth-century thinking about both types.

A "Creole" in its original meaning was "a person born or naturalized in the country [usually the West Indies or other tropical dependency] but of European (usually French or Spanish) or of African Negro race: *the name having no connotation of color,* and in its reference to origin being distinguished on the one hand from being born in Europe or Africa and on the other from being aboriginal" (*OED;* emphasis mine). The word thus speaks of a double differentiation or exile and opens the question of race while distinctly providing no answer to it. For the *Larousse du XIXe siècle,* that

repository of French *idées reçues,* the racial ambiguity is the same: a Creole
is "a person born in the American colonies of parents foreign to America."
They see the etymology as "dubious" but perhaps from the Spanish *criar,*
"to breed, to rear" (the *OED* speculates similarly). *Le créole* is the "language
spoken by the blacks of America." In the fascinating article that follows in
the encyclopedia, which I will quote, the manners of white Creoles are con-
trasted to those of black Creoles. The surprise in that article, as in the paragraph from Baudelaire below, is that there is no question of a real racial
distinction to be made between white Frenchmen and white Creoles, yet every
sign points in that direction:

> Je me suis souvent demandé, sans pouvoir me répondre, pourquoi
> les créoles n'apportaient, en général, dans les travaux littéraires,
> aucune originalité, aucune force de conception ou d'expression. On
> dirait des *âmes de femmes, faites uniquement pour contempler et
> pour jouir.* La fragilité même, la gracilité de leurs formes physiques,
> leurs yeux de velours qui regardent sans examiner, l'étroitesse sin-
> gulière de leurs fronts, emphatiquement hauts, tout ce qu'il y a
> souvent en eux de charmant les dénonce comme des *ennemis du
> travail et de la pensée.* De la langueur, de la gentillesse, une *faculté
> naturelle d'imitation qu'ils partagent d'ailleurs avec les nègres,* et
> qui donne presque toujours à un poète créole, quelle que soit sa
> distinction, un certain air provincial, voilà ce que nous avons pu
> observer généralement dans les meilleurs d'entre eux. [L'Art ro-
> mantique: Réflexions sur mes contemporains," section 9, "Leconte
> de Lisle," p. 778; emphasis mine]

> I have often wondered, and have never been able to answer, why
> Creoles in general bring to literary works no originality, no strength
> of conception or expression. It is as if they had *the souls of women,
> made exclusively to contemplate and to enjoy.* The very fragility, the
> gracility of their physical forms, their velvet eyes, which look without
> examining, the singular narrowness of their foreheads, emphatically
> high, everything in them that is often charming, denounces them as
> the *enemies of work and thought.* The langour, the gentility, a *natural
> faculty of imitation, which they share with Negroes,* and which gives
> to a Creole poet of whatever distinction a certain provincial air: this
> is what we have been able to observe generally in the best among
> them.

   From the depths of their "women's souls" to their actual "physical
shapes," Creoles have the appearance of another race. This is the first paragraph of an 1861 essay on Leconte de Lisle, the poet, whose parents were
both French, born in France, but who emigrated to La Réunion, a French
island in the Indian Ocean. Yet, as was common in writings by the metropolitan
French about their Creole cousins, the discourse seems drawn to distinctions

one would normally associate with race, not just geography: it was a question of having not merely a tan but a certain hair color and width of forehead. In this passage we have the "physical personality" of the Creole: the "fragility," the shape of the forehead, the quality of the gaze. Even though the only difference between the French Creole and the French of France is climate and culture, that difference is radicalized and expressed as if it were a question of race. In the 1855 Exposition article, Baudelaire wrote that beauty was dependent on "environment, climate, customs, and *race*"; here it is as if these were all one thing.[15]

In spite of being born and raised in the tropical world, constantly surrounded by the bizarre and the barbarous, the Creole is in fact no better than the academic for producing beauty: the Creole has no differential perspective on his perfumed and volcanic islands, so they are no better than that "vast unity, monotonous and impersonal." He is too much a part of the raw materials to be able to redeem and process them into beauty. The Creole therefore cannot make beauty; he or she must be *made beautiful;* the Creole cannot make color; he or she must "be colored": this, we shall see, is the project of the sonnet "A une dame créole."

Baudelaire does not assume that these barbarians hold any special mode of thought like Gobineau's "imagination"; he assumes that thought and creativity are one. The Creole is thus "academic" in the pejorative sense because he has "no originality, no force of conception or expression." It is ironic that these French people abroad, exposed surely to the "bizarre" on a day-to-day basis, have no faculties with which to "work and fashion" it into art. Baudelaire is thwarting the ancient tradition in a sense, for he reproaches his

15. The perception of Creoles as another people, almost as another race, does not appear to have been an isolated phenomenon in nineteenth-century France. The ambiguity of the word itself contributes to the feeling that white Frenchmen abroad take on attributes of other races; still, it is strange to assume that a Creole such as Leconte de Lisle, whose parents were both born in France and settled on Réunion island, should be physically distinguishable from Frenchmen who have not emigrated. Yet the *Larousse du XIXᵉ siécle* writes: "C'est dans les grands yeux spirituels des femmes *créoles* qu'on trouve le contraste si rare d'une douce langueur et d'une vivacité piquante. Elles sont surtout remarquables par la beauté de leur chevelure, qui est d'un noir incomparable, et par la petitesse de leurs pieds cambrés. . . . Ils [les créoles] sont généreusement bien faits et d'une taille avantageuse. . . . Leurs membres sont presque toujours doués d'une souplesse qui les rend éminemment propres à tous les exercices du corps." The *Larousse* goes on to compare white Creoles with black ones and winds up with a formula not unlike Louis XIV's *bon mot* addressed to Prince Aniaba ("Il n'y a donc plus de différence entre vous et moi que du noir au blanc"; see p. 32, above): "La seule différence qui existe entre eux [blacks born in the colonies] et les *créoles* blancs consiste à peu près dans la couleur de la peau et dans la forme de la chevelure." Nineteenth-century French encyclopedias in general insisted on both the moral and physical differences between metropolitan Frenchmen and French Creoles, frequently blurring the distinction between changes that could be attributed to the climate ("taille mince," "teint livide et plombé") and those that we would consider genetic ("le front haut"). See *Encyclopédie moderne* (Paris: Firmin Didot, 1847). José Juan Arrom has traced the history of the word *creole* in several languages, showing its shifts of meaning between black and white until the point when, with the Atlantic slave trade abolished, all slaves were born in the New World and *Creole* came to mean *white* ("Criollo: Definicion y matices de un concepto," in *Certidumbre de America* [Madrid: Gredos, 1971], pp. 11–26).

Creole for having qualities the African was reproached for *not* having: "contemplation" was the word used by Bossuet to describe the intellectual, reflexive faculty which the idolater did not possess. De Brosses' idea of a
"brutish and savage natural state" was based on the absence of "any reflexive
idea or any imitation." Now the practice of contemplation and imitation by
the Creole makes him an "enemy of thought," one of the strongest insults
in Baudelaire's battery. This is because these terms have slipped along the
scale of meanings and lost their status as the "work of reason" in Baudelaire's
lexicon. Like Gobineau's "imagination," they represent a degraded mode of
thought, like that of a cow with "velvet eyes that look without examining."
But there is still a critical difference between Baudelaire's Creole and Gobineau's black: the Creole, while an "enemy of thought," does not represent
a nullity. The Creole regresses every day toward an immanent state but never
reaches it, a regression seemingly caused by the "volcanic and fragrant isles"
he inhabits, where "the human soul . . . unlearns every day the exercise of
thought." Every day brings him closer to a goal he will never reach, that of
complete release from thought. Baudelaire's Creole is thus an *asymptotic,
gerundive version of Gobineau's black* and fits perfectly into the scheme of
the *Essai sur l'inégalité.*[16]

The tropical poet is the new topic, and in this case, he gets off easy:

> M. Leconte de Lisle est la première et l'unique exception que j'ai
> rencontrée. En supposant qu'on en puisse trouver d'autres, il restera,
> à coup sûr, la plus étonnante et la plus vigoureuse. Si des descriptions,
> trop bien faites, trop enivrantes, pour n'avoir pas été moulées sur
> des souvenirs d'enfance, ne révélaient pas de temps en temps à l'oeil
> du critique l'origine du poète, il serait impossible de découvrir qu'il
> a reçu le jour dans une de ces îles volcaniques et parfumées, où
> l'âme humaine, mollement bercée par toutes les voluptés de l'at-
> mosphère, désapprend chaque jour l'exercice de la pensée. Sa per-
> sonnalité physique même est un démenti donné à l'idée habituelle
> que l'esprit se fait d'un créole. [P. 778]

> M. Leconte de Lisle is the first and only exception I have met.
> Supposing that one could find others, he would still remain, certainly,
> the most astonishing and the most vigorous. If some descriptions,
> too well done, too intoxicating to have not been modeled on child-
> hood memories, did not reveal from time to time to the critic's eye

16. There are many reasons not to risk a comparison of Gobineau and Baudelaire and only
one reason to do so. Gobineau is in a sense unreadable in our times; he manages to offend all
current assumptions about the nature of man. There is no reason to think that Baudelaire ever
read the *Essai.* Yet I hope to have proved here that the comparison of their two texts establishes
a dialogue that aids in understanding both of them better, that is, that an intertextual relationship
is at work.

the origin of the poet, it would be impossible to discover that he was born on one of those perfumed and volcanic islands where the human soul, gently rocked by all the caresses of the atmosphere, unlearns each day the exercise of thought. His physical personality itself is a denial of the usual idea one holds about Creoles.

Leconte de Lisle is "one of our dearest and most precious poets," moved by a "sentiment of intellectual aristocracy," who can be compared "without absurdity" only to Théophile Gautier. Leconte de Lisle is undone only "from time to time," and then by a list of atavistic habits that might not seem entirely undesirable in a poet: *description, memory, inebriation, origin, voluptuousness*. One recognizes in this list the outline of "exoticism," of an "anterior life" holding the promise of "total existence," that is commonly read into Baudelaire's own poetry.[17] Assuming that this category has some validity, "exoticism" is a poetic discourse that is drawn back by memory into a descriptive mode (as opposed, one supposes, to a more reflexive, meaningful mode), attaining a place of origin, a primal island where the soul gives itself over to the unthought. This process is formulated here as a reproach to a poet who goes too far ("trop bien faites, trop enivrantes"), but within that reproach lies the foundation of the "bizarre beautiful," unsought and unconscious: unthought. The poet's project (be it Leconte de Lisle's or Baudelaire's) of unstitching the work of academic thought stands in contrast to the critic's demand (here at least) for thought as the work of reason. These desires work at cross-purposes in the essay "Leconte de Lisle," where Baudelaire the critic could easily be criticizing the opening of his own sonnet "A une dame créole."

The conflicting aims that we have seen so far within Baudelaire's corpus can be explained—with considerable oversimplification—as the struggle between two discourses. Poetic discourse, for lack of a better term, is that which gives itself over to absence, darkness, exile, and dream and, as such, is subject to contempt in an essay such as "Leconte de Lisle," which is written in a discourse of thought. Thought discourse (in Foucault's sense) respects meaning and plenitude, which the poetic frustrates. The difference is in the object of desire. Poetic discourse is capable of seeking "the void and the black and the naked," of slipping out from under the massive Western prejudice against darkness and difference, and of actively desiring that which spells the end of desire. But poetic discourse, by allowing darkness to become an object of desire, recuperates darkness as light: the light of art and literature ("la lumière a marché vers le sud, et maintenant elle jaillit de l'occident")

---

17. Edward Ahearn, "Black Woman, White Poet," p. 217: "in ["La Chevelure"] he has discovered an inebriating sense of *total* existence. . . . The essential significance of these poems, then, resides in the movement toward a state of intensified being, perhaps having communal overtones, certainly involving an enrichment of the experience of the self and deriving its value from its participation in an abundant, non-European nature."

are founded on the darkness of the unthought ("non voulue et inconsciente"). The immediate aims of any utterance are ultimately subject to this reversible foundation.

The Creole Lady

A person tropes in order to tell many-colored rather than white lies to himself.

Harold Bloom

Subject, figure, and biography conspire in "A une dame créole" to make Baudelaire the butt of his own criticism of Leconte de Lisle. This sonnet was written "on the scene" during Baudelaire's visit to the island of La Réunion in 1841. Dedicated to Madame Autard de Bragard—his host's wife—the poem was first sent in a letter to her husband ("As it is right, decent, and proper that verses addressed to a lady by a young man should pass through her husband's hands"; p. 942). "A une dame créole" was published first in May, 1845, in *L'Artiste* and was the first poem Baudelaire printed under his own name. It is not without a certain symbolism that Baudelaire first names himself as a poet above this particular poem, whose narrator must be precisely one of those "intelligent men of the world" (as Baudelaire was to write ten years later) who, having traveled to exotic lands, can return, with "wisdom in his pocket," to play upon "the immense clavier of *correspondences*!" ("L'Exposition universelle," p. 213).

Whether the descriptions in "A une dame créole" are "too well done," "too inebriating," to have been taken from anything but real life, is a judgment each reader can make for himself. It is true that the "volcanic and perfumed isles" that were the undoing of Leconte de Lisle return here as a "perfumed country caressed by the sun"; the "eyes that look without examining" are now part of a more complex scheme, in which laziness rains down from the trees:

> Au pays parfumé que le soleil caresse,
> J'ai connu, sous un dais d'arbres tout empourprés
> Et de palmiers d'où pleut sur les yeux la paresse,
> Une dame créole aux charmes ignorés.

In the perfumed country caressed by the sun, / I have known, under a canopy of all-empurpled trees / And of palms raining indolence, / A creole lady of unknown charms.

In this literally purple poetry, dripping with figures of liquidity and sensual saturation, the question of *knowledge* is confronted from a point of view opposite to that in "Leconte de Lisle." There "unlearning" was the negative role of the other, of the stupefied and stupefying Creole; here the speaker is

drawn into the realm of the unknown *by his own knowledge:* "I knew . . . a
lady . . . unknown." He has learned to unlearn. The lady's charms are unknown, or had been before the speaker's act of witnessing brought them to
the light. The first stanza is rife with contrasts between light and dark, known
and unknown: *soleil / arbres empourprés, yeux / paresse, connu / ignorés.*
The locus where the two sides meet and divide is the Creole lady, and the
mechanism by which the attraction and repulsion work is the speaker's discourse. The question posed by the first stanza is thus: Does the presence of
the first-person narrator, the sun, and knowledge constitute a redemption of
the Creole lady, a victory of one domain over the other, a translation of
darkness and ignorance into light and knowledge? Or does the encounter with
darkness cause a general contamination and reordering of the categories, as
was the case in "Obsession"? Grammatically speaking, are the charms of
the lady brought to the light of familiarity by the speaker, or do they remain
undigested within his presence and his knowledge?

The question of redemption is essential to the readings of Baudelaire over
the past century, and its moral dimension cannot be ignored. The discourse
of most criticism cannot but read darkness and ignorance as evil, light as
truth, and art as the passage from one to the other:

> Roughly speaking, art would be seen as the process of *rescuing*
> the image from chaotic darkness and oblivion: its illumination and
> ordering into beauty and remembrance. *Les Ténèbres* . . . is the
> nearest thing to a close adherence to that scheme.[18]

> Art, to Baudelaire, is artifice. And artifice is his means of trans-
> forming moral evil into artistic good, darkness into light.[19]

We have already read the first half of "Les Ténèbres" as a double bind
between creation and destruction, similar to the closing tercet of "Obsession,"
where darkness and light are no longer opposable categories but where the
tension between them remains the essential motor of the discourse. Returning
parenthetically to the end of "Les Ténèbres," one notices that the appearance
of a feminine figure is one of those moments seen by critics as a redemption,
a transformation of darkness into light:

> Par instants brille, et s'allonge, et s'étale
> Un spectre fait de grâce et de splendeur.
> A sa rêveuse allure orientale,

> Quant il atteint sa totale grandeur,
> Je reconnais ma belle visiteuse:
> C'est Elle! noire et pourtant lumineuse.

18. Pasinetti, "The 'Jeanne Duval' Poems," pp. 90–91; emphasis mine.
19. James C. McClaren, "The Imagery of Light and Darkness in *Les Fleurs du mal*,"
Nineteenth-Century French Studies 7, nos. 1 and 2 (Fall–Winter, 1978–79): 32.

Momentarily shines, and stretches, and spreads / A ghost made of
grace and splendor. / From its dreamlike oriental allure, // When it
reaches its total height, / I recognize my beautiful visitor: / It is
She! black and yet luminous.

Baudelaire wrestled with these tercets for a long time before he was satisfied;
the switch from a grammatical masculine *(le spectre)* to a feminine *(belle
visiteuse)* was an "embarrassment." That hinge between masculine and feminine coincides with the change from "chaotic darkness' to "illumination and
order." Yet the figure "Elle," for all its condensation, is itself still a hinge,
defined as "black *and yet luminous.*" The figure of unity and order, by virtue
of this "and yet" between polar opposites, calls into question the security of
the redemption. If blackness is "chaos," what is it doing here within the
realm of "order?" What is clearly a *desire* for redemption in the poem
becomes an accomplished fact for some readers. The part of darkness
within any scheme of light, and vice versa, seems to continually assert itself.

The commerce set up by the first stanza of "A une dame créole" is simply
that of making the unknown known, of redeeming darkness into light. My
interest is in asking what price is paid for that light and that knowledge. This
sonnet is on the surface an innocuous love poem, "a pleasantly turned compliment";[20] but the performative it describes is in effect that of the poetic
mercantilism seen in the 1855 Exposition article on progress in the arts.
Making the Creole lady known to and in the metropole, making her *perform
beauty,* will take away as much as it gives.

This brings us back to the second stanza of "Dame créole":

Son teint est pâle et chaud; la brune enchanteresse
A dans le cou des airs noblement maniérés;
Grande et svelte en marchant comme une chasseresse,
Son sourire est tranquille et ses yeux assurés.

Her complexion is pale and warm; the dark enchantress / Has in
her neck nobly mannered airs; / Tall and svelte, walking like a
huntress, / Her smile is tranquil and her eyes self-assured.

The consciousness of the poet has already been qualified by its environment,
contaminated with contemplation and laziness, knowledge of things unknown:
now out of this optic comes the object known and unknown, the Creole lady.
The dreamlike, inebriated, and heady atmosphere of the first stanza prede-
termines the appearance of the lady as already a kind of disappearance (a

---

20. "*A une dame créole . . .* qui n'est qu'une piéce de circonstance et un compliment agré-
ablement tourné" (Pascal Pia, *Baudelaire* [Paris: Seuil, 1952], p. 22).

projection onto a screen of darkness, nonvolitional and unconscious) and as a wish-fulfillment. The discourse of dreams—determined by a distance called sleep and producing the objects of desire—is another model for the dialectic of appearance and disappearance in this poem.

The play of light and dark continues, etiolated, removed from the poles of white and black, in the first verse of the second stanza. The lady is at once pale and brown. Since we cannot be certain, in the phrase *brune enchanteresse,* which is the noun and which is the adjective, we do not know whether the reference is to a woman with brown hair and white skin (which is certainly the most likely) or, in a rarer usage of the word *brune,* confirmed by the *Trésor de la langue française,* to a woman with (pale) brown skin, as Baudelaire writes in "Sed non satiata": "Bizarre déité, *brune* comme les nuits, . . . Sorcière au *flanc d'ébène.*"[21] While competent French-speakers will normally choose the former over the latter interpretation, I do not think that the ambiguity can be dismissed. The poem is *about* ambiguity and the possibility of moving along a scale of colors and places, from the purple islands, where ignorance rains from the trees, to the banks of the Seine and the green Loire: from the Ile de la Réunion, where the sonnet was written, to the Ile de France, the center of the center. The hypothesis of the two tercets is that of a translation of Creole or pseudo-nobility to proper nobility in the "*true* land of glory" as opposed to what must have been a false land of glory. On the surface, there is one continuous movement of elevation from beginning to end, an uninterrupted song of praise:

> Si vous alliez, Madame, au vrai pays de gloire,
> Sur les bords de la Seine ou de la verte Loire,
> Belle digne d'orner les antiques manoirs,
>
> Vous feriez, à l'abri des ombreuses retraites,
> Germer mille sonnets dans le coeur des poètes,
> Que vos grands yeux rendraient plus soumis que vos noirs.

> If you went, Madame, to the true land of glory, / On the banks of the Seine or of the green Loire, / Beauty worthy to decorate the antique manors, // You would spawn, in the shelter of shady retreats, / A thousand sonnets in the hearts of poets, / Whom your big eyes would subjugate more than your blacks.

But two phrases in the poem seem to call for a reevaluation of that movement, namely "noblement maniérés" (verse 6) and "digne d'orner" (verse 11). The sixth verse of the poem is perhaps the most difficult and the most

---

21. Victor Hugo follows the same usage in referring to his *obi,* a character of three-quarters black blood, as having a "brune poitrine" (*Bug-Jargal ou la révolution haïtienne* [Fort-de-France, Martinique: Désormeaux, 1979], p. 376).

interesting. Her neck is the locus of her airs: the neck is neither head nor body, but it is "on the way" toward both.[22] The "collar" of the 1868 version ("A dans le *col*") represents one step further away from either object. As an object in the symbolics of the body, the neck is indeterminate between the light of reason in the head and the darkness of ignorance in the body. It is neither reflection (of thought or of light) nor total absorption. The neck is the approach of both these sides and is therefore the perfect figure of the Creole or of "creolization" as etymology describes it: the approach of the black, the continual act of unlearning without ever unlearning everything—in other words, the vision of the Creole in Baudelaire's "Leconte de Lisle." The Creole is the gradual advance of the darkness of ignorance; the neck bears the same structure *en abîme*.

That which emanates from her neck is equally ambiguous: "nobly mannered airs." The nobility is the *head* portion of society, that which learns, knows, and controls the rest of the body politic. Etymologically, noble means "worthy of being known," from the Latin *noscere*, "to learn to know." The lady would thus be redeemed, and a superior status would be attributed to her, by virtue of the speaker's "learning to know" ("J'ai connu") her—which is to say, making her noble. As a counterexample, remember what Bossuet said about the slave, that he "has no state, *no head*."[23] By being known, the lady is set free from some sort of primal subjugation of which we thus far know nothing.

To see what happens to the Creole lady when she is made noble, we must delve a little deeper into the notion of nobility and the "racial" history of France, a subject that will be more adequately covered in my discussion of Rimbaud's "Mauvais sang." To be "noble" in French is closely related to the idea of being "frank," "Frankish," and "free," since the nobility was literally understood to be descended from the Franks, and *Franc* was defined as "Libre. *Noble*. Sincère."[24] The play of these meanings had manifest juridical ramifications. In 1315, when Louis X wanted to free the serfs, his decree read:

> Comme selon le droit de nature chacun doit NAISTRE FRANC, Et par aucuns usages ou coustumes, qui de grant ancienneté ont esté entroduites et gardées jusques cy en nostre royaume, . . . moult de

22. The sexual fetish for Freud is the perverse overinvestment of a part of the body that is "on the way" to the sexual organs: "Perversions are sexual activities which . . . linger over the intermediate relations to the sexual object which should normally be traversed rapidly on the path towards the final sexual aim" ("The Sexual Aberrations," in *Three Essays on Sexuality,* trans. James Strachey [New York: Basic Books, 1962], p. 16).

23. "L'esclave ne peut rien contre personne qu'autant qu'il plaît à son maître: les lois disent qu'il n'a point d'état, point de tête, *caput non habet;* c'est-à-dire que ce n'est pas une personne dans l'état" ("Sur les lettres de M. Jurieu," *Oeuvres complètes* [Paris: Chez Lefèvre, 1836], 6:503).

24. La Carne de Sainte-Palaye, *Dictionnaire de l'ancien langage français* (Paris: n.p., 1879); emphasis mine.

personnes de nostre commun pueple, soient encheues en lien de servitudes et de diverses conditions, qui moult nous desplait. *Nous considerants que nostre royaume est dit, et nommé le royaume des Francs, et voullants que la chose en verité soit accordant au nom. . . . Que . . .* telles servitudes soient ramenées à franchises.[25]

As according to the right of nature each man must be BORN FREE, and by such habits or customs, which from great antiquity have been introduced and preserved up to now in our kingdom, . . . the lot of many of our common people is that of servitude and of diverse conditions, which greatly displeases us. *We consider that our kingdom is called and named the kingdom of the Franks [of the free], and desirous that the fact be in agreement with the name. . . .* That . . . such servitudes be made free [be given the franchise].

The kingdom of the Franks must be the kingdom of the free. After serfdom ended and black slavery began, this slippage of the word across its meanings was to engender a doctrine, if not an actual practice, that any slave who set foot on the soil of France was to be freed.[26] It should be noted, however, that the *franchises* in Louis X's decree, like those of the current word "franchise" in English as well, had to be *bought* ("Certain compositions, by which sufficient recompense be made to us from emoluments"); the state of being *affranchi* can never equal that of being *franc "tout court."* To be *affranchi* is to be the object of someone else's action, the result of a projection, a gift from a superior agency. It is a mediated phenomenon rather than an immediate birthright.[27] For this reason the Creole lady's noble, frank-ish state is described as a function of her *airs,* a fleeting perception on on the part of the one who

25. François-André Isambert, *Recueil général des anciennes lois de France* (Paris: Plon, n.d.), 3:103. Isambert comments: "Pourquoi donc faire acheter à des hommes un droit que la nature leur donne?"

26. "Ainsi se posa la question: Quelle était, une fois qu'ils avaient débarqué sur le sol du royaume, la situation de ces nègres? Le principe n'était pas douteux: ils devaient être libres. Mais . . . dans la pratique, on ne tarda pas à s'ingénier pour l'éluder" (Lucien Peytraud, *L'Esclavage aux Antilles françaises avant 1789* [Pointe-à-Pître: Emile Désormeaux, 1973], p. 376). Diderot's *Encyclopédie,* in its article "Franc," states: "Franc signifie quelquefois une *personne libre,* c'est-à-dire *qui n'est point dans l'esclavage,"* and it quotes Loysel to the effect that "toutes personnes sont franches en ce royaume, & que si-tôt qu'un esclave a atteint les marches d'icelui en se faisant baptiser, il est affranchi. Ce que dit cet auteur n'a pas lieu néanmoins à l'égard des esclaves nègres qui viennent des colonies françaises en France avec leurs maîtres, pourvu que ceux-ci ayent fait leur déclaration en arrivant à l'amirauté, qu'ils entendent renvoyer ces nègres aux îles."

27. In a fascinating article called "Du noir au blanc, ou la cinquième génération," Michèle Duchet demonstrates to what extent the gradations of race in mixed-blood Caribbean peoples were dependent on two absolutes: white ("la couleur blanche, elle, ne semble pas menacée: elle n'est que l'absence de couleur") and black. The latter can never become the former, no matter how many generations later: "ni l'octavon, ni ses descendants (la cinquième génération), ni les gens de couleur, ni les affranchis ne deviennent jamais *semblables* aux Blancs. L'assimilation est un leurre." By the same token, a freedman can never be the same as a free man: "'Les libres sont des affranchis ou des descendants d'affranchis: à quelque distance qu'ils soient de leur origine, ils conservent toujours la tâche de l'esclavage et sont déclarés incapables de toute fonction

holds the power, the speaker. The lady is ennobled, given her freedom, accorded a head, but only as a result of the narrator's ability to distribute these gifts. One definition of *noble* is of "an animal whose behavior is *frank* or whose demeanor is *dignified*" ("dont le comportement est franc ou dont l'allure est digne"—*Grand Larousse*) (the Creole lady will be seen as *digne,* worthy, later in the poem); similarly, the *créole* is described by the *Larousse du XIXᵉ siècle* as "franc, affable, généreux." In both of these definitions, as in "A une dame créole," the act of ennoblement is also one of condescension, one for which something is forfeited.

The story of the poem thus far can be summarized in the etymology of the word "noble," "to learn to know," which is closely related to the notion of "making frank/free/Frankish/noble" *(affranchir):*

> J'ai connu
> J'ai appris à connaître
> J'ai ennobli   } une dame créole.
> J'ai affranchi

But, as already indicated by the word *airs,* the substance of her nobility and freedom is dubious. Immediately it is thrown into doubt by the term *maniérés.* Although this comes as a surprise to the linguistic habits of French-speakers, *franc* is listed as an antonym of *maniéré* by the *Grand Larousse,* and it seems clear to me that an opposition exists between simple frankness (defined above as sincerity) and the pirouettes of mannerism. (Maniéré: "Qui montre de l'affectation, manque de naturel ou de simplicité."—*Robert.* ["Showing affection, lacking naturalness or simplicity."]) Mannerism is opposed to both frank-ness and nobility, for affectations are not "worthy" but base. To be mannered is to imitate that which you are not, to put on *airs;* the nobility does not need to do so.[28] The lady is noble in a fashion that proves her lack

---

publique'" (quoting *Instructions pour la Martinique*) (Michèle Duchet, "Du Noir au blanc, ou la cinquième génération," in *Le Couple interdit: entretiens sur le racisme,* proceedings of a colloquium held at Cérisy-la-Salle, May, 1977, edited by Léon Poliakov [Paris: Mouton, 1980], p. 185).

28. Cf. Mme Rose de Saulces de Freycinet on Creole ladies' manners on the Ile Maurice: "Je trouve que les créoles ont bien tort, car elles seraient beaucoup mieux en vêtements simples que parées des plus belles étoffes. Il y a beaucoup de jolies personnes, mais peu de vraiment belles. . . . Elles sont *remplies de prétentions et calculent tous les mouvements.* J'ai vu au bal de M. Smith l'une de ces beautés, reconnues pour avoir une main et un bras superbes, *affecter* [emphasis mine] non seulement d'ôter ses gants toutes les fois qu'elle valsait, mais encore de poser sa main le plus avantageusement possible, et, de retour à sa place, elle s'informait près de sa mère si sa main et son bras avaient été dans la position la plus favorable. Même dans nos villes si perverties, on n'en voit pas tant! Ce sont là cependant *ces simples créoles* [author's emphasis] qu'on nous dit dépourvues de toute espèce d'art et parées seulement des grâces de la nature" (*Journal* [1817–20] [Paris: Société d'Editions géographiques, maritimes et coloniales, 1927], p. 27). Cf. J. Arago: "Les Créoles, en général, sont les femmes les mieux faites que j'ai jamais vues. Mais je voudrais un peu moins de *décision* dans leur démarche" (quoted in Freycinet, ibid., p. 27n).

of nobility: by aping their manners she defines herself as other, inferior. The lady is therefore:

> noblement maniérée
> noblement ignoble
> sincerely affected
> frankly unfrank
> worthily false
> freely enslaved

The proud Diana who marches through the two last verses of this stanza is thus carrying with her a very problematical status: a head that is not a head, a nobility that debases. Yet still in these verses there is a deepening of her personality, a passage from silhouette to the illusion of depth. Verse 7 presents her outline as a whole; verse 8 gives her a face, a mouth, eyes, and even expression—the signs of a growing subjectivity. It would be possible to interpret the whole poem as the presence of beauty to the narrator, to read the superficial placidity of this discourse as the entirety of the problem, but only at a certain cost, which I hope will become clear.

The two tercets make one grammatical proposition in the conditional mood: "Si vous alliez . . . vous feriez." The idea is that of translating the Creole nobility of the lady to the land of the legitimate nobility, and the hypothesis is that she would conquer and surpass the French nobility, reducing it lower than the low. As the lady hypothetically emigrates to France and acquires the title "Madame," she is pronounced "worthy." But worthy to do what? "Digne d'*orner*": worthy to decorate, to fulfill the function of a piece of furniture or a painting, to add beauty, to be *bizarre*. "Digne d'orner" reproduces exactly the structure of "noblement maniéré," for to decorate is to proliferate signs in the absence of something real.

Taking those two phrases as signs of ambivalence within an otherwise placid movement of elevation, one must look at the end of the poem, in which a violent reversal takes place, and in which reference is made to the oppressive social order—the slave society—of which Creoles are a part.

The fiction of the poem has been that of continuity and communication between extremes. Nothing is black or white, everything is *créole*, that is, determined in reality but ambiguous in reading: "Creole" means of one race or another but doesn't say which. The colors in the poem contribute to this myth of movement. As the lady goes to France, the Loire is green, the color Baudelaire said blended the most easily with the other colors, as the lady is called to do socially. The interchange and harmony of colors on the spectrum, which is analogous to the interchange between peoples and races of the world: this is the basis of the poem's movement. But when we read the last two words, *vos noirs,* a problem arises. Black in art criticism was the "solitary

and meaningless zero,'' excluded and yet referred to in the harmony of meaningful colors; the *noirs* in the Creole context are the subjugated slaves, whose
presence Frenchmen saw as a large corrupting influence in the lives of white
Creoles.[29] Blacks, as slaves, could never be part of the fiction of movement
and social climbing of this poem.

The significant ambiguity of the referent "Creole" becomes much more
pronounced in the phrase "vos noirs." Are "your blacks" the possessions,
the slaves, of a white woman, or are they her brothers in slavery? We know
that Madame Autard de Bragard was white. But if one were to take some
interpretive liberty, if "brune" were understood to refer to the lady's complexion as well as her hair, then one could even go so far as to read verse 11
phonetically, as "Belle digne d'orner les antiques, *ma Noire*," my black
woman.[30] I do not think this poem "refers" to a black woman, but the
possibility is written into its discourse. That trouble in the house of the referent
is only part of the larger unhappiness of the poem's rhetoric, which promises
nobility as it takes it away.

The intervention of "blackness" at the end of the poem seems to reorient
meaning and leave us with two distinct interpretations. On the one hand, we
witness the elevation of a white Creole lady, who, while fully "bizarre," is
brought to France to reverse the dependency of poets on raw materials. At
the end, her eyes reduce both the poets of France and the slaves of her native
land to crawling at her feet. This in a sense reverses the relationship described
in the 1855 article: the poet, dependent on the bizarre to make beauty, can
be enslaved by the object of his desire. A system of submission is therefore
reversed but kept intact.

29. "In places where this execrable institution still reigns, no despot ever received more
sycophantic attention, or was surrounded with more groveling flatterers, than the Creole child"
(*Larousse du XIXe siècle*). Complicity in the cruelty of slavery played a part in Baudelaire's
perception of America: "Brûler des nègres enchaînés, coupable d'avoir senti leur joue noire
fourmiller du rouge de l'honneur . . . tels sont quelques-uns des traits saillants, quelques-unes
des illustrations morales du noble pays de Franklin, l'inventeur de la morale du comptoir, le
héros d'un siècle voué à la matière" (*Curiosités esthétiques*, "Notes nouvelles sur Edgar Poe,"
p. 628). The article entitled "Nègre" in the *Larousse du XIXe siècle* states that "noir" referring
to a man takes account only of his *color* and allows the possibility that a *noir* who is not a *nègre*
may not be from Africa and may not be a slave. Baudelaire eliminates that ambiguity with his
phrase *plus soumis* or *plus rampants*, leaving us with the word *noir* (the "*idea* of color," as
Larousse puts it) making a bridge between this poem, its social context, and the esthetic theory
of color. *Larousse:* "Le substantif noir ne fait considérer l'homme que sous le rapport de sa
couleur. *Nègre* se dit proprement des noirs originaires de l'Afrique, et il ajoute ordinairement à
l'idée de couleur celle de la servitude, du travail forcé, de l'état presque sauvage, parce que
toutes ces choses ont pesé sur les hommes tirés de ce pays. A un autre point de vue, le mot *noir*
s'applique à des hommes dont la couleur peut être moins foncée que celle des nègres proprement
dits, de sorte que les *nègres* sont les plus *noirs* des *noirs*."

30. One French encyclopedia of the nineteenth century restricted the definition of *créole* to
blacks born in the New World, stating that only the Spanish *criollo* referred to whites (Ch.
Dezroby and Th. Bachelot, *Dictionnaire général de biographie et d'histoire* [Paris: Librairie
Ch. Delagrave, 1876]).

On the other hand, the lady, either black or white, is still handed her promotion by one of those poets, who controls the process from a position of centrality and superiority. She is still made to perform only a pseudo-nobility; she is still only nobly *mannered,* worthy to *decorate.* The hypothesis of elevation can be proffered only by him who has seen and known both worlds.

The last word of the poem forces an interpretive choice on the reader, and some, by inclination, will prefer to leave the poem unperturbed. But my point is that the promise of social and geographical nobility is analogous to the promise of harmony and meaning in Baudelaire's characterization of color. Poetry is, "like" the art of color, a function of infinity, as in the "thousand sonnets" of the last tercet. Poetry and color are the privilege of the North, to be given and taken away by the academic world. But the academic North cannot do without the barbarous South to provide it with raw materials, and when the transport takes place and the barbarous revivifies the academic with its strangeness, the result is the left-handed compliment of "A une dame créole."

Of course, Baudelaire is never doing only one thing at a time; while with his left hand he may be following the pattern I have described, with his right he may not. The "subject" of "A une dame créole," or rather our reading of it as either stable or instable, depends on our frame of reference. Within the enclosure of belles-lettres, the subject may be as much slave as master, may not distinguish between projection and perception, may deal in equal exchange rather than centralized domination. This is the Baudelaire who says, "I do not wish to assert the supremacy of one nation over another." But from the moment supremacy is mentioned, as in the reference to slavery at the end of "A une dame créole," inequality seems to assert itself. The act of breaking the strictly self-referential, Eurocentric frame in which literature is normally "deconstructed" and placing the subject in a world full of objects, even unstable ones, seems to reveal an unequal set of rules by which meaning is indicated. One object must be suppressed in order for another to rise: black for color, line-drawing for painting, zero for number, Creoles for poetry.

I do not, however, present the model of harmony, color, and colonialist economics as an all-encompassing model in Baudelaire's works. The question is a troubling one, which I hope to draw out further by reading "Sed non satiata," in which "black power" is evoked; "La Belle Dorothée," whose protagonist is given a measure of ironic subjectivity; and finally "Le Cygne," where the emphasis shifts from irony to allegory.

But Not Satisfied

Sed non satiata

Bizarre déité, brune comme les nuits,
Au parfum mélangé de musc et de havane,
Oeuvre de quelque obi, le Faust de la savane,
Sorcière au flanc d'ébène, enfant des noirs minuits,

Je préfère au constance, à l'opium, au nuits,
L'élixir de ta bouche, où l'amour se pavane;
Quand vers toi mes désirs partent en caravane,
Tes yeux sont la citerne où boivent mes ennuis.

Par ces deux grands yeux noirs, soupiraux de ton âme,
Ô démon sans pitié! verse-moi moins de flamme;
Je ne suis pas le Styx pour t'embrasser neuf fois,

Hélas! et je ne puis, Mégère libertine,
Pour briser ton courage et te mettre aux abois,
Dans l'enfer de ton lit devenir Proserpine!

[*Oeuvres*, p. 28]

Bizarre deity, brown like the nights, / Perfumed with a mix of
musk and tobacco, / The work of some obiman, Faust of the sa-
vanna, / Sorceress with ebony flank, child of the dark midnights, //
I prefer to Constance wine, to opium, to Nuits-Saint-Georges, /
The elixir of your mouth, where love struts about; / When toward
you my desires leave in caravan, / Your eyes are the oasis where
my ennui drinks. // Through those two great black eyes, ventila-
tors of your soul, / O demon without pity! unleash a lower
flame; / I am not the Styx to embrace you nine times, // Alas! and
I cannot, libertine Megaera, / To break your courage and keep you
at bay, / In the hell of your bed become Proserpina!

The power relations within "A une dame créole," between center and periphery, subject and object, male and female, revealed a certain ambiguity
by which the inferior object could exercise control almost by virtue of inferiority. "Sed non satiata" may have been written as early as 1842, soon after
Baudelaire's aborted trip to the tropics; its discourse is quite precisely that of
the "bizarre beautiful" and of the economic geography of poetry described
in 1855, yet here the possibility of reversed power has become the central
theme. The result is a nightmare of hell, dominated by a black demoness of
insatiable lust who exhausts the male narrator. I would like to explore briefly
the question of what this figure represents by looking at the ways in which
the sonnet reaches out toward other texts for a vocabulary of the bizarre.

The woman here is first of all a "deity," a goddess from mythology instead
of a legitimate "divinity"; her status is extravagant, baroque, and dubious.

Her power is that of a "sorceress" producing elixirs of love that the speaker cannot help but prefer to the more academic recreational drugs of Constance wine, opium, and Nuits-Saint-Georges wine. Yet this description of her powers does not prepare for any *real* power on her part: "deity" connotes a distancing of the speaker from any belief in the woman's power. It is only in the second strophe that the dynamics become clear; the speaker surrenders to the other power without a fight, by his own *preference* for the bizarre. By a masochistic choice his desires "leave in caravan" toward his own destruction in the flames.

The lexicographical adventurousness and playfulness of this sonnet, especially in the first stanza, have a specifically Africanist profile. It has been observed that Baudelaire managed to use every rhyme of -*avane* in the French language; that jaunty artificiality nevertheless gives a certain form to the object—one that mere play cannot account for. His use of "obi," a word of allegedly African origin via English (referring to a "witch doctor") has had lexicographers guessing for a long time. The word is not in *Littré; Grand Larousse* refers to Baudelaire as its originator; Claude Pichois, in his notes to the Pléiade edition, cites Pétrus Borel's tale "Three-Fingered Jack" (1833), set in Jamaica and featuring an "obi, whose purpose is the bewitching of the poor world, or the consumption by *diseases of languor, spleen.*"[31] Perhaps that last word caught Baudelaire's eye, as a link between the consumptive ennui of the academic world and the magic of the barbarian. In "Sed non satiata," it is the speaker's *ennuis* that drink at the well of the woman's eyes before he is consumed by her flames. Pichois rightly points out the contrast between the exotic Orientalist and Africanist vocabulary on the one hand (*obi, caravane, savane*) and the domestic, Western, "psychological" register on the other (*désir, ennui*). Borel, the self-styled "Lycanthrope" or Wolf-Man of sensationalistic Romanticism, had found in the violent, drunken, and fetishistic Negro of his own invention a man after his own heart; Baudelaire in his turn may have been an admirer of Borel's esthetic of the bizarre.

But it is at least as likely that Baudelaire got the word "obi" not from Borel's tale but from Victor Hugo's *Bug-Jargal*, in its definitive version of 1826 (the short version of 1818 makes no mention of an obi). *Bug-Jargal* is Hugo's fictionalized account of the Haitian slaves' revolt of 1791, that first and indelible image of reversed power, black power, which rocked France for decades. Hugo's preface of 1832 states that the events in his book represent a "struggle of giants," with "three worlds concerned by the question, Europe and Africa as combatants, America as the battlefield."[32] The story juxtaposes a stereotype of the "good Negro," *le nègre généreux et révolté,* named Bug-Jargal, to that of the "bad Negro," the "bizarre" obi. It is of course the

---

31. Petrus Borel, "Three-Fingered Jack, l'obi," in *Champavert* (Paris: Montbrun, 1947), p. 99.

32. Hugo, *Bug-Jargal*, p. 156.

demonology that is of more concern to us in relation to "Sed non satiata," whose black sorceress is called a "child of black midnights," suggesting a black Mass. These excerpts from *Bug-Jargal* expand on the suggestions of Baudelaire's sonnet:

> Je n'aimais pas cet esclave. Il y avait quelque chose de trop rampant dans sa servilité; et si l'esclavage ne déshonore pas, la domesticité avilit. J'éprouvais un sentiment de pitié bienveillante pour ces malheureux nègres que je voyais travailler tout le jour sans que presque aucun vêtement cachât leur chaîne; mais ce baladin difforme, cet esclave fainéant, avec ses ridicules habits bariolés de galons et semés de grelots, ne m'inspirait que du mépris. . . . Et quand [les autres esclaves] le voyaient passer au milieu de leurs cases avec son grand bonnet pointu orné de sonnettes, sur lequel il avait tracé des figures bizarres en encre rouge, ils se disaient entre eux à voix basse: *C'est un obi!* [see figure 3]. [P. 173-74]

> I disliked that slave. There was something too groveling in his servility; and if slavery does not dishonor, domesticity degrades. I felt benevolent pity for those unfortunate Negroes whom I saw working all day with hardly any clothing to cover their fetters; but this deformed buffoon, this idler slave, with his ridiculous clothes dripping with laces and strewn with little bells, inspired nothing but contempt in me. . . . And when the other slaves saw him pass among their huts with his high pointed bonnet, decorated with bells and on which he had traced bizarre figures in red ink, they said to each other in low voices: *He is an obiman!* [See figure 3]

> L'obi . . . était assis, les jambes repliées, tenant sa baguette droite, immobile comme une idôle de porcelaine dans une pagode chinoise. Seulement, à travers les trous de son voile, je voyais briller ses yeux flamboyants, constamment attachés sur moi. [P. 264]

> The obi was seated, his legs crossed, holding his stick straight up, immobile like a porcelain idol in a Chinese pagoda. However, through the holes in his veil, I saw his flaming eyes shining, staring at me constantly.

> Dès que leur cercle fut formé, elles [les griotes] se prirent toutes la main, et la plus vieille, qui portait une plume de héron plantée dans ses cheveux, se mit à crier: *Ouanga!* Je compris qu'elles allaient opérer un de ces sortilèges qu'elles désignent sous ce nom. Toutes répétèrent: *Ouanga!* La plus vieille, après un silence de recueillement, arracha une poignée de ses cheveux, et la jeta dans le feu en disant ces paroles sacramentelles: *Malé o guiab!* qui, dans le jargon des nègres créoles, signifient: —J'irai au diable. Toutes les griotes, imitant leur doyenne, livrèrent aux flammes une mèche de leur che-

Ils se disaient : *c'est un obi !*

Figure 3. Victor Hugo's "obi." Engraving by Adolphe François Pannemaker from *Bug-Jargal* (Paris: J. Hetzel, 1866). Reproduced from a copy in the University of Michigan Library.

veux, et redirent gravement: —*Malé o guiab!* . . . Je fermai les yeux
pour ne plus voir du moins les ébats de ces démons femelles. [Pp.
254–56]

Once their circle was formed, they [the female griots] joined hands,
and the oldest of them, who wore a heron's feather stuck in her hair,
started to cry: *Ouanga!* I understood that they were about to perform
one of those spells that is designated by that name. They all repeated:
Ouanga! The oldest, after a contemplative silence, pulled out a clump
of her hair and threw it into the fire, pronouncing these sacramental
words: *Malé o guiab!* which, in the jargon of creole Negroes, means:
"I will go to the devil." All the griots, imitating their headwoman,
threw a lock of their hair into the flames and repeated gravely: *"Malé
o guiab!"* . . . I closed my eyes so at least I would no longer see
the sportings of these female demons.

   If black power is divided between good, represented by Bug-Jargal, and
evil, evil is divided between male and female, *obi* and *griote*. The latter in
Bug-Jargal, as in "Sed non satiata," are subservient to a masculine master;
they are his "works." Of course the novel has whole pages on this theme,
which the sonnet simply invokes through the word *oeuvre*. The situation of
the narrators is similar to some extent: both the speaker of "Sed non satiata"
and the French nobleman who is the narrator of *Bug-Jargal* fall entirely into
the clutches of the sublime other power; the difference is that Hugo offers
the possibility that the good will triumph:

   Seul de mon espèce dans cette caverne humide et noire, environné
   de ces nègres pareils à des démons, balancé en quelque sorte au
   penchant de cet abîme sans fond, tour à tour menacé par ce nain
   hideux, par ce sorcier difforme, dont un jour pâle laissait à peine
   entrevoir le vêtement bariolé et la mitre pointue, et protégé par le
   grand noir [Bug-Jargal], qui m'apparaissait au seul point d'où l'on
   pût voir le ciel, il me semblait être aux portes de l'enfer, attendre la
   perte ou le salut de mon âme, et assister à une lutte opiniâtre entre
   mon bon ange et mon mauvais génie. [P. 384]

   Alone of my species in this damp, black cavern, surrounded by these
   Negroes like demons, as if suspended above this bottomless abyss,
   in turn threatened by this hideous dwarf, this deformed sorcerer,
   whose motley clothing and pointed miter were barely illuminated by
   the pale light, and protected by the tall black man, who was visible
   to me at the only point where the sky could be seen, it seemed to
   me that I was at the gates of Hell, waiting for the loss or the salvation
   of my soul, attending a bitter struggle between my guardian angel
   and my evil genie.

The power relations in the sonnet are more difficult to analyze, if only because the subject hands himself over to a force of his own making, whereas in Hugo the forces are perceived as purely outside the self. It is typical of Baudelaire that his figure of the sorceress suggests a large element of complicity between subject and object: while dominating the speaker, she is still only a result of his preference and desire ("jaillissant de mon oeil par milliers"). On the level of what is explicitly stated in the poem, the speaker "prefers" to make himself subservient to the sorceress and inadequate to her demands. On the level of discourse analysis, one can see that terms such as *bizarre, déité, obi, savane, sorcière,* and *caravane* are so heavily laden with exotic connotations that their denotations of power are undercut. The flash of the exotic, the invocation of an Africanist discourse, by then recognizable as such, forms an obstacle to the simple meaning of the words as much as it succeeds in meaning. The bizarreness of the referent places its power within the understood borders of a distant realm; the deity can mug and threaten on the stage as much as she likes, but the audience can leave at any moment. In this, the articulation of the masculine and the feminine in the third verse is significant: she is an *oeuvre*—feminine grammatically and actually—but she is the *oeuvre* of an obi, a Faust, a man. Here the text invites an autoreferential interpretation, for the *oeuvre* is both the deity and the poem—both created by a man who has made his pact with the devil.

Placing the poet and/or the speaker in a parallel relation with the obi, the paradox of power in the poem becomes clearer. The obi is a figure who has power, but only outside the realm of Western belief. The poet is recognized as creator in the West; but within "Sed non satiata," the *speaker,* representative of the poet, becomes impotent in his relations with the black goddess ("Je ne suis pas le Styx. . . . Je ne puis . . . devenir Proserpine!"), and his loss of power corresponds to the take-over by the forces of the bizarre. But it is the poet's discourse, not the speaker's fictive experience, that counts in the end, and it is on this level that the esthetic of the bizarre complicates the project of power reversal. The woman becomes omnipotent and all-consuming only by virtue of being an *oeuvre,* both of the obi and of the poet. As with "A une dame créole," it seems that the terms in which power or nobility are handed to the outside world complicate the gift. There will always be some level on which the superiority of the center asserts itself.

This is not to deny the growing and finally all-embracing power of the deity in "Sed non satiata," only to show in what frame it is cast. Already in the fourth verse she passes from being a "work" to being a sorceress in her own right, creating and destroying on her own. And to ascribe delimitations to her reality, even those given through the speaker's "voice," is not to say that he maintains that rational perspective. Quite the contrary. But it is also interesting to note that the growing lopsidedness of power toward the

end of the poem coincides with a shift from Africanist to mythological discourse, from an Other in space to an Other in time. I will reserve my discussion
of the articulation of Virgilian allusions with Africanist themes for my analysis
of "Le Cygne."

The first sentence of Baudelaire's private notebook, "Mon coeur mis à nu,"
may serve to put "Sed non satiata" in perspective, along with "A une dame
créole":

> De la vaporisation et de la centralisation du *Moi*. Tout est là.
>   [*Oeuvres,* p. 676]

> On vaporization and centralization of the Self. Everything is there.

This seems an accurate description of the question posed by these two early
poems. There is a tension between, on the one hand, the center, the writer,
the white, the male, and, on the other, the periphery, the object of desire,
the black, the female. Poems, we have been taught, represent the devapor-
ization of the object, its promotion to a state of light and centrality. But
reading these poems has indicated a contrary movement as well, by which
the center loses some of itself in the vapor of alterity. Another quotation from
"Mon coeur mis à nu" comes to mind:

> Foutre, c'est aspirer à entrer dans un autre, et l'artiste ne sort jamais
> de lui-même. [P. 702]

> Fucking is the hope of entering inside an other, and the artist never
> goes outside of himself.

As with many of Baudelaire's aphorisms, the opposite claim is also true, and
Baudelaire states it himself:

> Le poète jouit de cet incomparable privilège, qu'il peut à sa guise
> être lui-même et autrui. Comme ces âmes errantes qui cherchent un
> corps, il entre, quand il veut, dans le personnage de chacun. ["Les
> Foules," p. 291]

> The poet enjoys the incomparable privilege of being able to be, as
> he chooses, either himself or someone else. Like those souls wan-
> dering in search of a body, he enters, when he wants, the personality
> of each one.

The poet is constantly leaving himself, or trying to, and losing himself, a
little each time, in the vapor. Even if he cannot do it "nine times" like Victor

Hugo,[33] the proposition of entering inside the Other is made simultaneously with the realization that it cannot be done.

"La Belle Dorothée"

La tête le plus bas possible, c'est le secret du bonheur.
　　　　　　　　—Flaubert, *La Tentation de Saint Antoine*

Il méprisa l'Afrique, brûlant, à grandes étapes, là où il s'en était écarté, l'abîme qui le séparait de la prestigieuse civilisation blanche.
　　　　　　　　—Yambo Ouologuem, *Le Devoir de violence*

Equality seems to be a thorny issue in Western discourse. The Christian tradition, based on an ultimate difference—God—and structured by hierarchies, held the figure of the snake in contempt as that which knows no hierarchy, no difference between head and body. The African, being somehow metaphorically connected to the snake, was a figure of the Devil: the whole pack of them "cleaving to the ground with head, tail, and middle part" (Saint Jerome, *The Homilies,* 1:33). Now Baudelaire's volume of *Les Petits poèmes en prose* presents itself as a snake, as a series of writings in which equality and a certain arbitrariness have supplanted the dictatorship of the head:

> Mon cher ami, je vous envoie un petit ouvrage dont on ne pourrait pas dire, sans injustice, qu'il n'a ni queue ni tête, puisque tout, au contraire, y est à la fois tête et queue, altérnativement et réciproquement. Considérez, je vous prie, quelles admirables commodités cette combinaison nous offre à tous, à vous, à moi et au lecteur. Nous pouvons couper où nous voulons, moi ma rêverie, vous le manuscrit, le lecteur sa lecture; car je ne suspends pas la volonté rétive de celui-ci au fil interminable d'une intrigue superflue. Enlevez une vertèbre, et les deux morceaux de cette tortueuse fantaisie se rejoindront sans peine. Hâchez-la en nombreux fragments, et vous verrez que chacun peut exister à part. Dans l'espérance que quelques-uns de ces tronçons seront assez vivants pour vous plaire et vous amuser, j'ose vous dédier le serpent tout entier. [*Oeuvres,* p. 275]

> My dear friend, I am sending you a little work about which one could not say, without injustice, that it has neither tail nor head, because everything, on the contrary, is its head and tail, alternatively and reciprocally. Consider, please, the admirable conveniences this combination offers all of us, you, myself, and the reader. We can

---

33. Pichois speculates that Baudelaire's "nine embraces" in "Sed non satiata" are an allusion to Victor Hugo's alleged performance on his wedding night.

cut off where we like: me, my reverie; you, the manuscript; the
reader, his reading; for I do not suspend the mulish willfulness of
the reader on the interminable thread of a superfluous plot. Take
away one vertebra, and the two pieces of this tortuous fantasy will
join back up, effortlessly. Chop it in many fragments, and you will
see that each can exist on its own. In the hope that some of these
sections will be lively enough to please you and amuse you, I make
bold to dedicate the whole serpent to you.

Simply stated, this means that the reader can begin and end anywhere he
pleases—in effect, compose the book for himself. This claim to a certain
abdication of authority by the author, in favor of the reader's "mulish willfulness," is a daring move toward equality in discourse. Are we to understand
this as affecting the internal relationships of the poetry to follow, the ways
in which they produce meanings? If everything, including the force of the
writer's desire, were "head and tail, alternatively and reciprocally," then a
radical equality, of a type we have not yet seen, would have come to pass.

"La Belle Dorothée" is not officially understood to be the prose counterpart
of "A une dame créole," although their similarities invite the comparison.
The prose poem is supposed to be linked rather to "Bien loin d'ici" by "the
same memory of La Réunion" (*Oeuvres,* p. 1333; "beauty of tropical nature;
ideal of black beauty," ibid., p. 1118). "Bien loin d'ici" is a relatively static
poem, roughly equivalent to the ninth paragraph of "La Belle Dorothée,"
lacking the general movement of elevation and degradation the two longer
poems share. "Dorothée" and "Dame créole" are typical of the perceived
difference between the verse poem and the prose poem: the latter may share
the same "subject" but flattens, elongates, and generally undoes the crystalline miracle of the former.[34]
I would like to read "La Belle Dorothée" in function of three themes:
imitation, exchange, and *hierarchy.*

> Le soleil accable la ville de sa lumière droite et terrible; le sable
> est éblouissant et la mer miroite. Le monde stupéfié s'affaisse lâche-
> ment et fait la sieste, une sieste qui est une espèce de mort savoureuse
> où le dormeur, à demi éveillé, goûte les voluptés de son anéantisse-
> ment.
>   Cependant Dorothée, forte et fière comme le soleil, s'avance dans
> la rue déserte, seule vivante à cette heure sous l'immense azur, et
> faisant sur la lumière une tache éclatante et noire.
>   Elle s'avance, balançant mollement son torse si mince sur ses
> hanches si larges. Sa robe de soie collante, d'un ton clair et rose,
> tranche vivement sur les ténèbres de sa peau et moule exactement

34. For a study of this problem in the prose poem as a genre, see Barbara Johnson, *Défigurations du langage poétique* (Paris: Seuil, 1979).

sa taille longue, son dos creux et sa gorge pointue.

Son ombrelle rouge, tamisant la lumière, projette sur son visage sombre le fard sanglant de ses reflets.

Le poids de son énorme chevelure presque bleue tire en arrière sa tête délicate et lui donne un air triomphant et paresseux. De lourdes pendeloques gazouillent secrètement à ses mignonnes oreilles.

De temps en temps la brise de mer soulève par le coin sa jupe flottante et montre sa jambe luisante et superbe; et son pied, pareil aux pieds des déesses de marbre que l'Europe enferme dans ses musées, imprime fidèlement sa forme sur le sable fin. Car Dorothée est si prodigieusement coquette, que le plaisir d'être admirée l'emporte chez elle sur l'orgueil de l'affranchie, et, bien qu'elle soit libre, elle marche sans souliers.

Elle s'avance ainsi, harmonieusement, heureuse de vivre et souriant d'un blanc sourire, comme si elle apercevait au loin dans l'espace un miroir reflétant sa démarche et sa beauté.

A l'heure où les chiens eux-mêmes gémissent de douleur sous le soleil qui les mord, quel puissant motif fait donc aller ainsi la paresseuse Dorothée, belle et froide comme le bronze?

Pourquoi a-t-elle quitté sa petite case si coquettement arrangée, dont les fleurs et les nattes font à si peu de frais un parfait boudoir; où elle prend tant de plaisir à se peigner, à fumer, à se faire éventer ou à se regarder dans le miroir de ses grands éventails de plumes, pendant que la mer, qui bat la plage à cent pas de là, fait à ses rêveries indécises un puissant et monotone accompagnement, et que la marmite de fer, où cuit un ragoût de crabes au riz et au safran, lui envoie, du fond de la cour, ses parfums excitants?

Peut-être a-t-elle un rendez-vous avec quelque jeune officier qui, sur des plages lointaines, a entendu parler par ses camarades de la célèbre Dorothée. Infailliblement elle le priera, la simple créature, de lui décrire le bal de l'Opéra, et lui demandera si on peut y aller pieds nus, comme aux danses du dimanche, où les vieilles Cafrines elles-mêmes deviennent ivres et furieuses de joie; et puis encore si les belles dames de Paris sont toutes plus belles qu'elle.

Dorothée est admirée et choyée de tous, et elle serait parfaitement heureuse si elle n'était obligée d'entasser piastre sur piastre pour racheter sa petite soeur qui a bien onze ans, et qui est déjà mûre, et si belle! Elle réussira sans doute, la bonne Dorothée; le maître de l'enfant est si avare, trop avare pour comprendre une autre beauté que celle des écus!

The sun crushes the city with its straight and terrible light; the sand is dazzling, and the sea reflects. The stupefied world flops down and takes a nap, a nap that is a kind of savory death in which the sleeper, half awake, tastes the sensuality of his fall into nothingness.

Meanwhile, Dorothy, strong and proud like the sun, moves along the deserted street, the only living being at this hour under the

immense azure, and making on the light a sparkling and black
stain.

She moves along, softly balancing her slim torso on her wide hips.
Her clinging silk dress, of a light and pink color, contrasts vividly
with the darkness of her skin and molds precisely her long figure,
her hollow back, and her pointed breasts.

Her red parasol, sifting the light, projects on her dark face the
bloodlike rouge of its reflections.

The weight of her enormous head of hair, almost blue, draws her
delicate head backwards and gives her a triumphant and languid air.
Heavy ringlets twitter at her sweet ears.

From time to time the sea breeze lifts the corner of her floating
skirt and shows her shiny and superb leg; and her foot, the same as
those of the marble goddesses that Europe locks in museums, imprints
its shape faithfully on the fine sand. For Dorothy is so prodigiously
coquettish that the pleasure of being admired outweighs the pride of
being a freed woman, and, although she is free, she walks without
shoes.

Thus she walks along, harmoniously, happy to be alive and smiling
a white smile, as if she perceived a mirror in the distant space
reflecting her bearing and her beauty.

At the hour when even the dogs whine with pain under the sun
that bites them, what powerful motive causes the languid Dorothy
to move, beautiful and cold like bronze?

Why has she left her little hut, so coquettishly arranged, whose
flowers and tablecloths, although inexpensive, make a perfect boudoir; where she has such pleasure combing her hair, smoking, having
herself fanned, or looking at herself in the mirror of her great feather
fans, while the sea, beating the shore a hundred paces away, gives
a powerful and monotonous accompaniment to her indecisive rev-
eries, and while the iron pan, where a stew of crabs with rice and
saffron cooks, sends her its exciting perfumes from the back of the
courtyard?

Perhaps she is going to meet some young officer, who on far-off
shores heard of the famous Dorothy from his mates. Without fail the
simple creature will beg him to describe the Opera, and will ask him
if one can go there with bare feet, like at the Sunday dances, where
the Cafrines themselves get drunk and furious with joy; and again,
if the most beautiful ladies of Paris are more beautiful than she.

Dorothy is admired and pampered by everyone, and she would be
perfectly happy if she did not have to pile piaster on piaster to redeem
her little sister, who is all of eleven and who is already mature, and
so beautiful! She will doubtless succeed, will Dorothy; the child's
master is so greedy, too greedy to understand any beauty other than
that of coins!

The poem opens, as did "A une dame créole," in the stereotyped atmosphere of the tropics, with laziness raining down and enveloping the inhab-

itants. But here it is the sun rather than rain that is the source of stupefaction: the source of light, by the force of its burning power, produces a reversed effect of darkness, sleep, and annihilation. Between the first word of the first paragraph and the last word, there is a complete difference, which is none-theless given as a unified experience.

The second paragraph bears an imitative relationship to the first. Dorothée is "like the sun": she is strong and proud as the sun is straight and terrible, and she is isolated as the only living element in the picture. The sun alone "crushes," and all the other actions are passively responsive to it. Dorothée is the "only living being" in the immense dead universe the sun has created. But if she is a principle of light, the imprint she leaves is darkness: "making on the light a sparkling and black stain." She thus reproduces the effect of the sun: *soleil* (source of light and life) / *anéantissement; Dorothée (seule vivante)* / *tache noire.*

The imitation is thus a question of *exchange,* a sort of commerce between black and white. Similarly, the third paragraph describes a harmonious contrast between color and noncolor in a formula taken almost exactly from Baude-laire's comments on "La Mort de Cléopatre" seen here earlier *(Curiosités esthétiques,* p. 11):

> L'ajustement vert et rose de la négresse tranche heureusement avec la couleur de sa peau. / Sa robe de soie collante, d'un ton clair et rose, tranche vivement sur les ténèbres de sa peau.

> The green and pink apparel of the Negress contrasts happily with the color of her skin. / Her clinging silk dress, of a light and pink color, contrasts vividly with the darkness of her skin.

The "color" of her skin is actually the noncolor of darkness: a harmonious difference is established between the zero and the infinite spectrum of colors— zero plays a part within the system, but only as an Other within it. A gap is thus the determining factor for this harmony, whose mechanism is again represented in the fourth paragraph: "Her red parasol, sifting the light, projects on her dark face the bloodlike rouge of its reflections." Dorothée's colorless, somber face is a blank screen onto which light and its consequent colors are projected. The gap between the parasol and the face represents the difference between light and darkness, between Europe and a quasi-African island, and between the *perceived* red light of the parasol and the *projected "fard sang-lant"* on Dorothée's face. One color is originary, the other is artificially imposed, like so much makeup; throughout the poem Dorothée will proceed to imitate—to try to coincide with the source of light and thus to escape the projected nature of her universe.

The poem creates an Africanist object caught in the act of parodying Europe. Dorothée is of the world of "contemplation," of "huts," "bare feet," and

"Cafrines," but she is "the same as" *(pareil aux)* the marble goddesses that Europe shuts up in museums. *Pareil* is the strongest kind of simile, connoting likeness to the point of identity; in an uncanny combination of opposites, Dorothée's foot represents the closing of the distance between Europe and Africa. But once she is placed on this pedestal, it is easy to see that the free exchange between the goddesses and her casts them all as equally "bizarre" elements in a scheme of beauty conceived for a nonbizarre subjectivity. The exchange makes Dorothée part of a hierarchical system.

By virtue of being bare, the foot represents vanity overpowering the semiotics of emancipation; the sign of freedom (shoes) is sacrificed for the vain (narcissistic and hopeless) imitation of European goddesses. Dorothée is an *affranchie*: freed, frank, French, but always in a derived condition. If she is free *(libre)* to roam the sands, it is only as an illusion, for in fact she is only *affranchie*. The reversal is perfect: the goddesses of Europe are locked up in museums, while the slave goes free. But Dorothée's status as a goddess is effected to the detriment of a sign of freedom in her own world, and she remains the slave of imitation. Freedom is left behind in order to seduce, submit, and faithfully imitate. The form that Dorothée "imprints faithfully on the fine sand" is a form she receives from Europe; it is makeup projected onto the blank surface of her nothingness.

The tenth paragraph finds Baudelaire writing in a specifically Africanist topos, the unreflexive stuff of idolatry, given over to "passions and vices," with "no inkling of a future state." This comes as part of the further lampoon of Dorothée's parody, as the extreme clash of the academic (the Opera ball) and the barbaric (the dance of the old *Cafrines*). One detail shows how Baudelaire has remodeled his inheritance: these "Cafrines." The word *Cafre* (from Arabic *kafir*, "infidel"), coined in the eighteenth century, was already outdated by Baudelaire's time, for its designation, "inhabitant of Africa south of the Equator," referring to "little-known peoples" (*Larousse du XIXe siècle*, article "Cafrerie"), no longer reflected the state of geographical knowledge. The feminine *Cafrine* may have been Baudelaire's invention, and it represents an "unnecessary" insistence on the feminine gender.[35] *Une Cafre* or *femme caffre* would have sufficed (see figure 4); Malte-Brun had written, "Tous les

35. The word *Cafrine* is not to be found in *Grand Larousse*, *Littré*, or *Grand Robert*. The *Trésor de la langue française* lists *Cafre* as "(Celui, *celle* [emphasis mine]) qui habite la Cafrerie," but it adds: "On rencontre dans la documentation le substantif féminin *Cafrine*." The only source it gives is a work from 1904. "Cafre" is typically Africanist in its arbitrary application of an inherited term to the totally unknown. Some idea of the appeal it had for Baudelaire comes through in his angry protestation addressed to Gervais Charpentier about unapproved changes in "La Belle Dorothée": "Croyez-vous réellement que *'les formes de son corps,'* ce soit là une expression équivalente à *'son dos creux et sa gorge pointue'*? [Baudelaire's emphasis]—Surtout quand il est question de *la race noire des côtes orientales* [emphasis mine]?" (*Oeuvres*, p. 1333). The black and the oriental are figments of an imaginary geography in Baudelaire's mind, into which one cannot read more precision than was written; the choice of the dated, inexact, and possibly factitious *Cafrine* illustrates this.

FEMME CAFFRE.

Figure 4. "Caffre Woman," from François Levaillant's *Voyage dans l'intérieur de l'Afrique* (Paris: Desray, 1791). Reproduced by permission of the Sterling Memorial Library, Yale University. Levaillant was Baudelaire's great-uncle, and in a letter to his mother (dated February 6, 1834[?]), young Baudelaire, away at school, asks to have this work brought to him.

membres d'*une jeune Cafre* ont le contour arrondi et gracieux, qui est le signe d'une santé parfaite'' ("All the limbs of a young Cafer woman have rounded and gracious contours, which is the sign of perfect health''; *Larousse*). Baudelaire is thus using a lexical exaggeration that harks back to the assumptions of the previous century.

The double feminine coincides with his most frankly Africanist scene. Racial thinking in the nineteenth century frequently expressed itself in sexual terms, and it is worth digressing briefly to explore the connection. Gobineau constantly employs male and female metaphors to characterize the races. His "feminine populations of Ham and of Shem" (*Essai,* p. 315) are the black and the Jew. His "male races" would possess "a more precise, abundant, and richer language than the female races" (p. 187), whereas the feminine peoples, being sensually oriented, are credited with esthetic superiority. The sexual and the racial are both totalized in language for Gobineau, in that language follows a "preestablished order" (p. 189) which applies sounds to things and ideas that are innate to each race. He concludes: "The hierarchy of languages corresponds exactly to the hierarchy of the races" (p. 203). The self-professed Negrophile writer of 1839, Gustave Eichtal, expresses a similar thought, although his value judgment is the opposite:

> Le noir me paraît être la *race femme* dans la famille humaine, comme le blanc est la *race mâle*. De même que la femme, le noir est privé des facultés politiques et scientifiques; il n'a jamais créé un grand état, il n'est point astronome, mathématicien, naturaliste; il n'a rien fait en mécanique industrielle. Mais, par contre, il possède au plus haut degré les qualités du coeur, les affections et les sentiments domestiques; il est homme d'*intérieur*. Comme la femme, il aime aussi avec passion la parure, la danse, le chant; et le peu d'exemples que j'ai vus de sa poésie native sont des idylles charmantes.[36]

> The black seems to me to be the *woman race* among the human family, as the white is the *male race*. Like the woman, the black is bereft of political and scientific faculties; he has never created a great state, he is not an astronomer, a mathematician, or a naturalist; he has accomplished nothing in industrial mechanics. But, on the other hand, he is possessed to the highest degree of the qualities of the heart, the affections, and the sentiments of the home; he is a man of *interiors*. Like the woman, he has a passionate love for dressing up, dancing, singing; and the few examples that I have seen of his native poetry were charming idylls.

36. Gustave d'Eichtal and Ismayl Urbain, *Lettres sur la race noire et la race blanche* (Paris: Chez Paulin, 1839), p. 22. Quoted partially in Léon-François Hoffmann, *Le Nègre romantique* (Paris: Payot, 1973), p. 203.

Without resorting to barnyard locutions, it should be obvious in these sexualizations of race who is doing what to whom. Dorothée is a black prostitute and thereby participates in a physical, geographical, sexual, and economic hierarchy, a condition of total dependence. Dorothée's whole subjectivity is determined from the outside, colonized and coopted, primping itself in that mirror "far-off in space"—that mirror which is France. Her thoughts are "worked and fashioned" by France, as by the young officer's discourse, helping her to conform. That effort will always be experienced as a failure and a difference.

Now it is expressed as an economic lack, a need to close a gap in a hierarchy, to end the separation from her sister by "piling piastre on piastre." Translating the sexual into the economic, the irredeemably other is "redeemed" *(racheté)* by the illusion of progress: exchange occurs, permitting Dorothée to slip along the scale of values and make changes. Prostitution is the means by which a pseudo-equal exchange takes place, money for sex. But money, while a precondition of freedom and power, does not make Dorothée equal; it only confirms her dependence. The sister, enslaved, is excluded from the illusion of upward mobility: she has "no state, no head," and cannot participate in any movement. Progress is the piling of coin on top of coin, the illusion of a passage along the spectrum to another state. But that movement will only preserve the present order of things. When the sister is bought out of slavery, "redeemed," she will be in Dorothée's position, possessed of a head, a state that Europe gives to her, literally sells to her. Then the labor of illusion and imitation can begin again.

Dorothée the prostitute has a counterpart in the nameless, faceless woman of "La Chevelure" (the verse poem), reduced to the pure fetish-figure of her head of hair. The poem describes the speaker's investment of that figure with "a whole world, far off, absent, almost passed away"—also described as "languid Asia and burning Africa"—that is largely a passive container for commodities the speaker desires ("You contain, ebony sea, a dazzling dream"; "An echoing port where my soul can drink"). The speaker continues to describe what he takes out of that source (perfume, sound, color; "You render unto me the azure of the sky immense and round"), until, in the last stanza, he mentions the price he must pay:

> Longtemps! toujours! ma main dans ta crinière lourde
> Sèmera le rubis, la perle et le saphir,
> Afin qu'à mon désir tu ne sois jamais sourde!
>
> [*Oeuvres,* p. 27]

For a long time! Forever! my hand in your heavy mane / Will sow rubies, pearls and sapphires, / So that to my desire you never turn a deaf ear.

He must sow in order to reap; but, as with Dorothée, there is an insurmountable economic imbalance underlying the illusion of exchange. The poet plays with that illusion, as a tease.

A play between continuity and absolute difference characterizes both "A une dame créole" and "La Belle Dorothée." Together, they project a permanent state of exile and desire onto the black and creole mind, an "aspiring-after-France" like that of Villault de Bellefond's natives of Guinea, an experience of the self as a lack and a difference.[37] Across the gap between Europe and the black world, the traffic is imitation, parody, and desire for sameness. Illusions of progress are produced within that framework: nobility, status, redemption, freedom. But at the moment when the barrier seems to have been crossed, a term arises to reveal the projected, dependent, attributed status of the illusion. The nobility is a mannerism, the freedom is only an emancipation given by the master, the redemption is an access to a state not of fulfillment but only of continuing desire.

But there remains a distinction to be made between the rhetoric of "La Belle Dorothée" and that of "A une dame créole." Whereas the discourse of the earlier poem seemed implicated in a certain economy of exploitation, that of "La Belle Dorothée" is much more ironic, harder to qualify ideologically. Perhaps it is logical that a poem written sixteen years after Baudelaire's voyage to Réunion should be more detached than one written on the spot. There is no first-person narrator here; the rhetorical questions—"Quel puissant motif? . . . Pourquoi a-t-elle quitté?—belong to no one but the rhetoric itself. Although Dorothée is demeaned in the poem's terminology as a "simple creature" yearning for legitimacy and admiration, prostituting herself to the image of France, she is nevertheless allowed a measure of self-expression. A gesture is made toward her subjectivity in an approximation of free indirect discourse ("qui est déjà mûre, et si belle!"). Free indirect discourse is in principle the halfway point, the perfect combination of communication (Baudelaire) and consciousness (Dorothée). But rather than as a happy marriage between the two voices, this poem is best understood as the irony between them, allowing a double optic that exposes an oppressive structure of imitation while simultaneously mocking its victim.

There is a certain ideological "enlightenment" to be seen in the writing of "La Belle Dorothée," in the expressivity lent to this black woman and the sympathy it implies. But the poem as discourse is represented exactly by that mirror "far off in space" in which Dorothée would define herself. This

37. Cf. Baudelaire's "A une malabaraise" (1846), *Oeuvres,* p. 174: "Pourquoi, l'heureuse enfant, veux-tu voir notre *France,* / Ce pays trop peuplé que fauche la souffrance, / Et, confiant ta vie aux bras forts des marins, / Faire de grands adieux à tes chers tamarins? . . . Comme tu pleurerais tes loisirs doux et *francs,* / Si, le corset brutal emprisonnant tes flancs, / Il te fallait glaner ton souper dans nos fanges" (emphasis mine).

is the crux of the poem's irony; for that mirror is France, and what it reflects is a pathetic desire to be identical. The other subjectivity comes into its own here as a wish to be not "other" at all. Again, the discourse seems to debase as much as it elevates. The concession to Dorothée, therefore, does not seem to conform completely to the model of the snake, in which everything is "head and tail, alternatively and reciprocally"; for even if no single voice reigns, the irony that remains is a principle of inequality rather than equality. Strangely, it will be in reading one of Baudelaire's more monumental poems that equality will stand a better chance.

The Swan, the Slave, and the Rhetoric of Nostalgia

Le dernier jour du nègre est son jour le plus beau

. . . .

Sous la terre d'exil alors je dormirai

. . . .

O cher et doux rivage, ô lieux de ma naissance,
Chaque instant, entre nous, fait croître la distance!
        —Edouard Alletz, "L'Abolition de la traite des noirs"[38]

The Negro's last day is his day sublime . . . / Under exile earth then shall I sleep . . . / O dear and sweet shore, O place of my birth, / Each moment, between us, makes the distance expand!

Quand moi verra ma patrie
Oh! quel grand plaisir pour moi
Toute la peine s'oublie
Quand l'on retourne chez soi
Bons amis vous caressent
Pour vous tout est plaisir
Soupirs et pleurs de tendresse
S'échappant vous font jouir.
        —Mme Rouxel, *Le Nègre comme il y en a peu*[39]

When I sees my homeland / Oh! what big pleasure for me / All pain be forgot / When you go home / Good friends soothe you / For you all is pleasure / Sighs and cries of tenderness / Rising give you joy.

Ce nègre se consume en serviles travaux
Pour creuser le sillon qui nourrit ses bourreaux

. . . .

Il se tait . . . seulement, en regardant les mers,
Une larme muette a tombé sur ses fers.
Le malheureux, chargé d'entraves inhumaines,
Redemande à ses dieux les plages africaines,

38. (Paris: Chez Delaunay, 1832), p. 9.
39. (Nîmes: Gaude, 1822), p. 36.

Ces palmiers au front vert, ces arbres aux fruits d'or
Dont sa bouche altérée exprimait le trésor . . . .
      —Anne Bignan, "L'Abolition de la traite des noirs"[40]

The Negro is devoured by servile labor / To dig deeper the
furrow that feeds his oppressor . . // He is silent . . . only,
while looking at the sea, / A silent tear has fallen on his
chains. / The wretch, loaded with inhumane shackles, /
 Implores his gods for the African shores, / Those green-topped
palms, those golden-fruited trees / That his thirsty mouth so
treasured.

Je ne reverrai plus ce palmier tutélaire
Dont le feuillage épais et l'ombre hospitalière
Protègent la cabane où je reçus le jour!
Non: ces objets chéris sont perdus sans retour. . . .
      —Martial Barrois, "L'Abolition de la traite des noirs"[41]

I shall never again see that guardian palm / Whose thick foliage
and hospitable shade / Protect the hut where I was born! / No:
these cherished objects are lost without return. . . .

Je pense à la négresse, amaigrie et phtisique,
Piétinant dans la boue, et cherchant, l'oeil hagard,
Les cocotiers absents de la superbe Afrique
Derrière la muraille immense du brouillard;

A quiconque a perdu ce qui ne se retrouve
Jamais, jamais! à ceux qui s'abreuvent de pleurs
Et tètent la Douleur comme une bonne louve!
Aux maigres orphelins séchant comme des fleurs!

Ainsi dans la forêt où mon esprit s'exile
Un vieux Souvenir sonne à plein souffle du cor!
Je pense aux matelots oubliés dans une île,
Aux captifs, aux vaincus! . . . à bien d'autres encor!
      —Baudelaire, "Le Cygne" (1860)

I think of the Negress, emaciated and consumptive, / Stamping
in the mud and seeking, with haggard eye, / The absent palms
of superb Africa / Behind the immense wall of fog; / Of
whoever has lost that which cannot be regained / Ever, ever! of
those who quench their thirst with tears / And are suckled by
Pain like a good she-wolf! / Of hungry orphans drying up like
flowers! // Thus in the forest where my mind is exiled / An old
Memory bellows forth from the horn! / I think of sailors
forgotten on an island, / Of captives, of conquered ones! . . . of
many others more!

40. (Paris: Firmin-Didot, 1823), pp. 6–7.
41. (Paris: Firmin-Didot, 1823), p. 9.

Aside from the forty-year gap that separates "Le Cygne" from the other poems above, is the only difference that between "good poetry" and "bad poetry"? One cannot help but feel that this is a factor. The corpus of poetry produced in the Académie Française competition of 1823 (including the Alletz, Bignan, and Barrois poems above) spoke a language of melodramatic urgency aimed at performing a legislative end.[42] The principal gesture of the antislavery poetry was to glorify the suffering of the slave, to *affranchir,* to emancipate and elevate through the power of a transcendent reflexion that was projected onto him. The slave takes up first-person discourse, and, by the force of his desire and nostalgia, articulates and therefore transcends (attempts to transcend) the distance between the "dear and sweet shore" of home and the "land of exile." That articulation can be happy, as in the case of the Rouxel vaudeville above, where the wish is being fulfilled, or it can be tragic, as in the other passages above, where paradise is "lost without return." The driving force is the same in the two modes: a dream of lost palm trees, beaches, golden fruit, grass shacks, birth, and death. In either case, the slave still "consumes himself in servile labor," digging himself deeper into the experience of exile and difference even as he is depicted attempting to escape. The abolitionist slave, although attributed a discourse and a subjectivity of his (or her) own, is still a *machine*, built by European discourse, whose function is to desire. Like a machine, the slave speaks only the language he is programmed to speak, and the springs that make him work are always hidden. The slave-machine proceeds through the labor that both constitutes it and consumes it.

By the time Baudelaire wrote "Le Cygne," his reference to the Negress and the palm tree were immediately recognizable, belated programs within French poetic discourse. "Le Cygne," amidst its proliferation of allusions and symbols, revisits a topos of early nineteenth-century poetry, the slave's reverie. By the use of this *négresse,* a word that "adds to the idea of color that of *servitude*" [*Larousse*], i.e., slavery, the poem revives an issue that had become "academic." Slavery had been abolished in 1848 (for the second time), and yet the slave's *exile* continued. The slave's juridical enslavement had ended; his position was still subordinate. So the words *nègre, négresse* had ceased to mean literally "slave," as in "Ce nègre se consume en serviles travaux," while still evoking a *past* or *foreign* condition of enslavement. The word thus itself describes the distance between "Le Cygne" and its predecessors of abolitionist fervor; but the distance is double in that the topos of slavery always designates a distance from Africa, from a native state of undifferentiated unity.

42. For a discussion of the Academy competition, see Yvan Debbasch, 'Poésie et traite: L'Opinion française sur le commerce négrier au début du XIXe siècle," *Revue française d'Histoire d'outre-mer* 48 (1961): 311–52; see also Hoffmann, *Le Nègre romantique*, p. 203.

"Le Cygne" is from beginning to end a series of "thoughts": "Je pense
à vous . . . je ne vois qu'en esprit . . . Je pense à mon grand cygne . . . et
puis à vous, Andromaque . . . Je pense à la négresse . . . aux matelots . . . Aux captifs, aux vaincus!'' ("I think of you . . . I see only in my
mind's eye / Only in spirit . . . I think of my great swan . . . and then of
you, Andromache . . . I think of the Negress . . . of sailors . . . Of captives,
of conquered ones!'') Any reading of the poem must therefore take account
of both the distance described by each figure (between Andromache and Troy,
the swan and its native lake, the Negress and Africa) and the distance from
each of these figures in which the discourse of the poem establishes itself.
The abolitionist poems sought to create an illusion of perceptual depth: to
recreate before the senses (caresse . . . bouche altérée) both the present in-
justice and the absent paradise. By using an enslaved first-person narrator,
these poems project a present voice and a familiarity with the oppressed that
serve the political purpose but that also take full possession of the other's
subjectivity. The worst of this is obviously the petit nègre of the Rouxel
vaudeville, but even in the nobler poems the slave and his sufferings are
domesticated and elevated, then sold on the poetic market.

The Baudelaire poem is "too late" to influence any situation, and it speaks
a language of detachment, impotence, and removal. Its first-person narrator
is completely disembodied, its négresse is a slave after the fact of emancipation
but still in exile, a symbol removed from its potential meaning. The denial
of a voice to the négresse (and to all the other figures in the poem except the
swan) is thus the expression of an appropriate noninterference in the consciousness of the other, leaving it removed from any pretense of total com-
petence and control on the part of the speaker. Rather than a puppet, an
"oppressive image."

But it is not enough to speak of a simple removal as the structure of "Le
Cygne," a poem that articulates complex rhythms of spatial and temporal
distance: simple physical distance, temporal removal; memory, dream, and
nostalgia; symbol and allegory. It will, of course, not be possible to discuss
here even a good portion of the ramifications of "Le Cygne," but certain
aspects must be chosen.

The first half of the poem establishes three principal figures: first Andromache, the mourning widow of Hector, exiled and enslaved; then the city of
Paris, consuming itself in the renovation of its few remaining medieval hovels,
building the new Carrousel; and the swan, escaped from its cage, seeking
water amidst the sterile hurricane (ouragan) of urban renewal. We have
already seen that each of these is set off by the frame of thought, the narrator's
voice, which, having no present tense or incarnation, creates each figure as
an act of memory. The only utterances in the present tense are Je pense and
je vois, which lead immediately to something past or foreign. The present is

created only as the process of emptying itself into the past. Spatially, the present object is but a pathetic mirror leading to a resplendent past. Each figure is a point of articulation.

> Andromaque, je pense à vous! Ce petit fleuve,
> Pauvre et triste miroir où jadis resplendit
> L'immense majesté de vos douleurs de veuve,
> Ce Simoïs menteur qui par vos pleurs grandit,
>
> A fecondé soudain ma mémoire fertile,
> Comme je traversais le nouveau Carrousel.

> Andromache, I think of you! This little river, / Pitiable mirror where once shined / The immense majesty of your widow's grief, / This false Simoïs, which widens with your tears, // Suddenly pricked my fertile memory, / As I crossed the new Carrousel.

The poet thinks of Andromache through the fertility of his memory; Andromache thinks of Troy and, by the process of thinking, widens the gap that separates her from it. The Simoïs itself is elsewhere; Andromache's tears widen a stream that is merely an imitation, a representation. But the temporal and the spatial cross in the figure of the stream, in that it once *was* resplendent: "où *jadis* resplendit." The false Simoïs was apparently once "true" and served then as a mirror for a majestic act of mourning that is assigned no time or tense and that remains missing as a scene. So, as Andromache weeps, *it is both the medium of retrieval and the barrier of exile that grow*. The object of desire approaches and recedes at the same time. The nostalgia that seeks to recreate the Simoïs and cross over it to Troy produces the tears that enlarge the obstacle and prevent passage to the other side. Similarly, the optimistic fecundation of a "fertile memory" is later expressed negatively, as "seeing only in the mind": the memory that tries to make things present again to the mind is also the wall that holds them away, keeps them "*only* in the mind" or "*only* in spirit."

Whatever type of primal re-collecting or remembrance would *not* be only in the confines of the mind, we do not know: it is absent from "Le Cygne." It would be a miraculous destruction of time and space, a perception determined only by the object. But everything in the poem conspires to strip the present, actual, real world of its contents; the present remains as a vacuum ("an empty tomb"; "the old Paris is no more"; "the silent air"; "a stream without water"; "the sky . . . cruelly blue"). Meanwhile, the past and the foreign are "filled," overinvested with nostalgia and desire ("immense majesty"; "heart filled by his beautiful native lake"; "memories heavier than rocks"). This overload reaches a crisis point in the beginning of the second half of "Le Cygne":

> Paris change! mais rien dans ma mélancolie
> N'a bougé! palais neufs, échafaudages, blocs,
> Vieux faubourgs, tout pour moi devient allégorie,
> Et mes vieux souvenirs sont plus lourds que des rocs.

> Paris is changing! But nothing in my melancholy / Has moved!
> New palaces, scaffolds, building-blocks, / Old districts, everything
> for me is becoming allegory, / And my old memories are heavier
> than rocks.

The emptying of the present world has led to the point where *everything becomes other*. Allegory, etymologically, is "speaking otherwise than one seems to speak" *(OED)*. But what is the logical connection between allegory in the third verse above and memory in the fourth verse? It should be noted that the allegories of "Le Cygne" are described as acts of memory and vice versa. Andromache, a mythical figure (i.e., out of an apocryphal past), seen performing her own act of memory ("Hector, je pense à vous!"), is conjured up by the fertile memory of the narrator at the same moment that his memory establishes the difference between the old and the new Paris. Andromache *allegorizes*, or states otherwise, the poet's act of memory; she acts out his sorrow over losing the old Paris when she mourns Hector.

Returning to the phrase "Je ne vois qu'en esprit" ("I see only in my mind/ only in spirit"), a double potential becomes evident. To see *en esprit* means to see only through the mind's eye, with the real eyes shut, cut off from the object but still seeing. But it also means to see "otherwise," to lend spirit to the object and give it meaning. To see otherwise, to allegorize, is to give meaning. Thus "all this confused debris" in the present is immediately superseded by an image from the past, a menagerie; Paris changes, but melancholy will not budge; the swan produces the allegorical *Travail* (Labor) and eventually *Douleur* and *Souvenir* (Pain and Memory). Each sign points to another that precedes it, imparts meaning to it, and yet shows it, the present sign, to be empty. *The process of giving meaning to the present is the same as showing the present to be empty.* Allegory and memory work together, synonymously, to form the "pure anteriority" that Paul de Man, in his influential article "The Rhetoric of Temporality," saw as determining the allegorical sign.[43] Everything becomes allegory; everything points to something else as its predetermination, excusing itself and acquiring a meaning for itself.

---

43. "In the world of the symbol it would be possible for the image to coincide with the substance, since the substance and its representation do not differ in their being but only in their extension . . . . Their relationship is one of simultaneity . . . whereas, in the world of allegory,

But if everything is allegorical, nothing is. A state where everything is other is a state where the word "other" has lost its oppositional power and no longer means anything. If everything is pushed to one side of the barrier that divides present from past and sign from meaning, then the barrier no longer exists and the universe stagnates. The "allegorizing intentionality"[44] of the poem, by constantly intending something *else*, now suggests its own destruction in a world where there would be nothing left to intend or desire. De Man's "allegory," for example, is postulated as such an end of desire:

> Whereas the symbol postulates the possibility of an identity or iden-tification, allegory designates primarily a distance in relation to its own origin, and, *renouncing the nostalgia and the desire to coincide,* it establishes its language in the void of this temporal difference. [P. 191; emphasis mine.]

But it is certainly not pointing out anything that Paul de Man did not realize himself to contend that such a world of allegory, in which only difference is postulated, is a world of nothing but *identity:* the barrier falls away, nostalgia is nullified, and *pure difference becomes pure identity.* This is the moment of the purely "academic," according to Baudelaire's "De l'idée moderne du progrès":

> Tout le monde conçoit sans peine que, si les hommes chargés d'ex-primer le beau se conformaient aux règles des professeurs-jurés, le beau lui-même disparaîtrait de la terre, puisque tous les types, toutes les idées, toutes les sensations se confondraient dans une vaste unité, monotone et impersonnelle, immense comme l'ennui et le néant. La variété, condition *sine qua non* de la vie, serait effacée de la vie.[45]

---

time is the originary constitutive category. . . . It remains necessary, if there is to be allegory, that the allegorical sign refer to another sign that precedes it. . . . It is of the essence of this previous sign to be pure anteriority" ("The Rhetoric of Temporality," in *On Interpretation,* ed. Charles S. Singleton [Baltimore: Johns Hopkins University Press, 1969], p. 190). It should be noted that, in the interpretation of de Man that follows, I discuss only half of his "The Rhetoric of Temporality," the part devoted to allegory. The second half is about *irony,* which, according to de Man, is, along with allegory, "a truly temporal predicament"; but whereas irony "comes closer to the factitiousness of human experience as a succession of isolated moments lived by a divided self . . . , allegory exists primarily within *an ideal time* that is never here and now but always a past or an endless future" (p. 207; emphasis mine). It is the "idealization" of that ideal time that concerns us here. On irony, see "The Ironic Negro," below, pp. 155–57.

44. Victor Brombert, "Le Cygne de Baudelaire: Douleur, Souvenir, Travail," *Etudes bau-delairiennes,* 3 (1973): 256: "En fait, c'est bien cette tendance fixative [to immobilize experience] que Baudelaire associe à l'intentionalité allégorisante." For Brombert, the reign of the present indicative in the second part of the poem tends toward immobility, but I see it more as a constant flight away from the present by means of thought and analogy.

45. *Curiosités esthétiques,* pp. 214–15. Note that this is also a rewriting of "Correspon-dances": "Comme de longs échos qui de loin se confondent / Dans une ténébreuse et profonde unité, / Vaste comme la nuit et comme la clarté."

Everyone can understand without difficulty that, if the men responsible for expressing beauty conformed to the rules of the judge-
professors, beauty itself would disappear from the earth, because all
types, all ideas, all sensations would be confused in a vast unity,
monotonous and impersonal, immense like boredom and nothingness. Variety, the sine qua non condition of life, would be erased
from life.

If everything is "bizarre" (beautiful), then nothing is. This is inevitably
described as a plunge into a world of darkness. In "Voyage à Cythère,"
darkness and allegory are part of the same experience:

—Le ciel était charmant, la mer était unie,
Pour moi tout était noir et sanglant désormais,
Hélas! et j'avais, comme en un suaire épais,
Le coeur enseveli dans cette allégorie.
                                                [*Oeuvres*, p. 119]

The sky was charming, the sea was one, / For me all was black
and bloody from then on, / Alas! and my heart, as in a thick
shroud / Was enveloped in this allegory.

Africanist discourse has been from the beginning a specific series of means
for saying something "else," for describing difference and otherness; allegory
would logically be a privileged mode of expression within that discourse. We
have now come across, quite unexpectedly, a confluence of texts that explicitly
articulate the relations between a theory of alterity, allegorical poetry, and
Africanist thematics. To understand this, we must pursue two radical attitudes
toward allegory, back a century from Baudelaire and forward a century to
Charles de Brosses and Paul de Man.

We have already seen how de Man's allegory, by insisting on pure difference, implied pure identity. Perhaps it is inevitable that in debunking a language of totalization, "The Rhetoric of Temporality" ultimately turns to its
own language of totalization and almost religious belief:

Wide areas of European literature of the nineteenth and twentieth
centuries appear as regressive with regard to the *truths* that come to
light in the last quarter of the eighteenth century. For the *lucidity* of
the pre-romantic writers does not persist. It does not take long for
a symbolic [opposed to allegorical] conception of metaphorical language to establish itself everywhere. . . . But this symbolical style
will never be allowed to exist in serenity; *since it is a veil thrown
over a light one no longer wishes to perceive,* it will never be
able to gain *an entirely good poetic conscience.* [P. 191; emphasis
mine]

If allegory is the realm of the "entirely good," perhaps the only "pure anteriority" is God or a world where god and matter are one. Clearly, this is the world of de Brosses' fetish, produced by a people stuck at the beginning of time, in a "perpetual childhood," that is, a pure anteriority.[46] The fetish represents the total otherness of a world where everything has become God: "These divine Fetishes are nothing other than the first material object that it pleases each nation or each person to choose . . . . : it's a tree, a mountain, the sea, a piece of wood, a lion's tail" (pp. 18–19). Pure anteriority for de Brosses was a monstrous miscarriage of religion, but only because it carried the religious impulse *too far,* into a state of pandemic, and therefore nullified, transcendence. If everything is a god, nothing is.

But *Du Culte des dieux fétiches* becomes pertinent all over again because that fear of excessive alterity, expressed principally in the figure of the fetish, is also channeled into a subtext about allegory itself. *Du Culte* is interspersed with little outbursts against allegory, whose crime is *universality:*

> D'ailleurs l'allégorie est un instrument universel qui se prête à tout. Le système du sens figuré une fois admis, on y voit facilement tout ce que l'on veut comme dans les nuages: la matière n'est jamais embarrassante; il ne faut plus que de l'esprit et de l'imagination. . . . Aussi l'usage du figurisme a-t-il paru si commode, que son éternelle contradiction avec la Logique & le sens commun n'a pu encore lui faire perdre aujourd'hui dans ce siècle de raisonnement le vieux crédit dont il a joui durant tant de siècles. [Pp. 6–7]

> Furthermore, allegory is a universal tool that serves all purposes. Once the system of figurative meaning is admitted, one can see anything one wishes, as in the clouds: matter is never an obstruction; all that is necessary is a mind and an imagination. . . . And the use of figurism appeared to be so convenient that its eternal contradiction with Logic and common sense has not yet diminished, in this century of reason, the old influence it has enjoyed for so many centuries.

De Brosses writes, with resentment, from within the historical moment of the rise of allegory that de Man described. For de Brosses, allegory is the manifestation of an atavistic, primitive "figurism," which, much like fetishism, respects no material determinations and produces precisely "any figure that you wish." This is not to say that allegory and fetish are completely synonymous for de Brosses; allegory does designate a distance ("The Bible depicts it [the religion of Egypt] not as an emblem *or as an allegory* but as a pure direct Zoölatry" [p. 97]), but allegory represents an arbitrary abuse

46. Charles de Brosses, *Du Culte des dieux fétiches* (Paris: n.p., 1760), p. 12.

of figural thinking. Universality and arbitrariness are the common denominator between fetish and allegory.

De Brosses' project of discrediting both fetish and allegory led him to attack figural thinking in the broadest possible terms. He implies that "the system of figural meaning"—apparently, tropes of any kind—must be wholly abandoned in favor of logic and common sense. His "century of reasoning" is a world without tropes. De Man's project of dethroning symbol produced an opposite hypothesis, in which the illusion of immediacy would be replaced by a fully tropological consciousness that recognizes itself as such. His "entirely good poetic conscience" obeys a logic and a common sense opposed to de Brosses' by admitting the role of figural meaning in everything and by inhabiting a world where everything is a trope. De Brosses' plea for immediacy led to an overstated rejection of anything figural; yet his indictment must obviously be made through a series of *figures ("instrument . . . comme dans les nuages . . . Logique . . .")*, of which the *fetish* is the most striking example, the allegory of figurism itself. De Man's rejection of immediacy seemed obliged to have recourse to a language that implies immediacy: truth, light, serenity, conscience. By *desiring* allegory, one alters its differential purity: entering the world through a language of totalization, allegory became a fetish in "The Rhetoric of Temporality."[47]

But the problem of the total loss of perspective, of pure difference, is not the world of "Le Cygne," a poem that hangs on the edge of its own destruction but does not go over. Baudelaire did not write "Tout pour moi *est* allégorie"; he left the universe in a constant state of *becoming* other, fired by the same "nostalgia and desire to coincide" of which a "pure" allegory would be the end. The poem describes allegory as a process by which desire reaches toward an object it knows full well to be unreachable. The object is recognized as irretrievable: "that which cannot be regained / Ever, ever!" Yet the exiles within the poem are "consumed by a desire without respite," be it ever so "ridiculous." The barriers (the Simoïs, the ironic sky, the immense wall of fog) will never be transcended: the narrator's condition will never permit him to *actually recall* anything, to make anything present again in his memory, that is, to perform a perceptual identity with the lost object (*Wahrnehmungsidentität*, "taking for real"). For his memory is itself allegorical (*Souvenir*) and representational. Still, the trumpet blast of memory will call the poet to go on remembering, "otherwise."

But what is the part of the Negress, the slave, in this plan? Andromache, after the fall of Troy, became a slave and a consort to the conqueror Pyrrhus

---

47. Professor de Man's reaction to an early version of these remarks on allegory in "The Rhetoric of Temporality" was, first, to point to the irony section of the article in its relation to "Le Cygne"'s "ciel ironique" and, second, with his inimitable grin, to "disavow the article completely."

("adjugée par le sort à un maître et [entrée] comme captive dans le lit du vainqueur!");[48] when Pyrrhus' attention wanes, she is abandoned to a fellow-Trojan fellow-slave, Helenus, and thus becomes "the slave of a slave" ("Moi esclave à son esclave Hélénus"). This sort of slavery, a dividing of spoils following a "just war," is part of a completely different world and a completely different concept.[49] Virgil's words are *servitio* and *famula famulaque*, referring to a general notion of servitude that could be simply domestic and familiar ("serviteur, domestique, esclave, suivant, compagnon" are alternative definitions for *famulus* in the *Dictionnaire de la langue latine* by Theil, 1866). However, in nineteenth-century translations of the *Aeneid*, the word *esclave* was consistently used instead of its milder, more domestic counterparts.[50] Historical differences were thus glossed over in favor of an image of unmediated subjugation. The antislavery poet Jacques Delille even added "irons" in his translation where there were none in the original.

And yet, with Andromache, as with the *négresse* and the swan in "Le Cygne," the reference is to a previous state of captivity and a current state of "ironic freedom."[51] Each has been emancipated, *affranchi*, but actually only delivered over to a new condition of desire. Aeneas finds Andromache surrounded by idols of Troy ("falsi Simoentis . . . une petite Troie, un Pergame qui *reproduit* le grand");[52] Baudelaire's Andromache, as we have seen, is caught in a self-perpetuating nostalgia that further separates her from primal satisfaction. The *négresse* performs two actions: *piétinant* and *cherchant*. She "makes walking movements *while resting in place*" (*Grand Larousse;* emphasis mine), scratching at an indestructible, formless, muddy surface, looking for something that is almost synonymous with absence in Western discourse: Africa.[53]

48. Virgil, *L'Enéide,* annotated by M. Sommier, translated into French by M. A. Desportes (Paris: Hachette, 1862), p. 38.

49. See David Brion Davis, *The Problem of Slavery in Western Culture* (Ithaca: Cornell University Press, 1966), esp. chap. 3, "Slavery and Sin: The Ancient Legacy."

50. Cf. *L'Enéide,* trans. Jacques Delille (Paris: Chez Giguet et Michaud, 1804), p. 43: "J'ai rampé sous un maître, et, par mille revers, / Passé de Troie en cendre à l'opprobre des *fers.* / Bientôt, nouveau Paris, jusqu'à Lacédémone / Mon dégaigneux époux court ravir Hermione; / Et, fuyant des plaisirs par la force obtenus, / Il m'abandonne *esclave à l'esclave* Hélénus." Cf. the translation by Louis Planchon (Lyon and Paris: Périsse frères, 1846), p. 50: "un jeune orgueuilleux / . . . dans la servitude nous a rendue féconde: puis afin de suivre / La fille de Léda, Hermione, afin d'épouser une Lacédémonienne, / Il m'a transmise *esclave à l'esclave* Hélénus pour que je fusse à lui." Cf. also the translations by A. Desportes (see note 44), p. 38: "L'orgueilleux Pyrrhus . . . m'abandonna, *moi esclave, à son esclave* Hélénus"; André Bellessort (Paris: Société d'Editions Les Belles Lettres, 1962), p. 71: "Il m'a passée moi son *esclave à son esclave* Hélénus, comme *une chose.*" (Emphasis mine, in each case.)

51. Lowry Nelson, "Baudelaire and Virgil: A Reading of 'Les Cygnes,'" *Comparative Literature* 13, no. 4 (1961): 337.

52. *Aeneid,* verse 350; trans. Bellessort, p. 72.

53. The closing two verses of Baudelaire's early poem "A une Malabaraise" are evidently an earlier version: "L'oeil pensif, et suivant, dans nos sales brouillards, / Des cocotiers absents les fantômes épars!" ("With pensive eye, and following, in our dirty fog, / The scattered phantoms of the absent palms.")

One is left with only the scratching, searching gesture of allegory: "All slips and is deadened on her granite skin" ("Allégorie," *Oeuvres,* p. 116). Thus the *négresse* consumes herself slowly, literally, in phthisis, consumption. Allegory is desire chasing after an object it will never reach nor yet completely lose; it is the movement of *piétinant* deeper into the mud, haggard, but seduced by the conviction that something "superb" exists over there. By the temporality of their plight, reducing everything to an act of memory; by their spatial relationship to a barrier that is always also a medium of transport; by the whole complex system of desire feeding on its own productions ("ceux qui s'abreuvent de pleurs"), Andromache and the *négresse* are, like allegory itself, perfectly caught between the ecstasy of memory and the pain of loss.

The *négresse* and the Africa she contemplates are thus neither fetishes nor "pure" allegories; they are midway between the total identity of the one and the total difference of the other. The nineteenth century may never have produced a more profoundly sympathetic role for the black than in this small passage of "Le Cygne." The otherness of the *négresse* is allowed to exist in serenity, in a European (Greco-Parisian) context that neither vulgarly assimilates the other to itself nor rejects it as a monstrous aberration.

Equality and Hierarchy

The middle path described by "Le Cygne" does not hide the fact that elsewhere in Baudelaire's works a different discourse imposes itself. I have no intention of excusing in one place, accusing in another, of standing in judgment at all. The movement of simultaneous elevation and degradation in both "A une dame créole" and "La Belle Dorothée" are part of a specific discourse that leaves no room for compromise. Constantly involved in the problematics of nobility, slavery, reflection, and blackness, those two poems describe a world of hierarchies where relationships are always defined as superior or inferior. In "Le Cygne," however, it would seem that all elements are horizontally dispersed and equally alienated. All beings are "equal" before the forces of time, exile, and loss; the narrator, Andromache, the swan, and the slave all share the same tragic vision. Is the allegorical mode the key to describing the other—happily—within Western discourse without either forced domestication or monstrous alienation? "Le Cygne" allows Africa its alterity without prejudice because alterity is seen as endemic: the old Paris is as "absent" as the coconut palms of Africa.

But if the word "allegory" is taken in its broadest sense, as designating a distance between discourse and its object, all Africanist utterances are allegorical. In fact, we have observed this since the beginning of this study: if there is a quality of Africanist discourse, it consists in a certain overextension and incongruity between the European utterance and the African object. On the surface, this difference most often expresses itself as the perception of a nullity, a barbaric, originary, unattainable other, be it monstrous or idealized. Thus Gobineau's "artistic genius," founded in "irreflection" as a material imagination, is an allegory where the academic and the barbarous, the discourse and the object, cannot coincide. His "irreflective reflection" is an allegory of the unbridgeable gap between the two cultures and of his own inability to understand that gap for what it is.

Such a discourse is not lacking in Baudelaire: the violent domestication of the "Dame créole" and the sad parody of "La Belle Dorothée" leave subjectivity, meaning discursive power, entirely in the European corner, so that any access to freedom and reflection is to be conferred by France. Thus again the self-contradictory movements within the two poems allegorize a European perception that is itself "in two parts parted," half way between perception and projection. Like images "perceived" in the dark, "spurting out from my eye by the thousands," these allegories are written "on" (on the subject of and determined by) a nullity and yet have all the appearances of being reflections of the real world. Thus the same notions are found in "A une dame créole" as in the *Larousse* encyclopedia article. The contemplation of France, the "true land of Glory," from within an African or creole subjectivity creates that subjectivity as fully dependent on France: left to its own devices, the other subject dreams of France and defines itself according to what France would like not to be.

"Le Cygne," by transcending the simple kind of allegory that thematizes a single distance, constitutes an allegory of an allegory. Much of Baudelaire's poetry could be considered "allegorical." But it would seem that, from the moment the word "allegory" itself is mentioned, allegory is read and pressed out again as a figure of itself: as a woman with skin of granite ("Allégorie"), as a total loss of perspective ("Un Voyage à Cythère"), or as the menace of that loss ("Le Cygne"). It is interesting that the reversal of perspective—from the black contemplating France to the black in France dreaming of Africa—coincides with the advent of this doubly allegorical mode. In a world on the verge of collapse, where everything is becoming something else, a solitary black woman looks at the empty sky, searching for her native land. Her dream is the opposite of Dorothée's; it is a dream of a return to "authenticity" (the dream that will move African literature a century later). The reversed point of view and the self-consciously allegorical discourse go together: in "Le Cygne" there is no longer a nobility, a "true land of Glory"; we are in it, and it is nothing but a series of signs pointing elsewhere.

But this is not a reversal of the hierarchy. Africa as a sign cannot hold the privileged position that France holds in "Dame créole" and "Dorothée"; it is "superb" only because of its absence. The black woman of "Le Cygne" and the Africa of her dreams are thus equal in a universe where equality, being everywhere, has lost its meaning. The only discourse that allows the Africanist object the tranquillity of its otherness is a discourse that perceives otherness in everything. If the *négresse* has as much of a head as anyone, it is because everyone's head is in jeopardy.

There is one element that prevents total equality: the poetic subject. Everything in "Le Cygne" is framed by the phrase "*Je* pense à . . . ," which repeats itself and imposes itself as the instigator of the whole process. That narrator represents the head without which no discourse of headlessness can exist. The reigning equal exchange of allegories is defined by a principle that is not equal. The total destruction of cultural, geographical, and discursive hierarchies is a hierarchical decision that inevitably affirms the superiority of the one who makes it. This is only to say that "Le Cygne" holds itself back from the disaster of a world without barriers, where everything is absent: Africa remains absent here by comparison to a voice that is "less" absent if not really present. The narrator's voice is an allegory of the presence that remains in a world where everything is becoming absent; it is his voice that represents the power of a discourse to confer the "superb" absence of Africa and that invites a political reading—an analysis of power relations—such as the one I have proposed here.

If reading Baudelaire has left us with some sense of the unequal, hierarchical nature of the poetic "self," some inescapable residue of a presence in the world that observes the absence around it, then reading Rimbaud from an Africanist perspective will re-"orient" that notion of the self, taking Baudelaire's "intelligent man of the world" and destroying his privilege of centrality. For with Rimbaud, as we shall see, the center cannot hold.

3

"Je est un Nègre," or Rimbaud's Africanist Adventures

Introduction

The works of Arthur Rimbaud, in their brevity and obscurity, have persistently been surrounded by a complex zone of myths and mythologies concerning the author's life, his renunciation of literature, and his career as a trader in Africa. Editors, critics, and readers have always been aware of a vague Africanist topos in Rimbaud's works and have reacted with varying gestures of either interpretation or denial of the need to interpret. The problem that confronts one immediately in approaching Rimbaud with an Africanist interest is the conflation of autobiographical elements with the stuff of his poetry: this is where the adventures begin. The autobiographical fallacy has gone to further reaches of absurdity with Rimbaud than with, perhaps, any other writer, as a comparison of his letters from Ethiopia with their "literary" interpretations will show. It is as if the fact of having written poems causes a permanent access to significance, along with a troubling inability to signify more than "mythically." Rimbaud, they say, did not write poems, cease to do so, go to Africa and die; rather, he mysteriously foresaw his future life in works of quasi-religious *voyance*, went forth to meet his destiny, and died redeemed. The difference between the first proposition and the second is one of interpretation and mythification, which reads as the impossibility to think difference, to conceive of sequence without consequence. It is my contention that the later phase of Rimbaud's life has nothing to do with his poetry and that the importance of the African period per se is limited to a footnote in the French encounter with Africa. But the entanglement of myths and fables that we face in studying Rimbaud inevitably leads to reflections on the process of editing, interpreting, and myth-making itself, and for that reason it is important to read and study the fallacy rather than ignore it. Rimbaud's contribution to Africanist discourse consists of two very distinct domains: first the utterances "by," for, and about blacks and Africa within Rimbaud's poetry, which together constitute "le mythe du nègre chez Rimbaud"; second, the critical, historical, and anecdotal discourse of other writers concerned with Rimbaud's time in Africa, making up the "mythe de Rimbaud chez les nègres." Reading these two as distinct—in the critical difference that separates them, yet brought them together in the first place—is the task of this chapter.

The Poetry

It is customary in approaching the poetry of Rimbaud to issue warnings about its obscurity, its instability, its refusal to obey the rules of identity and non-contradiction; for one is faced with "an inquisitive, quibbling, cantankerous poetry which abuses language"[1] and with "a certain obstinate silence and a certain troubling dispersion: the silence of Rimbaud himself, the dispersion of 'his meaning.' "[2] The absence of solid meaning provokes two fundamental reactions: either a renunciation of the search for meaning, leaving obscurity unredeemed, or a reinsertion of irrationality within a rational system. The first is the despairing gesture of Jacques Rivière, discussing "Les Illuminations":

> At bottom, what Rimbaud says has no meaning. . . . The incoherence of his language is but the reflection of his ignorance in regard to the type of thing he speaks about.
>
> It is impossible for him to prepare us for what he is going to say, because he does not know in advance, because he learns it himself only at the moment of utterance.[3]

The incoherence is a result of automatism, produced by a machine-man who knows nothing of what he is about. The system is alien to the designation of a preexisting meaning; the object is projected without intention because there is no subject capable of intending; the only reflection is that of ignorance and is thus null.

Rivière's pejorative tone should not obscure the fact that a tenacious otherness is recognized by all as fundamental to Rimbaud's poetry. To all but the most brutal rationalists, the question will involve the inability to say what one means.[4] For some, the only thing holding back critical despair is the power of the word "I" to offset alterity, as in the famous formula "I is an other" ("Je est un autre"). If one believes sufficiently in the power of subjectivity, that one word can be made to reduce any otherness to a game played within the house of the subject, any enigma to an intention.

"Mauvais sang"

There is one poem that lies at the root of both the "mythe du nègre chez Rimbaud" and the "mythe de Rimbaud chez les nègres." It is "Mauvais

---

1. Philippe Bonnefis, "Onze notes pour fragmenter un texte de Rimbaud," *Littérature* 11 (October 1973): 48, referring to *Derniers vers*.

2. Atle Kittang, *Discours et jeu: Essai d'analyse des textes d'Arthur Rimbaud* (Grenoble: Presses Universitaires de Grenoble, 1975), p. 13.

3. *Rimbaud* (Paris: Kra, 1930), pp. 53, 121. Quoted in Kittang, pp. 28–29.

4. For Ernest Delahaye, however, there is no problem of the sort, as we will see in relation to "Démocratie" (*Les Illuminations" et "Une Saison en enfer" de Rimbaud*, ed. E. Delahaye [Paris: Albert Messein, 1927]).

sang" in *Une Saison en enfer,* a prose poem six pages long, divided into eight parts, and interpreted by Antoine Adam in his notes to the Pléiade edition as autobiographical ("describes his own character . . ."; the "profound idea" of the poem is that "His glory is all within himself" [p. 957]).[5] It is also the locus of a first-person discourse attributed to a "nègre," as one among the metamorphoses of the narrator, and it contains the famous prophecy of Rimbaud's departure for Africa. Thus, to read through the first word of the poem, we are immediately caught in the web of myths: "J'ai de mes ancêtres gaulois l'oeil bleu blanc, la cervelle étroite, et la maladresse dans la lutte" ("I get from my Gallic ancestors white-blue eyes, a small brain, and awkwardness in fighting").

To read that "I" as an "other," one must read it neither as an ironclad, autoreferential subjectivity in a world cut off from the outside nor as totally determined by what one perceives that world to be. I propose to read "Mauvais sang" between two aspects of its complex structure: the theme of the racial history of France, and the problem of temporality that prevents that history from ever being realized.

"French, that is to say, German"

The authors of the third and fourth centuries almost always
mean *French* when they use the word *German.*
        —Mézeray, *Abrégé de l'histoire de France* (1668)

Et, pour Astérix, vaincre le problème noir en France—problème
de Gaulois et de Romains, c'est-à-dire de Nègres et de Blancs,
somme toute . . . .
        —Yambo Ouologuem, *Lettre à la France nègre* (1968)

The impulse to attribute origins to oneself has produced an enormous variety of theories in France, theories that appear always to serve current political ends. Based on slender evidence, racial history reads more as a political allegory than a disinterested science. Opinions on the origins of "the French race" boil down to two opposite but complementary propositions. The French, the "true" inhabitants of the "land of glory" (Baudelaire), could be the descendants of the Germanic Franks, who conquered the Gauls, gave France its name, and were the "ferocious originators of liberty," "tall, blond, white-skinned," feared by the Romans, and whose very name meant "brave, valiant, and daring"[6] or "free, noble, sincere" (La Curne de Sainte-Palaye, *Dictionnaire historique,* 1879). The freedom that was concomitant to their nobility resulted from depriving others of their freedom, that is, from subjugating the

---

5. The notes in parentheses will refer to the Pléiade edition of Rimbaud, *Oeuvres complètes,* edited by Antoine Adam (Paris: Gallimard, 1972).

6. Jacques Barzun, *The French Race: Theories of Its Origins and Their Social and Political Implications Prior to the Revolution* (Port Washington, N.Y.: Kennikat Press, 1960), pp. 80, 119, 68.

Gauls. The opposing theory therefore simply attributes true Frenchness to the other side: in Jacques Barzun's words, "The French are all Gallo-Romans, who, in casting off the shackles imposed through the centuries by a few German conquerors and their descendants, regained in the French Revolution their original liberties" (p. 41). Léon Poliakov attributes to François de Belleforest (1579) the coining of a phrase often heard in nonroyalist circles in France: "Nos ancêtres les Gaulois."[7] The Gauls' native language was "Romanic or Romance"; under the Frankish yoke their identity was lost; the Revolution, in the eyes of writers such as the Abbé Sièyes, was to succeed in purging the Frankish oppressors. Poliakov (p. 41) quotes "a certain Ducalle," who asks, "How much longer will you suffer us to bear the infamous name of French? . . . we are of the pure blood of the Gauls." The two theories divide France against itself in a simple see-sawing of sovereignty and truth, of the self as either oppressor or oppressed.[8]

The first phrase of "Mauvais sang" advances the Gallic proposition while holding itself back from total commitment. Instead of the singleness of Belleforest's formula, there are "some" Gallic ancestors here; the others are to remain unspecified. Classical order in grammar dominates the opening of the poem (the first sentence has three direct objects, the first paragraph has three sentences), while a temporal dialogue is established between the time of the ancestors (referred to only once, "Les Gaulois *étaient*" ["The Gauls *were*"]) and the speaker's present, which in turn refers to the past as an explanation, "D'eux, j'ai . . ." ("From them I get"). That simple structure of origin and inheritance will be increasingly discombobulated by an onslaught of fragmented sentences, ambiguous references, and an indeterminate temporality.

> J'ai de mes ancêtres gaulois l'oeil bleu blanc, la cervelle étroite, et la maladresse dans la lutte. Je trouve mon habillement aussi barbare que le leur. Mais je ne beurre pas ma chevelure.
>
> Les Gaulois étaient les écorcheurs de bêtes, les brûleurs d'herbes les plus ineptes de leur temps.
>
> D'eux, j'ai: l'idolâtrie et l'amour du sacrilège;—oh! tous les vices, colère, luxure,—magnifique, la luxure;—surtout mensonge et paresse.

7. Léon Poliakov, *Le Mythe aryen* (Paris: Calmann-Lévy, 1971), p. 33.

8. The other vital tribal division of France is even more persistent and runs through the quarrels over Rimbaud's works: that between Catholics and anticlerics. The following passage from J.-M. Carré's *Vie aventureuse d'Arthur Rimbaud* (Paris: Plon, 1926) manages to encompass both sides: "Paterne Berrichon, qui prétend avoir pénétré les arcanes d'*Une Saison en enfer*, déclare . . . qu'elle est 'depuis les cathédrales gothiques l'affirmation la plus dense, la plus substantielle du christianisme, un témoignage poignant de la réalité catholique.' Je n'en crois rien et je partage sur ce point l'avis, diamétralement opposé, de M. Marcel Coulon. *La Saison* est pour moi l'expression de la dernière crise morale du poète et s'achève par 'le refus de Dieu' " (p. 129). One is left to wonder what demon lurks in those last quotation marks. Is it a refusal or not?

I get from my Gallic ancestors white-blue eyes, a small brain, and awkwardness in fighting. I find my clothes as barbaric as theirs. But I don't butter my hair. The Gauls were the most inept animal-flayers and grass-burners of their time. From them, I get: idolatry and the love of sacrilege;—oh! all the vices, anger, lust—magnificent, lust; especially lying and laziness.[9]

The image of Gaul is of a primal subjugation and inferiority prior to or independent of any superior entity. The vices of Gaul are innate, as if they flowed in the veins. The barbarous, sacrilegious idolater cannot be conceived, however, except in relation to a civilized, faithful monotheist; there can be no Gaul without the Frank (what the Frank will come to represent: the noble) to make him so. Yet everything in these paragraphs works to deny that derived nature of alterity. Gaul is asymmetrically negative: its proper qualities involve fragmentation, destruction, and vice, all fighting a battle against nothing. Thus, in the second chapter, the uprising is impotent: "Il m'est évident que j'ai toujours été race inférieure. . . . Ma race ne se souleva jamais que pour piller" ("It is obvious that I have always been of inferior race. . . . My race never rose up except to pillage"). The verb *se soulever* is designed to reverse and conserve the model of submission, but the Gauls rise up only to tear down distinctions, not to appropriate them.

Thus, when we learn at the end of the first chapter that the speaker's family "owes everything" to the Declaration of the Rights of Man ("J'entends des familles comme la mienne, qui tiennent tout de la déclaration des Droits de l'Homme"), the sense of that "everything" is amplified. The Gauls have been nothing save an agglomeration of negative qualities, and the document that declares their rights appears here as not only their redeemer but also as their very creator. The first definition of *tenir de* is "to resemble, to present an analogy with" someone or something, and perhaps the Gauls are "like" the Declaration in that the act of writing brought them into being: the Gauls, as in the tracts of the Revolution, have only a paper reality. Through the performative language of the Declaration ("The National Assembly *recognizes* and *declares . . .* that men are born and remain free and equal in rights"), as we shall see presently, a writing hand intervenes and bestows existence. But this use of *tenir de* seems equally prone to interpretation in the second, archaic, and odd definition *(Grand Larousse):* "Tenir d'un seigneur, être son vassal ou tenancier" ("To be the vassal or tenant of a lord"). The speaker's family is vassal, subjugated to the document that ends their subjugation and gives them their rights. Equality can only be accorded by an unequal agency that may efface itself but must yet remain superior.

9. Cf. André Maurois, *A History of France*, trans. Henry L. Binsse (New York: Minerva Press, 1960), p. 18: "The Franks . . . attended council meetings clad in the skins of wild animals or in short tunics, their hair smelling of rancid butter, their bodies of garlic."

The project of equality is advanced in tentative fragments in the first chapter of "Mauvais sang": "J'ai horreur de tous les métiers. Maîtres et ouvriers, tous paysans, ignobles. La main à plume vaut la main à charrue" ("I abhor all walks of life. Masters and workers, all peasants, ignoble. The hand with a pen is worth the hand with a plow"). Equality here is a matter of reducing hierarchies to their lowest elements, so that everyone is now ignoble; the head and the body become two equal bodies. Equality is sameness and is horrible. The writing hand and the plowing hand are given the same value in a discourse that devalorizes everything. Thus far "Mauvais sang" is the story of *missing oppositions,* of inferiority to nothing, of equality with nothing.

Does the authority of historical discourse present an alternative? The Declaration of the Rights of Man appears as a semantic anchor, connecting the shifting elements of the poems to a known object. The reference establishes an opposition in two senses: it designates a commonly recognized text from a single moment in history, and it thereby permits the *difference* that precedes and gives meaning to "equality." Before the Revolution, a state of inequality existed that was the condition of possibility for the Declaration. Within its pages, the "writing hand," the "hand with a pen," confers equality by virtue of its superiority; at the same time, the referent makes the rest of the poem beholden to it for positive grounding. The privilege of historical discourse is to hold an authority to which other elements owe *(tenir de)* their status. Bearing in mind that this referent is itself only another text, I would still read the end of the first chapter of "Mauvais sang" as an attempted insertion of history, which is the ability to be this instead of that, now instead of then, equal instead of unequal.

If the first chapter attempts to set up a dialogue between origin and inheritance and ends by articulating a historical referent, the second chapter names the problem explicitly as history and throws it into various problematical lights. A series of sentences within the chapter presents differing perspectives on the relationship between the individual and history:

> Si j'avais des antécédents à un point quelconque de l'histoire de France!
> Mais non, rien.

> If I but had antecedents at some point in the history of France!
> But no, nothing.

The word "antecedents" applies equally to genealogy and grammar, but the function of this sentence is to have grammar deny the reality of genealogy. The speaker's antecedents or ancestors were to have been decided in the first chapter, yet now the conditional mood acts to deny the accession to history that the Declaration of the Rights of Man would provide. The speaker has antecedents, his Gallic ancestors, but none of them qualifies for a part in something called the history of France. "Mais non, rien" defines the exclusion of Gaul from France, of the barbarous from the civilized, of nonhistory from history. History is the history of France; the plowing hand has no access to history except through the good graces of the writing hand. The experience of this sentence is thus exile and loss: the ancestors may have existed, but they cannot be recalled because they are alien to the system of recall, which is writing.

In contrast, the second mention of history works perfectly. "Je me rappelle l'histoire de France fille ainée de l'Eglise" ("I recall the history of France, eldest daughter of the Church"). The legitimacy of France and of its consti- tuted Church contrasts with the idolatry and sacrilege of Gaul. The structure of these two propositions reveals two different projects: first *to have* ante- cedents, which unite past and present in a single possession; second, *to recall* history, an intellectual act recognized as such. The first is described in the most tentative and dubious mood, then renounced; the second is performed simply in the present indicative, without complication. The phantasm of Christianity that follows, however, shows a double possibility within the act of recollection itself. First: "J'aurais fait, manant, le voyage de terre sainte" ("I would have made, as a roisterer, the voyage to the Holy Land"). He would have made the pilgrimage, but under what conditions we cannot know. The object approaches and recedes at once. Simultaneously, a phrase of crystalline definition arises: "je suis assis, lépreux, sur les pots cassés et les orties, au pied d'un mur rongé par le soleil" ("I am seated, leprous, on the broken pots and nettles, at the foot of a wall eaten away by the sun"). This is more a perceptual identity with the past, describing the phantasm as real and present.

Between these two examples, the recollection of history is as ambivalent as the inability to recall nonhistory. The past cannot be fully recovered, yet one cannot cease to perceive it: "Je ne me souviens pas plus loin que cette terre-ci et le christianisme. Je n'en finirais pas de me revoir dans ce passé" ("I remember nothing further than this land and Christianity. I would not be done seeing myself in this past"). Lastly, the past is defined negatively as the impossibility to find genealogy, to make connections and explain inher- itance: "Mais toujours seul; sans famille; même, quelle langue parlais-je? . . . Qu'étais-je au siècle dernier: je ne me retrouve qu'aujourd'hui" ("But always alone, without a family; for that matter, what language did I speak? . . . What was I in the past century: I find myself only in the present day").

The reign of the present follows the victory of Gaul ("La race inférieure a tout couvert" ["The inferior race has covered everything"]), and with it the threat of silence. After evoking, in parody, the perfect world of bourgeois science, progress, and philosophy as a "new nobility," the speaker seems on the point of short-circuiting his own discourse. Against the accession of Gaul to Frankish status, against the repression of what are now called *pagan* impulses, silence is the only reply:

> La science, la nouvelle noblesse! Le progrès. Le monde marche!
> Pourquoi ne tournerait-il pas? . . .
> Je comprends, et ne sachant m'expliquer sans paroles païennes,
> je voudrais me taire.

> Science, the new nobility! Progress. The world marches on! Why
> wouldn't it turn? . . .
> I understand, and, not knowing how to express myself without
> pagan words, I would like to fall silent.

Paganism is the hinge between the second and third chapters of "Mauvais sang," between the Other as a European antecedent and the Other as Negro. "Paganism" does not refer in its etymology to any belief system or form of worship; the Latin *paganus* means simply "villager," "perhaps because paganism was maintained longer in the countryside than in the cities" *(Grand Larousse)*. The pagan is: (1) A follower of polytheistic cults; (2) One not yet evangelized; (3) Greco-Latin; (4) Having no religious belief *(Grand Larousse)*. The first definition represents paganism as all religions, the last as no religion. In either case the usage of the word has tended to project the image of an Other within the realm of the same, of a European having all beliefs or no beliefs but understood as being *prior to* true belief in a monotheistic god. The pagan, unlike the idolater, is not "stuck" in a "perpetual childhood" (de Brosses, *Du Culte des dieux fétiches);* he is on his way to conversion.

What, then, are the "pagan words" without which the speaker cannot explain himself? They might be the unrecordable, irretrievable words of the plowing hand, which cannot write—words that remain prior to explanations and histories. Is the formula "pagan words" an oxymoron, indistinguishable from the silence between the second and third chapters, or does the third chapter consist of those words captured alive?

There is general agreement that Rimbaud's poetic project involved an attempted return to some "natural immediacy," a "world of substance" represented by the Negro and by Africa, but that the project failed and that Rimbaud, in the words of Yves Bonnefoy, "fell back under the spell of the categories he was fleeing."[10] But what are the contours of this supposed immediacy? What is the return of "pagan blood"?

> Le sang païen revient! L'Esprit est proche, pourquoi Christ ne
> m'aide-t-il pas, en donnant à mon âme noblesse et liberté. Hélas!
> l'Evangile a passé! l'Evangile! l'Evangile.

10. Yves Bonnefoy, *Rimbaud par lui-même* (Paris: Seuil, 1961), p. 127.

J'attends Dieu avec gourmandise. Je suis de race inférieure de
toute éternité.

Pagan blood is returning! The Spirit is near; why doesn't Christ
help me by giving my soul nobility and freedom. Alas! the Gospel
has passed by! the Gospel! the Gospel.
    I await God gluttonously. I am of a race inferior from all eter-
nity.[11]

"Blood" and "pagan" are not, strictly, words of the same category. Blood
is the stuff of racial theories, of Gauls and Franks and Negroes, whereas
paganism is defined as nonparticipation in a religious or social system. A
pagan could be of any race, of any blood. By evoking paganism in the terms
of race, "Mauvais sang" prepares to turn itself toward an alterity that is
complete, that of the Negro.[12] If paganism becomes a racial trait in this return,
if its alterity is pushed to the limit, then it must also be admitted that the
domestic elements (the Church, etc.) follow a similar pattern of radicalization.
Christianity, through the Eucharist, is conceived of as cannibalism: "J'attends
Dieu avec gourmandise,"[13] and, later, "j'ensevelis les morts dans mon
ventre" ("I entomb the dead in my belly"). The return appears as the raising
of paganism to the status of Christianity, of Frankness, noble and free, and
the lowering of Christianity to the status of paganism.

Me voici sur la plage armoricaine. Que les villes s'allument dans
le soir. Ma journée est faite; je quitte l'Europe. L'air marin brûlera
mes poumons; les climats perdus me tanneront. Nager, broyer
l'herbe, chasser, fumer surtout; boire des liqueurs fortes comme du
métal bouillant,—comme faisaient ces chers ancêtres autour des
feux.
    Je reviendrai, avec des membres de fer, la peau sombre, l'oeil
furieux: sur mon masque, on me jugera d'une race forte. J'aurai
de l'or: je serai oisif et brutal. Les femmes soignent ces féroces infirmes retour des pays chauds. Je serai mêlé aux affaires politiques.
Sauvé.
    Maintenant je suis maudit, j'ai horreur de la patrie. Le meilleur,
c'est un sommeil bien ivre, sur la grève.

11. Note that what the speaker asks for is precisely *affranchissement* in the sense we saw in
"A une dame créole": nobility and freedom.
12. That turning, from an Other in time (the Gaul) to an Other in space, is the thematic
armature of the whole poem and was not in itself a new idea. Nicolas Louis de la Caille wrote
in 1763: "La vie des Hottentots est à peu près la même que celle des Gaulois sauvages, dont
César fait mention dans ses Commentaires" (*Journal historique du voyage fait au cap de Bonne-
Espérance* [Paris: Chez Guillyn, 1763], p. 257). De Brosses' *Du Culte des dieux fétiches* is of
course the strongest text on this point.
13. "Il avait écrit, avec une arrière-pensée de blasphème: 'J'attends Dieu avec gourmandise'" (Louis Jalabert, "Rimbaud en Abyssinie," *Etudes* 76, no. 238 [1939]: 188).

Here I am on the Breton shore. May the towns light up in the evening. My day is done; I am leaving Europe. The sea air will burn my lungs; lost climates will tan me. Swim, tread on the grass, hunt, especially smoke; drink liquors strong, like boiling metal,—as did those dear ancestors around their fires.

I will return, with limbs of steel, dark skin, a furious eye: from my mask, I will be seen as coming from a strong race. I will have gold; I will be idle and brutal. The women care for these ferocious invalids back from hot lands. I will be mixed up in politics. Saved.

For the moment I am damned; I abhor my country. The best is a very drunken sleep, on the strand.

There is no sense denying the spooky relationship between these paragraphs and Rimbaud's African destiny, but that is a problem to be left for later in this chapter. For the moment, I would like to offer a version of the critical consensus on Rimbaud, adapted to the terms of this study, and see where it leads. The proposition is this: that Rimbaud, setting off on an Orientalist conqueror's dream, returns with an Africanist experience of dis-orientation. The fantasy quoted above is more precisely Orientalist, in its conception and format, than Africanist: the Orient, we are told, represents "the plenitude of light. . . . To return to the Orient is to go back to the beginning, to rejoin the world of innocence prior to civilization."[14] The Negro, to whom the speaker will later assimilate himself, is a being with his "eyes closed to your light."

What happens to the self in the creation of this fantasy is quite unexpected. The Other is a recreator of the self, a "lost climate" in which the lost self finds itself in the form of "those dear ancestors around the fires." The Other is encompassed and domesticated in a link of parentage, existing only in the terms the self establishes for it. This is nothing new. But by the same token the self has come to require the Other in order to be realized. The self knows itself as a being only through the intervention of the "strong race"; the Other gives being to the self. The speaker is, in fact, reminiscent of the moon in the crucial metaphor invented by Gobineau. Ethiopian civilization, said Gobineau *(Essai sur l'inégalité des races humaines),* may be compared to the moon in that it has no light, no presence of its own; it simply passes on what it receives from the outside. We can perceive the primitive world in this passage of "Mauvais sang" only through the passivity of the speaker, *"on his mask"* (like the moon's two-dimensional disk). The speaker is thus a new phenomenon in the history of Africanist discourse—a discourse that has previously passed itself off as a tour de force of objectification and projection, casting objects outward in order to deny any originary stake in their concep-

14. Marc Eigeldinger, *Rimbaud et le mythe solaire* (Neuchâtel: La Baconnière, 1964), p. 49.

tion. Now, within the house of the writing personage, the speaker-*nègre* acts out the process of paradoxical reflexive irreflection that has previously been wholly projected onto the Africanist object. That subjectivity now reflects without thinking, taking on the shape of an Other that is before him. That Other is an independent entity, with strength and wealth of its own: gold, steel, and the constituted systems of politics. The speaker is "saved" from nothingness by the intervention of this Orient-as-presence. The only question is whether the "Orient" can sustain the burden of being completely absent (known only as a reflection on the speaker's face) and completely present (as a positive, life-giving force). Therein lies the dilemma of the whole Orientalist fantasy: brought back alive and made present again, the ancestral primitive becomes mere dead representation.

The fourth chapter bursts the illusion with a gesture similar to that at the beginning of the second chapter ("Mais non, rien"). "On ne part pas.— Reprenons les chemins d'ici, chargé de mon vice." ("We are not leaving. Let me again take to the paths of this place, bearing my vice.") The shifter *ici,* along with *maintenant* at the end of the preceding chapter, represents the tyranny of the present, of the reality principle, over the fantasy, which had come to appear real. Instead of a happy Orientalist illusion, in which the primitive world has form and substance that can be represented, the speaker is left with a primal, undefined vice. Having set out to conquer and be conquered, he finds he cannot leave a pandemic present to which nothing opposes itself, a vast screen of unintelligibility. This is expressed in the language of idolatry:

> A qui me louer? Quelle bête faut-it adorer? Quelle sainte image attaque-t-on? Quels coeurs briserai-je? Quel mensonge dois-je tenir?—Dans quel sang marcher? . . .
> —Ah! je suis tellement délaissé que j'offre à n'importe quelle divine image des élans vers la perfection.

> Lease myself to whom? What beast must one worship? What sacred image to attack? What hearts shall I break? What lie must I support? In which blood to march?
> Ah!—I am so forlorn that I offer to any divine image impulses to perfection.

The series of questions places the speaker in a doubly negative position— opposed to each object, but with total indecisiveness, awash among equal choices without meaning. Idolaters "choose as a god . . . the first thing they meet in the morning, be it bird, snake, or other animal" (André Thévet, *Les Singularitez de la France antarctique* [1570]). *N'importe quelle* ("Any . . . whatsoever") expresses a perverse lack of discrimination in regard to that which should be the most discriminated, the godhead. Paganism, the Other within the same, is pushed one step further, so that it bears this specifically idolatrous characteristic.

So, as the Orientalist dream dies, the surprise is to find Africa within the self. The end of the fourth chapter (" . . . suis-je bête!" ["I am a fool!"]) is only a step away from the moment of the *poète-nègre* ("Je suis une bête, un nègre" ["I am a fool, a Negro"]). The speaker has thus far been a Gaul, a pagan, a semi-Christian, an imperialist or Orientalist mogul, and a fool, a beast *(bête)*. Each of these hypotheses has approached, become impossible not to see, and yet remained caught within the confines of thought. Each has been necessary but none sufficient to establish a coidentity between the self and the past or the Other. The ancestral past and its racial mythology would have produced a simulacrum of coidentity: inheritance. The Christian and Orientalist fantasies remove the speaker from that realm, but only in attempts to find it elsewhere. Gradually the past is rejected in favor of the Other, the "strong race," contemporary but distant. Coincidence with that object is destroyed by "the paths of this place," and the poem turns to the Africanist alternative.

> Oui, j'ai les yeux fermés à votre lumière. Je suis une bête, un nègre. Mais je puis être sauvé. Vous êtes de faux nègres, vous maniaques, féroces, avares. Marchand, tu es nègre; magistrat, tu es nègre; général, tu es nègre; empereur, vieille démangeaison, tu es nègre: tu as bu d'une liqueur non taxée, de la fabrique de Satan.— Ce peuple est inspiré par la fièvre et le cancer. Infirmes et vieillards sont tellement respectables qu'ils demandent à être bouillis.—Le plus malin est de quitter ce continent, où la folie rôde pour pourvoir d'otages ces misérables. J'entre au vrai royaume des enfants de Cham.

> Yes, my eyes are closed to your light. I am a fool, a Negro. But I can be saved. You are false Negroes, you maniacs, ferocious and greedy. Merchant, you are a Negro; magistrate, you are a Negro; general, you are a Negro; emperor, you old itch, you are a Negro: you have drunk an untaxed liquor, made by Satan.—This population is inspired by fever and cancer. Invalids and old codgers are so respectable that they ask to be boiled.—The smartest thing is to leave this continent, where madness prowls to provide these wretches with hostages. I am entering the true kingdom of the children of Ham.

At the heart of the "mythe du nègre chez Rimbaud" is the critical ambiguity between *nègre* and *faux nègre. Nègre* is first given in apposition to *bête,* as if it were synonymous with animality and stupidity, blindness to the light. The *nègre* is one cut off from light and reason; he can be saved, but this only confirms his condition of damnation. The speaker presents himself as a true *nègre,* which is also a *bête* or a false human being. But the sentence addressed to "you" complicates the scheme—those people are apparently false versions of the speaker, false *nègres.* They are false falsehoods, and no truth seems opposable to anything here. The new Other, *vous,* is defined as "maniaques, féroces, avares," each of which falls back on the speaker himself. In the Greek root of *maniaque* is "humeur sombre, délire prophétique" ("dark humor, prophetic delirium"—*Grand Larousse*), which describes the narrator's dark skin coming "back from hot lands," his prophetic pronouncements: "C'est oracle, ce que je dis" ("It's an oracle that I'm speaking"); *féroces* was also used in the fantasy of the pagan's return ("ces féroces infirmes"; "l'oeil furieux"); *avares* links with "J'aurai de l'or." The other subject is thus yourself; there is no opposition that does not collapse, no falsehood that is distinguishable from a sovereign truth. The emperor, the merchant, and the whole hierarchy of imperial France between them are all *nègres,* in a state of false "Negritude" that is a removal from truth and falsehood.

Yet the myth persists as a postulation of authenticity, origin, and escape. In spite of the collapse of oppositions at the beginning of the paragraph, an opposition arises between, on the one hand, present madness, misery, imprisonment, and disease ("la fièvre et le cancer . . . la folie rôde . . ."), and, on the other hand, the "true kingdom of the children of Ham." As with the "*true* land of Glory" in Baudelaire's "A une dame créole," this establishes the other as false—"this continent" is a false country of the children of Ham, peopled by false *nègres.* Lurking somewhere is an ideal, true Negritude, a black promised land.

Invoking the curse of Ham is a strange way to point to an ideal. The second son of Noah, Ham drew a curse upon all his descendants by looking on his father's nakedness. David Brion Davis remarks, "The fact that the curse was laid on Canaan, and not Ham, his erring father, caused considerable confusion through the ages."[15] What is even more confusing is the glib conflation made through the ages between the sons of Ham and the "black race": "Such is the story from the Holy Scripture, which explains the existence of the Negro races and the sort of subjection in which they find themselves relative to the white races," comments the *Larousse du XIXe siècle* in its article "Cham." At the period of Rimbaud's arrival in Africa, the Catholic Church was engaged in a concerted effort, "prepared by divine mercy, to put an end to the curse of the poor race of Ham," i.e., the Africans.[16] What, then, would be a return to this "kingdom"? A life both "primitive and without hypocrisy"?[17] To the extent that "the children of Ham" is merely a periphrasis for "Black Afri-

---

15. *The Problem of Slavery in Western Culture* (Ithaca: Cornell University Press, 1966), p. 451.

16. Cardinal Lavigerie, quoted in Pierre Charles, "Les Noirs, fils de Cham le maudit," *Nouvelle Revue Théologique* 55 (1928): 722.

17. Suzanne Bernard, ed., *Oeuvres de Rimbaud* (Paris: Garnier, 1981), p. 462n.

cans,'' a screen of transparent language, that kingdom could be interpreted as such, and that is the desire expressed in Rimbaud's phrase. But to be a child of Ham is to be not a king but a slave: the curse made Canaan ''a slave of the slaves of his brother'' (Gen. 9:25). This ''true kingdom'' is more like a slave-dom, a headless other of a kingdom.

The ''black'' narrator of the end of the fifth chapter, at the height of the Africanist myth, has been painfully derived through a series of hypotheses. His artificial Africanness consists of an image that persists in European discourse, that of the free reign of desire, of removal from the mediation of language and the rules of repression:

> Connais-je encore la nature? me connais-je?—*Plus de mots.*
> J'ensevelis les morts dans mon ventre. Cris, tambour, danse, danse, danse, danse! Je ne vois même pas l'heure où, les blancs débarquant, je tomberai au néant.
> Faim, soif, cris, danse, danse, danse, danse!

> Do I still know nature? do I know myself?—*No more words.* I entomb the dead in my belly. Cries, drum, dance, dance, dance, dance! I do not even see the hour when, with the whites disembarking, I will fall into nothingness.
> Hunger, thirst, cries, dance, dance, dance, dance!

There is nothing new in the depiction of Africa as a dance fest; what is more interesting is the representation of that world as on the brink of destruction. The next chapter describes the arrival of the disembarking whites, unseen before, as the advent of colonialism and Christianity at once. A new order is imposed: violence (''canon''), religion (''baptême''), repression (''s'habiller''), and work (''travailler''): ''Les blancs débarquent. Le canon! Il faut se soumettre au baptême, s'habiller, travailler.'' Just at the moment when the language of subjectivity had come into being, through the hard opposition of oppressor and oppressed, the one who submits *ceases to exist.* He is now assimilated, appropriated, killed as an Other and made same. Or rather he is just about to be. The black narrator is crushed into submission, reduced to nothingness: but that nothing—in fine Africanist fashion—takes the form of precisely an accession to form: the birth of reason and constituted religion. Before, the black was blind; now he sees the light: ''Sans doute la débauche est bête, le vice est bête; il faut jeter la pourriture à l'écart. . . . Adieu chimères, idéals, erreurs'' (''Undoubtedly, debauchery is foolish, vice is foolish; rottenness must be thrown aside. . . . Farewell chimeras, ideals, errors''). The vocabulary of the early part of the poem returns, to be superseded by reason: ''La raison m'est née'' (''Reason is born in me''). Reason is good and is linked to religion, which in turn is part of the violent new order of things: ''Le chant raisonnable des anges s'élève du navire sauveur'' (''The reasonable chant of the angels rises from the savior ship''). The *poète-*

nègre has come into existence only to be crushed by the order of the outside.

In the history of Africanist discourse, this is an important moment. If the common denominator of French texts about Africa from Alphonse de Sainctongeois (1559), through Charles de Brosses (1760) and Gobineau (1854), is, as I contend, a certain involvement with the problem of negativity, absence, and nullity, then a far more ambiguous, modern approach has developed in "Mauvais sang." Rimbaud invokes specifically Africanist topoi—the curse of Ham, idolatry, the negation of language, the surrender to desire—which come out of a tradition with certain established attitudes. Confident of the absence of an oppositional object of knowledge, Africanist writers produced a discourse that had to deny the existence of the object it was trying to describe. Yet, paradoxically, that object was represented with adamantine certitude, as truly other, cut off from the world of the writing subject. Such discourse represented difference as a *stable* distance between the self and the Other. But the peculiarity of the "Africanist" Other is that he, she, or it does not exist—and can be known only through the intervention of the outside. How, then, could the difference be stable? Readings of these texts tend to show that the differences the writers project are protean figures of various desires, and from that moment the reader looks more skeptically at the absence of the third dimension of the moon, at the reality of an object such as "idolatry." Then the reading of difference becomes a question of the difference between what the discourse desires and what it claims to produce. That difference cannot be stable, for it is no longer grounded in the perception of any object as *real*.

It is that grounding that is absent in "Mauvais sang." Antoine Adam, in his paraphrastic notes to the poem, has this to say about the fifth chapter:

> Here we find the idea that he [the narrator] is of the race of Ham, that he is a Negro [*nègre*] faced with the whites disembarking to conquer the country. This is certainly a reminder of the *Livre nègre*, but it is of course impossible to determine the relation between the former project and the text of "Mauvais sang."
>
> This presence of elements foreign to the definitive work explains how difficult it is to bring all the parts of "Mauvais sang" into accord. In the first part, the Damned [*le Maudit*] was a blue-eyed Gaul, and now he is a Negro. [P. 957]

Suzanne Bernard writes in the notes to the Garnier edition: "Faced with the contradictions of the text, one might think—wrongly—that it was not revised and worked through" (p. 461).

The resistance of the text to accord is its most basic armature. "Mauvais sang" proposes a series of identities and differences between the subject and various others, in conjunctions and juxtapositions that apply the famous formula "Je est un autre." Racial categories form the most basic template of

identity and difference, engaging a series of outside determinants that help
to explain the inner relationships of the poem. "There has never been a French
race"[18] (or, for that matter, a monolithic "black" race), but the category is
used to fortify the notion of identity. Now when we read in the racial history
of France such utterances as "French (i.e., German),"[19] based on the idea
that the people who gave their name to France were *Germanic Franks*, it is
possible then to see the part of difference in any identity. If you are as French
as French can be, you are German. "Mauvais sang" follows this pattern:
"French, that is to say, German"; self, that is to say, other; *Je, c'est-à-dire,
Autre; Gaulois*, that is to say, *nègre*. This "presence of foreign elements"
and the lack of accord between any opposites is the most essential point
of the poem. Each hypothesis approaches on the basis not of equality
(Je = Autre) but of perverse identity *(Je est un Autre)*.[20] Each is called up
from a different level of temporality and geography, and each, while "being"
both self and other, cannot demonstrate equality in difference. Equality is
appropriated by identity; to make the other equal to yourself, you must make
him identical, expunge his difference. Thus the *nègre* comes into being as
one voice with the narrator's, then immediately recounts his inability to be
different, to be a voice of the "true kingdom of the children of Ham." Instead
of "no more words" (the project of perfect otherness), words follow that
erase any possibility of difference. The subject is born as an Other doomed
to destroy his otherness from the minute he opens his mouth and spouts forth
this catechism of submission:

> La raison m'est née. Le monde est bon. Je bénirai la vie. J'aimerai
> mes frères. Ce ne sont plus des promesses d'enfance. Ni l'espoir
> d'échapper à la vieillesse et à la mort. Dieu fait ma force, et je loue
> Dieu.

> Reason is born in me. The world is good. I shall bless life. I shall
> love my brothers. These are no longer childhood promises. Nor the

18. Maurois, *A History of France*, p. 4. Cf. Céline, *Voyage au bout de la nuit* (Paris:
Gallimard, 1952), p. 16: "'Y en a pas deux comme lui pour défendre la race française, vu
qu'elle n'existe pas!'"

19. "Not only the Salic law, so profitable to the kingship, but the practices of primogeniture
and apanage, are likewise prudent provisions derived from French (i.e., German law)" (Jacques
Barzun, *The French Race*, p. 71. This is from a chapter explicating the historian Estienne
Pasquier (1529–1615), "the first historian of France to call the successors of the Romans in
Gaul—namely the Franks—*Français*, and at the same time, to call the Gauls 'our good old
fathers,' adding 'these *braves français*' in time became naturalized in the country as 'legitimate
Gauls'" (p. 66). Pasquier would thus be at the root of the understanding that "French" means
"from the outside," Frank, therefore German.

20. Cf. Martin Heidegger, "The Principle of Identity," in *Identity and Difference*, trans.
Joan Stambaugh (New York: Harper & Row, 1969), p. 23: "The usual formulation of the principle
of identity reads: A = A. . . . The formula expresses the *equality* of A and A" (emphasis
mine).

hope of escaping from old age and death. God is my strength, and
I praise God.

"Mauvais sang" reads the condition of possibility of racial identity as an
unstable difference, constantly shifting from self to other with no grounding
in a real (perceptual) object. There is thus little heroic optimism to be seen
in the evolution of a *poète-nègre* in the 1870s. This is not the moment of any
new racial understanding or harmony; it is rather a perception of discord as
the basis of any fictive identity. The poet becomes *nègre* as the impossibility
to be *nègre* and poet at the same time: the *nègre* must die out because he has
"No more words" and cannot be represented. The *Livre nègre*—of which
"Mauvais sang" is presumed to be at least a palimpsest (see Adam, p. 954)—
was never written because here, in the fifth chapter, the project came into
being, short-circuited, and died, all at the same time. The *Livre nègre* would
have brought the Africanist object back alive, as the primordial cry beyond
language, as the free reign of desire beyond repression; and it would have
failed as all others have. The success of "Mauvais sang" is in documenting
the teetering and collapse of that project into nothingness.

The Ironic Negro

A second critical pastiche thus presents itself as a conclusion: that, having
set out to make the poetic revolution that the stillborn *Livre nègre* would have
been, Rimbaud returned with irony. The *nègre* dies out, and all that remains
at the end is a discourse of legitimate authority: "la vie française, le sentier
de l'honneur" ("French life, the path of honor"). The language of conquest
and annihilation alone remains ("En marche!"["March!"]), as a serene and
"honorable" discourse, between quotation marks, i.e., ironic. After the meta-
morphosis of the speaker into a being of reason and religion, this "French
life" sounds a heavy and hollow note in contrast with the Gaul, the *nègre,*
etc. The noun "France" occurred twice before as a figure that excluded the
speaker from history and religion; the poem has returned on a spiral to the
same place at a different level. But by contrast with those previous moments,
being French (free, noble, emancipated) is divided against itself; the statement
both affirms and denies; it is ironic.

A linguist has recently written:

> Irony consists of expressing underneath judgments of valorization a
> judgment of devalorization. . . . It is not always easy to figure if the
> use of a word such as "nigger" [*nègre*] actually connotes racism,
> or if, by functioning on the "second degree," it claims to deride
> those who use the word in the first degree.[21]

21. C. Kerbrat-Orecchioni, *L'Enonciation de la subjectivité dans le langage* (Paris: Colin,
1980), p. 71. Quoted in Christiane Chaulet-Achour, *Langue française et colonialisme en Algérie:
De l'abécédaire à la production littéraire,* Dissertation, University of Paris III, 1982, p. 430.

Some current revisionist criticism consists of attributing that second-degree irony as a stable force in the works of nineteenth-century writers, thus making them readable again.[22] Rimbaud's *nègre* could be seen in such terms, designed to satirize those who use the term seriously. The myth of the *nègre* would be encompassed and transcended by the utterance "Je suis une bête, un nègre"; since the speaker is obviously not a beast, both terms are shown to be pure epithets, which could therefore mean quite the opposite of what they seem to say. Rimbaud would thus already be writing a sort of Negritude poetry *avant la lettre*, sharing a project with Aimé Césaire of "reclaiming their pagan identity," with Rimbaud "identifying himself rather well with the Negroes, to the point of anticipating the principal themes of neo-African literature."[23]

The last paragraph of chapter five consists of words following the emphatic "No more words!" The words "cri, tambour, danse, danse, danse, danse," would be the only stable utterances of Negritude on its own. Yet something is already wrong, for "no more words" is followed by more words. The poetic project of the pagan return involves valorizing that which is inferior, "la race inférieure de toute éternité . . . une bête, un nègre." But then inferiority, having become an object of desire, is no longer inferior: if you desire something that is "worse," it must be because in some way it is better. The *nègre*, being desired in and for his inferiority (in his "true kingdom of the children of Ham"), must fall into nothingness, be uplifted and obliterated; he must now speak the language of France and follow the path of honor. It is only through the intervention of the outside ("its existence can be noticed only from the moment that a force of opposite nature presents itself . . . the moment of the appearance of the white race among the blacks"—Gobineau) that the primordial moment becomes knowable and therefore passes into nothingness: "Je tomberai au néant." Rimbaud's *nègre* is created as an exile from Negritude. "Mauvais sang" describes the evolution of this self-destroy-

22. Jules Verne wrote the following dialogue in *Five Weeks in a Balloon* (trans. V. G. Bebbington [London: Allen & Unwin], p. 18): "'We thought you were being attacked by natives.'—'Luckily they were only monkeys,' the doctor replied.—'From the distance there's little difference, old man.'—'Nor near to, either,' Joe replied." But a passage from *Nord contre Sud* has recently been cited to support the theory that Verne is only "ridiculing the prejudices he had heard in the salons of Nantes" (O. Dumas, "La Race noire dans l'oeuvre de Jules Verne," in *Jules Verne: Colloque de Cérisy* [Paris: 10/18, 1979], p. 269). That passage, which occurs in chapter 8, reads: "Des noirs qui ne sont plus esclaves! . . . C'est contre nature! Oui, contre nature!" The *distance* of that voice makes it manifestly ironic, but can it be said to represent the presence of a diametrically opposed opinion?

23. Jonathan Ngate distinguishes between a "Rimbaud-Nègre" and Rimbaud and regards the former as a mere mask over the latter, an intellectual exercise: "S'il est vrai . . . que Rimbaud-Nègre s'identifie assez bien aux nègres, au point d'anticiper les principaux thèmes de la littérature néo-africaine, il est malheureusement vrai aussi que Rimbaud ne s'identifie pas avec Rimbaud-Nègre" ("'Mauvais sang' de Rimbaud et *Cahier d'un retour au pays natal* de Césaire: La poésie au service de la révolution," *Cahiers Césairiens* no. 3 (Spring, 1971): 29. Cf. Léopold Sédar Senghor, *Liberté III* (Paris: Seuil, 1977), p. 75: "Arthur Rimbaud s'était déjà réclamé de la Négritude"; p. 89: "Si les Gaulois ne sont pas nos 'ancêtres,' à nous les Nègres, ils sont nos cousins."

ing voice of the *nègre* as an inability to say what one means. The supposed ability of Rimbaud to say precisely what he means through "stable irony" appears to be much more problematic. Reading such texts will always leave passages that are "not easy to figure out," "difficult to bring into accord"; in the final analysis, attributing a first- or second-degree status to the *nègre* in "Mauvais sang" would be purely a matter of taste.

In his letter of May, 1873, to Ernest Delahaye, Rimbaud wrote: "Je travaille pourtant assez régulièrement, je fais de petites histoires en prose, titre général: Livre païen, ou Livre nègre. C'est bête et innocent. O innocence!" ("However, I'm working fairly regularly; I'm doing some little stories in prose, general title: Pagan Book, or Negro Book. It's foolish and innocent. O innocence!") "Tu es nègre" is *bête* in the first degree, connoting racism in the speaker, *innocent* in the second degree, as an impotent and absent myth, which, applied to everyone from emperor to peasant, has lost all meaning. The point is not in the value judgment; the significance lies in the critical necessity and inability of the poet to demonstrate that one thing *is* another, to say "this is that." If Sartre's formula is inevitable, if the *nègre* in French discourse is he for whom there will always be "a slight and constant gap separating what he says and what he means, from the moment he talks of himself,"[24] then Rimbaud is the *"nègre"* of French poetry.

"Démocratie"

The meanings of the word *nègre* conspire to form not only a *mythe du nègre chez Rimbaud* but also a *mythe de Rimbaud-nègre*. Rimbaud is his own "ghost-writer," spouting the discourse of an Other, never saying precisely what he means himself to say.

DÉMOCRATIE

"Le drapeau va au paysage immonde, et notre patois étouffe le tambour.
"Aux centres nous alimenterons la plus cynique prostitution. Nous massacrerons les révoltes logiques.
"Aux pays poivrés et détrempés!—au service des plus monstrueuses exploitations industrielles ou militaires.
"Au revoir ici, n'importe où. Conscrits du bon vouloir, nous aurons la philosophie féroce; ignorants pour la science, roués pour le confort; la crevaison pour le monde qui va. C'est la vraie marche. En avant, route!"

24. "Il n'est pas vrai pourtant que le noir s'exprime dans une langue 'étrangère,' puisqu'on lui enseigne le français dès son plus jeune âge et puisqu'il y est parfaitement à son aise dès qu'il pense en technicien, en savant ou en politique. Il faudrait plutôt parler du décalage léger et constant qui sépare ce qu'il dit de ce qu'il voudrait dire, dès qu'il parle de lui" ("Orphée noir," in *Anthologie de la nouvelle poésie nègre et malgache* [Paris: PUF, 1948], p. xix).

DEMOCRACY

"The flag goes with the filthy country, and our lingo is drowning
out the drum. In the centers we shall feed the most cynical prostitution. We shall massacre the logical revolts. To the pungent and
sodden lands!—in the service of the most monstrous industrial or
military exploitations. Till we meet again here, anywhere. Conscript
volunteers, we shall have a ferocious philosophy; ignorant for science, broken down for comfort; may the world outside drop dead.
That's real progress. Forward, let's go!''

For Antoine Adam and Ernest Delahaye, "Démocratie" is "without mystery" a "true evocation": it is, respectively, Rimbaud's "passage in the Dutch
Foreign Legion at Java in 1876" (Pléiade ed., p. 1017), and "nothing other
than a departure of conscripts that he saw in the county seat" (p. 113).
Trivializing literalism has the merit at least of not being exhaustive; some
troubling details remain here. To take only one, the "conscrits du bon vouloir": Adam reproaches the formula for its "obscurity" ("Are we to understand that this is a way of saying that these soldiers are volunteers? It must
be admitted that the formula is clumsy" [p. 1019]). Clumsy, gauche, sinister,
improper, foreign to its own meaning, "Démocratie" continues the discourse
of the end of "Mauvais sang" from the point of view of those who silence
the pagan drums instead of those who play them: this is "the path of honor,"
fraught with irony. The draftees are forced yet want to be forced. They cannot
help but want what they are forced to want. Philosophy, the love of knowledge
and the desire for it, is violent; science is ignorant; comfort is to be found in
a physical breakdown. Each of these obscurities reproduces the relationship
between the title and the general movement of the text: democracy, the free
reign of the people's desires, produces a violent repression of some other
people's desires, the "most monstrous exploitation." This is not democracy.
But Rimbaud, being the *nègre,* cannot say "democracy is this"; instead he
says what it is not, in words not his own.[25]

Rimbaud "chez les nègres"

If the discourse of the "nègre chez Rimbaud" is characterized by the inability
to make "this" be "that," the discourse of Rimbaud in Africa is caught up
in the opposite problem. Writings on the subject tend toward a wild proliferation of meanings and interpretations. Rimbaud could be: "perhaps the
most audacious model of the explorer"; a slave trader and a gun-runner; a

25. Cf. André Guyaux, preface to Farnier, *Oeuvres,* p. i: "Rimbaud reste le poète de la
parodie. Sa poésie est toujours le miroir d'une autre, fût-ce la sienne." Guyaux comments on
"Démocratie": "Le texte entier est encadré de guillemets et celui qui parle dit *nous,* comme
s'il reproduisait un discours qui ne serait donc pas nécessairement ni exactement le sien"
(p. 538n).

devout Catholic who "taught letters to the little brown children . . . and who confusedly loved Christ in his humble black brothers of . . . Abyssinia"; he could be a pagan and even an idol, "crouching on the seat of a chair, guarded by two savages, worshipped by two others who are prostrate like carpets on the floor."[26] Jean-Marie Carré claims to cut through all the mystification of Rimbaud as either an angel ("voyant . . . saint") or a devil ("fumiste . . . crapaud") when he assigns him the status of "undoubtedly the most prestigious adventurer of the ideal and of the real who has ever existed" (p. ii). Rimbaud is whatever you want to make of him, for underneath all the myths he does not exist.

Perhaps the most forthright response to all the mystifications surrounding Rimbaud's Abyssinian period is that of Yves Bonnefoy:

> I find it indecent that one who chose to return to an anonymous existence should be so persistently tracked down. Let us not try to find out if he who sought to one day *steal fire* was a merchant of this rather than that. [P. 173]

But having disobeyed Bonnefoy's proscription, and having found out how justified it is, I still believe that this corpus holds interesting lessons about Africanist evidence and interpretations, and we will see that the gap between the two is most impressive.

The Myth of Writing

The evidence comes mainly from the letters of Rimbaud "aux siens," written from Africa, starting in 1880. Occupying more than half of the current Pléiade edition, this corpus is nonetheless of dubious authenticity. Antoine Adam warns the reader that many of the letters' originals have been lost and that in many cases a letter is printed only on the mendacious authority of Paterne Berrichon, whose "willfully committed omissions and falsifications" have been well documented.[27] Adam marks with a star the letters he has been able to consult in their original form. Of the letters and documents written prior to Rimbaud's death, more than a third are inauthenticated, and it is particularly the early African period where Berrichon's version is all that is left. In several cases, Berrichon increased amounts of money Rimbaud was supposed to have received, to make him appear a more prosperous businessman than he was; and Adam, faced with Berrichon's "nasty habit" of falsification, is forced to admit defeat, for "it would not be prudent for an editor to substitute another

26. Jean-Marie Carré, quoted in René Etiemble, *Le Mythe de Rimbaud: Structure du mythe* (Paris: Gallimard, 1952), p. 236, 262, 258. Jalabert, "Rimbaud en Abyssinie," p. 188.
27. Adam, note to the Pléiade edition, p. 1066; see also Marcel Coulon, *La Vie de Rimbaud et de son oeuvre* (Paris: Mercure de France, 1929), pp. 333 ff.

figure arbitrarily'' (p. 1122). ''It is impossible to establish the authentic text''
(p. 1122). The faithful Pléiade reader, who pays dearly for nothing if not for
authenticity, is left with nothing but a bowdlerized text and a *caveat emptor*.

Immediately after Rimbaud's death, Isabelle Rimbaud (the sister) and Berrichon, who would later marry, began the process of mythification. Their
correspondence is printed in the Pléiade, and it is fascinating to observe the
comminglings of these two pious minds as they bear their fruit, a new, heroic
Arthur Rimbaud: ''En religion, Arthur Rimbaud était foncièrement un grand
croyant . . . à Aden, en Egypte, en Abyssinie, si vous saviez que d'actions
généreuses et saintes il a accomplies!'' (''In religion, Arthur Rimbaud was
basically a great believer. In Aden, in Egypt, in Abyssinia, if you only knew
how many generous and saintly deeds he performed!''; p. 751). While scholars
these days do not take Isabelle very seriously, she was the first critic to
articulate a view that many hold today. In the next sentence from the letter
quoted above, Isabelle begins the myth of Rimbaud's African writings:

> Over there, in Harar, he wrote some very serious pieces, descriptions
> of the country, curious details on the habits and institutions of the
> races that live there. I will not surprise you when I say that the
> description and the style were remarkable. Of course you wouldn't
> find the dreamlike language and magical music of the *Illuminations:*
> it was clear, precise, though always cloaked in an extremely har-
> monious and personal form.

This elaborate dance of Isabelle's comes immediately after, as if trying to
exorcise the demon of the sentence she had just had to write: ''Il n'écrivit
plus'' (''He wrote no more''). The break with Europe is the break with writing:
''No more words!'' Jacques Brosse comments, ''Is this not the basic scandal
of Rimbaud's life, that he fell silent, never again to speak?''[28] The silence of
Rimbaud is illicit and inadmissible, so Isabelle comes up with two responses:
he *did* continue to write (those very serious pieces), and he *would have* written
a heroic work about his ''cruel and touching odyssey'' amongst the ''accla-
mations, protestations, and tears of the Abyssinian peoples he had forever
conquered with his goodness and his charity.'' He might even have produced
''something divinely good and incommensurably beautiful.'' Other writers
have found the Abyssinian ''corpus'' to be equally worthy of attention. Marcel
Coulon, although no admirer of Isabelle's, sees the letters of Rimbaud as ''an
autobiographical document as precious as *Une Saison en enfer*. And isn't it
the story of an infernal season even more real than the other one?'' Even if
the letters are ''foreign to Art . . . closed to the idea that Art exists,'' for
Coulon they are a better mirror to nature than ''Art'' itself (p. 326). Suzanne

28. ''Le Silence de Rimbaud,'' in *Rimbaud* (Paris: Hachette, 1968), p. 205.

Briet sees in the African letters a relatively "literary quality" and refers to them as "the African part of the works of Rimbaud."[29]

The most recent work on the subject, Duncan Forbes' *Rimbaud in Ethiopia,* still shares certain of Isabelle's basic assumptions, and he too refers to the works Rimbaud "would have written":

> Although he had turned his back on poetry and on the society of poets, the urge to write was still in him. It was growing in another direction. If he had been able to accomplish his projected expeditions into the unknown and into Shoa, he would probably have written about them. . . . But it is not as a trader that he sees himself now. He will be the explorer, not charting the unknown channels of the mind, as he did in the *Illuminations,* but mapping mountain and river on the earth itself. . . . The poet in action is the explorer. . . . In the nineteenth century, when the last great unknowns of the earth's surface were being penetrated by men of courage and willpower, he was everybody's hero.[30]

This is that: the poet "is" the explorer. The gap of metaphor reads as the denial of any gap, as the continuity of one process, the process of writing. Geography is "earth-writing"; all Rimbaud did was to change genres; the dream did not die. The imperialist heroics of conquest and penetration that Forbes seems to accept may be necessary carryovers in the Western attitude toward writing. The writer, like the explorer, must defeat and subjugate his object through an exercise of superior will and courage; in order to "chart," he must "penetrate," puncture, rupture, destroy. But at the same time, Forbes points out that Rimbaud was as complete a "failure" at exploring the earth as at penetrating the "dark regions of the mind" (p. 39) (has anyone ever succeeded?): "There is actually no evidence that Rimbaud undertook any journeys into unknown territory" before he published his "Report on the Ogaden," which "left it to appear as if he himself had been on the trip" (pp. 39–40). So underneath the falsified and mythified Rimbaud produced since his death lies the real Rimbaud, falsifying and mythifying himself.

The Myth of the Slave Trade

Perhaps the best way to understand the problem is to take a single case, the most controversial one, and see how evidence and proof never completely coincide but chase each other furiously, nevertheless. No question has been more contested than that of "Rimbaud négrier": "Slave-trader or not?" The

29. *Rimbaud notre prochain* (Paris: Nouvelles Editions Latines, 1956), p. 422.
30. Forbes, *Rimbaud in Ethiopia* (Hythe, Eng.: Volturna Press, 1979), pp. 22–24.

wide dissemination of the allegation is largely due to Enid Starkie's *Rimbaud en Abyssinie,* in which a British Foreign Office report is quoted as referring to "the French trader Rembau" *(sic).* This trader was reported to be traveling with a caravan of slaves.[31] Forbes devotes a chapter to the subject and argues that keeping company with slave-traders is not the same as being a trader yourself. He effectively demonstrates that no proof exists, that there is no conclusive evidence; he advances the verdict of "not proven" (p. 93). Indeed, the circle of clues is vicious, loaded with rumors and hints but few affirmations. "This hypothesis is not based on any document," said André Tian, the son of an associate of Rimbaud's (Forbes, p. 95); "Starkie *assumed* . . ." (Forbes, p. 94); there are "slips in the spelling of names, two on the part of the Italian copyist and one on the part of the translator"; the Foreign Office report "bears little weight" (p. 99). An associate of Rimbaud's in Africa wrote: "J'ai vécu sa vie, il lui aurait été impossible de faire la traite sans que je m'en aperçoive" ("I lived his life; it would have been impossible for him to engage in the trade without my noticing"), but such is not precisely to say that he never did so. To prove that someone never did something is rhetorically more complicated than to prove that he did. The negativity has no positive object, referring to an act that never was, and can never have the authority of an affirmation, such as "He never traded in slaves."[32]

The utterances of Rimbaud himself on the subject are contradictory, a fact that has not been sufficiently emphasized. In 1885, after five years in Africa, he wrote to his family: "N'allez pas croire que je sois devenu marchand d'esclaves. Les m[archandises] que nous importons sont des fusils" ("Don't believe that I have become a slave merchant. The goods we import are guns"; Pléiade, p. 409). Again the utterance is just short of a fully positive denial; "no one would dare say it, it is forbidden to say it," but is it true? But in 1889 Rimbaud writes to Alfred Ilg: "Je vous confirme très sérieusement ma demande d'un très bon mulet et de deux garçons esclaves" ("I confirm very seriously my request for a very good mule and two slave boys"; p. 602). The publication of this "smoking pistol" letter in 1965 confirmed that Starkie had been at least half right, if for the wrong reasons. She had had access only to Ilg's reply: "Quant aux esclaves, pardonnez-moi, je n'en ai jamais acheté et je ne veux pas commencer. Je reconnais absolument vos bon[nes] intentions, mais même pour moi je ne le ferai jamais" ("As for the slaves, forgive me, I have never bought any, and I don't want to start. I absolutely

31. Starkie, *Rimbaud en Abyssinie* (Paris: Payot, 1938), pp. 143–60.
32. Cf. Mario Matucci, *Le Dernier visage de Rimbaud en Afrique* (Paris: Marcel Didier, 1962), p. 100: "Mais où est la preuve? Miss Starkie n'a pas réussi, jusqu'alors, à retrouver dans les archives du *Foreign Office,* la minime allusion au prétendu trafic d'esclaves qu'aurait pratiqué Rimbaud. La dernière preuve n'a pas été trouvée, car tous ceux qui approchèrent le poète au cours de son séjour africain, explorateurs français, italiens, etc. . . . , n'ont jamais fait aucune allusion à cet égard." What is thus proved is that proof is absent.

recognize your good intentions, but even for myself I will not do it''; p. 638).

Slavery, as a forbidden activity and subject, must veil itself from the light of knowledge. Both slaving and gun-running, Forbes writes, ''had to be conducted with the appearance of secrecy, if not . . . with the reality'' (p. 93). But secrecy is nothing but an appearance, and, once that appearance changes, the underlying facts tend to be altered. The object of knowledge (or secrecy), once brought to light, is diminished in force: if someone were a real slave-trader, he would dissemble the traces (if the French had begun trading with Black Africa in the fourteenth century, they would have had to keep it a secret to protect their priority). Thus, for Forbes, Rimbaud's involvement in slaving is only ''technical'' (''two boy slaves do not make a trade'' [p. 93]); it is there to be read positively in a letter, but it limits itself to this act of writing, for Rimbaud never actually received the slaves. For Starkie, the proof was still absent, present in a lost letter, but the culpability is much greater: ''Rimbaud was involved in the slave trade'' (p. 155). The appearance of secrecy accompanies the reality of guilt. For Suzanne Briet, the hermeneutic character of slavery explains Rimbaud's involvement: ''Rimbaud had a nostalgia for the ancient world. He sees slavery as a traditional and antique custom. Slavery had, as in Antiquity, a familial character'' (*Rimbaud notre prochain*, pp. 176–77). Rimbaud's slave-trading would be a sort of translation of ''Mauvais sang'' into action. For Jalabert, the moral slip is ''black'' but forgivable: ''It would not be surprising if, left vulnerable by a morality that had already accommodated itself to so many things, his poor conscience gave in, one particularly dark and distressful day, to this lamentable weakness'' (*Etudes*, p. 185).

What emerges is the image of an inscrutable Rimbaud involved in inscrutable affairs behind a screen of unintelligibility. A friend of Rimbaud's later wrote: ''Rimbaud did not speak very often, but when he spoke he sometimes used expressions that could have been misinterpreted by people who didn't know him well.''[33] According to Henri Dehérain, Rimbaud was at first ''uncommunicative'' with other Europeans.[34] Alfred Ilg wrote: ''I did not know him well, but he remains in my memory as a taciturn, uncommunicative man, who sought no company'' (quoted in Dehérain, p. 446). Yet he was also alleged to have ''a wit, verve, and skill in conversation that were truly French'' (Jules Borelli, a friend of Rimbaud's, quoted in Forbes, p. 94). ''He was a stupefying conversationalist: immediately he could make you laugh and laugh.''[35] Rimbaud is finally a sort of Africanist idol, an oracle speaking only in riddles, unveiling the truth only in a veiled manner: ''C'est très-certain,

33. Jules Borelli, quoted in Forbes, *Rimbaud in Ethiopia*, p. 96.

34. Henri Dehérain, ''La Carrière africaine d'Arthur Rimbaud,'' *Revue de l'histoire des colonies françaises* 4 (1916): 446.

35. Victor Ségalen, *Le Double Rimbaud* (N.p.: Fata Morgana, 1979), p. 31.

c'est oracle, ce que je dis.'' He is ''an implacable force brooding over an inscrutable intention,'' in a world where ''the truth is hidden—luckily'' *(Heart of Darkness)*. He is Kurtz, and those who travel upriver toward him will encounter certain difficulties. He is a *myth*.

Rimbaud and Myth

The name of Rimbaud seems to be inextricably tied to the word ''myth.'' *Rimbaud and the Myth of Childhood* (Fowlie), *Le Mythe de Rimbaud* (Etiemble), *Rimbaud et le mythe solaire* (M. Eigeldinger), ''Le mythe du nègre chez Rimbaud'' (M. Courtois), etc. *Nègre* is another word that continually occurs in conjunction with ''myth'': Léon Fanoudh-Siefer's *Le Mythe du nègre et de l'Afrique noire* is one of the most important studies. The function of the myth is there defined as a deformation of the object; its end ''is to condense the object into a simple, impoverished, general image, even a caricature''; myths ''reduce reason to silence.''[36]

The word seems to connote some altered relationship with truth. In popular usage (and for Fanoudh-Siefer as well), myths are useless mystifications, screens of superfluous complication between the subject and the truth. This particular kind of truth, conceived with the assumptions of Realism and positivism as being opposed to fiction, is absent from ''mere myth.'' But in literary usage, myth can be seen as a detour through fiction that reveals a different, deeper kind of truth. The *Oxford Dictionary* definition: ''A purely fictitious narrative usually involving supernatural persons, actions or events, and embodying some popular idea concerning natural or historical phenomena. Properly distinguished from *allegory* and *legend*.'' The *Larousse du XIXᵉ siècle* defines myth in Antiquity as a ''tradition which, under the figure of allegory, reveals a great historical, physical, or philosophical generality.'' The ''generality'' or the ''popular idea'' must be the altered truth that myth creates. *Larousse* hazards an ultimate etymology in the Sanskrit *mû*, meaning ''to link.''[37] Myth is saying ''this is that,'' linking two elements together to form an idea or generality: ''The poet in action *is* the explorer''; ''Je *suis* une bête, un nègre; Je *est* un autre.'' Myth is the risky assertion of identity in difference.

As with all the modes of discourse that typify Africanist writing—and the mode ''discourse'' itself—the relationship is an articulation of distance, the hauling-in of an object that by definition recedes. Arthur Rimbaud may never have laid eyes on an African before he went there; the interpreters of his African sojourn, even Isabelle, can never know why he went there or what he did or what it all could mean. The absolute answer to this is Rimbaud's

---

36. *Le Mythe du nègre et de l'Afrique noire dans la littérature française (de 1800 à la 2ᵉ Guerre mondiale)* (Paris: Klincksieck, 1968), p. 12.

37. ''Mythe . . . gr. *mythos*, fiction, légende, probablement du même radical que *musterion*, savoir, *muein*, initier, proprement serrer, fermer, de la racine sanscrite *mû*, lier.''

refusal to write, Bonnefoy's refusal to read; that alone will break the cycle of one thing continually becoming another. For those who do read and do write, the impulse to bridge gaps and make connections is inevitable. But linking and translating pay a price for the sense they make. The desire for clarity, identity, and closure produces the distance it seeks to transcend; the similarity between the poet and the explorer, the speaker and the *nègre,* is also the tension that holds them apart. They could not be similar if they were not different; they cannot be identical from the moment you say they are.

Thinking about identity, equality, and difference in relation to Baudelaire and Rimbaud has led us to two basic observations. With Baudelaire, the project of describing a distant object as equal or even superior to France tended to reassert the centrality and thus the superiority of the writing subject, and we were left with an impression of power in discourse, if only the power to write. But Rimbaud's role as a poet and as a figure in literary history is to show how the writer's engagement with the Africanist object tends to destabilize his own identity as a writer. Writing about the Negro as a figure outside of your language, with "no more words," makes you into a "Negro": a ghost-writer *(nègre)* for yourself, because your meaning is alien to your language. The identity of the writer and the authority of the words he writes are questions to bear in mind as we continue readings of white, European, male, and (mostly) French authors, as we shift from those who wrote poetry to those who wrote novels.

Part Three
Africanist Narrative

Le roman, c'est l'histoire de gens qui, le plus souvent,
n'entreront pas dans l'Histoire. Par lui, été sauvée la mémoire
de quelques héros obscurs de la brousse. Par le roman encore,
le public a appris à mieux connaître les Noirs, "ces ombres de
nous-mêmes," et le décor dans lequel ils passent, aiment et
souffrent.

—Gaston-Denys Périer,
Nègreries et Curiosités congolaises (1930)

4

The Discoursing Heart:
Conrad's *Heart of Darkness*

Le nègre n'a pas parcouru les étapes de notre civilisation; il
observe encore les coutumes de sa vie barbare comme le
faisaient nos pères germains du Niebelungenlied.
—Charles Buls, *Croquis congolais* (1899)

One's literary life must turn frequently for sustenance to
memories and seek discourse with the shades.
—Conrad, *A Personal Record* (1912)

Today fell into a muddy puddle. Beastly. The fault of the man
that carried me. . . . Getting jolly well sick of this fun.
—Conrad, *Congo Diary* (1890)

Africa and the Novel

If Africanist discourse had not existed prior to the advent of the modern novel,
one would have had to invent it. There is a "blank" in the science of narrating
that can be filled with any figure one likes and that "Africa" has been made
to fill with its emptiness. That coincidence, between a place in the interpretation of literature and a place supposedly in the world, is the object of the
last part of this study. The repeated moves of Africanist discourse seem to
be as old as the Western narrative tradition itself, beginning in the first verses
of Homer's *Odyssey;* but if the two phenomena are of equal age, they are
obviously not "necessary" to each other. The pattern exists outside of what
we consider narrative (in poetry and the graphic arts) and vice versa. There
are thus two questions to be differentiated. First, what is the place, the blank
within any narrative that a figure such as "Africa" is eligible to fill? Second,
what happens to the figure of Africa when it is inserted in a narrative scheme?

I would like to consider the implications of the second question first. How
can "Africa" be narrated? How can a "perpetual childhood," a "pure anteriority," with "no more words" be made to tell a story? If narrative is the
translation of time into language, what language can express the absence of
time before time began? If the passage of time is an element no Western novel

can do without, constituting the genre's most basic armature, then the role
of the Africanist figure, persistently depicted as *stuck* in time, will be to resist
narration from within. Africa's supposed incompatibility with time and progress thus becomes the focus—the heart—of a literary product built around
an essentially resistant core, and Africanist narration will be a reflection of
one of the genre's central concerns. Our task is thus to decipher the process
of representivity by which an inert element is placed within a living, progressing, organic body of narrative and represented as its heart. The political
implications of the European novel, representing itself as *progress* and evolution made literature, should not go unnoticed (see the epigraphs by Périer
and Buls). We will thus be reading a temporal metaphor—progress as opposed
to stasis—crossed with a spatial metaphor—centrality, together with the related image of a central organ that controls a unified process of growth.

The initial perception of a discourse as "Africanist" would perhaps not be
possible without the perspective afforded by reading Conrad's *Heart of Darkness,* the strongest of all Africanist texts, first published in 1899.[1] That perspective is so fundamental to this study that any analysis of *Heart of Darkness*
itself risks appearing redundant. But since there is no more condensed Africanist narrative, it is essential to begin here with a few basic remarks.
    Heart of Darkness reads as an allegory of all other Africanist texts; it
defines the condition of possibility of Africanist discourse, time and time
again, within its narration:

> We were cut off from the comprehension of our surroundings; we
> glided past like phantoms, wondering and secretly appalled, as sane
> men would be before an enthusiastic outbreak in a madhouse. We
> could not understand because we were too far and could not remember
> because we were travelling in the night of the first ages, of those
> ages that are gone, leaving hardly a sign—and no memories. [P.
> 105][2]

It has been evident from the beginning that Africanist writers felt themselves
to be cut off from comprehension in some way; but they would thematize
this by depicting the African mind as cut off from representation and signification. *Heart of Darkness* is the master text in which it becomes possible,

1. *Heart of Darkness* has been seen as a key text in the development of narrative modernism.
Peter Brooks has called it the "subversion of the traditional structures of narrative" ("Un rapport
illisible: *Coeur des ténèbres,*" *Poétique* 44 [November, 1980]:472–89), and in *Reading for the
Plot* (New York: Knopf, 1984) Brooks discusses *Heart of Darkness* as a "detective story gone
modernist," with its "constant reference to the inadequacy of the inherited orders of meaning"
(p. 283). Tzvetan Todorov has interpreted *Heart of Darkness* as an allegory of the reading process
(in "Connaissance du vide," *Nouvelle Revue de Psychanalyse* 11 [Spring, 1975]: 145–54).
    2. The notes in parentheses refer to the Signet Classics edition, *"Heart of Darkness" and
"The Secret Sharer"* (New York: New American Library, 1950).

perhaps for the first time, to transform that ancient mode of projection into an epistemological perception, where it is not so much the African object as the Africanist subject—the explorer, the writer—who is called into question. For *Heart of Darkness* is a self-conscious meditation on misunderstanding, and its self-consciousness is what places it at a highly significant crossroads between an old and a new mode of Africanist expression, between the projection of a corrupt and ignoble Africa and the later critique of that projection and its political outgrowth, colonialism. It is for this reason that *Heart of Darkness* elicits such ambivalence among readers nowadays: it is neither colonialistic enough to be damnable nor ironic enough to be completely untainted by "colonialistic bias."[3] The net effect is a subversion of Africanist discourse from within.

Narrating Backwards

Going up that river was like travelling back to the *earliest beginnings of the world,* when vegetation rioted on the earth and the big trees were kings. An empty stream, a great silence, an impenetrable forest. The air was warm, thick, heavy, sluggish. There was no joy in the brilliance of sunshine. . . . The broadening waters flowed through a mob of wooded islands; you lost your way on that river as you would in a desert, and butted all day long against shoals, trying to find the channel, till you thought yourself bewitched and cut off for ever from everything you had known once—somewhere—far away—in another existence perhaps. There were moments when *one's past came back to one,* as it will sometimes when you have not a moment to spare to yourself; but it came in the shape of an unrestful and noisy dream, remembered with wonder amongst the overwhelming realities of this strange world of plants, and water, and silence. And this stillness did not in the least resemble a peace. It was the stillness of an implacable force brooding over an inscrutable intention. It looked at you with a vengeful aspect. I got used to it afterwards; I did not see it any more; I had no time. I had to keep guessing at the channel; I *had to discern, mostly by inspiration, the signs of hidden banks.* . . . When you have to attend to things of that sort, to the mere incidents of the surface, the reality—the reality, I tell you—fades. The inner truth is hidden—luckily, luckily. [Pp. 102–3; emphasis mine]

This often-quoted passage and its most basic armature—the phrase "travelling back"—are a paradigm of Africanist narration. Whereas the pre-anthropologists (such as de Brosses) and the "ethnologists" (such as Gobi-

3. Frances B. Singh, "The Colonialistic Bias of *Heart of Darkness,*" *Conradiana* 10, no. 1 (1978): 41–54. Todorov also refers to an alleged "ethnocentric paternalism of Conrad's" ("Connaissance du vide," p. 149).

neau) we have read in this study depicted the primitive world as static and
isolated, the project of narration as seen in this passage will be to reach back
to that frozen past and make it real in writing. Traveling back means bringing
the primitive world forward, or, more accurately, projecting the primitive
world as an anteriority that can be reached geographically: "We were travelling in the night of the first ages" (p. 105). The temporal and the spatial
are conflated in such a way that physical travel will take one "back to the
earliest beginnings of the world." Narration, which would normally be the
recounting of sequential events (a model from which it can never wholly
escape if only because one word, one paragraph, must follow another), is
here literally a "backwards" process. As V. S. Naipaul writes in *A Bend in
the River,* the strongest Africanist narration since *Heart of Darkness:* "I am
going in the wrong direction."[4]

But the immediate corollary of that backwards narration is the loss of
directionality itself, for the primitive world into which one penetrates is a
place where "backwards" and "forwards" have no more meaning. There is
only a litany of negativity: "an empty stream, a great silence, an impenetrable
forest." The stream is "empty," one supposes, in the sense that there is no
one there, it is devoid of life; yet the narrator is there to bear witness to its
emptiness. The silence is impenetrable in its meaning because it has no form
to be interpreted. The forest, and later the desert, are two principal Africanist
figures for the loss of directionality. Penetration into this world is a process
of "discerning, mostly by inspiration," because the referents by which one
could determine direction (*sens,* "meaning" in French) keep slipping away:
"Sometimes I would pick out a tree a little way ahead to measure our progress
towards Kurtz by, but I lost it invariably before we got abreast" (p. 109).
Africa is represented as dismantling European concepts of measure and progress. The forward movement of the steamship, progressing toward Kurtz, is
all but canceled out by the vast emptiness on which the traveler can make no
impression nor find his way: "leaving hardly a sign—and no memories."
The ability to make distinctions between past and present, this and that—
which is the ability to narrate—is crippled in a world without substance: "The
rest of the world was nowhere, as far as our eyes and ears were concerned . . . swept off without leaving a whisper or a shadow behind." In this
context, it is no mere lapse into deconstructionist doggerel to assert that what
is being narrated is the impossibility of narration.

The referent of *Heart of Darkness* is so commonly understood to be Africa,
and specifically the Congo Free State at the time of King Leopold II's reign
of terror and profit at the end of the nineteenth century, that it may come as
a surprise to learn that "Africa" is never specifically named as its referent.
The fact that a referential interpretation works so perfectly, as a "slightly

4. V. S. Naipaul, *A Bend in the River* (New York: Knopf, 1979), p. 4.

fictionalized record'' of Conrad's own experience in the Congo,[5] makes it all the more interesting to read this passage, in which Marlow first describes his image of Africa. Here the referent is named, then almost immediately repressed:

> "Now when I was a little chap I had a passion for maps. I would look for hours at South America, or Africa, or Australia, and lose myself in all the glories of exploration. *At that time there were many blank spaces on the earth,* and when I saw one that looked particularly inviting on a map (but they all look that) I would put my finger on it and say, 'When I grow up I will go there.' The North Pole was one of these places, I remember. Well, I haven't been there yet, and shall not try now. The glamour's off. Other places were scattered about the Equator, and in every sort of latitude all over the two hemispheres. I have been in some of them, and . . . well, we won't talk about that. But there was one yet—*the biggest, the most blank, so to speak*—that I had a hankering after.
>
> "True, by this time it was not a blank space any more. It had got filled since my boyhood with rivers and lakes and *names. It had ceased to be a blank space* of delightful mystery—*a white patch* for a boy to dream gloriously over. *It had become a place of darkness.*"
> [Pp. 70–71; emphasis mine]

Everything Africanist is there except "Africa" itself, which is mentioned as one among "many blank spaces." Here, then, is Conrad's description of the empty space in narrative (in Marlow's tale) that Africa can come to "fill." But the fashion in which Africa is inserted in that space is highly perverse. The description fits Africa perfectly: the boyhood fantasies produced by nineteenth-century adventure stories,[6] the exchange of white (the North Pole) with black through the word "blank," a felicity that French does not permit. But when the moment comes to name the object of his hankering, Marlow says only "one . . . the biggest, the most blank." That principal blank space is most definitely not identified as "Africa." The point at which the link is

---

5. Albert J. Guérard, introduction to the Signet edition, p. 13. See also Norman Sherry, *Conrad's Western World* (Cambridge: Cambridge University Press, 1971), pp. 9–125, and Gérard Jean-Aubry, *The Sea-Dreamer,* trans. Helen Sebba (N.p.: Archon Books, 1967), p. 159: "Marlow, who is Conrad himself."

6. The point at which Africa became the property of boys' adventure stories is a matter of some interest. Conrad tells of his own experience, in his short essay "Geography and Some Explorers," about his youthful fascination with geography: "And it was Africa, the continent out of which the Romans used to say some new thing was always coming, that got cleared of the dull imaginary wonders of the dark ages, which were replaced by exciting spaces of white paper. Regions unknown! My imagination could depict to itself there worthy, adventurous and devoted men, nibbling at the edges, attacking from north and south and east and west, conquering a bit of truth here and a bit of truth there, and sometimes swallowed up by the mystery their hearts were so persistently intent on unveiling" (*Heart of Darkness,* ed. Robert Kimbrough [New York: Norton, 1971], p. 102).

made between *Heart of Darkness* and its supposed referent is the point where the question is begged; nowhere in the rest of the novel is "Africa" mentioned after this. Concern for propriety of course accounts to some extent for this "repression of the referent": so that *Heart of Darkness* would not become a mere political tract (perhaps banned in Belgium), Africa becomes the "heart of darkness," and Brussels becomes "a city that always makes me think of a whited sepulchre" (p. 73). The silence and the void of Africa that *Heart of Darkness* is claimed to depict are thus reflected in the literal absence of the word "Africa," which absence is in turn an appropriate reflection of a continent and a state never seen by its sole outright owner, Leopold II.[7] Just as the referential tree is lost by Marlow each time he tries to establish his position, so is the reader—teased into thinking he is reading a book "about" Africa—led into a void that in fact has no name but "heart of darkness."

Several changes between the original hand-written version of *Heart of Darkness* and the final version reveal a consistent effort to replace direct references with hints, allusions, and intimations. Ian Watt points out the suppressed references to "some third-rate king," too readily identifiable as Leopold of the Belgians.[8] Further checking of the manuscript reveals that Conrad had originally included certain references to Africa—place-names— which he later took out. For example, when Marlow has set off from Europe, the manuscript reads: "I left in a French steamer, and *beginning with Dakar* she called in every blamed port they have out there."[9] The final version reads: "I left in a French steamer, and she called in every blamed port" (p. 77).

---

7. The political intertextuality of *Heart of Darkness* is of course very rich, involving, as it does, the controversy that raged over the Congo Free State at the turn of the century. Leopold II, King of the Belgians, made himself not only the sovereign but also the sole owner of the Congo, saying, "The Congo has been, and would have been, nothing but a personal undertaking. There is no more legitimate or respectable right than that of an author over his own work, the fruit of his labor. . . . My rights over the Congo are to be shared with none; they are the fruits of my own struggle and expenditure" (quoted in Ruth Slade, *King Leopold's Congo* [New York: Oxford University Press, 1962], p. 175). The most useful reading to complement *Heart of Darkness* could be the "Report of the Commission of Enquiry in the Congo Free State," translated by E. A. Huybers for the Federation for the Defence of the Belgian Interests Abroad (Brussels: Hayez, 1905). The commissioners, sent into "the heart of Africa," which was "steeped in the lowest barbarism," where "atrocious massacres were of constant occurrence," found that the system of forced labor then in place had its evils (those not providing their quota of rubber were alleged to have had their hands cut off; the quota became one of severed hands exacted out of the Force Publique rather than buckets of rubber out of the populace); but on a continent where the "mutilation of dead bodies is an ancient native custom" (p. 90), why should not a Kurtz do likewise? "Native witnesses . . . saw seven sexual organs which had been removed from natives killed during the fight, and which were suspended to a cord tied to two sticks in front of the hut of a European" (p. 89). Cf. *Heart of Darkness,* p. 132, when Marlow comes upon Kurtz's house: "I had expected to see a knob of wood there, you know . . . and there it was, black, dried, sunken, with closed eyelids—a head that seemed to sleep at the top of that pole."

8. *Conrad in the Nineteenth Century* (Berkeley: University of California Press, 1979), p. 158.

9. Conrad, *Heart of Darkness,* autograph manuscript, Beinecke Rare Book Library; emphasis mine.

Similarly, the manuscript shows: ''we passed various places: Gran'Bassam, Little Popo, names out/names that seemed to belong''; the final version: ''we passed various places—trading places—*with names like* Gran'Bassam, Little Popo, names that seemed to belong to some sordid farce'' (pp. 77–78; emphasis mine). The only African place-names left in *Heart of Darkness* after Marlow's description of the ''blank space'' are thus transformed from fact to simile, from places with names to places with names ''like'' these—perhaps these names themselves, perhaps not.

Is Africa thus ''repressed'' in anything but name? The word is practically synonymous with absence in Western discourse, as we have seen since the beginning of this study. Now in a text where every detail points to Africa, ''Africa'' alone is missing, encoded in a new phrase, ''heart of darkness.'' That phrase can never be wholly identified as either a repressed, encoded real referent or a fictive pseudo-referent, independent of the real world. *Heart of Darkness* is in fact deeply engaged in both projects at once.

Kurtz, like ''Africa,'' is only a name for an absence, having substance only to the extent that he *discourses* (a word that Conrad uses). Kurtz cannot be a fixed goal or object for the text, even though that is the role he is assigned.

> ''There was a sense of extreme disappointment, as though I had found out I had been striving after something altogether without a substance. I couldn't have been more disgusted if I had travelled all this way for the sole purpose of talking with Mr. Kurtz. Talking with . . . . I flung one shoe overboard, and became aware that that was exactly what I had been looking forward to—a talk with Kurtz. I made the strange discovery that I had never imagined him as doing, you know, but as *discoursing*. . . . The man presented himself as a *voice*.'' [P. 119, emphasis mine]

A great ambivalence lies in Conrad's use of the word ''voice'': ''He was very little more than a voice'' (p. 120); yet ''The privilege was waiting for me.''[10] When he finally speaks, a stream of dark gibberish is all that emerges, which it is no privilege to hear: '''Save me!—save the ivory, you mean. Don't tell me. Save *me*! Why, I've had to save you''' (p. 138). At the center of the story, one action takes place: ''Kurtz *discoursed*. A voice! a voice! It rang deep to the very last. It survived his strength to hide in the magnificent folds of eloquence the barren darkness of his heart'' (p. 146; emphasis mine). ''Discoursing'' is the heart of the matter—a detached, empty spewing of words in which emptiness (''barren'') and plenitude (''heart'') cross. If the

10. The ''privilege of the voice'' in Western metaphysics is the subject of Jacques Derrida's *La Voix et le phénomène* (Paris: PUF, 1967). His explication of that privilege could account to some extent for the insistence on ''loyalty'' and ''faith'' to the voice of Kurtz: its *magical* quality needs no outside determinant; it is purely autonomous and present.

continent the young Marlow looked at was blank—white and then black—
Kurtz's discourse is the central agency by which black and white cross and
interchange: "all Europe" made him, yet his was an "impenetrable darkness," most un-European (p. 147); his only product, the only way to know
he exists upriver, is the "precious trickle of ivory" (p. 84), a stream of white;
yet the "powers of darkness claimed him for their own" (p. 121); he is an
"apparition *shining darkly*" (p. 135), in a perfect Africanist oxymoron.

"Heart" and "Darkness": Condensing and Lying

Ian Watt asks the right questions about the title "Heart of Darkness":

> The more concrete of the two terms, "heart," is attributed a strategic
> centrality within a formless and infinite abstraction, "darkness";
> the combination defies both visualization and logic: How can some-
> thing inorganic like darkness have an organic centre of life and
> feeling? How can a shapeless absence of light compact itself into a
> shaped and pulsating presence? And what are we to make of a
> "good" entity like a heart becoming, of all things, a controlling part
> of a "bad" one like darkness? [*Conrad in the Nineteenth Century*,
> p. 200]

Those are, of course, the questions that this study has been constantly con-
fronting: the representation of a "shapeless absence," the congealing of nothingness into a figure. Watt goes on to compare Conrad's title to another
"fateful event," the oxymoron of the title "Les Fleurs du mal." Earlier, we
saw how Baudelaire's art criticism conceived of darkness as "the insignificant
and *solitary* zero," unitary in its opposition to the infinity of color. Darkness
is at the same time "one vast unity, monotonous and impersonal, immense
like boredom and nothingness,"[11] and also "les ténèbres" (as in *Coeur des
ténèbres*), multiple, formless, and without unity. There is only one darkness,
but it behaves as a refractory "formless and infinite abstraction." Negativity
cannot always be made to identify itself as either a singular force or as a
zero, a nullified force. In Conrad's title that indeterminate negative, "darkness," is condensed into a lifelike unity, with reality and presence. The
conceptualization of darkness brings it within the realm of light; the workings
of discourse lend life to nothingness. Thus darkness gets a "heart."

By virtue of its singularity, "heart" is usually expressed as "the heart,"
as in Graham Greene's *The Heart of the Matter* (1948), an Africanist successor
to *Heart of Darkness*. In his correspondence Conrad repeatedly refers to his
manuscript as "*The* Heart of Darkness" (Norton ed., pp. 130–31). Why the

---

11. Charles Baudelaire, "Exposition universelle de 1855," in *Curiosités esthétiques* (Paris:
Garnier, 1962), p. 215.

change? Without the definite article, "heart" is deprived of its singularity, as in a partitive usage; "heart" no longer has the power to define the life of a body. It is less of an organ, more of an abstraction. The title "Heart of Darkness" denies the singularity of form to the heart; but the narrative inside remains more "loyal." Within the body of the text, Conrad consistently uses the definite article in ways that give a singularity and presence to that which can have none:

"We penetrated deeper and deeper into *the* heart of darkness" [p. 105]; "the deceitful flow from *the* heart of an impenetrable darkness" [p. 120]; "the brown current ran swiftly out of *the* heart of darkness" [p. 145]; "A voice! a voice! It rang deep to the very last. It survived his [Kurtz's] strength to hide in the magnificent folds of eloquence *the* barren darkness of *his* heart" [p. 146]; "the beat of the drum, regular and muffled like the beating of a heart—*the* heart of a conquering darkness" [p. 152]; "the tranquil waterway . . . seemed to lead into *the* heart of an immense darkness" [p. 158]. [Emphasis mine]

"Heart of Darkness" thus becomes more real and present in narration than in the title; narration makes a specific, concrete locus out of the formless void, echoing what Marlow recounts happened to the image of Africa in his nineteenth-century boyhood: "It had ceased to be a blank space . . . . It had become a place of darkness." In its turn, darkness must be taken as an entity rather than as nothingness, given a unity and a heart, made recountable. Narration in *Heart of Darkness* is an act that makes something out of nothing, a black out of a blank, oneness out of zero.

That process is described as an act of loyalty, a desperate dedication to negativity. The "yarn" that Marlow tells and that someone else repeats is built on that premise: in a world of "utter silence," searching for something "altogether without a substance" (p. 119), "you must fall back upon your own innate strength, upon your capacity for faithfulness" (p. 122). Marlow repeats the idea that he must "be loyal to the nightmare of my choice" (p. 141), "to show my loyalty to Kurtz once more" (p. 148). At the same time that the reality of experience is denied—it is only a "shadow," a "nightmare," or a "weary pilgrimage among hints for nightmares"—it must be recounted and given some positive form. The narration is faithful to something it simultaneously asserts to be untrue, unfounded, insubstantial. *Heart of Darkness* is built on the false premise that Kurtz "had something to say. He said it"; that his cry "The Horror! The horror!" constituted "an affirmation, a moral victory"; in short, the premise is that darkness has a heart and a meaning. The truth of Kurtz's cry, his "summing-up," comes from beyond "the threshold of the invisible" and cannot be brought back out of the heart of darkness *as truth:* when Marlow is called upon to repeat that truth to

Kurtz's anxiously waiting fiancée, his Intended, back in Europe, he finds he must lie:

> "'I heard his very last words . . . .' I stopped in a fright.
> "'Repeat them,' she murmured in a heart-broken tone. 'I want—I want—something—something—to—to live with.'
> "I was on the point of crying at her, 'Don't you hear them?' The dusk was repeating them in a persistent whisper all around us, in a whisper that seemed to swell menacingly like the first whisper of a rising wind. 'The horror! The horror!'
> "'His last word—to live with,' she insisted. 'Don't you understand that I loved him—I loved him—I loved him!'
> "I pulled myself together and spoke slowly.
> "'The last word he pronounced was—your name.'" [P. 157]

Marlow's stated reason for lying is that telling the truth "would have been too dark—too dark altogether."

"Those Savages"

In a world so assiduously painted black, what manner of consciousness does Conrad attribute to the dark people who are part of the heart of darkness?: "those savages" (p. 84), "black shapes," "bundles of acute angles" (p. 82), "whirl of black limbs" (p. 105). The local population is first described in such inanimate terms, as pure material objects passing before Marlow's consciousness; presently they are revealed to be human victims of "these high and just proceedings" of colonialism:

> "They passed me within six inches, *without a glance,* with that complete, deathlike indifference of unhappy savages. Behind *this raw matter* one of the *reclaimed,* the product of the new forces at work, strolled despondently, carrying a rifle by its middle. He had a uniform jacket with one button off, and seeing a white man on the path, hoisted his weapon to his shoulder with alacrity. This was simple prudence, white men being so much alike at a distance that he could not tell who I might be. He was speedily reassured, and with a large, white, rascally grin, *and a glance* at his charge, seemed to take me into partnership in his exalted trust. *After all,* I also was a part of the great cause of these high and just proceedings." [Pp. 80–81; emphasis mine]

The oppressed are so thoroughly oppressed as to be pure "raw matter," deprived of any known consciousness and of the glance that is its sign. Their state of debasement leaves little to be described; it is almost uninteresting. Conrad is more intrigued by what he calls the "improved specimens" (p.

106), those Africans whom the Europeans have selected to "evolve" out of their primitive state.[12] The soldier in the passage just quoted is one of those "reclaimed" (as in *racheté*, "redeemed"; cf. Baudelaire's "La Belle Dorothée"): he is an incomplete version of a European soldier, a parody of what he ought to be. He is shown in this portrait to have evolved to the point of claiming a glance of his own, the right to see the white man and to look down on his inferiors. It is thus a matter of some significance that the last sentence of the paragraph is written, in free indirect discourse, from the black soldier's "point of view,"[13]

> "Their headman, a young, broad-chested black, severely draped in dark-blue fringed cloths, with fierce nostrils and his hair all done up artfully in oily ringlets, stood near me. 'Aha!' I said, just for good fellowship's sake. ' "Catch 'im,' he snapped, with a bloodshot widening of his eyes and a flash of sharp teeth—'catch 'im. Give 'im to us.' 'To you, eh?' I asked; 'what would you do with them?' 'Eat 'im!' he said curtly, and, leaning his elbow on the rail, looked out into the fog in a dignified and profoundly pensive attitude. . . . They [the headman and his chaps] had been engaged for six months (I don't think a single one of them had *any clear idea of time, as we at the end of countless ages have. They still belonged to the beginnings of time—had no inherited experience to teach them as it were*) . . . ." [P. 111; emphasis mine]

These people are thus stuck in time, prior to time, and outside it, in a "perpetual childhood." There is nothing anterior to their present moment, nothing to inherit from; time begins with the arrival of the whites and, as we shall see, with the arrival of their genre, the novel. Thus the fireman on board had only "a few months of training" and "ought to have been clapping his hands and stamping his feet on the bank, instead of which he was hard at work, a thrall to strange witchcraft, full of improving knowledge" (p. 106).[14] For him, the steam engine contains "an evil spirit" that must be controlled. The "countless ages" of Europe have produced this technological wonder,

12. "The workmen, like the soldiers, but in a less degree, constitute a class of partly civilized men" ("Report of the Commission of Enquiry," p. 120).

13. Free indirect discourse combines the expressivity of direct speech with the grammar of narration. The expression can be attributed to a character other than the narrator, in this case the soldier, who is overheard reasoning, "*After all*, he is also a part of the great cause." The "dual voice" of free indirect discourse thus helps increase the irony of the "proceedings," particularly when one considers that this coming-into-consciousness of an African is performed in a technique that, by "doubling" the voice, confounds the notion of voice itself. African consciousness is born as the inability to be autonomously conscious. For a useful interpretation of free indirect discourse, see Claude Perruchot, "Le Style indirect libre et la question du sujet dans *Madame Bovary*," in *La Production du sens chez Flaubert* (Paris: Union Générale d'Editions, 1975), pp. 253–85.

14. Cf. Rimbaud, "Mauvais sang": "Les blancs débarquent. Le canon! Il faut se soumettre au baptême, s'habiller, travailler" (*Oeuvres complètes*, Pléiade edition [Paris: Gallimard, 1972], p. 98).

which the savage can interpret only as a fetish. Even the improved and useful ones are only a few months removed from total savagery and still do not understand the difference between animate and inanimate objects.

But what Conrad is actually describing is a *mutual* fetishism: for the African, the machines of Europe are animated by gods; for the European, everything African is moved by the troublesome darkness and its heart. The African performs a simple investment of matter with spirit; the European works at cross-purposes, labeling his object a mere shadow without substance while insisting that it has a life of its own, a heart. The fetishist is one who makes something out of nothing; this is what Kurtz has done with his power over *words:* "This was the unbounded power of eloquence—of words—of burning, noble words. There were no practical hints to interrupt the *magic* current of phrases" (p. 123; emphasis mine). Kurtz's "unsound method" consists of taking himself for a god in the Africans' eyes (we "must necessarily appear to them in the nature of supernatural beings"). His "high place among the devils of the land— . . . literally" (p. 122) comes from his ability to make magic, a fetish, out of language.

If narrative is time made language, and if fetishism is "reducing history to nature,"[15] then, according to the patterns of European Africanist thought, the African will never have narration or history because he has no time, only immanent nature, a perpetual childhood. But the European, on the other hand, when he attempts to describe Africa and the African, will be drawn "back" into the production of fetishes in a double reduction of time to language and language to nature. In seeking to describe fetishism, Africanist narrative must perform fetishistic reductions, of "heart" to "the heart," of "utter silence," "altogether without substance," to fine overwrought phrases such as "an implacable force brooding over an inscrutable intention" (p. 103) or "an exotic Immensity ruled by an august Benevolence" (p. 123). Mere words become magic, eliciting "loyalty" and "faith." Language is bewitched in its attempt to reach back to a point where words and things were one—and nothing. The people on the other side of the barrier know no difference between past and present, matter and spirit, word and thing; when European discourse describes "those savages," its own categories will be discombobulated. *Time becomes language becomes history becomes nature* in a continually backsliding, atavistic takeover by things themselves.

That relentless emptying of the present moment in favor of an unattainable prior object is reminiscent of Baudelaire's "Le Cygne." Conrad's fetishization of darkness works on a principle similar to Baudelaire's allegory: both leave the present as a moment of "calm, of critical delay, of time circumstantially at a standstill,"[16] and both look back (or up) toward abstractions made nature:

15. Paul de Man, *Allegories of Reading* (New Haven: Yale University Press, 1979), p. 142.
16. Edward Said, *Joseph Conrad and the Fiction of Autobiography* (Cambridge: Harvard University Press, 1966), p. 94. See also Said's comparison of Baudelaire and Conrad, ibid., p. 103.

"sous les cieux . . . le Travail s'éveille"; "la Douleur"; "Souvenir"; "exotic immensity"; "inscrutable intention"; "My Intended"; "the heart of darkness." Allegory is at bottom the production of a literary fetish, reaching back to the point where an object of desire can be conceived as a Thing.

Conrad and Rimbaud

There are rumblings among critics to the effect that Conrad's production of those highfalutin allegorical phrases may be a fig leaf over the fact that he really doesn't know what he means. F. R. Leavis finds that the effect of Conrad's "adjectival insistence upon inexpressible and incomprehensible mystery" is "not to magnify but rather to muffle." He concludes that "the actual cheapening is little short of disastrous."

> Conrad must here stand convicted of borrowing the arts of the magazine-writer (who has borrowed his, shall we say, from Kipling and Poe) in order to impose on his readers and on himself, for thrilled response, a "significance" that is merely an emotional insistence on the presence of what he can't produce. The insistence betrays the absence, the willed "intensity" the nullity. He is intent on making a virtue out of not knowing what he means.[17]

The pejorative tone should not hide the fact that Leavis is "right," if for the wrong reasons: note that in passing he produces a perfect explication of "Le Cygne": "an emotional insistence on the presence of what he [Andromache, the swan, the Negress] can't produce." The impotence is indeed proportional to the insistence.

Frederick Crews says that Conrad "indulges our fears of isolation, neglect and victimization by maligning higher powers—the fears of an anxious infant—without locating their source" (quoted in Watt, *Conrad,* p. 238). This brings to mind another "infant" who "made a virtue out of not knowing what he meant": Rimbaud. In fact, Conrad presents a reversed image of Rimbaud in that Conrad's African junket was the origin rather than the destruction of his literary career. Jean-Aubry writes, "We are justified in thinking that this voyage to the Congo and its deplorable consequences played a big part in turning Captain Korzeniowski into the novelist Joseph Conrad" (*Sea-Dreamer,* p. 175). According to your wishes, Africa is either the principle of literary inspiration or the force that swallows up that inspiration and reduces you to silence. In either case, Africa is lent the force of myth.[18]

17. F. R. Leavis, *The Great Tradition* (London: Chatto & Windus, 1948), p. 180.
18. For Watt, it is Kurtz rather than Conrad himself or Marlow who resembles Rimbaud: "Kurtz is a poet, a painter, a political radical, a man with the power of words; and in his final liberation from all the constraints of civilisation, he becomes a symbolic parallel to the career of Arthur Rimbaud, who, in Verlaine's words, had aspired 'to be that man who will create God,' but who had turned his back on European civilisation in 1875" (*Conrad in the Nineteenth Century,* p. 164).

Heart of Darkness and the French

If one of the threads running through the Africanist tradition in French and European literature in general is the writer's experience of alienation from his own meaning, of alienation as meaning itself, then the facts of Conrad's literary existence—as an exile, writing in a foreign language—are highly significant. Joseph Conrad's protestations notwithstanding, English *was* a language he learned in late adolescence; he was hard to understand when he spoke it, and he used it in a quirky, original fashion when writing it.[19] Writing for Conrad was necessarily an act of translation, a loss of one meaning in order to gain another. Looking back to the myth of Rimbaud as ghost-writer for himself and forward to a whole literature founded on such a principle (that of black Africans writing in French), Conrad's position seems all the more interesting.

There is no *Heart of Darkness* in French literature—no text with such a singularity of influence, producing so many rewritings and interpretations. In the aftermath of the scramble for Africa in the late nineteenth century, it was generally felt that the colonial endeavor should be accompanied by an appropriately grand body of literature. Territorial rivalry was echoed by literary competition. The French at times admitted to a feeling of "impotent rage and jealousy" in regard to the English imperial success;[20] there was an "unadmitted envy" of that towering, Shakespearean precursor . . . Kipling. That it was Kipling who reduced the French to silence rather than Conrad is one of the great ironies of literary history. Kipling's success was prolific, and his style, according to the anglophile critic André Chevrillon, was capable of "total effects," "probing reality, finding the essential and effective detail"; for "he is English" and has "left the illusory world of ideas behind, [and] belongs to the respected world of facts."[21] The whole network of influences

19. Might Conrad have written in French, or was English his natural, necessary means of expression in Western European literature? The question persists, with Conrad himself at the head of a school arguing that the recourse to English was *not* arbitrary but somehow destined: "The truth of the matter is that my faculty to write in English is as natural as any other aptitude with which I might have been born [the English of the Congo diaries seems to contradict this]. I have a strange and overpowering feeling that it had always been an inherent part of myself. . . . If I had not written in English I would not have written at all" (author's note to *A Personal Record*, quoted in Zdzisław Najder, *Joseph Conrad: A Chronicle* [New Brunswick, N.J.: Rutgers University Press, 1983], p. 115). Najder deflates Conrad's mystification: "He protests too much. . . . The French language, which in many circumstances he would have preferred to use, also tempted him as a literary medium: more than once he advanced the possibility of writing in French" (ibid.). Whether *Heart of Darkness* "might have" been originally created as *Coeur des ténèbres* is in fact irrelevant. *Heart of Darkness* is a seminal text within French and all European Africanist discourse not because of its immediate influence on living writers but for what it teaches us now about how to read the figure of Africa: for the light it sheds—so to speak—on the discursive practice of European writers of whatever language.

20. Martine Astier-Loutfi, *Littérature et colonialisme: L'expansion coloniale vue dans la littérature romanesque française, 1871–1914* (Paris: Mouton, 1971), p. 92. I am particularly indebted to chapter 3, "Thèmes impérialistes," for the literary history of this period.

21. André Chevrillon, *Revue de Paris* (March–April, 1899), pp. 35, 54.

and intimidations between England and France, with Conrad as the odd man out and winner in posterity, is an interesting question, outside the scope of this study. But leaving that causal issue aside, we can take stock of what kinds of literature were produced.

A search for "the" *Heart of Darkness* in French leads, appropriately, into a jungle of voices, a discourse, rather than to any single work.[22] Malraux' *La voie royale* describes a journey into an inextricable forest, but its object is Orientalist rather than Africanist. The mediocrity of Pierre Loti's *Le Roman d'un spahi* puts it in another class from anything Conrad wrote, in spite of its considerable thematic interest.[23] Dozens of colonial novels in French and English describe Europeans in Africa who "go native," "go fantee,"[24] as in one effort of 1946, *Le Blanc qui s'était fait nègre,* by René Guillot. The commonest theme in these works is a voyage into the incomprehensible depths of Africa to rescue a European who has become "unsound." The voice of that wayward son becomes the focus of the novel's discourse.

The two most interesting "rewritings" or echoes of *Heart of Darkness* in French are from entirely different periods; my choice of them is deliberately heterogeneous, for their discourse, rather than the intentions of their authors, is the object of interest here. The Marquis de Sade's *Aline et Valcour,* an epistolary novel subtitled *Le Roman philosophique,* contains a sort of diptych of the good and evil savage, the good being pseudo-Tahitian, the evil being African. In each of the two parts the discoursing of a half-European savage is the main armature. The double portrait is given in two letters, which occupy almost half of the novel.

Céline's *Voyage au bout de la nuit,* which, like *Aline et Valcour,* describes peregrinations reaching far beyond both Europe and Africa, devotes approximately a hundred pages to a stopover in the colony of "Bambola-Bragamance," between the cry of "Go for Africa!" and the "surprise, if ever there was one," of waking up in a slave galley in New York Harbor.[25]

22. Ivo Vidan lists four main rewritings: Gide's *Voyage au Congo,* Malraux' *La Voie royale,* Céline's *Voyage au bout de la nuit,* and Genet's *Les Nègres* ("Heart of Darkness in French Literature," *Cahiers d'Etudes et de Recherches Victoriennes et Edouardiennes* 2 [1975]: 167–204).

23. See "Pierre Loti ou la vision tragique de l'Afrique," in Léon Fanoudh-Siefer, *Le Mythe du nègre et de l'Afrique noire* (Paris: Klincksieck, 1968), pp. 51–110.

24. See Watt, *Conrad in the Nineteenth Century,* p. 144.

25. In his biography of Conrad, Frederick R. Karl gives the title "Journey to the End of Night" to a chapter on Conrad's time in the Congo and comments that "Louis-Ferdinand Céline's version of his African journey, which owed much to Conrad's 'Heart of Darkness,' stresses the same sense of reflected madness" (*Joseph Conrad: The Three Lives* [New York: Farrar, Straus, Giroux, 1979], p. 285n). Zdzisław Najder titles his chapter on the same subject "To the End of Night" (*Joseph Conrad,* pp. 123–42).

5

No One's Novel:
Sade's *Aline et Valcour*

J'ay vû l'Afrique, mais je n'y ay jamais mis le pied.
— Jean-Baptiste Labat,
Nouvelle Relation de l'Afrique occidentale (1728)

This initiated wraith from the back of Nowhere honoured me
with its amazing confidence before it vanished altogether.
— *Heart of Darkness*

Framing Disruption

It is generally conceded that no single true voice within his works can be
attributed to the Marquis de Sade, nor can any point of view that plainly
represents the view of the man who lived and wrote. The "thought" of Sade
is impossible to isolate among the conflicting voices he adopts like so many
masks. Sade is finally "No One: . . . an elusive lack of specific attributes."[1]
The conventions of the epistolary novel allow the author to efface himself
among the voices of others and to write under other people's names, as a
pseudo-*nègre* or ghost-writer. The "editor" of an eighteenth-century novel—
one like Sade at least—casts himself as writing for someone else and would
thus never be the sole proprietor of his meaning. The editor meticulously
manipulates the relations between all the other voices but just as carefully

1. Jane Gallop, *Intersections: A Reading of Sade with Bataille, Blanchot, and Klossowski*
(Lincoln: University of Nebraska Press, 1982), pp. 8–9. Cf. Maurice Blanchot, *Lautréamont et
Sade* (Paris: Editions de Minuit, 1963), pp. 18–19: "Non seulement son oeuvre, mais sa pensée
restent impénétrables,—et cela, bien que les développements théoriques y soient en très grand
nombre . . . qu'il raisonne de la manière la plus claire et avec une logique suffisante. Le goût
et même la passion des systèmes l'animent . . . il semble qu'il ne devrait y avoir rien de plus
facile à entendre que l'idéologie. . . . Cela non plus n'apparaît pas clairement . . . . C'est que
ses pensées théoriques libèrent à tout instant des puissances irrationnelles auxquelles elles sont
liées." I quote Blanchot at length because his remarks are of prime significance in the interpretation that follows. See also Roger Mercier, "Sade et le thème des voyages dans *Aline et Valcour*,"
Dix-Huitième Siècle 1 (1969): 352: "D'abord Sade, au lieu d'exposer ses propres idées, donne
la parole aux représentants de thèses contraires." I would disagree with Mercier's assertion that
"Il n'y a cependant là que le souci d'un écrivain qui ne veut pas transformer son roman en
exposé didactique."

keeps his own voice to himself. For this reason, the critic attempting a "political reading" of Sade's work is faced with a protean ideology, an author "having his characters speak and act according to the ideology he chose for them without, however, feeling any concern of his own . . . . The truth [is] in a perpetual state of laceration."[2] In a note to *Aline et Valcour*, Sade writes a sort of manifesto of the *nègre:*

> Quelques lecteurs vont dire: Voilà une bonne contradiction; on a écrit quelque part avant ceci qu'il ne fallait pas changer souvent les ministres de place: ici l'on dit tout le contraire.—Mais ces vétilleux lecteurs veulent-ils bien nous permettre de leur faire observer que ce recueil épistolaire n'est point un traité de morale dont toutes les parties doivent se correspondre et se lier; formé par différentes personnes, ce recueil offre, dans chaque lettre, la façon de penser de celui qui écrit, ou des personnes que voit cet écrivain, et dont il rend les idées: ainsi, au lieu de s'attacher à démêler des contradictions ou des redites, choses inévitables dans une pareille collection, il faut que le lecteur, plus sage, s'amuse ou s'occupe des différents systèmes présentés pour ou contre, et qu'il adopte ceux qui favorisent le mieux, ou ses idées, ou ses penchants.[3]

> Some readers will say: This is quite a contradiction; it was written somewhere before this that ministers must not often be moved: here quite the opposite is stated.—But will these quibbling readers please permit us to point out that this collection of letters is not a moral treatise whose every part must correspond and link; formed by different persons, this collection offers, in each letter, the writer's way of thinking, or that of persons whom this writer sees and whose ideas he renders: thus, instead of trying to sort out contradictions and redundancies, which are inevitable in such a collection, the wiser reader must be amused or occupied with different systems presented pro and con, and he must adopt those that most favor either his own ideas or his penchants.

Aline et Valcour, ou le roman philosophique, largely ignored by Sadean criticism, uses the vehicle of around-the-world peregrinations and the materials of preanthropological observation that were circulating in late eighteenth-century France to string together a loose narrative in which anything is possible. *Aline et Valcour* is Sade's venture into "realistic" fiction; the novel is heartily seasoned with facts and descriptions of life in the primitive world,

---

2. Jean-Marie Goulemot, "Lecture politique d'*Aline et Valcour,*" in *Le Marquis de Sade* (Paris: Colin, 1968), pp. 122–23.

3. *Aline et Valcour,* in *Oeuvres complètes du Marquis de Sade,* 15 vols. (Paris: Cercle du Livre Précieux, 1962), 4:109–10n. (Subsequent references in parentheses are to this volume, unless otherwise noted.)

taken from the *Voyages* of Captain Cook and others; Sade's efforts are credited
with "a care for documentation and an attentiveness to exactitude which have
been traits of his personality little known up to now" (Mercier, "Sade," p.
343). Yet this work of obvious interest has fallen somewhat between the
boards of criticism: its adulterated Sadism makes it less appealing to those
interested in pure libertinism, while its absence among Africanist bibliographies may be symptomatic of the author's still-repressed status within the
canon of literature.[4] The Africanist section of the novel is of capital importance
to us in that it stands at the confluence of Africanist observation and another
current of thought, libertinism. The location of that intellectual event is in
Letter XXXV, titled "Histoire de Sainville et de Léonore," and Letter
XXXVIII, "Histoire de Léonore," which together constitute almost half of
the novel.[5] Both Sainville and Léonore, the separated lovers, blunder into the
fictive African kingdom of Butua, in the "center of Africa," "inhabited by
man-eating peoples, whose customs and cruelties surpass in depravity everything that has been written and told up to now" (p. 189). There, *"libertinage
becomes law"* (p. 224).

In stark moralistic contrast stands the South Sea utopia of Tamoé, to which
Léonore flees, in a perfect blend of intertextual trendiness and plot, aboard
a vessel accompanying Captain Cook (p. 250). The description of Tamoé is
made in a subsection of the "Histoire de Sainville et de Léonore," called
"Histoire de Zamé"—Zamé being the island's benevolent ruler. Following
hard on the heels of Butua's thrilling debauchery, of which more presently,
the bland goodness of Tamoé seems more than insipid and, paradoxically,
less than desirable. Sade addresses this problem in the "Avis de l'éditeur"
that precedes *Aline et Valcour:*

> Personne n'est encore parvenu au royaume de Butua, situé au
> centre de l'Afrique; notre auteur seul a pénétré dans ces climats
> barbares; *ici ce n'est plus un roman, ce sont les notes d'un voyageur
> exact, instruit et qui ne raconte que ce qu'il a vu.* Si par des fictions
> plus agréables il veut à Tamoé consoler ses lecteurs des cruelles
> vérités qu'il a été obligé de peindre à Butua, doit-on lui en savoir
> mauvais gré? Nous ne voyons qu'une chose de malheureuse à cela,
> c'est que tout ce qu'il y a de plus affreux soit dans la nature, et que
> ce ne soit que dans le pays des chimères que se trouve seulement le
> juste et le bon. [Pp. xxvii–xxviii; emphasis mine]

4. *Aline et Valcour* is not included in either Roger Mercier's *L'Afrique noire dans la littérature
française* (Dakar: Université de Dakar, 1962) or in Léon-François Hoffmann's *Le Nègre romantique* (Paris: Payot, 1973), although Hoffmann does mention the scene in *La Nouvelle Justine*
that we will discuss below.

5. Letter XXXV, our primary concern here, was published separately by 10/18 Editions,
edited by G. Lély.

No one has yet arrived in the kingdom of Butua, situated in the center of Africa; our author alone has penetrated these barbaric climes; *at this point this is no longer a novel but the notes of an exact and educated traveler who recounts only what he has seen.* If with pleasanter fictions of Tamoé he wishes to console his readers from the cruel truths he was obliged to depict in Butua, must we hold it against him? We see but one unfortunate thing in this, that all that is the most awful is to be found in nature and that it is only in the land of dreams that the just and the good are to be found.

Unlike the self-condemning narrative voice of *120 Journées de Sodome,* which labels itself "the most impure narrative that has ever been made in the earth's existence" (*Oeuvres,* 13:60), the discourse of *Aline et Valcour* claims that "the horrifying *colors* [*sic*] which have been used to depict vice will not fail to render it detestable" ("les couleurs effroyables dont on s'est servi pour peindre le vice ne manqueront pas de le faire détester"; p. xxvii). The transcription of evil into literature would therefore be a redeeming act; telling about the darkness serves the light, the truth. The truth, as in *Heart of Darkness,* is dark, "cruel"; but the narration escapes complicity in the evil it recounts by recounting it, out of pure obligation. But that loyalty to the Real must destroy the convention of fiction, reducing the *roman par lettres* to "les notes d'un voyageur." Storytelling becomes pure History, in the service of, as Sade has it in *Idée sur les romans,* verisimilitude regarding customs and geography: "Your local descriptions must be real."[6] The dark truth of Butua is outside the bounds of the novel; the idyll in Tamoé is offered as a pure distraction for the reader.

If service to the truth is the defined purpose and frame of "Histoire de Sainville et de Léonore," that truth is also the force that periodically breaks through the frame and calls the whole project into question. Butua is described principally through the voice of Sainville; his voice is embedded in a letter written by Déterville, addressed to Valcour, the suitor of Aline. The story of Sainville and Léonore echoes that of Aline and Valcour, which surrounds it: Aline de Blamont and Léonore (whose real name turns out to be Claire de Blamont) are sisters; Valcour and Sainville are their respective suitors. Each frame is surrounded by another frame that resembles it (see diagram, p. 188).

On the innermost level, Sainville "discourses."[7] Déterville in turn writes in the first person to the absent Valcour, who will in turn write to other

6. "Je ne te pardonnerai ni une invraisemblance de moeurs, ni un défaut de costume, encore moins une faute de géographie: comme personne ne te contraint à ces échappées, il faut que tes descriptions locales soient réelles, ou il faut que tu restes au coin de ton feu" (*Idée sur les romans* [Paris: Editions Ducros, 1970], p. 57).

7. The resemblance to *Heart of Darkness* includes the structure of embedded narrative, of Kurtz's discourse within Marlow's within someone else's.

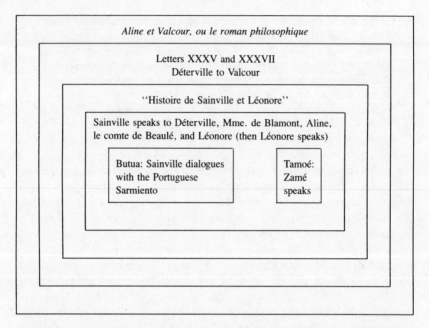

persons, so that all the frames in fact "correspond and link up," though not
without contradictions and redundancies. But, within Sainville's discourse,
an Africanist scandal erupts and threatens to break up the scene of narration
and the painstaking overall structure of the narrative. No sooner has Sainville
hinted at "the horror" he is about to depict than Aline heads for the door:

> . . . j'affaiblirai sans doute ce que cette relation pourra présenter
> d'indécent; mais pour être vrai, je serai obligé quelquefois de révéler
> des horreurs qui vous révolteront. Comment pourrai-je autrement
> vous peindre le peuple le plus cruel et le plus dissolu de la terre?
>   Aline ici voulut se retirer, mon cher Valcour, et je me flatte que
> tu reconnais là cette fille sage, qu'alarme et fait rougir la plus légère
> offense à la pudeur. Mais Mme de Blamont soupçonnant le chagrin
> qu'allait lui causer la perte du récit intéressant de Sainville, lui
> ordonna de rester, ajoutant qu'elle comptait assez sur l'honneur et
> la manière noble de s'exprimer de son jeune hôte, pour croire qu'il
> mettrait dans sa narration toute la pureté qu'il pourrait, et qu'il
> gazerait les choses trop fortes. [P. 189]

> I shall probably weaken the indecent aspects of this narration; but
> in order to be true, I shall sometimes be obliged to reveal horrors
> that will revolt you. How else can I describe for you the cruelest
> and most dissolute people on earth?
>   Aline wanted to retire at this point, my dear Valcour, and I flatter
> myself to think that you will recognize from this description that

prudent girl, in whom even the slightest indecency causes alarm and embarrassment. But Madame de Blamont suspected the sorrow that missing Sainville's interesting account would cause her and ordered her to stay, adding that she would count enough on the honor and noble manner of expression of her young guest to believe that he would put all the pureness he could into his narration and that he would gloss over things too strong.

The Comte de Beaulé then intervenes with an opinion that echoes the "Avis de l'éditeur": "Ceci n'est pas une historiette indécente: monsieur ne va pas nous faire un roman" ("This is not some ribald little tale. The gentleman is not going to give us a novel"). Loyalty to verisimilitude thus offsets the "feminine" concern for *pudeur*. But that argument of service to the truth, while permitting the innermost frame to be developed, must belie the label on the outermost frame: "le *roman* philosophique."[8] Revulsion at the African story is not the only cause of parabasis or of calling forward the narrative agency in *Aline et Valcour*, but significantly, in "Histoire de Zamé," the interruptions are occasioned by expressions of delight and eagerness rather than expressions of horror.[9] In all cases, the Comte de Beaulé intervenes to set the narrative back on its track, protecting it from the dual traps of attraction and revulsion.

If "anthropological" information and realism are the declared organizing *raison d'être* of *Aline et Valcour*, they are apparently a principle of disruption at the same time. Sade's "Avertissement" makes it clear that the heart of the novel is darkness, an unspeakable truth, "cruelles vérités"; the entire narrative structure referred to in the diagram is simply a pretext for the revelation of these truths. Yet no sooner is the truth approached than the structure is momentarily disorganized. Interruption and disorganization are given as integral parts of the scheme.

The Body Dis-organized

Les indigènes qui m'entourent se nomment Paoins ils sont
notoirement anthropophages—
    Ce qui me permet d'assister à des petites scènes que l'on
pourrait surnommer à coup sûr "tranches de vie"—
        —Céline, Letter to Simone Saintu, June 28, 1916

Africanist material is thus posed as a threat to the organization of the narrative from the beginning. But, once back on the track, the inner frame of Sainville's description of Butua grows into a full pseudo-anthropological study. This is

8. For a historical perspective on this problem, see Georges May, *Le Dilemme du roman au dix-huitième siècle* (New Haven: Yale University Press, 1963).
  9. See pp. 258, 289, 306, 370.

not effected without producing yet another voice, that of Sarmiento, a "totally denaturalized" Portuguese who "had adopted both the morals and the customs of the nation where he found himself" (p. 196). Sarmiento is one of the earliest avatars of the European "gone native"; he is an essential ancestor of Kurtz. Rather more loquacious and articulate, however. His discourse and that of Sainville will constitute a "philosophical" dialogue in which no single argument will ever prevail, in which manners and morals will be endlessly compared from opposed viewpoints.

Sarmiento, sixty-six years old, has been in Butua for about twenty years; taken prisoner, he came to be the monarch's most trusted aide. He arrived predisposed to the native vices, with the baggage of "superstition" and idolatrous Roman Catholicism that Sade sees as innate in the Portuguese.[10] As Sainville and Sarmiento sit down to their first meal together, the Portuguese pronounces his "Bénédicité." Sainville, upon discovering that the *plat du jour* is "the thigh or buttock of one of the young ladies" that the despot king has just had sacrificed to his bloodthirsty idol, utters the following denunciation:

> —Malheureux! m'écriai-je en me levant de table, le coeur sur les lèvres, ton régal me fait frémir . . . j'expirerai plutôt que d'y toucher. . . . C'est donc sur ce plat effroyable que tu osais demander la bénédiction du ciel? . . . Terrible homme! à ce mélange de superstition et de crime, tu n'as même pas voulu déguiser ta nation . . . . Va, je t'aurais reconnu sans que tu te nommasses. [P. 196]

> "Wretch," I cried standing up from the table, my heart leaping forth, "Your feast makes me quake. . . . I will expire rather than touch it. . . . On this horrifying dish you dared invoke the blessing of heaven? . . . Terrible man! In this blend of superstition and crime, you haven't even tried to disguise your nationality. . . . I would have recognized you even if you had not identified yourself."

Sarmiento responds with the major theme of his speeches, the relativity of morals and customs. "It is folly," he says, "to believe that a moral good exists: all manners of behavior, absolutely indifferent in and of themselves,

10. Sarmiento is referred to most frequently as "le Portugais," making of him a national allegorical figure; Raynal, whom Sade cites repeatedly and with admiration throughout *Aline et Valcour,* had this to say about the Portuguese: "les vices et l'ineptie de quelques commandans, l'abus des richesses, celui de la puissance, l'ivresse des succès, l'éloignement de leur patrie, avaient changé les conquérans. *Le fanatisme de religion,* qui avait donné plus de force et d'activité à leur courage, ne leur donnait plus que de l'atrocité" (emphasis mine) (G. T. Raynal, *Histoire philosophique et politique des établissemens et du commerce des Européens dans les Deux Indes* (Paris: Costes, 1820), 1:238. A contemporary of Conrad's would write: "La nation [Belgium] y [in Africa] verra sombrer sa fortune, comme l'Espagne, ou abâtardir sa race, comme le Portugal" (Charles Buls, *Croquis congolais* [Brussels: G. Balat, 1899], p. xi).

become good or evil according to the country judging them. . . . In Butua I do as the Negroes do" (p. 197).[11] The immediate problem is solved by serving up a grilled monkey (which proves to be slightly tough); the more general problem, of values, discontinuity, and disorganization, remains.

Organisation in Sade is the body,[12] the living machine composed of various organs working together: "Is it astonishing that we feel such a noticable difference in our *organization* from one season to another?" ("Est-il étonnant que nous éprouvions une différence aussi sensible dans notre organisation d'une saison à l'autre?" [p. 218n]). There is no *désorganisation* in Sade's lexicon, only *éléments désorganisés,* that is, fragments of the body, elements severed from the living whole. Sarmiento argues that cannibalism is a perfectly good use of such elements: "It is absolutely indifferent whether disorganized elements be entombed in the bowels of the earth or those of men."[13] In a footnote, the editor (Sade?) states that "man-eating is certainly not a crime," and cites "Paw," "Meunier," and Captain Cook to assure the reader that cannibalism, like idolatry, "was general on our planet and is as old as the world."[14] The practice of returning "disorganized" organs to another "or-

11. Cf. Baudelaire, "Tout peuple est académique en jugeant les autres, tout peuple est barbare quand il est jugé" ("L'Exposition universelle . . . ," *Curiosités esthétiques* [Paris: Garnier, 1962], p. 212).

12. The original sense of the word in French, dating from the end of the fourteenth century, is: "Etat d'un corps, d'un être organisé; ce corps, cet être lui-même" *(Grand Larousse).*

13. Cf. Rimbaud, "Mauvais sang": "J'ensevelis des morts dans mon ventre."

14. "Paw" is Cornelius de Pauw, author of *Recherches philosophiques sur les Américains* (Berlin: Decker, 1768–69). This work, though it is obviously concentrated on America rather than Africa, contains some received ideas about Negroes: they "prefer the flesh of snakes and lizards to all others" (p. 17), and "Les *organes* les plus délicats ou les plus subtils de leur cerveau ont été détruits ou oblitérés par le feu de leur climat natal" (p. 182; emphasis mine). However, Pauw makes no mention of cannibalism among Africans. "Meunier" is Jean-Nicolas Démeunier (1751–1814), author of *L'Esprit des usages et coutumes des différens peuples, ou Observations tirées des Voyageurs et des Historiens* (Paris and London: Chez Pissot, 1776). This work was among those the marquis had with him in the Bastille when he was writing *Aline et Valcour* (Mercier, "Sade et le thème des voyages," p. 339); it consists, as its subtitle modestly admits, of a compilation of information gleaned from readings of *récits de voyage.* But Démeunier's attitude toward his own sources is paradoxical and fascinating: in his chapter devoted to "Different sorts of foods," he provides a long list of peoples in the world who have been said to be cannibals, along with careful references to the sources of his information. There are Mexicans, Peruvians, and many varieties of Africans. Démeunier warns the reader: "On n'examine pas quel degré de croyance il faut accorder à ces auteurs. Si quelques uns attribuent légèrement le terme d'antropophages [*sic*] aux peuples dont ils parlent, le point capital de la question n'en est pas moins avéré" (1:15–16). That "cruel truth" of cannibalism is nonetheless built on unsolid foundations, by Démeunier's admission: "Enfin on a prétendu qu'il y a des Nègres à physionomie de tigres qui sont antropophages par instinct, & qui déchirent même sur les vaisseaux, les autres esclaves avec lesquels ils se trouvent à bord. Cette assertion est dénuée de preuves; mais on a voulu expliquer par la constitution physique de l'homme, pourquoi il y a des antropophages" (1:27). Edna Lemay, who has analyzed the relationship between Démeunier and his sources as a question of numerical faithfulness, found that, "nine times out of ten, Démeunier copied exactly the original text," in spite of his own caveat: "Les voyageurs et les écrivains *dénaturent* d'ailleurs la plupart des usages, et comme ils n'en cherchent jamais l'origine, ils les *altèrent* par ignorance ou de *mauvaise foi,* pour les rendre plus piquants" (1:33–34;

ganization," instituted as "an organic law of state,"[15] is thus a return to the earliest organization of man. Cannibalism, Diderot's *Encyclopédie* will maintain, is a temporal, not a geographical, problem, the business of those who must still be "in the obscure beginnings of the long march toward the light" (article "Anthropophagie").

Disorganization in Butua is the law of state. Sade condenses the received ideas of his time into several pages of observations that will be familiar in the context of this study: the Africans have no past or future, no writing, history, or memorial; they are ignorant of arts, sciences, and politics; "they have no money, . . . nor sign that represents it; each lives from what he has" (p. 231). Butua disorganizes Sainville's notions of binary oppositions to the point where he is lost in a "world derisive of structures of meaningful opposition."[16] Through the mouthpiece of Sarmiento, the distinction between life and death itself is blurred:

> Reste à savoir maintenant si cette destruction est un aussi grand mal que l'on se l'imagine, et si, ressemblant aux fléaux que la nature envoie dans les mêmes principes, elle ne la sert pas tout comme eux. Mais ceci nous entraînerait bien loin: il faudrait analyser d'abord, comment toi, faible et vile créature, qui n'as la force de rien créer, peux t'imaginer de pouvoir détruire; comment, selon toi, la mort pourrait être une destruction, puisque la nature n'en admet aucune dans ses lois, et que ses actes ne sont que des métempsychoses et des reproductions perpétuelles; il faudrait en venir ensuite à démontrer comment des changements de formes, qui ne servent qu'à faciliter ses créations, peuvent devenir des crimes contre ses lois, et comment la manière de les aider ou de les servir peut en même temps les outrager. [Pp. 199–200]

> It now remains to be seen if this destruction is as great an evil as it is imagined to be, and if, like those disasters nature sends according to the same principles, it does not serve her just as they do. But this would lead us far: it would be necessary to analyze, first, how you, a weak and vile creature, who have the force to create nothing, can imagine yourself capable of destroying; how, according to you, death could be a destruction, since nature allows none in its laws, and since her acts are only metempsychoses and perpetual transformations; it would next be necessary to demonstrate how changes of

---

emphasis mine) (see Lemay, "Naissance de l'anthropologie sociale en France: J. N. Démeunier et l'étude des usages et coutumes au XVIIIe siècle," *Au siècle des lumières* [Paris and Moscow: SEVPEN, 1970], pp. 37, 39). Démeunier's faithfulness is thus a "bad faith" of his choice, invested in material he admits he distrusts. Sade's subsequent reliance on Démeunier for footnote material, for solid information on cannibalism, reproduces that problematical act of loyalty.

15. Beatrice C. Fink, "Sade and Cannibalism," *L'Esprit Créateur* 15, no. 4 (Winter, 1975): 405. See also Jean Biou, "Lumières et anthropophagie," *Revue des sciences humaines* 37 (1972).

16. Jane Gallop, "The Immoral Teachers," *Yale French Studies* 63 (1982): 125.

form, which serve only to facilitate nature's creations, can become crimes against her laws, and how a manner of helping them or serving them can offend them as well.

Individual lives, and life itself, are only a question of form and transformation; there is no hierarchy or hereafter to define relationships temporally or theologically; life can neither begin nor end. This view is reminiscent, first, of the "deeply ambivalent," and "grotesque" image of the body described by Mikhail Bakhtine in *Rabelais and His World,* in which "The artistic logic of the grotesque image ignores the closed, smooth, and impenetrable surface of the body and retains only its excrescences. It is a point of transition in a life eternally renewed, the inexhaustible vessel of death and conception."[17] If Bakhtine's thesis is valid, then Sade's Butua has its intellectual roots not in Africa but deep within European folk culture.

Such an etiology is beyond the limits of what can be proved here; a closer relation to Sarmiento's speech is to be found in the Abbé Demanet's "soft wax," "any figure you wish," in which form is all there is and form is always metamorphosing: in Sade's words, "des métempsychoses et des reproductions perpétuelles." Sarmiento's and Demanet's discourses differ only in valorization; Sarmiento is, however, the first character we have met to state the Africanist thesis in positive terms. What makes it possible for Sade to create such a point of view?

The soft-wax metaphor was only Demanet's way of explaining another image, that of the *machine*. Both discourses, Africanist and Sadean libertine, produce and make use of machines; by examining this common denominator we can perhaps understand their deeper condition.

Libertinism and the Figure of Africa

> Et la malheureuse [Justine] . . . se laisse faire machinalement.
> —*La Nouvelle Justine (Oeuvres, 7:402)*

Butua is ruled by Ben Mâacoro, but Ben Mâacoro is ruled by the single idol of the country, "a horrible figure, half man, half serpent" (p. 191), with an enormous appetite for virgins. Idolatry and cannibalism are one and the same system. On his arrival in Butua, Sainville is put to work as chief inspector of incoming women for the harem and the sacrifices of the despot. The women arrive each month as tribute paid to the king by the outlying provinces. Sainville's job proves to be arithmetically complicated: he must count not the heads—for they are veiled—but the more nether parts of the women, and from among them he must certify the virgins and maintain a constant set of

17. Mikhail Bakhtine, *Rabelais and His World,* trans. Helene Iswolsky (Cambridge: MIT Press, 1968), pp. 317–18.

two thousand. Sarmiento's explanation of the entire system is an elaborate exercise in numbers:

> Toutes les femmes du prince, continua Sarmiento, au nombre de douze mille, se divisent en quatre classes; il forme lui-même ces classes à mesure qu'il reçoit les femmes des mains de celui qui les choisit: les plus grandes, les plus fortes, les mieux constituées se placent dans le détachement qui garde son palais; ce qu'on appelle les cinq cents esclaves est formé de l'espèce inférieure à celle dont je viens de parler: ces femmes sont ordinairement de vingt à trente ans; à elles appartient le service intérieur du palais, les travaux des jardins, et généralement toutes les corvées. Il forme la troisième classe depuis seize ans jusqu'à vingt ans; celles-là servent aux sacrifices: c'est parmi elles que se prennent les victimes immolées à son dieu. La quatrième classe enfin renferme tout ce qu'il y a de plus délicat et de joli depuis l'enfance jusqu'à seize ans. C'est là ce qui sert plus particulièrement à ses plaisirs; ce serait là où se placeraient les blanches, s'il en avait. [Pp. 194–95]

> All the prince's women, continued Sarmiento, numbering twelve thousand, are divided into four classes; he forms these classes himself as he receives the women from the hands of the man who chooses them; the tallest, the strongest, with the best constitutions, are placed in the detachment that guards his palace. Those known as the five hundred slaves are formed from the next-lower species: these women are normally from twenty to thirty years old; the interior service of the palace, taking care of the gardens, and generally all the chores belong to them. He forms the third class from sixteen to twenty years; these are used for the sacrifices: it is among them that the victims burned to his god are found. Finally, the fourth class includes all those who are the most delicate and pretty, from childhood up to sixteen years. These are the ones who are used most particularly for his pleasures; it would be here that the white women would be placed if he had any.

Jane Gallop is correct—and justifiably perverse—in insisting on the arithmetical character of libertinism in Sade as part of a "long, concerted effort to subsume the body, sexuality, desire, disorder into categories of philosophy, of thought" (Gallop, "Immoral Teachers," p. 122). Butua is one of those disorderly, disorganized elements, seeking containment in this "roman philosophique." In another Sade text, chapter 20 of *La Nouvelle Justine*, two Negroes silently and complacently participate in the intricately organized *disfiguration* of the hapless heroine, and the passage serves as a good illustration of the scheme in which Sade is exploiting Africanist themes. The two men's "fierce aspect excites [Justine's] terror":

Les deux nègres avaient environ vingt-deux à trente ans: nul monstre ne fut membré comme ces deux Africains; l'âne le plus célèbre du Mirebalais n'eût été qu'un enfant auprès d'eux; et l'on ne pouvait croire, en les voyant, que jamais aucun être pût se trouver dans la possibilité d'employer de tels hommes. [*Oeuvres*, 7:391]

The two Negroes were about twenty-two to thirty years old: no monster was ever endowed like these two Africans; the most famous donkey in the Mirebalais would have been a mere child beside them; and seeing them, one could not believe that any being would ever be capable of employing such men.

The assembled libertines, "numbered twelve," "will each have a number, and, turn by turn, each will briskly inflict his or her assigned punishment on the patient." Justine is whipped one hundred times by each participant, mounted on a wheel, given one hour to rest, tied down to a round saddle having "not six inches in diameter" (p. 395); she is made to run the gauntlet of the twelve libertines, divided in two rows of six each, twelve times: "in six minutes, her miserable body is nothing but an open wound" [une plaie"]. All those numbers—and *Justine* is rife with them—are difficult to interpret. Are we supposed to draw charts and admire the symmetry of the debauchery, or are the figures throwaway details, with no significance?

The libertine machine is a means of *objectifying* the relationship with the victim, of having an impersonal orderliness intervene and control; it permits an unreflexive adherence to the form of things. The succession of numbers following, multiplying and dividing each other, mimics but excludes thought: it follows the same patterns but has no meaning of its own. "The tortures *had* to be applied in the order in which we have just named the characters," observes the narrator. He could as well be speaking for the king of Butua.

On this point the libertine and the primitive have been compared: "The libertine, like the primitive," writes A. M. Laborde, is engaged in the "rediscovery of his original forces, of those he would have enjoyed in a prior state, at the moment of the original creation." That process of rediscovery through ritual exercises a "fidelity to assigned place and the systematic ordering of activities according to certain geometrical figures."[18] Sadean ritual would thus represent an effort to "destroy the Historical Condition of being, in order to return to the state before Time, before Form, before the Fall of man" (Laborde, p. 137). Note that the description of that return is made in allegorizing, fetishistic capitals.

18. Alice M. Laborde, *Sade romancier* (Neuchâtel: La Baconnière, 1974), pp. 141, 144. Laborde's thesis in the chapter "Le rituel sadique" is based mostly on a comparison of passages from *Juliette* and a study by Mircea Eliade, *Myths, Dreams, and Mysteries,* trans. Philip Mairet (New York: Harper & Bros., 1960); it is regrettable that the comparison does not take account of *Aline et Valcour,* in which primitive ritual and libertinism are explicitly compared by Sade.

The libertine and the primitive are both creatures of, or seeking, a world prior to difference; their devotion to machinery, to numbers, and to form is similar to the process of idolatry: when practiced on a statue by Butuans, it is Africanist idolatry; when practiced on women by Europeans, it is libertinage. So says Ben Mâacoro:

> Vous êtes fous . . . , vous autres Européens, d'idolâtrer ce sexe; une femme est faite pour qu'on en jouisse, et non pour qu'on l'adore; c'est offenser les dieux de son pays, que de rendre à de simples créatures le culte qui n'est dû qu'à eux. [P. 192]

> You are mad, you Europeans, to idolize this sex; a woman is made to be enjoyed, not to be worshiped; it is an offense to the gods of one's country to give to simple creatures the adoration that is due only to them [the gods].

Sainville admits to an "idolatrous" love for Léonore ("ces attraits que j'idolâtre" [p. 195]; "O toi que j'idolâtre!" [p. 217]; "un sexe que tu méprises [Sarmiento] et que j'idolâtre" [p. 223]); but Sainville is no libertine. The European libertine in "Histoire de Sainville" would have to be Sarmiento, who is more an accessory to the primitive libertinism of the king. It is Ben Mâacoro who uses women as material objects. Sainville's idolatry is expressed as a spiritual metaphor—a nonfetishistic idolatry, if that were possible, reflecting the weakened meaning of the word "idol" after de Brosses. Sade's vocabulary is divided between the old and the new senses of the word: there is the idol of Butua, bloody and physical, and there is this verbal usage by Sarmiento, which is more in line with the modern "idolize," "teen idol," etc. There does not appear to be any lexical basis for Sade's distinction between the noun form and the verb form for the old and new senses, respectively. Ben Mâacoro the primitive and Sarmiento the Roman Catholic remain in the world of original idolatry. The religion of Butua is a peculiar kind of mono-idolatry, with only one idol for the whole country ("representing a horrible figure, half man, half serpent, having a woman's breasts and the horns of a goat; it was stained with blood. Such was the god of the country" [p. 191]). Sarmiento, as a Portuguese, is accused by Sainville of having a natural predisposition to all this, coming from a land with "your crucifixes, your reliquaries, your rosaries, your ciboria, all those idolatrous instruments with which superstition degrades the pure worship of the Eternal" (p. 207). Sainville, the voice of uncorrupted Europe, advocates a rational, metaphorical idolatry, recognized as such: emotionally attached to a material object without seeking to utterly destroy the difference of the object.

The libertine machine and the primitivistic idol represent materiality pushed to the extreme, to the point at which matter must be fragmented and disfigured in order to be an object. The libertine counts, orders, and arranges the *disfiguration* of his victim ("Justine . . . pâle, tremblante, *défigurée*" [*La Nouvelle Justine, Oeuvres*, 7:392]); the primitive sacrifices a fixed number of virgins each month to satisfy his idol, which is of course immune to satisfaction. Fidelity, loyalty to these "nightmares of your choice," involves violent gestures that leave the victim "without consciousness" (*Nouvelle Justine*, p. 399). To attain the object, the object must be disfigured, dismembered, and disorganized until it expires, ceases to exist. Africanist discourse has appeared to follow this practice from the beginning.

In the meantime, the narration of *Aline et Valcour* pursues the realism of its object, proliferating facts with numerous substantiating details, footnotes to prestigious voyagers and philosophers.[19] Each detail strengthens the truth-producing machine that the "Avertissement" inaugurates. Yet with each step toward that truth, with each effective turn of the narrative machine, the object is worn down a little more: like the word "Butua" itself, each utterance of which increases the illusion of realism while in fact demonstrating how much the author does not know. Sade included no maps in the original edition of *Aline et Valcour,* but he situates Butua verbally, for Sarmiento walks twenty-five leagues inland from the spot where he was washed ashore: "between Benguela and the kingdom of the Jagas, on the shores of the latter empire, near Cape Negre" (see figure 5). Butua appears to have been a real kingdom in what is now Zimbabwe: first a vassal state in the Monomotapa Empire, which was then, in its eighteenth-century heyday, an isolated, xenophobic power, ruling vast territories.[20] The word "Butua" or "Abutua" or "Toroa" appears on contemporary maps, described as "rich in Gold,"[21] but encyclo-

19. Sade's apparent source of Africanist imagery would be another book he had with him at the Bastille: Antoine Banier's edition of *Cérémonies et coutumes religieuses de tous les peuples du monde* (Paris: Rollin fils, 1741), which is interesting for its differences from Sade's text as much as for its similarities. In the kingdom of "Juda" there is a king with two thousand wives divided into three classes, none of which serves the Sadistic custom of sacrifice. The religious ceremonies are described in great mathematical and symmetrical detail, but there is nothing corresponding to the "cruel truths" of Butua. A passing reference, revealing in its glibness, to human sacrifice in the kingdom of the "Jagas" is the only disturbing detail (vol. 7, p. 266).

20. W. G. L. Randles, *The Empire of Monomotapa, from the Fifteenth to the Nineteenth Century,* trans. R. S. Roberts (Gwelo, Rhodesia: Mambo Press, 1981).

21. Sanson's map of the whole continent from 1656 shows "Butua" as a city within the Empire of Monomotapa (*L'Afrique en plusieurs cartes* [Paris: Chez l'Autheur, 1656]). D'Anville's map of 1727 appears to indicate that "Abutua" is a territory adjacent to Monomotapa (in Labat, *Nouvelle relation de l'Afrique occidentale* [Paris: Chez Theodore Le Gras, 1728], vol. 1), while a map of 1732, also by D'Anville, shows the "Royaume d'Abutua: peu connu où on tient qu'il y a des mines d'argent" (in Yussuf Kamal, *Monumenta cartographica Africae et Aegypti* [Cairo: n.p., 1927–37], vol. 5, map no. 1589). Butua also figures on maps of 1763, 1787, and 1822 (in Yussuf Kamal, nos. 1600, 1606, and 1621). The Cercle du livre précieux edition of *Aline et Valcour* includes two maps that show Butua: one signed by Robert de Vaugondy in 1749, another, unidentified, but appearing to be from the end of the eighteenth century (pp. 193, 241).

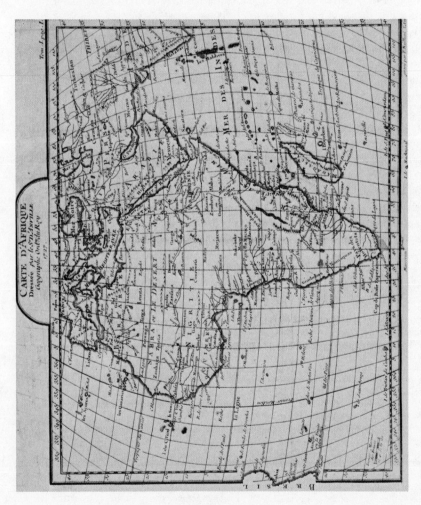

Figure 5. Jean-Baptiste d'Anville's map of Africa, from Jean-Baptiste Labat's *Nouvelle relation de l'Afrique occidentale* (Paris: T. Le Gras, 1728). Reproduced by permission of the Sterling Memorial Library, Yale University. Note "Abutua" at 40° longitude, 15° South latitude, near Benguela and between "Manamotapa" and "Giaga" (Jaga).

pedias and travel accounts, including those that Sade read, have almost nothing to say about it.[22] Sade seems to have deliberately picked one of those places about which, as Rousseau said, "we know nothing but the name." The advantages of this for a fictionalized account are obvious; but more pertinent to the exact status of "Butua" is Sade's apparently inaccurate choice of reference points: Benguela and the "kingdom of the Jagas." Benguela, a Portuguese seaport settlement in Angola since 1617, holds no mystery. But "the kingdom of the Jaga," the absolute counterpart to Butua in *Aline et Valcour,* about which masses of "information" were available to Sade, is now thought to have been nothing but a myth: "no such 'Jaga' ever existed outside the imaginations of missionaries, slave dealers, and Government officials who created these myths to justify or conceal their own activities in Africa."[23] Sade's placement of Butua between Benguela and the land of the "Jaga" thus becomes symbolic. Benguela is known, unexciting, and European; the Jaga are titillating and unknown but do not exist. Butua appears to have existed, but not in the way Sade described it. The effort to reach out into the unknown, the interior of Africa, and to promulgate a "récit intéressant" (both "interesting" and "advantageous") that will satisfy the reader ("Ceux qui aiment les voyages trouveront à se satisfaire") both produces the object and places it beyond the author's control.

The anthropological details are built on a foundation of fiction that swallows them up: their authenticity is certified by no one, or rather by that No One, our author, who is the only person, or nonperson, to have gone to Butua: "*Personne* n'est encore parvenu au royaume de Butua . . . ; notre auteur seul a pénétré dans ces climats barbares" ("Avis de l'éditeur"). The negative *personne,* no one, expands to become the sole determinant, the entire ground-

22. Neither Banier nor Démeunier mentions Butua; there is nothing in Diderot's *Encyclopédie,* although the article on Monomotapa asserts that the king of that empire "has under him many tributary princes." De Chévigny's *La Science des personnes de la cour* (Amsterdam: Chez les Frères Chatelain, 1713) lists Butua as one of the cities of Monomotapa (vol. 1, p. 214); the *Nouveau Dictionnaire historique géographique universel* (Basel: Chez Jean Rodolphe ImHof, 1766) shows "Butua, Royaume et ville d'Afrique dans le Monomotapa, sur la rivière Zambie" (p. 261).

23. Joseph C. Miller, "Requiem for the 'Jaga,' " *Cahiers d'Etudes Africaines* 13, no. 49 (1973): 121. It is certainly true that the "Jaga" were a catchall of evil and cruelty in the European imagination. Diderot's *Encyclopédie* describes the "Jaga" as a "peuple féroce, guerrier, et anthropophage, qui habite la partie intérieure de l'Afrique méridionale. . . . Nulle nation n'a porté si loin la cruauté et la superstition: en effet, ils nous présentent le phénomène étrange de l'inhumanité la plus atroce, autorisée et même ordonné par la législation. [Cf. Sade's Butua, in which "le libertinage devient loi."] . . . Ils n'ont point de demeure fixe, mais ils forment des camps volans . . . ; ils ne cultivent point la terre, la guerre est leur unique occupation." Their "lack of fixed dwelling" is emblematic of their status in the European mind, as a free-floating signifier. Sainville is eyewitness to a troop of Jaga returning from battle with the Butuans, "sadistically" tearing their prisoners limb from limb and devouring them (p. 186). It is also interesting to note that, according to recent scholarship, both "Butua" and "Jaga" may mean, etymologically, "foreigner" (Miller, "Requiem," p. 128; Randles, *Empire of Monomotapa,* p. 20).

ing of the novel.[24] Who has been to Butua? No one has: *No One,* who becomes the "exact and educated voyager who tells only what he has seen." Each succeeding realistic detail only digs the paradox a little deeper: just as the sources Sade actually cites contain relatively little information about Africa, so does this "author," who alone has been to Butua, disappear, leaving the story, which is wholly dependent on him, to proceed in the void.

Ultimately, narrative, like idolatry and libertinism, cannot "envelop" its objects completely, *Aline et Valcour* seems to tell us. Léonore later recounts in her own story: "I was told that gross material things could not envelop immaterial being . . . , that God could not be represented in an image . . . without worship becoming idolatrous" (*Oeuvres,* 5:118). But in a world where only representations are accessible, all worship is to a certain extent idolatry: loyalty to something one cannot have. Narration in *Heart of Darkness* and *Aline et Valcour* would seem to be an act of devotion to an object that cannot be totally enveloped, an act of faith in "the nightmare of your choice." By choosing "Africa" as the name for that object, these authors commit themselves to a referential stance that ultimately calls their act of reference into question.

24. Bakhtine cites a work of Latin literature, *Historia de Nemine* by Radulfus Glaber, a French monk: "the word *nemo* (nobody), which in Latin is used as a negation, was interpreted by Radulfus as a proper noun. For instance, in the Scriptures *nemo deum vidit* (nobody has seen God) in his interpretation became 'Nemo saw God.' Thus, everything impossible, inadmissible, inaccessible is, on the contrary, permitted for *Nemo*" (*Rabelais and His World,* pp. 413–14; this is also reminiscent of the Cyclops episode in the *Odyssey*). Bakhtine mentions the utopian dimension of this linguistic game, which brings to mind Pierre Favre's interesting but not very daring analysis of Butua as a "utopia of evil" in *Sade utopiste* (Paris: PUF, 1967), pp. 11–36. His is the only book-length study of *Aline et Valcour* to date.

6

Céline and the Night:
"Nothing to Report"

La nuit n'est pas parfaite, elle n'acceuille pas, elle ne s'ouvre
pas. Elle ne s'oppose pas au jour par le silence, le repos, la
cessation des tâches. Dans la nuit, le silence est parole, et il
n'est pas de repos.

—Maurice Blanchot,
L'Espace littéraire

Céline the Obscure

Si Céline est inconnu, il entend le rester. Ainsi lorsque, le 7
décembre 1932, *Marianne* publie les photos des éventuels
lauréats des prix, une place reste en blanc, celle de Céline.

—Yves Lavoinne

Laissez-moi dans l'ombre.

—Céline

If Africanist topoi in French literature involve writing on, within, and about
a blank space, the authors chosen here have each presented in their own way
an enigma, a critical blank to be filled in (or not). This was most evidently
the case with Rimbaud and Sade; it is also the case with "Céline," a name
covering over a problematical identity. Louis-Ferdinand Destouches made a
concerted effort to dissociate himself from the works of his pseudonym, to
leave himself blank and inscrutable in the annals of literary history. He is a
version of Sade's "no one": Céline "fashions a false face for himself . . . and
proceeds through his works dissimulated behind the masks of multiple characters, giving to each one of them limited views which are not properly his
own."[1] The enigma of Céline's biography, self-produced as a mixture of

1. Philip Stephen Day, *Le Miroir allégorique de Louis-Ferdinand Céline* (Paris: Klincksieck,
1974), p. 21. "Céline a toujours abusé ses biographes, laissant coexister dans ses écrits et dans
ses propos la vérité et le mirage . . . . L'énigme n'a pas arrêté de s'embrouiller à sa mort.
Lorsqu'on ouvre sa correspondance en vue d'effectuer des recoupements, on se perd dans un
dédale insensé. . . . Et comment situer l'oeuvre par rapport à l'écrivain?" (pp. 17–18). See J.
P. Dauphain and H. Godard, eds., *Cahiers Céline 1: Céline et l'actualité littéraire* (Paris:
Gallimard, 1976), p. 17: "Céline avait pensé, sous le couvert de pseudonym et moyennant
quelques précautions, mettre sa personne et son activité professionnelle à l'abri de toute exhibition
dans la presse." Quoting an interview with Céline: "Laissez-moi dans l'ombre. Ma mère même
ne sait pas que j'ai écrit ce livre, ça ne se fait pas dans la famille" (p. 22).

"truth and mirage," is not resolved by his correspondence, which is itself an "insane labyrinth" (Day, *Le Miroir*, pp. 17–18). The name of Céline is a mask draped over a face no one has seen; his identity is a question of difference; his *je* is an *autre*, a *nègre*. Those who choose to excuse Céline's involvement with fascism can refer to this labyrinth, ultimately, as a form of esthetic nihilism divorced from ideology. The "writer" is thereby excised from the "anti-Semite" (or racist), and the reading process is allowed to proceed in tranquillity.[2]

Along with the false name comes the peculiar status of Céline's texts. It is a little-known fact that the writings bearing his pseudonym are not wholly attributable to the hand of Louis Destouches, in that they were subject to extensive stylistic "correction" by others:

> [Céline] will not take an interest in his works from this point on and will refuse to read the galley proofs, not even letting anyone speak to him about them . . . . The typographers, confused by an unwonted punctuation, reinstate the periods and commas according to their own ideas, which are everyone's. The composition, the proofs, and the correction are started over again. Finally, at the last moment, the author can sign the indispensable "bon à tirer." He has seen nothing, read nothing, corrected nothing. For him, as he will say later, the typographical mutation makes the text lose all life.[3]

The editors of *Cahiers Céline 4: Lettres et premiers écrits d'Afrique* had the good judgment to print Céline as he had written, and a reading of those texts, with their highly unorthodox spelling, punctuation, and grammar ("Si vous n'avez rien de mieux affaire"),[4] can only make one wonder how the novels would read in an unretouched condition. Céline's refusal to be totally responsible for his text problematizes the idea of authorship and authority, for here is an author who apparently removed himself purposely from mastery and domination of his own meanings. He is another *nègre* or ghost-writer for himself, renouncing his work, surrendering it to others, in a fashion that our last author in this study, the African novelist Yambo Ouologuem, exploits

2. Day, *Miroir*, p. 167: "L'observation impartial est amené à conclure qu'il y a aussi loin du nihilisme de Céline dans *Bagatelles* à l'antisémitisme politique que la pensée nietzschéenne à la démagogie fanatique du nazisme. *Négligeons donc chez Céline l'antisémite pour ne plus considérer que l'écrivain*" (emphasis mine). Day has just referred to a quotation from Céline that illustrates the link between anti-Semitism and anti-black racism: "Le Juif est un nègre, la race sémite n'existe pas . . . ; le Juif n'est que le produit d'un croisement de nègres et de barbares asiates." The resemblance of that utterance to Gobineau calls to mind a similar defense of the text by its editor in the case of the *Essai sur l'inégalité des races humaines:* that Gobineau was not a "racist," he was a "poet" (ed. H. Juin [Paris: Belfond, 1967], p. xi).

3. Jean A. Ducourneau, ed., *Oeuvres de Louis-Ferdinand Céline*, 5 vols. (Paris: André Balland, 1966), 1:739. (Henceforth the notes in parentheses will refer to this edition of *Voyage*.)

4. *Cahiers Céline 4: Lettres et premiers écrits d'Afrique* (Paris: Gallimard, 1978), p. 19.

and reorients. How is the critic to say anything true about authors who so deliberately dissimulate their own truths?

The Endless Night

Voyage au bout de la nuit appeared in 1932, over 600 pages written half in proletarian argot, half in the belle-lettristic language of the novel:[5] a "monster" by Céline's own description.[6] If *Voyage* is (according to Paul Nizan) a book of "pure revolt," which can "lead anywhere" (quoted by Lavoinne, p. 9n), its lines are more or less those taken from the "real-life experiences" of L. F. Destouches, which are also those followed in *L'Eglise,* a play written before *Voyage* but published only in 1933 and never performed until 1973. Those three texts (including the "text" of Destouches' life) all follow the same seemingly haphazard path from the battlefields of World War I in Europe to colonial Africa to America and back again.

Voyage au bout de la nuit engages negativity in a way that is both reminiscent of and dissimilar to *Heart of Darkness. Voyage* is first of all linked to the tradition of travel accounts and to the novels (such as *Aline et Valcour, Gulliver's Travels,* and *Candide*) that imitate that genre. The voyage, whether to places imaginary or real, provides the basic armature of plot and progress. In stark contrast is this novel's name for the principle of negativity: *nuit* (night). Leaving aside for the moment what ramifications that word might acquire in the context of the novel, one should notice that its role in the title is ambiguous. One could be traveling to and thus beyond the edge or end of night into something different, such as day, or one could be traveling along, *at* the edge of night, along a boundary between dark and light, negative and positive ("sur les bords de cette nuit"; p. 127). The former interpretation is the more accepted one; the latter is the more interesting. This can make sense only within a reading of the word *nuit* itself in the novel.

The war, and the novel, begin for the narrator, Bardamu, when, sitting in a café, he is suddenly inspired to enlist in a regiment that is passing by in the street. The war will prove to be a movement toward solitude, disorientation, and darkness, a loss of perspective that creeps up slowly until it almost surrounds him, then changes direction. Darkness is the principal metaphor used to describe this progression, and "night" is the principal representative

5. Edmond Jaloux: "Le style est très inégal. Pourquoi M. Céline au début s'exprime-t-il comme un ouvrier qui monologue et dans un langage presque uniquement populaire, traversé d'argot, alors que, quelques pages plus loin, il reprend le langage d'un bon narrateur bourgeois?" (*Les Nouvelles littéraires,* December 10, 1932, quoted in Céline's *Oeuvres,* 1:796). Cf. Claude Lévi-Strauss: "Mais ce style compact et argotique qu'on dirait spécialement coulé pour la réalisation d'une oeuvre exceptionnelle, se marie parfois difficilement avec des formules et une écriture indices d'une pensée cultivée, bien éloignée de celle qui s'inscrit naturellement dans la langue des faubourgs" (*L'Etudiant socialiste,* January, 1933, quoted in *Oeuvres,* 1:808).
6. Yves Lavoinne, *"Voyage au bout de la nuit" de Céline* (Paris: Hachette, 1974), p. 5n.

of darkness. The war is a "dirty adventure" in the "darkness of these no-man's-lands" (p. 21). The passage that follows is an allegory of negativity, describing an experience similar to navigating toward the heart of darkness:

> A force de déambuler d'un bord de l'ombre à l'autre, on finissait par s'y reconnaître un petit peu, qu'on croyait du moins. . . . Dès qu'un nuage semblait plus clair qu'un autre, on se disait qu'on avait vu quelque chose. . . . Mais devant soi, il n'y avait de sûr que l'écho allant et venant, l'écho du bruit . . . qui vous étouffe, énorme, tellement qu'on en veut pas. . . . Je me disais toujours que la première lumière qu'on verrait ce serait celle du coup de fusil de la fin. [P. 21]

> By dint of ambling from one edge of the shadow to the other, you wound up knowing your way a little bit, or so you thought. . . . The minute one cloud looked brighter than another, you thought you had seen something. . . . But in front of you, the only sure thing was the coming and going of the echo, the echo of the noise . . . which smothered you, enormous, so much that you didn't want it to. . . . I always told myself that the first light we would see would be the rifle blast of the end.

Beginning and end, appearance and apparition, are confused. From that point on, images of darkness increase and come to have one dominant name: night.

> Mais bientôt les nuits, elles aussi, à leur tour, furent traquées sans merci. Il fallut presque toujours la nuit faire encore travailler sa fatigue, souffrir un petit supplément, rien que pour manger, pour trouver le petit rabiot de sommeil dans le noir. [P. 26]

> But soon the nights as well, in turn, were mercilessly hemmed in. It took almost the whole night to work through your fatigue, to pay a higher price, for nothing but to eat, to scrounge a little more sleep on the sly, in the blackness.

Night, practically speaking, is the refuge of those in "this profession of getting yourself killed" (p. 27), who must logically "flee the dawn" like vampires to avoid destruction: "We wound up looking forward to, desiring, the night. They fired on us less easily at night than in the day" (p. 26). But night, once it becomes an object of desire, takes strange forms and alters desire itself.

Hence the village named "Blackness": "Noirceur-sur-la-Lys." Bardamu is ordered to proceed "that night," "before daylight," to this "village of weavers, fourteen kilometers from the village where we were camped" (p.

28), to confirm the presence of the enemy. In the night, a voyage, perhaps a voyage to the "end" of night—but the passage ends with a pessimistic warning: "Il me sembla du coup partir en *voyage. Mais la délivrance était fictive*" ("I thought I was leaving on a journey. But the deliverance was fictive"; p. 28, emphasis mine). That fictive deliverance will nonetheless alternate with the night throughout the novel as the illusion of progress and hope, as *the "glow" Bardamu perceives on the way to a place called Blackness:*

> Noirceur-sur-la-Lys ça devait être encore à une heure de route au moins, quand j'aperçus une lueur bien voilée au-dessus d'une porte. Je me suis dirigé tout droit vers cette lueur. [P. 29]

> Noirceur-sur-la-Lys had to be at least another hour away by the road when I spied a glow, well veiled above a door. I headed straight for that glow.

At this point enters Robinson, Bardamu's alter ego, nemesis, bête noire, and savior, more a principle of change and gratuitous plot reversal than a character. Robinson appears briefly several times in the novel, at various points of maximum obscurity and loss; he is a creature of negativity, an agent of the night.

> —Faut nous dépêcher, qu'a ajouté ce Robinson. . . .
> C'est la nuit qu'il faut faire ça, le jour il y a plus d'amis. . . .
> Ce Robinson comptait donc sur la nuit pour nous sortir de là? . . .
> Il avait raison, Robinson, le jour était impitoyable, de la terre au ciel. . . . Alors il [le Maire de Noirceur] se mit à nous parler de l'intérêt général, *dans la nuit, là, dans le silence où nous étions perdus.* . . .
> Une longue raie grise et verte soulignait déjà au loin la crête du coteau, à la limite de la ville, dans la nuit; le Jour! Un de plus! Un de moins! Il faudrait essayer de passer à travers celui-là encore comme à travers les autres, devenues des espèces de cerceaux de plus en plus étroits, les jours, et tout remplis avec des trajectoires et des éclats de mitraille. [Pp. 34–36; emphasis mine]

> "Got to hurry up," added Robinson. . . . You've got to do this at night; in the day you've got no more friends. . . . So this Robinson was counting on the night to get us out of here? . . . He was right, was Robinson, the day was pitiless, from earth to sky. . . . Then [the mayor of Noirceur] started talking to us about the general scheme, there *in the night, in the silence where we were lost.* . . . A long gray and green stripe was already lighting up the distant crest of the hill, at the city limits, in the night; Day! One more! One less!

We would have to pass through this once again as through the others, like jumping through hoops, these days all filled with artillery and machine-gun fire.

The "journey to the end of night" has indeed led to "day," but a day that is only part of a larger night of which day is but a part, in which it is subsumed. The escape fashioned by Robinson is only a throwback to the war, in which "things and more things happened, which it isn't easy to tell about now, since people today would already be unable to understand them" (p. 66). But what is the point of this fall back into negativity, into "night"?

Perhaps no passage of modern criticism is more relevant to understanding Céline's night, and the nature of Africanist negativity in general, than this one from Maurice Blanchot's *L'Espace littéraire:*

> Dans la nuit, tout a disparu. C'est la première nuit. Là s'approche l'absence, le silence, le repos, la nuit. Là, . . . celui qui meurt va à la rencontre d'un mourir véritable, là s'achève et s'accomplit la parole dans la profondeur silencieuse qui la garantit comme son sens.
> Mais quand tout a disparu dans la nuit, "tout a disparu" apparaît. C'est l'*autre* nuit. La nuit est apparition du "tout a disparu." Elle est ce qui est pressenti quand les rêves remplacent le sommeil, quand les morts passent au fond de la nuit, quand le fond de la nuit apparaît en ceux qui ont disparu. Les apparitions, les fantômes et les rêves sont une allusion à cette nuit vide. C'est la nuit de Young, là où l'obscurité ne semble pas assez obscure, la mort jamais assez mort. Ce qui apparaît dans la nuit est la nuit qui apparaît, et l'étrangeté ne vient pas seulement de quelque chose d'invisible qui se ferait voir à l'abri et à la demande des ténèbres: l'invisible est alors ce qu'on ne peut cesser de voir. . . . Cette nuit n'est jamais la pure nuit. Elle est essentiellement impure. . . . Elle n'est pas la vraie nuit, elle est nuit sans vérité.[7]

In the night, everything has disappeared. This is the first night. Here absence approaches; silence, repose, night. Here . . . he who dies meets a true death, here the word is accomplished and finished in the silent depths that guarantee its meaning.

But when everything has disappeared, "everything has disappeared" appears. This is the *other* night. Night is the appearance of "everything has disappeared." It is that foreseen when dreams replace sleep, when the dead pass into the recesses of the night, when the recesses of the night appear in those who have disappeared. Apparitions, phantoms, and dreams are an allusion to this empty night. It is the night of Young, where darkness seems not dark

7. Maurice Blanchot, *L'Espace littéraire* (Paris: Gallimard, 1955), pp. 214–15.

enough, death not dead enough. That which appears in the night is the night appearing, and the strangeness does not come only from something invisible that would be seen in the shelter, and at the request, of the darkness: the invisible is then that which one cannot stop seeing. . . . This night is never pure night. It is essentially impure. . . . It is not true night, it is night without truth.

Africanist discourse has been from the beginning a question of incomplete, inefficient negativity, of that "glow" of desire drawing one into a darkness that was supposed to be total. Blanchot's "other" night speaks of the impossibility of total negativity, obscurity, darkness, or emptiness: it is "this *empty* night," which apparitions continue to fill ("From the moment one cloud seemed brighter than another, you thought you had seen something"). The general Africanist preoccupation with nullity and emptiness, we have seen, is altered by the necessity to thematize, to write "soft wax," "irreflection," "fetishism," or "night" instead of writing nothing at all. These "apparitions, phantoms, and dreams," in Blanchot's vocabulary, are the *reflection of that which has nothing to reflect* (thinking once more of Gobineau's moon); they are the persistent residue of form in the evocation of formlessness.

Blanchot's prose shows better than any other how, once negativity is totalized, that totality is necessarily reinscribed in a *discourse:* so I would interpret his use of the quotation marks, " 'Tout a disparu' apparaît." From that point on, reading becomes no longer a question of projected absolutes (blackness, blankness, darkness) but of the rigorous incompatibility between those absolutes and the system that projects them, between the "invisible" and "sight." Thus, as in Baudelaire's "Le Cygne," the invisible object, Africa, behind the "immense wall of fog," becomes in Blanchot's words "that which one cannot stop seeing."

If Céline's "night" has no real end, if any deliverance from it is "fictive," its similarity to Blanchot's "other night" of nonoppositional negativity, "essentially impure," could provide a useful perspective. The journey described thus far has gone to the end of night but proved to be caught in a system without ends or beginnings, without the guarantee of meaning that Blanchot's "first night" holds. "Everything has disappeared" will consequently reappear in another guise, this time an African one.[8]

8. The comparison of the rarefied metalanguage of Blanchot with the down-to-earth thematics of Céline may be reproached for contaminating the former with the latter, for soiling the purity of theory with the mud of interpretation. Breaking down that distinction has been fundamental to the procedure of this study; it reenacts the Africanist habit of giving positive form to that which should have none: the void. The desire for pure theory is inevitably involved in some way with thematic content; the coincidental occurrence of the word "night" in the "nonthematic" text of Blanchot's and in the "nontheoretical" text of Céline's is my pretext for violating a barrier that has been fortified by resistance to theory more than by the demands of theory itself.

In Bambola-Bragamance

Je soigne le plus de nègres possible, quoique je ne sois
nullement persuadé de leur utilité.
—Letter to Simone Saintu, October 12, 1916

The Africanist passage of *Voyage au bout de la nuit* uses "Africa" as another
name for its specific brand of negativity and continues, through concomitant
sets of images and assumptions, the baggage of early twentieth-century colonialism. The peculiarity that *Voyage* offers to the Africanist topos is a series
of observations on the insufficient distinction between material objects and
human beings, the failure of appearances to maintain barriers between the
immanent and the transcendent: "Over there, it's not only the men who are
hysterical; things get into it too" (p. 94). But prior to developing this point,
we will look at the plot situation as it moves into the Africanist context.

> Nous voguions vers l'Afrique, la vraie, la grande: celle des in-
> sondables forêts, des miasmes délétères, des solitudes inviolées, vers
> les grands tyrans nègres vautrés aux croisements de fleuves qui n'en
> finissent plus. Pour un paquet de lames "Pilett" j'allais trafiquer
> avec eux des ivoires longs comme ça, des oiseaux flamboyants, des
> esclaves mineures. C'était promis. La vie quoi! Rien de commun
> avec cette Afrique décortiquée des agences et des monuments, des
> chemins de fer et des nougats. Ah non! Nous allions nous la voir
> dans son jus, la vraie Afrique! Nous les passagers boissonnants de
> l'*Amiral Bragueton*. [P. 84]

> We rolled toward Africa, the real one, the great one: the one of
> unfathomable forests, of noxious miasmas, of inviolate solitudes,
> toward great Negro tyrants sprawling at the junctions of rivers that
> have no end. For a pack of "Pilett" razors I was going to trade with
> them for ivory tusks as long as that, flamboyant birds, under-age
> slaves. It was promised. Life, eh? Nothing to do with that watered-
> down Africa of companies and monuments, of railroads and almond
> cakes. Oh no! We were going to see it in the raw, the real Africa!
> We, the drunken passengers of the *Admiral Bragueton*.[9]

The enthusiastic (if ironic) "glow" of "truth," of the "true Africa," is
the illusion of escape that keeps the novel moving from episode to episode.
Voyage is not a novel about deliverance, and Bardamu's will is not always
the agency of change (as when he is taken to America as a captive), but he
sets off for Africa with the express purpose of setting himself to rights: "so

9. That "real" Africa is thus a constituted "image" put together from literature. By the time
Céline goes to Africa, a whole set of recognizable phrases and assumptions can come into play
in a way that was not possible at Rimbaud's period. For example, Céline writes in a letter that
he finds himself in "le tréfond de la plus noire Afrique" (*Cahiers 4*, p. 166).

that I could try and set myself up again in the colonies," in Africa, "where a bit of temperance and good behavior were enough to get you a position immediately" ("Pour que j'essaie de me refaire aux colonies . . . où, m'assurait-on, il suffisait de quelque tempérance et d'une bonne conduite pour se faire tout de suite une situation"; p. 83). In his letters from Africa, Céline wrote of a feeling of "great, total, absolute freedom," of being saved from anguish by his "great solitude."[10] Yet at the same time he found himself to be in the "antechamber of Hell" (*Cahier* 4, p.38). The "true" Africa toward which Bardamu now sails is prepackaged in his imagination with the same dual potential: the promise both of "life"and of a deleterious, unfathomable threat to life.

Bardamu is rowed to the African shore by "a shadow," an African "whose darkness [*obscurité*] concealed from me almost entirely his features and movements" (p. 92). What is to be found in the colony of "Bambola-Bragamance" is a portrait of Europeans in a state of decadence, "croaking off under the sun" in one of two ways: "getting fat or dying skin on bone." French people, awash in their own silliness, conducting nightly "fever contests" ("Tiens, j'ai trente-neuf!"), have devised various methods for bilking the Africans. The satire is double-edged, with demeaning portraits dealt out to both the colonizer and the colonized: "The natives barely functioned without being cudgeled—they preserve that bit of dignity—whereas the whites, perfected by public education, go along by themselves."[11] If the Africans are "shadows" that hardly exist, the Europeans are on their way toward that state, *falling away from* the constructs of civilization (the etymological sense of decadence): they "melt worse than butter." If they are becoming "hysterical," it is through this process of absurd and pathetic loss, of coming unstuck ("quelques blanches ci et là . . . que le climat décollait bien davantage encore que les hommes" ["a few white women here and there . . . whom the climate unglued even more than the men"; p. 110]).

"Unsound methods" on the part of a European who has fallen apart at a station upriver, and the long symbolic voyage "back" or up to his post: this is the theme from *Heart of Darkness* that *Voyage au bout de la nuit* reworks in its fashion. The whys and wherefores of Bardamu's assignment to the bush post are never made terribly clear; a vague imperative drives him: "I *should have to* travel upstream to get to the fine middle of my forest" ("Je *devrais* remonter pour atteindre, en barque, le beau milieu de ma forêt"; p. 111, emphasis mine). In the meantime he stops at *Topo,* a place named Place

10. *Cahiers 4,* p. 43: "Joignez à ce charmant tout, que je dois vivre exclusivement sur le pays c'est-à-dire à la nègre et vous aurez un enviable tableau de mon existence—Elle comporte cependant quelques compensation l'absence absolu de commentaires sur ma conduite—et la grande, totale absolue liberté" (*sic*).

11. For an analysis of the relations between the races in *Voyage,* see Henri Mitterand, "Le Discours colonial dans 'Le Voyage au bout de la nuit,' " *La Pensée* 184 (December, 1975): 80–88.

(Greek *topos*), an empty place-holder with no *raison d'être:* "No one came to Topo. There was no reason to come to Topo" ("On ne venait pas à Topo. Il n'y avait aucune raison pour venir à Topo"; p. 111). That "no one" and that lack of reason are of course bound to take shape as the problem itself, as the nullity to which Africanist narration dedicates itself. In fact, there are two "writers" at Topo: Lieutenant ("place-holder") Grappa and Sergeant Alcide, a sort of Tweedledum and Tweedledee association, who, living in the void, "Prepared in advance many reports of 'Nothing to report' " ("beaucoup d'états 'Néant' "), which are promptly filed with the governor general. The point is that they choose, with perfect faith in their nightmare, to file the word "nothing" rather than filing nothing at all.[12]

But Topo is not Bardamu's destination; he must still travel ten days upriver to the "almost theoretical dwelling place" (p. 121) of the man he is to replace, who will turn out to be Robinson.

The superficial similarity of plot between *Voyage* and *Heart of Darkness* is a sign of the common ground on which they are working, the problems they describe. If *Heart of Darkness* works by condensation, making something out of nothing and remaining faithful to it as to a fetish, then *Voyage* does the same but tells the other side of the story as well: if nothing can become a thing (a report of "Nothing to report"; an "unreadable report"), then things can become nothing again; and people can do both.[13] The Africanist section of *Voyage au bout de la nuit* is made up of constant metamorphoses of humans, animals, and objects along both of those axes. If one can discern a pattern among the utterances of *Voyage* it is this: that Europeans, who exist prior to their description as constituted selves, break down into their component parts and melt away in the tropics; that blacks, on the other hand, are unto themselves nothing but "shadows" (p. 93), "*pieces of the night* turned hysterical" (p. 123; emphasis mine), as Robinson will say. Things, meanwhile, work in both directions, becoming both "hysterical" and null (see pp. 94, 110, 129). The depiction of blacks is similar to that in *Heart of Darkness* in that they are "shadows," "bundles of acute angles" in the background, handled with a few thumbnail sketches and pathetic anecdotes. It is the discombobulation of the Europeans that occupies center stage.

12. A meticulous concern for the writing of reports is a commonplace in Africanist literature. The colonial official, living in the midst of nothingness, clings to the necessity of form. *Heart of Darkness:* " 'When one has got to make correct entries, one comes to hate those savages . . .' "; "In the steady buzz of flies the homeward-bound agent was lying flushed and insensible; the other, bent over his books, was making correct entries of perfectly correct transactions; and fifty feet below the doorstep I could see the still tree-tops of the grove of death" (Signet Classics ed., pp. 84–85). It is an "unreadable report" written by Kurtz that serves as the "pretext" for *Heart of Darkness*.

13. Cf. Lévi-Strauss, quoted in Céline's *Oeuvres,* 1:807: "On pense à Conrad, mais au Conrad dont les brumes de poésie et de mystère se seraient coagulées et solidifiées en arêtes coupantes, où les aventuriers sont plus simplement des exploiteurs et des escrocs, les indigènes secrets, des imbéciles, et le cerveau des Européens, troublé par le climat et l'atmosphère exotique, une masse moisissante d'alcool, de vérole et de fièvre."

Sous le climat de Fort-Gono, les cadres européens *fondaient* pire que du beurre. Un bataillon y devenait comme un morceau de sucre dans du café, plus on le regardait, moins on en voyait . . . .

On avait à peine le temps de les voir *disparaître,* les hommes, les jours et les choses dans cette verdure, ce climat, la chaleur et les moustiques. Tout y passait, c'était dégoutant, par bouts, par phrases, par membres, par regrets, par globules, ils se *perdaient* au soleil, *fondaient* dans le torrent de la lumière et des couleurs, et le goût et le temps avec, tout y passait. Il n'y avait que l'angoisse étincelante dans l'air. [Pp. 108, 110; emphasis mine]

In the climate of Fort-Gono, the European administrators *melted* worse than butter. A battalion would get like a cube of sugar in coffee; the more you looked at it, the less you would see . . . .

You hardly had time to see them *disappear,* the men, the days, and the things in this vegetation, this climate, the heat, and the mosquitoes. Everything passed, it was disgusting, by bits and by phrases, by sorrows, by globules; they *got lost* in the sun, *melted* in the torrent of light and of colors, taste and time going with them, everything passed by. There was only anguish sparkling in the air. [Emphasis mine]

Europeans are the appearance of that which is disappearing; Africans are the appearance of that which has already disappeared (pieces of the *night*). The specific role of Robinson is to appear, then disappear. His "appearance"—in both the narrative and the perceptual senses—is grudging, spooky, and brief. Arrived at Robinson's "almost theoretical dwelling place," Bardamu describes the slow process of identifying the strange man before him. Robinson is first a "figure": "a decidedly adventurous figure, a figure with well-etched angles" ("une figure décidémment aventureuse, une figure à angles bien tracés"; p. 122). His well-defined etchings nonetheless leave Robinson a purely enigmatic figure at this point. The stream of bizarre verbiage that the figure produces, riddled with points of suspension, is not equal to Kurtz's primal cry "The horror! The horror!" But Robinson's madness itself turns around one figure, the sounds of night, when perspective is lost.

"Le jour c'est la chaleur, mais la nuit, c'est le bruit qui est le plus difficile à supporter . . . . C'est les bestioles du bled qui se coursent pour s'enfiler ou se bouffer, j'en sais rien, mais c'est ce qu'on m'a dit . . . . Et les plus bruyants parmi, c'est encore les hyènes!" "Les nègres, vous vous en rendrez tout de suite compte, c'est tout crevés et tout pourris! . . . Dans la journée c'est accroupi, on croirait pas ça capable de se lever seulement pour aller pisser le long d'un arbre et puis aussitôt qu'il fait nuit, va te faire voir! Ça devient tout vicieux! tout nerfs! tout hystérique! Des morceaux de la nuit tournés hystériques! Voilà ce que c'est que les nègres, moi j'vous le dis! Enfin, des dégueulasses . . . . Des dégénérés quoi! . . ." [Pp. 122–23]

"In the daytime it's the heat, but at night it's the noise that's the hardest to put up with. . . . It's the vermin from that hole of a village who run around and stab each other or eat each other, who knows, but that's what I've heard. . . . And the noisiest of all are the hyenas!" "The niggers, you'll see right away, they're all dead and rotting! . . . In the daytime they're all crouching, you wouldn't think they'd be able to get up and piss on a tree trunk, and then, the minute it's night, watch out! They get all vicious! all nerves! all hysterical! Pieces of the night turned hysterical! That's what the niggers are, I'm telling you! Slobs, anyway . . . Degenerates!"

Bardamu will refer to this man as "ce ténébreux," the dark one, and as a jackal and a pirate who blurs all sense of reality: "Je n'étais pas très sûr que ce soit réel tout ce qu'il me racontait là" ("I wasn't very sure that all of what he told me was real"; p. 124). The substantiality of "this African hell," of "this night with all its monsters," increases: in Blanchot's terms, the presence of absence becomes impossible not to see. "Monsters," etymologically, are things "shown," signs (Latin *monstrum*, sign, warning); here they are condensations of the amorphous night. As Robinson takes shape and comes together within Bardamu's consciousness and memory, so does Africa.

Learning that the man's name is Robinson, Bardamu begins a difficult process of recollection, described as if it were the penetration of a jungle. "Traveling back," the fundamental Africanist verb, is applied to Bardamu's past and his effort to recollect it. The fact that the episode happens in Africa, at an isolated post to which Bardamu has just "traveled back," is the happy coincidence behind Céline's contribution to Africanist writing. As in *Heart of Darkness,* travel in Africa is linked to "traveling back" into one's own past and into the primordial history of man ("There were moments when one's past came back to one . . . like traveling back to the earliest beginnings of the world," *Heart of Darkness,* p. 102).

La figure de ce Robinson m'apparut encore une fois avant que j'éteignisse, voilée par cette résille d'insectes. C'est pour cela peut-être que ses traits s'imposèrent plus subtilement à ma mémoire, alors qu'auparavant ils ne me rappelaient rien de précis. Dans l'obscurité il continuait à me parler pendant que *je remontais dans mon passé* avec le ton de sa voix comme un appel devant les portes des années et puis des mois, et puis de mes jours pour demander où j'avais bien pu le rencontrer cet être-là. *Mais je ne trouvai rien.* On ne me répondait pas. *On peut se perdre en allant à tatons parmi les formes révolues.* C'est effrayant ce qu'on en a des choses et des gens qui ne bougent plus dans son passé. . . .

Je cherchais à l'identifier ce Robinson . . . .
C'est le nom même de Robinson qui me tracassait surtout. [P. 126; emphasis mine]

Robinson's face appeared to me once more before I turned out the light; it was veiled by a fabric of insects. Perhaps that is why his features were pressed on my memory more subtly, while before they had brought back nothing specific. In the darkness he went on talking to me while *I traveled back in my past* with the tone of his voice like a summoning before gates of the years, and then of the months, and then of my days to wonder where I could have met that being. *But I found nothing.* I was not answered. *One can get lost while groping among the dead shapes.* It's frightening what one has of things and people who no longer move in one's past. . . . I tried to identify this Robinson. . . . It was the very name of Robinson that bothered me above all.

The terminology of memory and perception (*figure, traits, rappeler, passé, appel*) mingles with that of travel in the jungle (*obscurité, remonter, se perdre, à tatons, formes révolues*). Identifying the Robinson of Noirceur-sur-la-Lys, "whom I had accompanied along *the edges of that night*," with the half-crazed Robinson of the jungle, bringing those two together, is thus a way of Bardamu's finding a lost part of himself at the farthest corner of the earth. Robinson is also so intricated in the Africanist scene that this process of "identifying" him takes on a broader significance, as an act transcending the immense wall of Memory (again, "Le Cygne" comes to mind). The tone of Robinson's voice is the lure this time, drawing Bardamu in to grope among the things and people of his past.

But the moment at which Bardamu succeeds in breaking through the wall of memory and brings the object into presence again is also the moment when that object *disappears*. Robinson, now identified, has already absconded, taking with him all objects of value.

Ce nom de Robinson finit cependant à force de m'entêter par me révéler un corps, une allure, une voix même que j'avais connus. . . . Et puis au moment où j'allais pour de bon céder au sommeil, l'individu entier se dressa, devant mon lit, *son souvenir je le saisis, pas lui bien sûr,* mais le souvenir précisément de ce Robinson, l'homme de Noirceur-la-Lys, lui, là-bas en Flandres, que j'avais accompagné *sur les bords de cette nuit* où nous cherchions ensemble un trou pour s'échapper à la guerre et puis encore plus tard à Paris. . . *Tout est revenu.* [P. 127; emphasis mine]

That name of Robinson, after I had persisted, finally revealed to me a body, a posture, even a voice that I had known. . . . And then at

the moment when I was just going to fall asleep for good, the whole
individual stood up, before my bed, the memory of him I grasped,
not him of course, but the memory exactly of that Robinson, the
man of Noirceur-sur-la-Lys, that one, over in Flanders, the one I
had gone with along the edges of that night when we were looking
for a hole where we could escape from the war and then later in
Paris. . . . Everything came back.

Immediately Bardamu calls to Robinson: there is "no answer." Bardamu is
alone, Robinson has "disappeared" (p. 129). Two critical phrases in the
passage above show the significance of that juncture where "everything" has
reappeared before disappearing again. The first is a rewriting of the title: "sur
les bords de cette nuit" ("on/along the edges of that night"), which makes
explicit the potential in the title of a night from which there is no escape
because it has no distinct boundaries; its "edge" is a fiction of deliverance
and hope. The second important phrase is a rewriting, so to speak, of Blanchot,
in which positive and negative are reversed: "Tout est revenu" instead of
"Tout a disparu." Allowing oneself to carry the paraphrase through, one
would get: "Quand tout est revenu, 'Tout est revenu' ne revient pas" ("When
everything has returned, 'Everything has returned' does not return"). On the
theoretical level, this means that the positive instead of the negative is totalized, then reinscribed in a discourse ("'Tout est revenu'") which imposes
the loss of the object that has been found. "Tout est revenu" is like "Tout
est allégorie": its absolutism cannot be stable; it places an unbearable strain
on the workings of its own expression. On the thematic level, this means that
Robinson and all that he represents—which is here named no less than "everything"—once recaptured, immediately disappears. Robinson cannot be circumscribed, identified, or held down; once he has returned in memory, he
will already be gone in fact. He is like the beasts of Céline's forest, through
which Bardamu is carried on a stretcher: "the moment one approached the
place of all their noise, nobody was there" (p. 132). The moment at which
everything has appeared in clarity is only a discursive precursor to loss and
disappearance, to "night": "I no longer tried to recognize the real among
the absurd things of my fever" (p. 132). The marriage of the real and the
absurd continues as Bardamu is carried out of the jungle into the Spanish
colony of San Tapeta, where he is given over to a priest, who sells him to
the captain of a slave-galley bound for New York. Thus ends the Africanist
section of *Voyage au bout de la nuit*.

What "returns" then? To what does one "travel back" in Africanist narrative?
For Céline, "the true Africa" is a place beyond truth, a twilight zone where
reality and hallucination mingle: "This night is never pure night . . . [nor]
the true night; it is night without truth" (Blanchot). The "hysteria" of things

and people, the appearances of things that have already disappeared, the reports of "nothing to report": these are the signs and portents (the monsters) of an insufficient negativity, incapable of maintaining barriers or of imposing silence. The texts we have read in this study have all flirted with nothingness, played a game of brinksmanship with pure negativity. The particularity of the narrative texts is to depict a progression toward that ultimate state of anteriority or blankness as a voyage. But at the end of that voyage one finds that the night has no end and no beginning; from the moment it is given a name, it "turns hysterical," constantly shuttling between appearance and disappearance, between "nothing to report" and nothing itself. Africanist figures are produced by the difference between those two versions of negativity.

When the European novel "visits" Africa, as in *Heart of Darkness, Aline et Valcour,* and *Voyage au bout de la nuit,* its inherent involvement with time and progress meets the Other of itself, a resistant, inert core. On the one hand, a presence "traveling back," "recollecting," "penetrating," and of course, writing. On the other, that place and those people outside of evolution, those "barbarous climes," those "shadows of ourselves," "pieces of the night," not completely containable in a discourse that insists on progress. The incongruity between the two forms the profile of the European Africanist novel.

Africanist writers, while working through problems of negativity, have coincidentally raised questions about their own authority, the stable identity of their writing presence. Writing about an Other, they each in their own way have become a sort of Other in relation to their own work—as we have seen, a *nègre*. The last author in this study, an African novelist, is one who seizes the irony of being a *nègre,* in both senses of the word, to add a new dimension to Africanist discourse.

7

Dis-figuring Narrative: Plagiarism and Dismemberment in Yambo Ouologuem's *Le Devoir de violence*

At its extreme, the myth of the Negro, the idea of the Negro, can become the decisive factor of an authentic alienation.
—Frantz Fanon, *Black Skin, White Masks*

The African and the Novel

Time can become constitutive only when the bond with the transcendental home has been severed.
—Georg Lukács, *The Theory of the Novel*

If the rise of the European novel is tied to the rise of the bourgeoisie,[1] it must also be tied to the rise of colonialism, the relationship with those exotic countries that supply raw materials destined to be, in Baudelaire's words, "marvelously worked and fashioned." The crude, unredeemed nature of the primitive element that makes it unable to "evolve" on its own also makes it perfect in a scheme where progress meets stasis and where the former is imposed on the latter by an outside agency: this is colonialism. In literary terms, the novel is arguably the genre that imposes "progress," the evolutionary conception of time, where before there was only "inertia." The relationship between this genre and its not completely digestible raw material is, as we have seen in reading Sade, Conrad, and Céline, central to the European novel written about Africa. Those three novels took advantage of

---

1. See Ian Watt, *The Rise of the Novel* (Berkeley: University of California Press, 1960), chap. 2, "The Reading Public and the Rise of the Novel." On the idea of progress in the interpretation of the novel, see Georg Lukács, *The Theory of the Novel,* trans. Anna Bostock (London: Merlin Press, 1971), p. 71: "The novel is the art-form of virile maturity, in contrast to the normative childlikeness of the epic (the drama form, being in the margin of life, is *outside the ages of man* even if these are conceived as *a priori* categories or normative stages). . . . The novel, in contrast to other genres whose existence resides within the finished form, appears as *something in process of becoming*" (emphasis mine). The significance of those "ages of man" need not be embellished.

the difference between their genre's penchant for progress, for "travel," and the Africanist material depicted as outside or prior to linear time. But the particularity of those works, unlike more mediocre colonial novels, was to show progress stymied rather than imposed.

What happens when Africa "writes back," when the people who previously played shadow-like roles in European literature take up a discourse of their own? Is this the moment when the Other is perfectly wedded to language, when raw material and finished expression coincide without violence? Such questions assume that the African novel will address itself to the concerns posed by the European discourse of Africanism. While the new African genre will come to be explicitly concerned with forging an authentic voice for itself, the inherent irony is, of course, that this discourse of one's own is written in the language of the Other. The novel is that which alienates the African from his own language, his own past; it will be both a barrier and a medium of retrieval. But in certain literary productions of the colonial period, it is as if a single discourse imposed itself, combining the French language, the genre of the novel, the European image of Africa, and colonialist ideology.

In *Le Fils du fétiche,* a novel by David Ananou, European religious values are espoused as the sign of progress and evolution away from "this very curable ill which glowers over the African continent,"[2] i.e., fetishism. Conversion to Christianity and the break with "ancestral conceptions" are necessary to "emancipate" Africa. Ananou uses the verb *émanciper,* but *affranchir* would be more suitable, because becoming free in this ideology is synonymous with losing your difference, becoming "Frank, free," French. Ananou asks, "What good is an emancipation of people still completely faithful to fetishistic practices?" (p. 216), and he warns that "the foreigners are watching our performance and are awaiting results": "Let us purify our customs . . . by dropping everything trivial and idolatrous. Let us put some light in our practices. Obscurantism is not favorable to progress" (p. 217). The terms of *Le Fils du fétiche* would be completely familiar to Charles de Brosses. It is in the novel that this story of imposed progress is told; it is the novel that serves the literary imposition of progress, i.e., colonization.[3]

Ananou's discourse might be compared to that of the domesticated versions of Aniaba and Zaga-Christ, in which otherness is obliterated in favor of

---

2. David Ananou, *Le Fils du fétiche* (Paris: Nouvelles Editions Latines, 1955), p. 9.

3. The fact that the novel is seen to be the depiction of change and progress makes it suitable for the importation of "maturity" (see the quotation from Lukács in note 1); the search for something "outside the ages of man" was more the concern of Negritude *poetry,* which is now being reproached for an idealized vision of the African past: "Le concept de la 'négritude' concerne plutôt les éléments permanents de la tradition" (Robert Pageard, "Individu et Société: La vie traditionnelle dans la littérature de l'Afrique noire d'expression française," *Revue de littérature comparée* 3–4 [July–December 1974]: 421). See "Wole Soyinka: 'La négritude ne me satisfait pas, je lui préfère l'africanisme,'" interview in *Jeune Afrique* 544 (June 8, 1971); Stanislas Adotevi, *Négritude et Négrologues* (Paris: Union générale d'éditions, 1972).

harmony. Zaga-Christ's epitaph should serve as a warning in approaching African literature: "Ci-gît le roi d'Ethiopie / L'original ou la copie" ("Here lies the king of Ethiopia / The original or the copy"). The question of originality has been a preoccupation of European Africanists for centuries: the supposed "earliest beginnings of the world," the "perpetual childhood," is a state of *origin* that Africanist discourse *desires*. In their radically divergent avatars, Aniaba and Zaga-Christ were made to either reflect or refute that desire. Ananou's discourse, by "copying" European discourse, addressed itself to European questions in terms that Europe would recognize as its own. In order to redeem Africa from its originary state, Ananou had to *copy* a discourse that put Africa there in the first place. His novel illustrates the type of conundrum in which African literature can get involved once a European question is asked of it. As with Chinese handcuffs, the more you struggle to get out, the more you are stuck.

The African novel in general is preoccupied with its own originality and authenticity, as well it might be for a genre imported from and usually edited in Europe and written in European languages. Thus, although there is no reason why the African novel should address any of the same questions that the European Africanist novel addresses, the very desire to break away and negate can lead African discourse back to certain ancient European preoccupations, namely, that of the origin and the copy. "Africa" is often used as a figure for a lost origin in African novels, as it is in European ones: the comparison of the two remains to be written. My purpose here is to look at one novel that consciously engages itself in the cross-cultural and interliterary "zone of interferences" between the two continents and does so not to forge a synthetic response but to exaggerate and undermine the whole tradition we have been reading. Yambo Ouologuem's *Le Devoir de violence* is not a work that can be held up as the African "answer" to the European Africanist tradition or as a work completely and authentically detached from the tradition. It is a negative response if, by "negative," it is understood that no true contradiction takes place, only a brazen act of trifling with the idols of literary creation, respecting the taboos of neither the African nor the European literary establishment. The problem is that Ouologuem engages the European Africanist tradition and leads one to expect a positive repudiation and refutation of it. My purpose here will be to show that it is not on the thematic level that Ouologuem's "answer" should be sought but in the symbolics of writing itself.

In the early 1960s, four hundred years after Zaga-Christ, Yambo Ouologuem, a student from Mali, arrived in Paris. He studied at the Ecole Normale Supérieure (roughly equivalent to being baptized by Bossuet), and his first and only novel was published in 1968. Hailed by *Le Monde* as a "great African novel," *Le Devoir de violence* was seen as a welcome antidote to the "savannas of pseudo-lyricism," the "complacency" of the African novel. This was not only a good novel; it was a "true" novel, opposed to others that must have been false. Indeed, it was "the first African novel worthy of the name."[4] *Le Devoir de violence* would thus be literally the original African novel. From *Le Monde* to the American *Today Show* on television, Ouologuem's success redounded, and his novel received the 1968 Prix Renaudot. The adulation began to be offset, however, by two objections: some Africans had found the book ideologically offensive, its violence and pessimism too open to anti-African interpretations, and some critics had begun to find an excessive amount of "borrowing" (the polite quotation marks showing that they didn't want to call it outright plagiarism). Confrontation of *Le Devoir de violence* with other texts, from the Bible to André Schwartz-Bart's *Le Dernier des justes* (1959) and Graham Greene's *It's a Battlefield* (1934), revealed a tissue of quotations, translations, and incorporations, which, depending on your point of view, would be either an "original" and creative exercise in intertextuality or "copied," plagiarized, tainted with crime. The ensuing *succès de scandal* was proportional to the initial *succès d'estime*. The literary establishment had been duped, and it might well have buried *Le Devoir de violence* under Zaga-Christ's epitaph.

The question of originality and plagiarism, once posed, generates a discourse with only one axis, that of truth and falsehood, paternity and kidnapping, white and black. It will be my contention that *Le Devoir de violence* cuts across those categories with its "operative gymnastics of writing" and that the continual rocking of those binary questions has precluded another reading of the novel: as an assault on European assumptions about writing and originality. Plagiarism as a problem in literary criticism tends to elicit two responses: either an accusation of criminality or a recuperation as originality. *Le Devoir de violence,* both in its narrative method and in its narrated content, posits destructive violence and theft as origin itself.

Plagiarism, Legally

> There is no more legitimate or respectable right than that of an
> author over his work, the fruit of his labor.
>
> —Leopold II

Identity of the Text

Copyright is a defense between one literary body and another, and plagiarism is a violation of that defense. To own a copyright is to delimit a certain sequence of words, sentences, and paragraphs from other sequences that might infringe on the integrity of the first. The right of the text is to not be copied

4. Matthieu Galey, "Un grand roman africain," *Le Monde,* October 12, 1968.

or reproduced, to remain identical to itself. At the same time, writers on plagiarism also emphasize that "there is nothing new under the sun," that the author's rights apply only to "creations of form and not to ideas."[5] It is form that must be original; no one can own an idea. Form is fortified and defended, often in military metaphors: the French Société des Gens de Lettres takes as its object, "aside from the safeguard of the interests of its members, the defense of French language and thought" (Françon, p. 93). What is defended is thus the very identity of the sole creator, the father of the text.

Plagiarism is kidnapping, a false fatherhood. The *Oxford English Dictionary* points to the Latin *plagiarus,* "one who abducts the child or slave of another, a kidnapper; a seducer; also . . . a literary thief." In 1613, Samuel Purchas wrote, "In the time of his childhood, he was by some Plagiary stolne away from his friends." The plagiarized text is likewise abducted; the plagiarist then passes himself off as its creator, although he is only a thief. Hence one kidnapping engenders another: the true creator is entitled to "begin by having the work seized" (Françon, p. 95) in order to restore the proper state of identity and noncontradiction.

Between the identity of the text and the crime of plagiarism, certain observations tend to blur the distinction. The author's rights apply only to form, not content, yet *Le Devoir de violence* was accused of plagiarism *in translation.* When a passage from Graham Greene's *It's a Battlefield* was printed alongside a passage from *Le Devoir,* the latter was found to be "a loose but stylish version of the other."[6] Translation would normally seem to involve the total transformation of a text, precluding unitary responsibility. Yet the author's rights are recognized as applying to translations, supposing that form is somehow limited not to the actual words but to the sequence of their differences. Translation in the physical sense involves moving the object intact to a different place ("his remains were translated"), and that is the sense in which plagiarism can occur in translation. If, in the passage from Greene, we take the author's rights as applying to his series of referents, then Ouologuem did kidnap and reproduce a literary object. But if literary productions are more than referential, then the fact of translation, and of "loose" translation, would introduce such differences of connotation, flavor, and culture that plagiarism would not be conceivable.

It's a Battlefield	*Le Devoir de violence*
(London: Heinemann, 1934)	(Paris: Seuil, 1968)
The kitchen was like a snow-drift with its white casement and white dresser and white	La cuisine évoquait un paysage de rêve, avec ses fenêtres blanches, son buffet blanc, son

5. André Françon, *La Propriété littéraire et artistique* (Paris: PUF, 1970), p. 9.
6. *Times Literary Supplement,* May 5, 1972, p. 525.

table and enamelled gas stove
and its deep blue walls and
ceiling. The lights in the back
rooms of the houses opposite
glinted on the walls; a car com-
plained in the mews between.
'You can see what everyone's
doing,' Kay Rimmer said,
standing at the window.
Through the chink of the curtains on a top floor she saw a
woman brushing her hair; a
great double bed waited for its
inhabitants; a maid laid breakfast; a man wrote letters; a
chauffeur leant from the window of a little flat above a ga-
rage and smoked his last pipe.
    'Everyone doing something
different,' she said, her eyes
going back to the double bed
and her thoughts on the pink
bedspread in the other room
and Jules and half a loaf is better than no bread. [P. 57]

ensemble blanc, son four à
charbon émaillé, ses murs et
son plafond bleu pastel.
    Par l'écartement des rideaux,
Awa aperçut, dans la maison
voisine, qui se brossait les cheveux, une splendide négresse,
nue, devant un miroir: un vaste
lit à deux personnes attendait
ses abonnés. Une ordonnance
mettait la table pour le petit dé-
jeuner du lendemain; ailleurs,
le capitaine Vandame écrivait,
devant un caporal au garde-à-
vous.
    ''Ils font tous quelque chose
de différent,'' murmura-t-elle,
cependant que son regard re-
venait au grand lit, et ses pensées vers la courtepointe rose,
dans la chambre de Chevalier,
puis vers Saïf. [P. 69]

The kitchen evoked a dream
landscape, with its white win-
dows, its white buffet, its white
furniture, its enameled coal
stove, its pastel blue walls and
ceiling. Through the gap in the
curtains, Awa glimpsed, in the
neighboring house, brushing
her hair, a splendid black woman, nude in front of a mirror: a
huge double bed was waiting
for its subscribers. An orderly
was setting the table for the
next day's breakfast; elsewhere,
Captain Vandame was writing,
in front of a corporal standing
at attention. ''They're all doing
something different,'' she mur-
mured, while her eyes returned
to the big bed, and her thoughts
toward the pink quilt, in Chevalier's room, then toward Saïf.

Seth I. Wolitz has analyzed in detail the stylistic and narrative differences between these two passages. His comparison tends toward reversing the accusations, attributing to Ouologeum the true creative powers: "an intelligence which knows how to chose and eliminate in order to tighten and intensify the narration."[7] Greene, the "original" writer, is judged guilty of being "cold and anodyne," "banal": "Greene presents us with a disjointed text, almost devoid of resonance; Ouologuem tightens and intensifies everything." Wolitz concludes that Ouologuem's translation has nothing to do with plagiarism. But it is interesting to note that his argument against plagiarism borrows the vocabulary of originality and falsehood, leaving the categories intact, with only the places exchanged: Ouologuem, instead of kidnapper and falsifier, becomes the avatar of authenticity and creation, the "*Urtyp* of the creator, of this fertile young Mandarin African literature."

One would be hard pressed to find a translation that did not manifest differences of tone, style, attribution, and grammatical aspect, all of which make a translation susceptible to value judgments in relation to its precursor. Translation is a relationship of distance as well as sameness; like plagiarism, it is understood as the removal of a single object to another place.

Once that distance is of sufficient magnitude, plagiarism is no longer a question. Passages from the Bible, the Koran, or Aesop's fables obviously have no copyright nor any single author, for that matter. It is difficult to imagine a plagiary of Shakespeare; even were some playwright to lift passages verbatim and use them in his own play, it *(a)* would not violate any existing copyright and *(b)* would probably be interpreted as creative intertextuality. If T. S. Eliot had not included footnotes in "The Waste Land," would that highly borrowful text have been considered plagiary? Like *Le Devoir de violence,* Eliot's poem is largely a patchwork of other texts, but, aside from the nature of the texts quoted (some of which had no copyright), those he quotes are safe between quotation marks or in italics. If distance is the relationship that plagiarism falsifies by producing a simulacrum of identity, then quotation marks, along with footnotes and italics, are the guardians of that distance, of good faith.

Plagiarism has played a curiously prominent role in the European Africanist tradition, to such an extent that one's perspective tends to be reversed by immersion, and one begins to see theft as origin itself. I began this study by quoting Pigault-Lebrun, who was copying Raynal. Labat plagiarized Loyer, who copied Villault, who lifted passages from Dutch travelers.[8] Reaching back far enough, one finds everyone copying Homer. The distance between

---

7. Seth I. Wolitz. "L'Art du plagiat, ou une brève défense de Ouologuem," *Research in African Literature* 4, no. 1 (Spring, 1973): 132.

8. William B. Cohen, *The French Encounter with Africans* (Bloomington and London: Indiana University Press, 1980), p. 29.

texts is violated as European writers attempt to close another distance, that between themselves and Africa.

But in the situation of the African writer, that distance has always already been violated from the moment he or she commences to write in French (or English or Portuguese). Any original African utterance in French must already be a translation from a more authentic source into a medium of useful communication but also of exile. A logic of alienation from one's own literary productions is thus implicit in Francophone writing. This is important to keep in mind while reading Ouologuem, an author who establishes his discourse frankly in the void of that distance.

The Purloined Quotation Marks

Discourse in the novel could be said to have two basic types: the unattributed, unquoted recounting of events, known as narration itself, and the speech of characters within that narration, framed by quotation marks. No real novel, of course, conforms to this division, for techniques such as embedded narrative, free indirect discourse, and "stream of consciousness" tend to blur distinctions. Narration, in this narrow definition, would be a direct perception of the world, opposed to the second-hand, mediated mode of quotation.

In the passage from *Le Devoir de violence* reproduced above, a mystery surrounds the status of the narrative discourse. After the *Times Literary Supplement* (May 5, 1972) had established the derived nature of the paragraph, Ouologuem defended himself in *Le Figaro Littéraire* (June 10, 1972) in the following terms:

> Thus the passage from Mr. Graham Greene incriminated as plagiarism, but in fact *cited between quotation marks* (as were some lines from Schwartz-Bart) *in my manuscript,* which I have given over to my lawyer, preceded a wild scene in which a White man . . . made a Black woman have intercourse with a dog. I am Black. It is obvious that if the facts I evoked had been the product of my imagination, my racial brothers would scarcely have forgiven me for having besmirched the Black race. . . . In these conditions, putting Mr. Greene's text in quotation marks was not an act of plagiarism, but a way to be not disavowed by my own people, by casting a legal fact in a literary light. [Emphasis mine]

Ouologuem goes on to say that the coupling of the Black woman and the dog "is a true fact, as are all the facts reported in my novel." In an article in *West Africa* (July 21, 1972), "K. W." reports on an interview with Ouologuem, in which,

> To demonstrate the injustice of the charges against him, he spent some time taking me through his original hand-written manuscript (in an old exercise book) of *Le Devoir de violence* showing me all the places where there had been quotation marks, if not actual mentions of his literary allusions and quotations. . . . I saw, for instance, where he had written "here ends The Last of the Just," a reference omitted like so many others, for whatever reason, from the published version. [P. 941]

Ouologuem's defense thus consists of two arguments: that the quotation marks he used to set off the passage from Greene had been lost, stolen, or otherwise waylaid, probably by the publisher;[9] and second, that while verisimilitude demanded the recounting of that certain sequence of events, fraternal feeling made it necessary to use someone else's voice. The text that Ouologuem showed to "K. W.," and which he claims was the one submitted to Editions du Seuil, would thus contain *narration between quotation marks*. Reading the passage over again with this change inserted (see pages 220–21, above) one is faced with a stylistic maelstrom. Unless some other narrative agency were inserted, such as "X then recounted that . . . "—and Ouologuem mentions no such clause as having been deleted—those additional quotation marks would belong to no one. Furthermore, they would alter the status of the marks that are already there, scrambling direct and indirect attributions.

Ouologuem's defense on the grounds of attributability, while working from the traditional assumptions about narrative, points the way to the general subversion that his novel perpetrates. By invoking some lost or stolen quotation marks, he would have us believe that his manuscript was constructed according to the strict rules of proper borrowing. One can only wish that his exercise book were available, for if it indeed cited and acknowledged all its sources, it would be a remarkable scholastic novel, with a whole new set of rules concerning voice and attribution. According to Ouologuem's self-defense, it is the publishers who are responsible for the crime that the final text commits. Yet a study of the borrowings already discovered reveals that no proliferation of quotation marks, italics, or footnotes could restore *Le Devoir de violence* to a primal state of pure textual autonomy in which each intertextual relationship is identified.[10] From the first words (which are taken from *Le Dernier des Justes*) on, throughout the two hundred pages of the work, this is a novel so highly refined and perverse in its manner of lifting titles, phrases, and passages from other texts that it makes the binary system

9. See Eric Sellin, "The Unknown Voice of Yambo Ouologuem," *Yale French Studies* 53 (1976): 151–57.

10. The most complete analysis of the intertextuality of *Le Devoir* is to be found in the thesis of Christiane Chaulet-Achour, "Langue française et colonialisme en Algérie: De l'abécédaire à la production littéraire" (Dissertation, University of Paris III, 1982), vol. 2, pp. 419–43.

of quotation and direct narration irrelevant. The symmetry of acknowledgment no longer applies. Ouologuem's defense appears to argue on the basis of those standard binary terms while, at the same time, subverting them.

In the context of a new literature trying to define its own ground, claim its own territory, Ouologuem's stance seems at first to respect the principles of identity and distinction that are necessary for such a literature to establish itself and to repress all awareness of an ironic, inevitable collapsing-together of self and Other when one writes in the Other's language. Respect for the rules of borrowing imitates respect of national borders, the delineation of distinct subjectivities. Thus far Ouologuem has argued on those terms. But this study has tended to show that involvement with an Other—Africa, "irreflection," the "night," the Negro—can blur the distinctions between subject and object: by describing the Other in your writing, your writing becomes the Other's. Thus our European authors have tended to become alienated from their own meanings, surrendering them to someone else, becoming a *nègre*. Ouologuem had some explicit remarks to make on this subject—remarks that upset the principle of sole authorship and property as well as the founding basis of authenticity.

Lettre à la France nègre

The logic with which Ouologuem opposed himself to his accusers and precursors was first developed in a quirky book of essays called *Lettre à la France nègre*. Published in 1969, at the high tide of the acclaim for *Le Devoir* and so before the controversy, the second book was greeted as "a pamphlet in every way inferior to his novel."[11] And no wonder: the irreverence of the *Lettre* is but a sign of its subversive intent. Its humor does not reason or argue but rather opposes itself asymmetrically: "I deliberately chose the path of pamphlet humor. I hope it will have been ferocious enough to begin the demise of that comedy, the brawling but untouchable Negro" (p. 11). The essays include such titles as "Letter to all those who don't know what a Black is or who have forgotten what a White is," "Letter to all those who frequent Negroes," and "Letter to the copy-pissers, Negroes [i.e., ghost-writers] of famous writers." The last title is the one that concerns us here.

Ouologuem exploits the double meaning of the word "nègre" in French, where *Negro*, originally synonymous with *slave*, came also to mean (since the eighteenth century) *ghost-writer*. If the plagiarist is a slave of another text, merely repeating it while passing himself off as its master and creator, then the ghost-writer/*nègre* is a master passing himself off as a slave. The

11. J. Mbelolo Ya Mpiku, "From One Mystification to Another: 'Négritude' and 'Négraille' in *Le Devoir de violence*," *Review of National Literatures* 2, no. 2 (Fall, 1971): 124. Ouologuem, *Lettre à la France nègre* (Paris: Edmond Nalis, 1968).

plagiarist kidnaps and rewrites someone else's words; the *nègre* sells his own words to be rewritten under someone else's name. In the "Lettre aux pisse-copies, nègres d'écrivains célèbres," Ouologuem likens the exploitation of the ghost-writer to that of the black, and he proposes a solution:

> Chère négraille,
>   . . . Vous êtes encore moins qu'un manoeuvre: car lui, n'est-ce pas, est salarié et peut, sans rougir, avouer sa profession. Mais vous! comment oseriez-vous confesser que vous avez un souteneur, lequel exploite votre tête fêlée, en brandissant l'opium de la gloire post-hume?
>   Vous seriez, en vous révélant obscurs tâcherons, plus que déclassés; on se garderait de vous admirer; ou, plutôt, on vous admirerait rétrospectivement.
>   C'est pour tous les pauv'gars de votre acabit, que moi, un Nègre, j'ai travaillé comme un Blanc: en pensant. Hihi! . . .
>   Voilà donc, à votre usage, une thérapeutique dénégrifiante, et rudement commerciale. . . .
>   Nègres d'écrivains célèbres, vous êtes terriblement frustrés, et châtrés dans votre génie par la loi du silence: je veux que par ces pages, vous sachiez comment faire pour être pisse-copie et rester blanc. [Pp. 165–66]

> Dear Nigger-Trash,
> You are even less than a manual laborer: at least he has a salary and can admit his profession without blushing, can't he? But you! How would you dare confess that you have an underwriter, who exploits your cracked head by brandishing the opium of posthumous glory? By revealing yourselves as dark jobbing-laborers, you would be more than *déclassés;* people wouldn't let themselves admire you, or, rather, they would admire you in retrospect. It's for all the poor blokes of your ilk that I, a Negro, labored like a white man: by thinking. Heehee! Here, therefore, for your use, is a denigrifying therapy, damned commercial. . . . Negroes/ghost-writers of famous writers, you are terribly frustrated and castrated in your genius by the law of silence: I want you to learn from these pages how to go about being a copy-pisser while remaining white.

The problem of "Nègres, Négrilles, Négraillons, and Négrillons" is already complicated enough, the author says, without these white *nègres* adding to the misfortune of fate. The *nègre*–ghost-writer is defined as an *écrivaillon,* half writer and half slave boy, from the terminology of the old slave codes and of Césaire's *Cahier d'un retour au pays natal* via *Le Devoir de violence.*[12]

12. Cf. Aimé Césaire, *Cahier d'un retour au pays natal* (Paris: Présence Africaine, 1971), p. 147: "La négraille aux senteurs d'oignon frit retrouve dans son sang répandu le goût amer de la liberté."

The *écrivaillon* is a debased, decapitated, castrated, nonthinking object that nonetheless persists in producing "copy," churning out or rather urinating verbiage. The *écrivaillon,* like the plagiarist, represents the inability of one literary body to "contain itself" completely—to hold back the impulse to excrete, spill over the edges, and invade other bodies.

The project of "denigrifying" the *nègre,* however, neither ends that interpenetration nor elevates the status of the ghost-writer. "Remaining white" is associated with "thinking," which, ironically, the ghost-writer does for a living anyway. But it is the "white," the overseer of the *nègre*–ghost-writer, who maintains the pretense of noninterpenetration and autonomy. The "famous writers" for whom the *nègres* produce copy are "white" in their false wholeness; the *nègre* is castrated and thus is not whole unto himself. But importantly, the project consists not in restoring wholeness to the *nègre* but in inventing a cleverer dismemberment. The author therefore proposes that the *nègre* become a plagiarist as well. He would thus become the controller of the interpenetration of textual bodies in a system that has become doubly perverse.

The "new gadget" proposed will permit the ghost-writer "to compose one after the other all the works [his] boss will order." It consists of reading, cutting, and pasting together "the finest vintage of the detective novel . . . , which should permit you to invent, in the corridors of your imagination, A BILLION NOVELS PAINLESSLY!" (p. 168). In the charts and tables that follow, including a large fold-out of passages from Ian Fleming, Carter Brown, and Simenon, numerous permutations are demonstrated.

> Encore une fois, c'est un exemple, mais non point la révélation absolue de toute la diversité de la gymnastique opératoire de l'écriture. . . .
>
> Sous cette forme, chère négraille, pour qui exécute ce travail avec une conscience très lucide de la demande du marche, *être le nègre d'un écrivain célèbre* c'est se donner, comme une liberté, la clé d'un langage envisagé dans ses puissances combinatoires—mises à la disposition de la clientèle. C'est un peu de l'algèbre, mais de l'algèbre pour petits enfants.
>
> Cet algèbre-là n'est pas une analyse d'objet, c'est une analyse d'action. [P. 176]

> Once again, this is an example, but not the absolute revelation, of the whole diversity of the operative gymnastics of writing. . . .
> In this form, dear nigger-trash, for whoever executes this labor with a keen awareness of the market's demands, *being the ghost-writer [nègre] of a famous writer* is giving to oneself, like freedom, the key to a language envisaged in its combinative powers, made available to the clientele. It's a bit of algebra, but algebra for little children. This algebra is not an object analysis but an action analysis.

The scheme of the "Lettre aux pisse-copies" restores the initiative, the missing member, the sign of control, to the formerly castrated *nègre*. But he does not thereby become simply another "master of thought" in a system of writing that remains intact; he rather engages in "the play of language" and turns the process of writing upside down. Writing now follows and is completely dependent upon reading instead of the other way around. The writer becomes first and foremost a reader and a compiler, and the originary character of creative thought is rendered moot.

Seen in the light of this essay, which blurs the distinction between creating and copying, engendering and kidnapping, the status of *Le Devoir de violence* is somewhat explained if not really clarified. Ouologuem's writing, according to his own description, would be a conscious effort to spoil the distinction between original and copy. No wonder that, when the scandal over *Le Devoir de violence* broke out, *Lettre à la France nègre* was denounced as "an all-too-real *modus operandi*."[13]

Narration in *Le Devoir de violence*

According to the model we have seen, narration in a novel such as *Le Devoir* would not be a matter of creation *ex nihilo* performed by a "master of thought"; rather, it would involve a surrender to the play of repetition, copy, and theft. While on the level of narratology *Le Devoir* is continually breaching the standards of single-subject creativity as well as (apparently) those of legality, on the level of narrated plot a similar story is unfolding. This is the violent history of a fictive African empire, the Nakem, and of its rulers, the Saïfs. As the writing of the novel plugs itself into other texts, borrowing, stealing, and violating, the characters within the plot become bodies cutting and cut up, raping and raped, in the success formula for the popular novel, sex and violence.

The opening section of *Le Devoir de violence,* "La Légende des Saïfs," while recounting a condensed history of the Nakem Empire, also constitutes an important, if ironic, meditation on the possibility of narrating African history. The chapter contains both sweeping condensations of time—moving from the year 1202 to the twentieth century in twenty pages—and a minute attention to detail, particularly to the exact fashion in which bodies are tortured and dismembered. But, from the first paragraph, there is a crucial tug-of-war between "true history" *(véritable histoire)* and "legend," a debate on the modes of historical epistemology when applied to Africa. The various alternatives include "narrative" ("récit"), speech, chant, "Arab historians," and "the African oral tradition." If we bear in mind that we are reading in a

---

13. Eric Sellin, "Ouologuem's Blueprint for *Le Devoir de violence*," *Research in African Literatures* 2, no. 2 (1971): 120n.

genre and a literature split between a European "form" (the French language, the genre of the novel) and an African-designated "content," "La Légende des Saïfs" could be read as a working-through of Mohamadou Kane's assertion that, in reading the African novel, "everything becomes clear from the moment one refers to the traditional [i.e., oral] literature."[14] Kane also writes that "the perspective in which the author [of Le Devoir] places himself proves to be authentically African." Does the opening of Ouologuem's novel constitute a return to the Urtyp of African literature, the looming precursor, the oral tradition? The text must be read carefully.

> Nos yeux boivent l'éclat du soleil, et, vaincus, s'étonnent de pleurer. *Maschallah! oua bismallah!* . . . Un récit de l'aventure sanglante de la négraille—honte aux hommes de rien!—tiendrait aisément dans la première moitié de ce siècle; mais la véritable histoire des Nègres commence beaucoup, beaucoup plus tôt, avec les Saïfs, en l'an 1202 de notre ère, dans l'Empire africain de Nakem, au Sud du Fezzan, bien après les conquétes d'Okba ben Nafi el Fitri.

> Our eyes drink the sun's glare, and, conquered, surprise themselves weeping. *Maschallah! oua bismallah!* . . . A narrative of the bloody adventure of the nigger-trash—shame upon the men of nothing!—would fit easily into the first half of this century; but the true history of the Negroes begins much, much earlier, with the Saïfs, in the year 1202 of our era, in the African empire of Nakem, south of the Fezzan, some time after the conquests of Okba ben Nafi el Fitri.

The simple "narrative" of the "nigger-trash," that shapeless nonclass who cannot represent themselves but must be represented, is depicted as hardly worth mentioning and fits into the time frame of French colonial domination. This implies that the *négraille* were produced by that colonialism, which contradicts the basic thesis of the novel: that when the French arrived, they were "already too late"; for the African notables, the Saïfs, had been busy oppressing for centuries, and any colonialism would be a pale neocolonialism by comparison (see *Devoir*, p. 31). Thus, opposed to a brief narrative from the first half of the twentieth century, which will come to occupy the major part of the novel, there is the "true history of the Negroes," which takes on much grander proportions. Now if that history corresponds to the authenticity of the African past, unfettered and not yet impinged upon by Europe, it is strange that it should be linked to the word "Negro." The mode of "true history" is linked to "the Negroes," but that group is immediately subsumed into the category of the Saïfs, the legendary rulers and oppressors of Nakem.

14. Mohamadou Kane, "Sur les 'formes traditionnelles' du roman africain," *Revue de littérature comparée* nos. 3–4 (July–December 1974): 549.

The "Negroes" will disappear as the novel proceeds, losing all status as a constituted group (the word *nègre* remains, uncapitalized, as an adjective). It is the *négraille*, those "nothing men" like Sade's No One, who are the counterpart of the Saïfs; it is they who will persist as the irredeemably oppressed and alienated "trash." The Empire reduces itself to a pure oppressor and a pure oppressed, Saïf and *négraille*, a binary opposition that knows no mediation. The Saifs are represented in this paragraph as assuming "true history" and Negritude unto themselves.

Simultaneously, the narrative moves toward an authentically African point of view, defined by the speech and the chant of the oral historian, the griot, and at the same time toward a negative interpretation of African history. Those who will proffer "true history" are not influenced by European ideas or preconceptions in any way; neither are they the voice of the *négraille;* they are the "ancients, notables and griots" (p. 9). Those who speak are the same as those who, claiming an obscure legitimacy, will establish dominion over the *négraille*. The history of violence that begins to unfold thus has a spoken and repeated, inherited status, and the chapter proceeds with such reminders as "they say"; "it is told in the talismanic annals of the wise Ancients, among the narratives of the oral tradition"; "our griots recount . . ."; etc. At one point, narration without quotation marks is interrupted thus: "There followed a pious silence, and the griot Koutouli, of precious memory, completed the exploit thus," and a quotation follows (p. 10).[15] But we did not know we were listening to the griot Koutouli or to his *chanson de geste;* in fact, the crossing of voices is so complex that no single narrator can be isolated.

The question that dominates the chapter is that of singularity and origin. The legitimacy of the Saïfs depends on the legend of the single original hero: "the tradition of the Saïf dynasty, at the origin of which is found the grandeur of one man alone, the most pious and devout Isaac El Héit, who, every day, would free one slave" (p. 12). Thus "detaching itself from this table of horrors, the fate of Saïf Isaac El Héit was of a prodigious singularity; rising well above common destiny, it endowed the legend of the Saïfs with the splendor in which the dreamers of the theory of African unity still slumber" (p. 11). The method by which Ouologuem disassembles that theory still lets it be known that legends are necessary things.

No sooner has the figure of Isaac El Héit been established than the following warning is issued:

> Ici, nous atteignons le degré critique au-delà duquel la tradition
> se perd dans la légende, et s'y engloutit; car les récits écrits font

15. That sentence introduces a quotation in two senses: the quotation that follows in the text and the other, unseen quotation that "preceded" it by ten years, the sentence from Schwartz-Bart's *Le Dernier des justes* on which it is modeled: "Suit un pieux commentaire et le moine achève ainsi sa chronique" (p. 12).

défaut, et les versions des Anciens divergent de celles des griots, lesquelles s'opposent à celles des chroniqueurs. [P. 11][16]

Here we reach the critical degree, beyond which the tradition is lost in legend and is swallowed up; for written accounts are lacking, and the versions of the Ancients diverge from those of the griots, which are opposed to those of the chroniclers.

The project of "true history," dependent on a certain accord of voices, is swallowed up and lost. If history for Africa is tradition, an inheritance and repetition of oral evidence, then this "critical degree" is Ouologuem's device for problematizing history. Described as a result of the absence of written records, this "black hole" in the text, with all its loss of authority, is the sine qua non of the legend that will emerge. The absence of writing is a pretext for fragmentation and mythification. The gap between the various accounts of the griots, the Ancients, and the chroniclers will be filled by the legend of the Saïfs' origin: "the splendor of a single man, our ancestor the black Jew Abraham El Héït, a half-caste born of a Negro father and an Oriental Jewish mother—from Kenana (Chanaan)" (p. 12).[17] The unity of that origin, the singleness of the hero, involves at the same time an outside determinant. Abraham El Héït's parentage ties Black Africa both with the West, through the Bible, and the East, in that his mother is "Oriental."

His heirs will exploit the prestige of this birthright to lord it over the *négraille:* the Saïfs, a dissenting voice will say later, "claim to be Jews . . . only for the delight of proving that [their] ascendance makes [them] superior to the Negro. . . . Because the Negroes couldn't get along on their own, direct themselves, govern themselves, could they?" (p. 64). The Saïf is a "fétichiste musulman et négro-juif" (p. 87), a multifaceted system of masks that has no one true face. Ouologuem's Saïfs thus reflect a conscious effort to be "any figure that you like"; they are an African exploitation of an Africanist myth.

Their legendary foreign origin permits the Saïfs to expropriate any incipient intervention in their empire and to pit their vassals against one another: "fomenting between the backward peoples . . . [in the words of one Saïf], 'as many misunderstandings as possible'" (p. 19). At the moment of the

16. Cf. Schwartz-Bart, p. 13: "Ici, nous atteignons le point où l'histoire s'enfonce dans la légende, et s'y engloutit; car les données précises manquent, et les avis des chroniqueurs divergent."

17. Cf. p. 59: "S'il est vrai . . . que le peuple de Cham dont parlent les Ecritures est le peuple maudit, s'il est vrai que nous sommes partis de ce peuple nègre et juif . . . ." This single ancestor is thus the link with both the "Orient" and the West, through the Bible. Rimbaud comes to mind for two reasons: first, Nakem is here postulated as a sort of "vrai royaume des enfants de Cham"; second, the singularity of origin, the sole person who defines the identity of the dynasty, is the one who makes that identity into an otherness, a link to the outside: "Je est un autre."

Arab conquest, the Saïfs and notables sell the *négraille* into slavery (pp. 24–25), and Islam proves to be a useful tool: the Saïfs affect great Islamic piety and "convert the fetishistic populace, dumbfounded by the blackness of its soul" (p. 29). At the time of the French colonial conquest, the Saïfs adopt a progressivist mask and make sure the new laws work to their benefit: "Since French law had to be made for someone, the notables made it be for the populace" (p. 64). While the Saïf dynasty is the only principle of unity, it is also the principle that resists identity, giving itself all identities in order to dominate consistently and denying any identity to the *négraille*. The dynasty is unopposable in two senses of the word: it is all things at once and therefore cannot be opposed symmetrically by any one thing; consequently, its dominion is total.

If that "critical degree" of obscurity is the necessary condition for the Saïfs' legend, then it is also a part of what was called "true history." Ouologuem's attitude toward that ambiguity between truth and fiction comes through in the following passage:

> Véridique ou fabulée, la légende de Saïf Isaac El Héït hante de nos jours encore le romantisme nègre, et la politique des notables en maintes républiques. Car son souvenir frappe les imaginations populaires. Maints chroniqueurs consacrent son culte par la tradition orale et célèbrent à travers lui l'époque prestigieuse des premiers Etats. . . .
> Mais il faut se rendre à l'évidence: ce passé—grandiose certes— ne vivait, somme toute, qu'à travers les historiens arabes et la tradition orale africaine, que voici: . . . . [P. 14]

> Whether fact or fable, the legend of Saïf Isaac El Héït still haunts Negro romanticism and the politics of the notables in many republics. For his memory appeals to the people's imaginations. Many chroniclers pay homage to him in the oral tradition and through him celebrate the grand epoch of the first States. . . . But one must face up to the evidence: this past—for all its glory—lived only, in the final analysis, through the Arab historians and the African oral tradition, which follows: . . . .

The net effect of these paragraphs is surprising. In the first paragraph, the epoch of ancient African civilizations is treated as if it were a romanticized fantasy, self-indulgent and politically expedient.[18] Yet within the context of the chapter, the denial is less of the history itself than of the good faith of

---

18. Ouologuem was not made popular in Africa or among some European critics by this cynical interpretation of a history still struggling to be discovered by the West. See Yves Benot, "*Le Devoir de violence* de Yambo Ouologuem est-il un chef d'oeuvre ou une mystification?" *La Pensée* no. 149 (January–February, 1970).

its uses in politics. "True or fabled," "original or copy," the legend persists; the veracity is less important than the persistence of the haunting traditions, this perpetual error. The second paragraph opens as if to set the record straight and finally define the status of history. But by saying that that past "lived only . . . through the Arab historians and the African oral tradition," the life of the legend is given substance—for how else would such a tradition persist in West Africa but through those two agencies? Yet the tone and grammatical restriction of the sentence give the impression that this is a diminished, inferior status—compared to what, we do not know. Is the narration that then follows a viable history, a living tradition growing organically out of a legitimate ancestry, or is it a mere fable, patched together, like the Saïf dynasty, out of usurpation and violence? The question is perpetuated rather than answered by this passage and by the novel as a whole.

The global effect is to depict the African past as a purloined, kidnapped, and usurped origin, as an originary violence that precludes the autonomy of any given object, leaving only a void. Wole Soyinka, in his sensible discussion of *Le Devoir* in *Myth, Literature, and the African World*, writes that it is "a fiercely partisan book on behalf of an immense historic vacuum." In answer to the most essential question—"What was the creative genius of the African world before the destructive alien intrusion?"—we find only "another rubble-maker of cultural edifices" trying to "stuff up the cultural black hole of the continent." Soyinka rightly points out that "the positive does not engage his [Ouologuem's] re-creative attention."[19] The violent partisanship that runs through the novel is opposed to everything and symmetrically counterbalanced with nothing.

On the smaller scale of immediate plot devices, sex and violence are the armatures by which human interaction proceeds through time: the primal usurpation of the Saïf dynasty by Saïf El Haram, who marries his mother and has the heir to the throne eaten alive by worms; the devouring of the sexual parts of defeated enemies (p. 22); the colonial administrator whose dogs have sex with a black woman (pp. 70–71); etc. Violent atrocities destroy the barriers between one life and another; sexual intercourse, which more often than not becomes violent, is depicted as a breach in the body's integrity, the opening of a wound. We are close to the "grotesque image of the body" described by Bakhtine and to the "disorganization" of Sade's Butua. Bearing in mind that cannibalism and the grotesque interpenetration of bodies was part of a European vision of the "earliest beginnings of man," one wonders to what end Ouologuem is exploiting these themes.

Tambira, the mother of the protagonist, Raymond-Spartacus Kassoumi, is forced to have sex with a sorcerer named Dougouli in order to gain his help

19. Wole Soyinka, *Myth, Literature, and the African World* (Cambridge: Cambridge University Press, 1976), pp. 104–6.

for her children. Their encounter is representative of the way in which any two bodies interact in *Le Devoir de violence:*

> L'oeil révulsé par le désir, les lèvres lourdes, les mains trem-blantes, *ils se dévisagaient.* Les cuisses nues de Tambira se miraient dans la flaque. . . .
> La flaque dansait devant les yeux de Tambira fascinée, attirait, mordait furieusement ses yeux ivres; les formes tourbillonnaient tou-jours, *s'emplumaient de violence* et de luxure où sa propre ignominie était insignifiante. . . . Et ce fut le néant. Plus rien que le reflet du sexe de Tambira, entrouvert au-dessus de la flaque. [Pp. 148–49; emphasis mine]

> Their eyes turned back by desire, lips heavy, hands trembling, they *stared at each other [disfigured each other].* Tambira's naked thighs were mirrored in the puddle. . . . The puddle danced in front of Tambira's fascinated eyes, it attracted her, furiously chewed at her drunken eyes; the shapes still flew about in a whirlwind, *fledged in violence* and lust, in which her own ignominiousness was insig-nificant. . . . And then nothing. Nothing but the reflection of Tam-bira's genitals, opening above the puddle.

Desire is at the same time the very process of turning away, of revulsion. The act of looking at each other involves a breach of the body's integrity: *dévisager,* which normally means "to stare someone down," means literally to dis-figure, to deface.[20] Later, under the magician's curse, Tambira dies, and her body is found with "worms crawling in her nostrils; her head stuck out from among the feces, held by a noose attached to one of the boards." Her husband, Kassoumi, "lifting up the sticky body of his beloved, washed it gently, . . . from time to time . . . sucking the nose and spitting out a worm." The head and the feces, love and putrefaction, commingle. Disfig-urement entails the violation of all oppositions: life/death, sex/violence, oral/anal, desire/revulsion. The human body in *Le Devoir de violence* is not an integrity but a "masse de pâte molle, plaies vives" ("mass of soft paste, live wounds"). Intercourse, even in its most positive instance (the homosexual affair between Raymond Kassoumi and a Frenchman), involves the destruction of the self, loss of "face": "soiling of his face," "wearing-away of the flesh." That destructive process is defined as "linking and opposing irre-mediably the White man and him [Kassoumi]." The act of linkage and union is immediately an opposition: attraction does not occur without revulsion; love cannot be distinguished from violence.[21]

---

20. *Grand Larousse:* "Dévisager—Déchirer le visage de quelqu'un, défigurer."
21. See Raymond O. Elaho, "Le devoir d'amour dans le devoir de violence de Yambo Ouologuem," *L'Afrique littéraire* 56 (1979): 65–69.

The creator, progenitor, and lover is also the kidnapper, murderer, and rapist. As *Le Devoir de violence* narrates violence and the flowing of one body into other bodies and into the world, the narration itself is *disfiguring* a prior text, violating the integrity of another literary body. Chaulet-Achour makes the following connection:

Le Devoir de violence, p. 144	Maupassant, *Boule de suif* (Paris: Librairie de France, 1934), p. 7.
Parmi les décombres de la guerre, Kassoumi rêvassait sous son bananier, promenant, au-delà des feuillettes grisâtres des fruits bourgeonnants, son pauvre regard sur la rive du Yamé, empestée par l'odeur saumâtre de carcasses de squelettes que les pêcheurs ramenaient souvent du fond de l'eau, dans leurs filets, *cadavre d'Allemand décomposé dans son uniforme, tué d'un coup de* lance ou de sabre, *la tête écrasée par une pierre ou* flanqué *à l'eau du haut d'un pont. Les vases du fleuve ensevelissaient ces vengeances obscures, sauvages héroïsmes inconnus, attaques muettes, plus périlleuses que les batailles au grand jour, et sans le retentissement de la gloire.*	Cependant, à deux ou trois lieues sous la ville, en suivant le cours de la rivière, vers Croisset, Dieppedalle ou Biessart, les mariniers et les pêcheurs ramenaient souvent du fond de l'eau quelque cadavre d'Allemand gonflé dans son uniforme, tué d'un coup de couteau ou de savate, la tête écrasée par une pierre, ou jeté à l'eau d'une poussée du haut d'un pont. Les vases du fleuve ensevelissaient ces vengeances obscures, sauvages et légitimes, héroïsmes inconnus, attaques muettes, plus périleuses que les batailles au grand jour et sans le retentissement de la gloire.
Among the ruins of the war, Kassoumi day-dreamed under his banana tree, letting his eyes wander beyond the grayish little leaves of the burgeoning fruit, to the bank of the Yamé, tainted by the brackish smell of skeleton carcasses, which the fisherman often hauled up from the bottom in their nets, a German's body rotting in his uniform, killed by a lance or saber, the head crushed by a rock, or thrown into the water from up on a bridge. The vessels of the river enshrouded these	Meanwhile, two or three leagues downstream from the city, toward Croisset, Dieppedalle, or Biessart, the sailors and fishermen often hauled up from the bottom some German's body, swollen in his uniform, killed by a knife or kicked to death, the head crushed by a rock, or shoved into the water from up on a bridge. The vessels of the river enshrouded these obscure, savage, and legitimate acts of vengeance, unknown heroism, silent attacks, more perilous than

obscure, savage acts of ven-	battles in broad daylight and
geance, unknown heroism, silent	without the resounding glory.
attacks, more perilous than bat-	
tles in broad daylight and without	
the resounding glory.	

I have italicized the words that are identical in the two passages. A sufficiently close reading could demonstrate that the alterations of Maupassant
in Ouologuem's text—the total change of context, the transplanting of the
scene to Africa—produce a completely new meaning. This is the thrust in
current criticism of Ouologuem.[22] It redeems the kidnapper, making him into
a creator, and the validity of the point is indisputable. But that redemption
should not deny the violent nature of Ouologuem's enterprise. The precursors
of *Le Devoir de violence*, as best seen in the passages I have just quoted, by
virtue of being lifted and reorganized, become swollen bodies with crushed
heads, both more and less than they used to be, with words added and words
deleted, worms crawling out of their orifices.

In the incongruously "harmonious" last section of the novel, "L'Aurore,"
which consists of a dialogue between Saïf and the European bishop Henry de
Saignac, the double tension of the novel is clarified:

>—Vous parliez du Nakem tout à l'heure.
>—Je voulais être seul, pur.
>—Mais la solitude s'accompagne d'un sentiment de culpabilité,
>de complicité . . .
>—Pardon, de solidarité, rétorqua l'évêque.
>—L'homme est dans l'histoire et l'histoire dans la politique. Nous
>sommes déchirés par la politique. Il n'y a ni solidarité ni pureté
>possible. [P. 201]

>"You were speaking of Nakem just now."
>"I wanted to be alone, pure."
>"But solitude comes with a feeling of guilt, of complicity . . ."
>"Excuse me, of solidarity," retorted the bishop.
>"Man is in history, and history is in politics. We are torn apart
>by politics. There is no possible solidarity or pureness."

Politics, a subset of human intercourse, is a force not of unity but of dismemberment and fragmentation. You cannot be pure, because other bodies
interfere with yours. According to the model of interaction as defacement,
solitude is spoiled by intervention from the outside, and the configuration of
solidarity is also out of the question. The closing section of the novel has

---

22. See, especially, the Chaulet and Wolitz works listed in the Bibliography.

been seen as an espousal of the Euro-Christian values of the bishop, as if corrupt Africa, in the person of Saïf, is reaching toward its last best hope. But the relationship between the two men is described as the sharing of a secret—"that they were the sole authentic conspirators of Nakem-Zuiko" (p. 203)—and as an uncanny tension between attraction and repulsion: "their stares linked them in an *unnameable strangeness*" ("leurs regards les liaient en une *indicible étrangeté*"; p. 203, emphasis mine).

Several pages earlier, the bishop tells a parable that comes close to naming that strangeness, which is the link between himself and Saïf, Europe and Africa, and even between *Le Devoir* and its precursors:

> Les Chinois ont un jeu: le trait d'union. Ils capturent deux oiseaux qu'ils attachent ensemble. Pas de trop près. Grace à un lien mince, mais solide et long. Si long que les oiseaux, rejetés en l'air, s'en-volent, montent en flèche et, se croyant libres, se grisent de batte-ments d'ailes, de grand air, mais soudain: crac! Tiraillés. . . .
> L'humanité est une volaille de ce genre. Nous sommes tous vic-times de ce jeu; séparés, mais liés de force. [Pp. 193–94]

> The Chinese have a game: the tether. They capture two birds, which they attach to each other. Not too closely. Using a thin but long and solid cord. So long that the birds, when they are thrown up into the air, take flight, rise like arrows, and, believing themselves free, get drunk on beating their wings in the open air. But suddenly: bam! Pulled short. . . . Humanity is a bird of that feather. We are all victims of that game; separated, but linked by force.

The Chinese game describes Ouologuem's vision of the world as a whole: a forced linking of unwilling opposites, which proceed to tear each other apart. The irony of the name "trait d'union" lies in the fact that the birds will eventually "peck each other's eyes out," and one or both will wind up dead, all because of this "union." But "trait d'union" also means "hyphen," a link by punctuation, which might describe the authorship of *Le Devoir de violence:* "Ouologuem-Schwartz-Bart," "Ouologuem-Greene," or "Ouo-loguem-Maupassant." The political violence to which the bishop's parable obviously refers is echoed by the separation and forced linkage between the text itself and its precursors, leaving authorship, authority, and authenticity "teased" ("tiraillé") between the two.

Ouologuem's "theory" and practice thus tend to apply the grotesque image of the body to the interrelations of literatures. *Le Devoir de violence,* in both its thematic content and its stylistic practice of plagiarism, violates the notion of an integral body, whole unto itself. That notion is generally taken for granted in the face-off between two literatures: one assumes that one knows which "corpus" one is reading. But there is another metaphor at work; for if two bodies exist side by side, one can or must be different from the other, probably older, and hence "better." This is the root of theories such as Lukács', which projects a hierarchy according to age, between "childlike-ness" and "virile maturity," between epic, drama, and novel. Lukács saw the novel as the genre of progress from one to the other, and a work such as *Le Fils du fétiche* fits perfectly into that scheme. But in the world of the grotesque, such closed, smooth bodies are unknown; and hierarchies, as with the Saïfs, are a matter of deceit. *Le Devoir de violence* is written in the excrescences, the orifices, and the intrusions between European and African literature, by a sort of *nègre franc,* if one permits a play on words: not only a "frank" ghost-writer, with no compunctions about the nonintegrity of his text, but also a "Frankish Negro," a perverse and "un-nameable strangeness" instead of a national identity. No wonder the novel was controversial.

Ouologuem is a dangerous writer to put in the context of this study, under the weight of the European Africanist tradition. *Le Devoir de violence* can too easily be interpreted as warmed-over European prejudice, especially when one thinks of the Saïf dynasty, taking on any figure it wants to, like soft wax, and of the *négraille,* the irredeemable nullity. But it is Ouologuem's willing-ness to face those phantoms that makes him an appropriate "answer": fully conscious of the Africanist tradition (even Aniaba appears in the novel at one point [p. 43]), Ouologuem is able to look it in the eye and disfigure it in his fashion. His relation to his European precursors defies the rules that would place him in the position of "childlikeness" compared with their "virile maturity." *Le Devoir de violence* is difficult to read because Ouologuem involves himself to such an extent in those myths while refusing to resolve them. He refuses to be either "original" or "copy."

Ouologuem and Libertinism

Do you know that some people said I was a black Sade?
—Yambo Ouologuem

Another text, attributed to Ouologuem, brings us back to the crossroads of libertinism and Africanist writing. *Les Mille et une bibles du sexe* is a work of episodic libertine adventures ostensibly "edited" by Yambo Ouologuem but, according to Jahnheinz Jahn, actually written by him.[23] One is reminded of Sade on two accounts: by the theme of sexual adventure and by the quirky narrative frame by which the author effaces himself. Ouologuem signs his

23. Jahnheinz Jahn and Claus Peter Dressler, *Bibliography of Creative African Writing* (Nen-deln, Liechtenstein: Kraus-Thomson, 1971). James Olney, whose treatment of *Les Mille et une bibles du sexe* I will discuss here, accepts this opinion, which certainly seems justified (*Tell Me Africa: An Approach to African Literature* [Princeton: Princeton University Press, 1973], p. 223n).

name to the preface and returns to introduce each episode, centered on a French foursome: Régis and Vive, Harry and Emmanuelle. The fact that one of their adventures leads them to Africa invites speculation on the role of Africa in erotic writing ("ce côté safari . . . qu'est-ce que c'est dans l'érotisme?")[24] or, more importantly, on the role of eroticism in Africanist writing.

The fictive Yambo Ouologuem of the preface is an editor at Editions du Seuil who is approached by a "great Parisian aristocrat" with a 2,400 page manuscript of "poker confessions" sorely in need of revision. This new genre is a combination of gambling, sex, and tale-telling, in that order, interconnected. A game is played with sex as the prize, all of which is then related in a "confession." The six hundred persons who had contributed their confessions had not been able, however, to go beyond "a pornography of dubious taste," as Ouologuem says. But due to apparent affinities between these texts and his own *Le Devoir de violence,* Ouologuem says he accepted the task of editing and correcting the work. Referring to the banning of *Le Devoir de violence* from certain African countries as if it had been out of prudery rather than politics, Ouologuem writes a small manifesto for erotic writing.[25] The poker confessions reveal, he writes, "all the originality of the freshest, the most troubling eroticism." Their freshness will not, however, be without resonance in the history of libertinism: an obsession with rules, numbers, counting, and recounting. The betting game depends on the quality of the tale one tells, thus on recounting *(conter);* eroticism is dependent on language and vice versa. Sex is "essentially irrational and marvelously visceral," but "eroticism alone speaks. . . . The metaphysical utterance is thus inseparable from eroticism."[26] Eroticism rises above mere physical sex and above pornography, which is apparently the rendering of sex in writing; eroticism is made to speak and promise.

This brings to mind remarks by Michel Foucault on sexuality and language since Sade:

> La sexualité n'est décisive pour notre culture que parlée et dans la mesure où elle est parlée. Ce n'est pas notre langage qui a été, depuis bientôt deux siècles, érotisé; c'est notre sexualité qui depuis Sade et

24. *Les Mille et une bibles du sexe* (Paris: Editions du Dauphin, 1969), p. 275.
25. "Si j'ai pris sur moi de présenter *Les Mille et une bibles du sexe,* c'est également parce que, *en raison de certains aspects érotiques* de mon premier roman, divers pays africains ont rejeté de leurs frontières *Le Devoir de violence.* J'étais, aux yeux de chefs d'Etats irresponsables ou incultes, j'étais, pour avoir osé dire du Nègre qu'il faisait l'amour, un cartiériste vendu à une France raciste, laquelle s'amusait de voir dénigrer par un Noir les moeurs des peuples noirs. Soit. Il est bon d'être primitif, certes, mais impardonnable d'être primaire. Tant pis pour les primaires qui se revent censeurs" (p. 18).
26. "Il a fallu dépeindre, autant que ces confessions, les arrières-mondes dont elles étaient lourdes. L'érotisme seul parle; la littérature n'apporte que la sensibilité cachée, inconsciente, inconnue de soi, qui allume l'intelligence des sens et vivifie ses données. . . . Le propos métaphysique est ainsi inséparable de l'érotisme à l'oeuvre: comme un chef d'oeuvre poétique" (p. 17).

la mort de Dieu a été absorbée dans l'univers du langage, dé-
naturalisée par lui, placée par lui dans ce vide où il établit sa sou-
veraineté et où sans cesse il pose, comme Loi, des limites qu'il
transgresse.

Sexuality is decisive in our culture only in spoken form and to the
extent that it is spoken. It is not so much that our language, for
almost two centuries now, has been eroticized; it is our sexuality
that, since Sade and the death of God, has been absorbed into the
universe of language, thereby denaturalized, placed in that void
where language establishes its sovereignty and ceaselessly poses as
Law the limits that it transgresses.[27]

Foucault insists that Sade was the first to lock sexuality inside a single discourse, of which "he suddenly became the sovereign" and in which a frus-
trating game of transgression and limitation takes place ad infinitum: "the
questioning of boundaries is substituted for the search for a totality" ("Préface
à la transgression," p. 753). The value judgment expressed by Foucault,
whereby language *denaturalizes* sexuality and establishes a dictatorship over
a void, is a common one. Discourse for Foucault is a means of repression in
which the "free circulation" of sex is chaneled, reduced, controlled (*Volonté*,
p. 25). The problem is that *any* discourse, even or *especially* a libertine one,
by unleashing the "secret" of sex confirms the repression it is combating.
This is why the entry of sex into language makes sex into both "something
to be said" (p. 45) and something "at once banished, denied, and reduced
to silence" (p. 10). Foucault can offer no positive vision of a world free from
all this, because any liberation is only transgression, confirming one's imprisonment. Yet, before Sade, things must have been better; Foucault cannot
help but imply that a renaturalized, nondiscursive sexuality is the object of
his obscure desire. In a critique of the libertine duality between surface
"natural animality" and the sought-after "Absence" ("Préface," p. 752),
can one escape creating a dualism of one's own, whose object is the escape
from dualism?
    Foucault states that language interferes in sexuality "in our culture," but
Ouologuem's eroticism, which "alone speaks" and is "inseparable from the
metaphysical utterance," seems caught in the same scheme. This is to say
that Ouologuem's eroticism is involved in a very European conceptualization
of itself and is understandable in terms of the libertine tradition, the dialectic
of law and transgression, exile and return.

    27. Foucault says that Sade was the first to place sexuality in a new discursive "realm of
irreality" (as we will see, Ouologuem's "cieux autres") (Michel Foucault, "Préface à la
transgression," *Critique* 19 nos. 195–96 [August–September 1963]: 751–69). A more recent
rendering of Foucault's thesis on language taking over sex is to be found in his *Histoire de la
sexualité: La volonté de savoir* (Paris: Gallimard, 1976), pp. 25–49.

That dialectic, a design for the release of tension, can therefore be seen as an obstacle to its own design. If the desire of the libertine is to reach back to a primal state of unity (the state "before Time, before Form, before the Fall of man"),[28] the observance of ritual is both a means toward that end and proof that one has not yet arrived. In Sade, at least, libertines seemed to be offered no alternative to the perpetual motion of their machines: "Justine . . . se laisse faire machinalement." The performances in *Les Mille et une bibles* seem to constantly involve the technology of the industrialized world: cars (mostly Rolls Royces and Jaguars), trains, elevators, even switchblade knives, telephone receivers, and so on. The process is more self-perpetuating than successful in producing perpetuity. On the one hand, there is this illusion of a return to Eden:

> Le couple couché se caresse, et s'abreuve de cris de gorge en galop. Aldo a les yeux d'Annabelle dans la gorge, et son corps se trahit. Aldo se crispe, il ne veut pas mourir. Annabelle sans cesse répète des sanglots qui emplissent l'espace. Et tous deux soudain sont comme au début. Quand la terre était oeuvre de Dieu, et l'homme le bout du monde. Ils ne savent pas si le soleil reviendra après la nuit, si la lune saluera le coucher du soleil. Ils vivent sans fin. [P. 100]

> The couple, lying down, caress each other, and each drinks in the cries from the other's throat. Aldo has Annabelle's eyes in his throat, and his body betrays him. Aldo shrinks back; he doesn't want to die. Annabelle ceaselessly repeats her sobs, which fill the space. And suddenly both of them are like at the beginning. When the earth was God's work, and man the edge of the world. They do not know if the sun will return after the night, if the moon will greet the setting sun. They live without end.

But, on the other hand, "living without end" is the problem itself, to which death is the only true answer: "Les hanches de Régis voyageaient à la mesure des râles de la femme qu'il prenait, et cette femme-là grondait à voix basse. Elle pleurait. Elle mourait. Elle s'éveillait de son agonie, puis s'affaissait tout doucement. . . . Comme tuée de plaisir. Inerte." (p. 48). ("Regis' hips were traveling in time with the death-rattle of the woman he was taking, and the woman groaned in a low tone. She was weeping. She was dying. She woke up from her agony, then eased herself back down. . . . As if killed by pleasure. Inert.") Those, in brief, are the two poles of the libertine dilemma.

The possibility of a geographically based solution is raised by James Olney in his discussion of *Les Mille et une bibles du sexe* and *Le Devoir de violence*.

---

28. Alice M. Laborde, *Sade romancier* (Neuchâtel: La Baconnière, 1974), p. 137.

In his reading of the former, Olney sees an important difference between the practice of libertinism in Europe and the promise of eroticism in Africa:

> The atmosphere of Africa that embraces the figures the moment they step from the plane seems somehow to offer promise in itself of a kind of fulfillment—the individual in relation to the surrounding, enveloping sensory universe—denied to the human creatures in the thin air of France. . . . Immediately they drown themselves in the abundant fruits of nature that in their variety and plenitude render any less natural satisfaction for the senses irrelevant. [*Tell Me Africa*, p. 226]

On the one hand, Olney sees a promise; on the other hand, actual "satisfaction." Nature—the fruits and vegetables that become synonymous with women's bodies—replaces machines: "the union of interior and exterior, the joining, 'beyond fear and death,' of the individual with nature, realizes itself in highly erotic sexual performances . . . [pointing to] mystic dissolution and natural reunion" (pp. 228–29). Nature is by definition that which needs no explanation, that which is self-evident and nonironic: if man and man's eroticism are sublated into Nature, then a solution has been found to the perpetual labor of the libertine machine. It is in such a reading of *Les Mille et une bibles* that Olney is able to assert the existence of a "straight face" in Ouologuem's writing, "somewhere behind the irony." If a straightforward eroticism or happy libertinism is meant to relieve the tension of European Africanist experience and writing, can we now close the book on the idols and fetishes that have peopled this study, or have we in fact created another one?[29]

Let us suppose that behind the irony of *Le Devoir de violence* and of the rest of *Les Mille et une bibles*, there is "Africa," an allegory of mystified eroticism. What happens in the African passage of *Les Mille et une bibles* to justify such an interpretation? The four principal libertines have met three

29. Is *Les Mille et une bibles* to *Le Devoir de violence* as Sade's South Seas utopia Tamoé is to his depraved African kingdom of Butua? The lost Léonore travels to Tamoé with Captain Cook, it will be recalled, and Sainville follows, setting up his long interview with the noble King Zamé, a mouthpiece of the idealism of the *philosophe*. Tamoé is indeed a land of justice and goodness; the first problem is that, once desire has been fulfilled, it can no longer be admitted or allowed: "A l'égard des crimes moraux . . . je ne reçois jamais ni un libertin ni une femme adultère," says Zamé (*Aline et Valcour* [Paris: Cercle du livre précieux, 1962], p. 300); in order for everything to be virtuous, everything must be controlled by the state, as Zamé declares: "l'Etat est tout ici" (p. 343; the conformity to Foucault's model is striking). Sainville's objection is also relevant: "Si vous avez peu de vices, vous ne devez guère avoir de vertus" (p. 297). But Tamoé's value as a foil to libertinism, as a solution to the endless vacillations of desire, is well destroyed by Sade's "Avis de l'éditeur" (quoted above, p. 186), which labels Tamoé a *pays de chimères*, alienated from *nature*. The ultimate return to nature is ultimately unnatural. Sade's "answer" is thus similar to Ouologuem's, or at least to Olney's interpretation of *Les Mille et une bibles;* the difference is that Sade tells us that his answer is illusory.

Africans from Liberia (the name of which becomes symbolic), who have given them round-trip airline tickets to Africa. Here the story is interrupted for a comment from Ouologuem the editor, who declares that he is "sorry to see Africa mixed up in this business" (p. 275) and that he would have preferred a "less collective exoticism." He concludes with some grudging admiration for the "poor great exoticism that dreamed the art of violence for the erotic banquet."

Africa welcomes them like an anxious lover: "naked earth, trembling in the air stirred by the last breath of the sirocco . . . the beaches, lined with palm trees, stretched out without end, licked by the Atlantic" (p. 283-84). If Africa "herself" is a sensuous woman, African women have become allegorical figures as well; landscape and humanity are metaphorically linked in their erotic appeal:

> Or le paysage était luxuriant de baroque, avec son folklore exu-
> bérant de carmins, de bougainvilliers, d'hibiscus, d'amaryllis de
> vermeille, d'orchidées de formes étranges, de couleur diabolique.
> [P. 284]

> And the landscape was baroque, luxuriant, with its folklore ex-
> uberant with carmine, bougainvillaeas, hibiscus, rosy amaryllis,
> strange forms of orchids in diabolical colors. [P. 284]

> Si l'on en croit le voyage de Régis et de ses compagnons, l'Afrique
> avait autant à dire, avec ses femmes noires aux seins insolents, avec
> ses joliesses en boubous lamés et sans corsage, leur démarche canaille
> de nonchalance, leurs silhouettes agrémentées de laisser-aller, leur
> fesses qui bombent au bas de leurs reins cambrés, leur sexe: crépu
> et électrique quand le frotte le pubis masculin, leurs poitrines: re-
> dondantes sous le soleil lourd, le robuste *ouvrage* de leur sensualité,
> née *comme du climat, débordant les corps* comme *la volupté de cieux
> autres* [P. 286: emphasis mine]

> If the voyage of Régis and his companions is to be believed, Africa
> has as much to say, with its black women and their insolent breasts,
> with its pretty young things in spangled boubous and no top, their
> rascally, insouciant gait, their silhouettes adorned with unconstraint,
> their buttocks bulging out from their well-set loins, their sex: frizzy
> and electric when the man's pubis rubs against it; their chest: su-
> perfluous under the heavy sky; the robust *work* [product] of their
> sensuality, born *as from the climate, overflowing the bodies* like *the
> voluptuousness of other heavens*.

The burden of idealization is literally stated to "overflow" the confines of the physical body in this second passage, and it seems to me that the role of artificiality ("*product* of their sensuality," "*like* the climate") is important. The differential, removed perspective from which this kind of writing must be done is seen in the phrases "formes *étranges*," "la volupté de cieux *autres*": this is more reminiscent of Baudelaire than anyone ("this vegetation, disturbing" to the eye of the traveling academic, "these men and women whose muscles do not move according to the classical gait of his own country").[30]

Traveling to Kenya, the four friends set off on safari with a local guide. The two couples wander into the bushes at one point and find themselves confronted by a lion, who "knew that the men were naked and making love" (p. 290). Unarmed, they must try to distract the beast, and sex is their method. The guide immediately takes his clothes off. Régis recommences intercourse with Vive, as the lion lies down and masturbates with his tail. Harry and Emmanuelle join the other two, but the black guide approaches the lion with a gourd and a forked stick. Stimulating the lion with the stick, to the point where the beast is incapacitated, the guide stuffs the gourd down the throat of the lion, who then dies in piteous contortions. The chapter ends there, and the next "confession poker" takes place in Europe.

It is in this African chapter that Olney sees Ouologuem's "descriptions of the sensual, the exotic, and the erotic take a rather new turn—more natural, less strained, less grotesque, and less pornographic" (p. 225).[31] But the difference seems *quantitative* to me and inadequate to prove a "union of interior and exterior," "of the individual with nature," or "beyond the irony, a straight face." The irony of libertinism, as I have tired to indicate, is that the persistence of its efforts makes unity and resolution recede before it. If a "natural libertinism" substitutes a black man, a gourd, a stick, a lion, and an African landscape for white men, elevators, cars, and Europe, has libertinism been released from its burden, lifted up and canceled out? The stakes have certainly changed, but in my opinion not toward any resolution of the problem.

The role of sex in Africanist writing has been a continual subtext in this study. On the one hand, there has been a close relationship between the opposition of races and the opposition of the sexes: "the Black seems to me the female race."[32] In reading works such as "Sed non satiata" or "La Belle

30. Baudelaire, "De l'idée moderne du progrès . . . ," in *Curiosités esthétiques* (Paris: Garnier, 1962), p. 212.

31. "Comparatively, the forms of sex in Africa, as Ouologuem renders them in *Mille et une bibles*, are natural—one to one, man and woman, the ordinary appendages and orifices, no foreign instruments such as smoking guns, telephone receivers, whips, fragile crystal flutes, switch-blade knives, 'godemichets,' etc. True, a lion does get into the act in Kenya, but even then the beast carries some of his nobility with him, and the passage is nothing like as depraved as the one that deals with the massive dog, the woman on a block of ice, and a crowd of voyeurists back in Paris, or the scene of Golda, Harry, the motorcycle policeman, and a hot Maserati automobile beside a French superhighway" (Olney, *Tell Me Africa*, p. 226).

32. Gustave Eichtal and Ismayl Urbain, *Lettres sur la race noire et la race blanche* (Paris: Chez Paulin, 1839), p. 22.

Dorothée,'' the relation of center to periphery seemed to conceal a relation of superiority, white over black, male over female. The act of poetic redemption—of bringing materials back from the tropics—implied simultaneous sexual submission. The libertine program demands passive submission and resignation to such an arrangement (''Justine se laisse faire . . . machinalement''). When a figure such as Africa is placed in a libertine context, therefore, the writer's liberation may well cost the African's liberty: in the Ouologuem passage above, Africa is made to speak (''l'Afrique avait autant à *dire*''), and her people thus become figures in a discourse of idealized sensuality, allegorical puppets.

On the other hand, seductiveness is a natural part of writing, and, if allegory exploits, pure irony cannot satisfy. Africa in *Les Mille et une bibles du sexe* is illustrative of this double bind. On the positive side, Africa makes a promise of fulfillment and erotic splendor. But the other side of the same coin is the fact that Africa is thereby reduced, for the millionth time, to the role of primitive, natural Garden of Eden, like Homer's Ethiopia, a playground for the gods (Olney: ''this perception of the countryside as an immense vagina,'' p. 228).

A look at the illustration for the African ''confession poker'' should make this clear. *Les Mille et une bibles* is something of a ''fine edition,'' carefully designed typographically, and illustrated with surrealistic drawings and photographs. On one level this is indeed a sign of some nonironic seductiveness, an embrace of the subject that *Le Devoir de violence* never permits itself. But the plate representing Africa looks like this: the dominant figure is a lion, roaring, his mane contiguous with the long blond hair of a naked woman, who is embracing a blond-haired man. The white couple are situated alongside, perhaps as part of, the lion's flank; but flat on his back, being trampled by the lion, with one hand on his own penis and the other apparently on the lion's, there is the black man, on whom the lion is ejaculating. The symbolism is excessively transparent: the couple represent Europe, the black man Africa, and the lion, it seems fair to say, is that discourse of mystified eroticism, ''la volupté de cieux autres.'' The ''naturalness'' of that discourse is both *derived*—the conscious, willed result of a difference and a need—and *unequal*—subjugating one figure in order to liberate another. The language of idealization and mystification seems to produce difference at the very moment it is claiming unity and identity.

When one looks beyond the surface, *Les Mille et une bibles du sexe* is actually a much less scandalous, less original, and more ''European'' work than *Le Devoir de violence*. The refusal of discourse in *Le Devoir* to obey the rules of European logic emerges as a triumphantly hopeless gesture, whereas the false hope erected in *Les Mille et une bibles* seems ill conceived and slightly treacherous.

8

Conclusion

The principal gesture of Africanist literature has appeared to consist of reaching out to the most unknown part of the world to bring it back as language. The incongruity between that world and the language that seeks to manipulate it, that overextension of discourse, is the source of its strength and its strangeness. Writers have insisted on the unredeemed, unknown state of the object they have just brought back and made known: "I knew a lady unknown"; "One is not obliged to make reason out of something that has none." The resistance of the object to rational explanation appears as part of its nature, as a hard fact before the reader's eye, whereas it is more probably the result of a question. The history of Africanist discourse is that of a continuing series of questions imposed on Africa, questions that preordain certain answers while ruling others out. It would be artificial to reduce that series—the discourse as a whole—to a single statement or historical condition, yet it seems that a certain artificiality is of its essence. One can assert with assurance that the relationship between Europe and Africa has continually been represented as simply North over South, light over dark, white over black: as an unmediated pairing of opposites. A discourse dependent on such a polarized logic has a hard time saying what it means, and it bears a perverse relation to truth.

What, then, are the questions that Europe asks of Africa? Perhaps the most compelling concern brought about by the historical relationship between the two is that of equality and identity. The problem is that, in desiring equality, one often imposes identity. Aniaba and Zaga-Christ were permitted to be equal to the peerage of France only in a social discourse that obliterated their different identity, leaving them equal but indifferently so. A black whose blackness has been erased is no longer a black. But writers who recognize difference have a hard time interpreting it as anything but a sign of inequality: de Brosses and Gobineau, Sade and Céline, all write in that mode.

The alternative to that maelstrom appeared to be the discourse of pandemic difference found in Baudelaire's "Le Cygne" and Rimbaud's "Mauvais sang," in which difference and otherness, expressed as unfulfilled desire, were recognized as the very foundation of identity. In this world the closer one comes to identification and closure with the self, the more one is contaminated by the outside. Since an identity must be defined in terms other than pure repetition of itself (A is A is A), alterity gets its foot in the door as that which constitutes the identity (A is X, Y, and Z). If you are French,

246

you are German and may as well be black African. This is analogous temporally to the allegorical process of giving meaning to the present by showing
the present to be empty, showing what identity is by pointing out difference.
The allegorical mode recounts difference while, in the meantime, it explodes
the "academic" notion of identity ("one vast *unity*, monotonous and impersonal, immense like boredom and nothingness"—Baudelaire). In "Le
Cygne" and "Mauvais sang" one finds the alluring prospect of an Other
rationally recognized as such, not assimilated, erased, or crushed by the arrival
of that "force of opposite nature." Such a discourse, in which light and
presence seem to engage in an equal exchange with darkness and absence,
is of course itself a dream, a desire for presence and light. It is essential to
recall that "Mauvais sang" ends not with allegory but with *irony* ("La vie
française, le sentier de l'honneur!"), just as, in "Le Cygne," nothing transcends the "*ironic* sky, cruelly blue": the moment of "pure" allegory is the
moment when ("with the whites disembarking") one falls into nothingness.

It would thus be a mistake—a noble mistake—to see hope for social justice
in a sympathetic depiction of the black such as "Le Cygne." The discourse
that will tell you what you want to hear—that equality and difference are
compatible—is a discourse that will tell you that you cannot have it.

The desire (which is everyone's in the age of liberalism) for an Other whose
otherness is neither denigrated nor expunged seems to meet relatively few
exponents in French literature,[1] at least as compared with literature in Spanish;[2]
historical factors certainly help account for this. By the mere continuation of
Spanish culture in the New World, and through the instance of universities
and the church, possibilities of assimilation were bound to develop, even into
a discourse of coexistence between black and white. The French involvement
in the Americas ended in Haiti, for example, with "black over white" as an
image that horrified "the true land of glory." Later, the colonial experience
would inaugurate the process of assimilation, but only on the basis of an
unmediated difference and a forced identity, when Africa became "French
Africa" and its people "French Africans."

Identity and difference are thus related to the self-styled advent of linear time,
of European progress in Africa. The time before was a "pure anteriority"

---

1. Léon-François Hoffmann finds in Xavier Saintine, author of "La Vengeance" (1825), "un
des rares, très rares Blancs qui n'ait pas donné de [l'Afrique] une image péjorative ou édulcorée.
Il y avait un certain risque à choisir pour protagonistes des Noirs que la culture occidentale n'a
pas dénaturés, n'a même pas influencés. N'en avoir fait ni des monstres, ni des saints ni des
paillasses mais des êtres complexes et dignes est une preuve d'originalité et de largeur d'esprit"
(*Le Nègre romantique* [Paris: Payot, 1973], p. 175).
2. See Magnus Mörner, "The History of Race Relations in Latin America," *Latin American
Research Review* 1, no. 3 (Summer, 1966): 17–44; H. Hoetink, *The Two Variants in Caribbean
Race Relations* (London: Oxford University Press, 1967).

and cannot be described; it was "vast and monotonous" in its stagnation; it was different from our time, therefore it did not exist. A novel such as *Heart of Darkness* recounts the confrontation between time and its Other as the penetration of a world whose people had no "clear idea of time," no "inherited experience to teach them." It is in this fashion that Africa fills a need in the European novel, a need for something outside itself on which to form its discourse, a need for raw materials to be fashioned and reworked. By traveling back to the point before there was time, where word and thing were one, the novel grounds itself in a world of Things. The desire is to prove the reality of that world, to put one's finger directly on it and bring back "the notes of an educated and exact voyager," who has been nowhere.

Reaching backward in time thus poses the other principal question of Africanist discourse: that of fullness and emptiness, presence and absence, desire and denial. If desire for presence is desire itself, how can a discourse so persistently seek "the void and the black and the naked"? Perhaps this is possible to the extent that the emptiness is "full": "as in the clouds," according to de Brosses, you can see anything you wish. The blank slate of Africa, with no past or future, can be made to fulfill the desires of your own present. From there it is only one step to the fulfillment of your nightmares as well: Villault's Africans crying welcome are merely the counterparts of Sade's monstrous cannibals. Ambivalence is the controlling force of Africanist discourse.

Favorable descriptions of Africa can be as detached from reality as negative ones: the axis between realism and fantasy does not run parallel to that of desire and loathing. Desire is the desire for realism, for the documented, reified presence of the object. The peculiarity of Africanist discourse has been the slight and constant tease between what the author proposes and what he can prove; for, as often as not, what he wishes to describe is the presence of an absence. Then what becomes of the notion of desire if one "wants nothing"? Wanting something, Freud tells us, ultimately makes it appear as real before the senses,[3] but we have seen that wanting *nothing* can do the same. Nothing then becomes a thing, and "no one" becomes a person, both taking shape and lending themselves to the process of description. The positively valorized instances of Africanist discourse could thus be defined as *wishing for something one cannot have* (Leavis on Conrad: "the emotional insistence on the presence of what he can't produce"). The negative versions would be

---

3. *The Interpretation of Dreams* (New York: Avon Books, 1965), p. 605: "Nothing prevents us from assuming that there was a primitive state of the psychical apparatus in which this path [between the psychic impulse and the mnemic image of a past perception] was actually traversed, that is, in which wishing ended in hallucination."

having something one does not wish for—provided that having is understood as that dubious end-product of a wish, hallucination.

But the difference between favorable and unfavorable Africanist utterances is not one that really advances our understanding, for nothing permits us to distinguish desire from loathing, dream from nightmare: did Sade "want" those "cruel truths"? Which particular meaning did Louis XIV intend when he spoke to Aniaba? Is the figure of the Negro in Rimbaud *bête* or *innocent?* Reading must take place in the ambivalent space between the two, in the midst of an ambivalent irony: it is there that the Africanist author tries to produce his object. But not being sure what he wants, he will neither produce its presence nor prove its absence. The author's inability to describe an object congruent with his language is thus related to his ambivalence: for his nightmare is "the nightmare of his choice."

Bibliography

In an effort to simplify, I have divided the bibliography into sections corresponding to the divisions of the text. The first section contains works of general, theoretical, or historical relevance to the study as a whole; the second section corresponds to the various topics in Part One; the remaining sections deal with Baudelaire, Rimbaud, etc., respectively. For more complete information the reader should refer to the bibliographies of Léon-François Hoffmann's *Le Nègre romantique* and Roger Mercier's *L'Afrique noire dans la littérature française.*

General Works

Astier-Loutfi, Martine. *Littérature et colonialisme: L'expansion coloniale vue dans la littérature romanesque française, 1871–1914.* Paris: Mouton, 1971.

Atkinson, Geoffrey. *Les Relations de voyage du XVIIe siècle et l'évolution des idées.* Paris: Champion, 1927.

Barthes, Roland. "Grammaire africaine." In *Mythologies.* Paris: Seuil, 1957.

Barzun, Jacques. *The French Race: Theories of Its Origin and Their Social and Political Implications.* New York: Columbia University Press, 1932.

Baudet, Henri. *Paradise on Earth: Some Thoughts on European Images of Non-European Man.* Trans. E. Wentholt. Westport, CT: Greenwood Press, 1965.

Blanchot, Maurice. *L'Espace littéraire.* Paris: Gallimard, 1955.

Bugner, Ladislas, ed. *L'Image du noir dans l'art occidental.* 3 vols. Paris: Bibliothèque des arts, 1979.

Cohen, William B. *The French Encounter with Africans: White Response to Blacks, 1530–1880.* Bloomington: Indiana University Press, 1980.

Cole, Charles Woolsey, *French Mercantilism, 1683–1700.* New York: Columbia University Press, 1943.

Coquery-Vidrovitch, Catherine. *La Découverte de l'Afrique.* Paris: René Julliard, 1965.

Curtin, Philip D. *The Image of Africa: British Ideas and Action, 1780–1850.* Madison: University of Wisconisn Press, 1964.

Davidson, Basil. *A History of West Africa to the Nineteenth Century.* New York: Doubleday, 1966.

Davis, David Brion. *The Problem of Slavery in the Age of Revolution.* Ithaca: Cornell University Press, 1975.

———. *The Problem of Slavery in Western Culture.* Ithaca: Cornell University Press, 1966.

De Man, Paul. *Allegories of Reading.* New Haven: Yale University Press, 1979.

Derrida, Jacques. *La Voix et le phénomène.* Paris: Presses Universitaires de France, 1967.

Devyver, André. *Le Sang épuré: La Naissance du sentiment et de l'idée de race dans la noblesse française (1560—1720)*. Brussels: Université de Bruxelles, 1973.

Diamond, Stanley. *In Search of the Primitive: A Critique of Civilization*. New Brunswick, NJ: Rutgers University Press, 1974.

Duchet, Michèle. *Anthropologie et Histoire au siècle des lumières*. Paris: Flammarion, 1977.

Dudley, Edward, ed. *The Wild Man Within: An Image in Western Thought*. Pittsburgh: University of Pittsburgh Press, 1972.

Encyclopédie, ou dictionnaire raisonné des sciences, des arts et des métiers par une société de gens de lettres, mis en ordre et publié par M. Diderot. Geneva: Chez Jean-Léonard Pellet, 1778.

Fanon, Frantz. *Black Skin, White Masks*. Trans. C. L. Markmann. New York: Grove Press, 1967.

Fanoudh-Siefer, Léon. *Le Mythe du nègre et de l'Afrique noire dans la littérature française de 1800 à la deuxième guerre mondiale*. Paris: Gallimard, 1969.

Foucault, Michel. *L'Archéologie du savoir*. Paris: Gallimard, 1969.

———. "Préface à la transgression." *Critique* 19, nos. 195-96 (August–September, 1963).

———. *Histoire de la sexualité: La Volonté de savoir*. Paris: Gallimard, 1976.

Fredrickson, George M. *The Black Image in the White Mind: The Debate, 1817–1914*. New York: Harper & Row, 1971.

Freud, Sigmund. *The Interpretation of Dreams*. Trans. James Strachey. New York: Avon Books, 1965.

Gates, Henry Louis. "The History and Theory of Afro-American Literary Criticism, 1773–1831: The Arts, Aesthetic Theory and the Nature of the African." Diss., University of Cambridge, 1978.

Gay, Jean. *Bibliographie des ouvrages relatifs à l'Afrique et à l'Arabie*. San Remo, Italy: J. Gay & fils, 1875.

Gilman, Sander. *On Blackness without Blacks: Essays on the Image of the Black in Germany*. Boston: G. K. Hall, 1982.

Gobineau, Joseph Arthur de. *Essai sur l'inégalité des races humaines*. (1853–55) Paris: Pierre Belfond, 1967.

Godefroy, Frédéric. *Dictionnaire de l'Ancienne langue française et de tous ses dialectes du IXe au XVe siècle*. Paris: Librairie des Sciences et des Arts, 1937.

Grand Larousse de la langue française en six volumes. Paris: Larousse, 1971.

Heidegger, Martin. *Identity and Difference*. Trans. Joan Stambaugh. New York: Harper & Row, 1969.

Herskovits, Melville J. *The Myth of the Negro Past*. Boston: Beacon Press, 1958.

Hoffmann, Léon-François. *Le Nègre romantique: Personnage littéraire et obsession collective*. Paris: Payot, 1973.

Hogg, Peter C. *The African Slave Trade and Its Suppression*. London: Frank Cass, 1973.

Jahn, Jahneinz. *Muntu: An Outline of the New African Culture*. New York: Grove Press, 1961.

Jameson, Fredric. *The Political Unconscious: Narrative as a Socially Symbolic Act*. Ithaca: Cornell University Press, 1981.

Johnson, Lemuel. *The Devil, The Gargoyle, and the Buffoon: The Negro as Metaphor in Western Literature*. Port Washington, NY: Kennikat Press, 1969.

Jones, Eldred. *Othello's Countrymen*. Oxford: Oxford University Press, 1965.

Jordan, Winthrop. *White Over Black: American Attitudes toward the Negro, 1550–1812*. New York: Norton, 1968.

Jourda, Pierre. *L'Exotisme dans la littérature française depuis Chateaubriand*. Paris: Boivin, 1938.

Jurt, Joseph. "L'Image de l'Afrique et des africains dans la littérature française: Un Etat présent des recherches." *Oeuvres et critiques* 3, no. 3 (Autumn, 1979): 219–28.

Kiernan, V. G. *The Lords of the Human Kind: Black Man, Yellow Man, and White Man in an Age of Empire*. Boston: Little, Brown, 1969.

Larousse, Pierre. *Grand Dictionnaire universel du XIXᵉ siècle*. Paris: Administration du Grand Dictionnaire universel, 1866–78.

Lebel, A. Roland. *L'Afrique occidentale dans la littérature française (depuis 1870)*. Paris: Emile Larose, 1925.

———. *Histoire de la littérature coloniale en France*. Paris: Larose, 1931.

Lévi-Strauss, Claude. *La Pensée sauvage*. Paris: Plon, 1962.

Littré, Emile. *Dictionnaire de la langue française*. Paris: Gallimard, 1962.

Lokke, Carl-Ludwig. *France and the Colonial Question (1763–1801): A Study of Contemporary French Opinion*. New York: Columbia University Press, 1932.

Lucas, Edith E. *La Littérature anti-esclavagiste au dix-neuvième siècle: Etude sur Mme Beecher Stowe et son influence en France*. Paris: De Boccard, 1930.

Lukács, Georg. *The Theory of the Novel*. Trans. Anna Bostock. London: Merlin Press, 1971.

Mannoni, Octave. *Prospero and Caliban: The Psychology of Colonization*. Trans. P. Powerland. New York: Praeger, 1956.

Marx, Karl. *Capital: A Critique of Political Economy*. New York: International Publishers, 1970.

McCloy, Shelby T. *The Negro in France*. Lexington: University of Kentucky Press, 1961.

———. "Negroes and Mulattoes in Eighteenth-Century France." *Journal of Negro History* 30 (1945): 276–92.

Memmi, Albert. *The Colonizer and the Colonized*. Trans. Howard Greenfeld. Boston: Beacon, 1985.

Mercier, Roger. *L'Afrique noire dans la littérature française: Les premières images (XVIIᵉ et XVIIIᵉ siècles)*. Dakar: Université de Dakar, 1962.

———. "Les Débuts de l'exotisme africain en France." *Revue de littérature comparée* 36 (1962): 191–209.

———. "L'Image de l'autre et l'image de soi-même dans le discours ethnologique du XVIIIᵉ siècle." *Studies on Voltaire and the Eighteenth Century* 154 (1976): 1417–35.

Montagu, Ashley. *The Concept of the Primitive*. New York: Free Press, 1968.

New Encyclopedia Britannica. Chicago: Encyclopedia Britannica, 1971.

Peytraud, Lucien. *L'Esclavage aux Antilles françaises avant 1789, D'après les documents inédits des Archives coloniales*. Pointe-à-Pitre: E. Desormeaux, 1973.

Poliakov, Léon. *Le Mythe aryen: Essai sur les sources du racisme et des nationalismes.* Paris: Calmann-Lévy, 1971.

Randles, W. G. L. *L'Image du Sud-Est africain dans la littérature européenne au XVIᵉ siècle.* Lisbon: Centro de Estudos Historicos Ultramarinos, 1959.

Robert, Paul. *Dictionnaire alphabétique et analogique de la langue française.* Paris: PUF, 1953.

Said, Edward. *Orientalism.* New York: Random House, 1979.

Sartre, Jean-Paul. "Orphée noir." In *Anthologie de la nouvelle poésie nègre et malgache.* Edited by Léopold Sédar Senghor. Paris: PUF, 1948.

Scharfman, Ronnie. "*Engagement* and the Language of the Subject in the Poetry of Césaire." Ph.D. diss., Yale University 1979.

Seeber, Edward Derbyshire. *Anti-Slavery Opinion in France in the Second Half of the Eighteenth Century.* Baltimore: Johns Hopkins University Press, 1939.

Sypher, Wylie. *Guinea's Captive Kings: British Anti-Slavery Literature of the Eighteenth Century.* New York: Octagon Books, 1969.

Todorov, Tzvetan. *La Conquête de l'Amérique.* Paris: Seuil, 1982.

Trésor de la langue francaise. Edited by Paul Imbs. Paris: Editions du Centre National de la recherche scientifique, 1973.

Watt, Ian. *The Rise of the Novel.* Berkeley: University of California Press, 1960.

Zemp, Ada Martinkus. *Le Blanc et le Noir: Essai d'une description de la vision du Noir par le Blanc dans la littérature française de l'entre-deux-guerres.* Paris: Nizet, 1975.

Chapter 1. "Telle figure que l'on veut"

Albertus Magnus. "De Natura Locorum." In *Opera Omnia.* Aschendorff, Germany: Monateserii Westfalorum, 1980.

Alfonce de Sainctongeois, Jean. *Voyages auentureux.* Poitiers: n.p., 1559.

Anchor Bible. Trans. Marvin Pope. Garden City, NY: Doubleday, 1977.

Anthiaume, Abbé A. *Cartes maritimes, constructions navales, voyages de découverte.* Paris: Dumont, 1916.

Archives Départementales de la Gironde, Bibliothèque Municipale de Bordeaux. MS. 828/65 (1741). "Quelle est la cause phisique de la couleur des Nègres, de la qualité de leurs cheveux, et de la dégéneration de l'une et de l'autre?"

Augustine. *The City of God.* Trans. E. M. Sanford and W. McA. Green. London: W. Heinemann, 1965.

Avezac, Armand d'. *Notice des découvertes faites au Moyen-âge dans l'océan Atlantique antérieurement aux grandes explorations portugaises du XVᵉcle.* Paris: Fain & Thunot, 1845.

Bontier, Pierre, and Jean Leverrier. *Le Canarien: Livre de la conquête et conversion des Canaries (1402–1422) par Jean de Bethencourt.* Rouen: Meterie, 1874.

Bossuet, Jacques. *Oeuvres complètes.* Paris: Lefèvre, 1836.

Brasseur, Paule. "Le Mot 'nègre' dans les dictionnaires encyclopédiques français du XIXᵉ siècle." *Cultures et développements* 8, no. 4 (1976): 79–104.

Caillié, René. *Voyage à Tombouctou.* Preface by Jacques Berque. Paris: Maspéro, 1982.

Castelnau, Francis de. *Renseigements sur l'Afrique centrale et sur une nations de Niam-niam ou "hommes à queue" qui s'y trouverait, d'après les nègres du Soudan, esclaves à Bahia*. Paris: P. Bertrand, 1851.

————. "Sur les Niam-niam ou hommes à queues." *Bulletin de la société de géographie* 4th ser., no. 2 (1851): 25–27.

Charlevoix, Pierre-François-Xavier. *Histoire de l'isle espagnole de Saint Domingue, écrite particulièrement sur des mémoires manuscrits du Père Jean-Baptiste Le Pers, jésuite, missionaire à Saint-Domingue, et sur les pièces originales qui se conservent au Dèpot de la Marine . . . .* Paris: Guérin, 1730–31.

De Brosses, Charles. *Du Culte des dieux fétiches, ou parallèle de l'ancienne Religion de l'Egypte avec la Religion actuelle de Nigritie*. Paris: n.p., 1760.

Debrunner, Hans Werner. *Presence and Prestige: Africans in Europe: A History of Africans in Europe before 1918*. Basel: Basler Afrika Bibliographien, 1979.

Demanet, Abbé. *Nouvelle Histoire de l'Afrique françoise*. Paris: Chez la veuve Duchesne, 1767.

Desanges, Jean. "L'Afrique noire et le monde méditerranéen dans l'antiquité (Ethiopiens et Gréco-Romains)." *Revue française d'histoire d'outre-mer* 62 (1975): 391–414.

Dictionnaire apologétique de la foi catholique. Edited by A. d'Alès. Paris: G. Beauchesne, 1925.

Diodorus Siculus. *Works*. Trans. C. H. Oldfather. Loeb Classical Library. Cambridge: Harvard University Press, 1935.

Dubois-Fontanelle, Jean. *Anecdotes africaines, depuis l'origine ou la découverte des royaumes qui composent l'Afrique jusqu'à nos jours*. Paris: Vincent, 1775.

Egli, J. J. *Nomina geographica*. Leipzig: Brandstetter, 1892.

Fall, Yoro K. *L'Afrique à la naissance de la cartographie moderne: les cartes majorquines: XIVᵉ–XVᵉ siècles*. Paris: Karthala, 1982.

Forbath, Peter. *The River Congo*. New York: Harper & Row, 1977.

Giffre de Rechac, Jean de. *Les Estranges evenemens du voyage de son Altesse le serenissime Prince Zaga-Christ d'Ethiopie, du grand empire des Abyssins*. Paris: Sevestre, 1635.

Grant, Douglas. *The Fortunate Slave: An Illustration of African Slavery in the Early Eighteenth Century*. London: Oxford University Press, 1968.

Hamilton, Paul. "Visitors to Mecca." In *Exploring Africa and Asia*. New York: Doubleday, 1973.

Herodotus. *The History*. Trans. A. D. Godley. Loeb Classical Library. London: Heinemann, 1921.

Histoire de Louis Aniaba, roi d'Essenie en Afrique sur la côte de Guinée. Paris: Aux Dépens de la Société, 1740.

Homer. *The Iliad*. Trans. Richmond Lattimore. Chicago: University of Chicago Press, 1951.

————. *The Odyssey*. Trans. S. H. Butcher and A. Lang. New York: Modern Library, 1935.

————. *The Odyssey*. Trans. George Chapman. Princeton: Princeton University Press, 1967.

————. *The Odyssey*. Trans. Robert Fitzgerald. New York: Doubleday, 1963.

————. *The Odyssey*. Trans. Richmond Lattimore. Harper Colophon edition. New York: Harper & Row, 1975.

————. *The Odyssey*. Trans. A. T. Murray. London: Heinemann, 1930.

Ibn Battuta. *Textes et documents relatifs à l'histoire de l'Afrique*. Trans. R. Mauny et al. Dakar: Université de Dakar, 1966.

Jantzen, John M., and Wyatt MacGaffey. *Anthology of Kongo Religion: Primary Texts from Lower Zaïre* Lawrence: University of Kansas Press, 1974.

Jeffreys, M. D. W. "Arab Knowledge of the Niger's Course." *Africa* 25, no. 1 (1955): 84–90.

Jerome. *The Homilies of Saint Jerome*. Trans. Marie Liguori Ewald. Washington, D.C.: Catholic University of America Press, 1964.

————. *Sancti Hieronymi Presbyteri*. Edited by D. Germanus Morim. Maredsoli: J. Parker, 1895.

Julien, Charles A. *Les Voyages de découverte et les premiers établissements français*. Paris: PUF, 1948.

Kimble, C. H. T. *Geography in the Middle Ages*. London: Methuen, 1938.

Labat, Abbé Jean-Baptiste. *Nouvelle relation de l'Afrique occidentale*. Paris: Th. Le Gras, 1728.

————. *Voyage du Chevalier des Marchais en Guinée, isles voisines et à Cayenne, fait en 1725, 1726, & 1727 . . . .* Paris: Chez Saugrain, 1730.

La Roncière, Charles de. *La Découverte de l'Afrique au Moyen Age: Cartographes et explorateurs*. Cairo: Société Royale de Géographie d'Egypte, 1925.

Le Cat, Claude-Nicolas. *Traité de la couleur de la peau humaine en général, de celles des nègres, en particulier, et de la métamorphose d'une de ces couleurs en l'autre, soit de naissance, soit accidentellement*. Amsterdam: n.p., 1765.

Leo Africanus. *Description de l'Afrique*. Trans. A. Epaulard. Paris: Librairie d'Amérique et d'Orient, 1956.

Long, Edward. *The History of Jamaica, or general survey of the ancient and modern state of that island: with reflections on its situation, settlements, inhabitants, climate, products, commerce, laws and government*. London: T. Lowndes, 1774.

Loyer, Godefroy. *Relation du voyage du royaume d'Issyny, côte d'or, païs de Guinée en Afrique*. Paris: Arnoul Seneuze and Jean-Raoul Morel, 1714. [This work is reproduced in its entirety in Paul Roussier, *L'Etablissement d'Issiny,* and references to it in this study are to the Roussier volume.]

Margry, Pierre. *Les Navigations françaises et la révolution maritime du XIVe au XVIe siècle*. Paris: Librairie Tross, 1867.

Mathorez, J. *Les Etrangers en France sous l'Ancien Régime*. Paris: Champion, 1919.

Mauny, Raymond. "Les prétendues navigations dieppoises à la côte occidentale d' Afrique au XIVe siècle." *Bulletin de l'Institut français d'Afrique noire* 12 (1950): 122–34.

Meek, C. K. "The Niger and the Classics: History of a Name." *Journal of African History* 1, no. 1 (1960): 1–17.

Monod, Théodore. "Un vieux problème: Les Navigations dieppoises sur la côte occidentale d'Afrique au XIVe siècle." *Bulletin de l'Institut français d'Afrique noire* ser. B 25, no. 2 (1963): 147–50.

New American Cyclopedia. New York: Appleton, 1858.

Pigault-Lebrun, Charles-Antoine. *Oeuvres complètes*. Paris: J. N. Barba, 1822.

Pintard, René. *Le Libertinage érudit dans la première moitié du XVIIe siècle*. Paris: Boivin, 1943.

Pliny the Younger. *The Natural History*. Trans. H. Rackham. Loeb Classical Library. Cambridge: Harvard University Press, 1938.

Pruneau de Pommegorge, Antoine Edmé. *Description de la Nigritie*. Amsterdam: Maradan, 1789.

Ptolemy. *Geographia*. Edited by Sebastian Münster (1540). Amsterdam: Theatrum Orbis Terrarum, 1966.

Raynal, Abbé Guillaume-Thomas-François. *Histoire philosophique et politique de l'établissement et du commerce des Européens dans les deux Indes*. (1770) 10 vols. Paris: Amable Costes, 1820.

Roger, F. Eugène. *La Terre sainte, ou description topographique . . . et une Relation véritable de Zaga-Christ Prince d'Ethiopie . . . .* Paris: Chez A. Bertier, 1664.

Roussier, Paul. *L'Etablissement d'Issiny*. Paris: Larose, 1935.

Sainville, Leonard. *Histoire du Sénégal depuis l'arrivée des Européens*. Saint-Louis du Sénégal: CRDS-Sénégal, 1972.

Santarem, Vicomte de. *Recherches sur la priorité de la découverte des pays situés sur la côte occidentale d'Afrique*. Paris: Dondey-Dupré, 1842.

Simpson, David. *Fetishism and Imagination: Dickens, Melville, Conrad*. Baltimore: Johns Hopkins University Press, 1982.

Snowden, Frank. *Blacks in Antiquity: Ethiopians in the Greco-Roman Experience*. Cambridge: Belknap Press of Harvard University, 1970.

Solinus, Caius Julius. *The Excellent and Pleasant Worke*. Trans. Arthur Golding. London: Thomas Hacket, 1587.

Taylor, Isaac. *Words and Places, or, Etymological Illustrations of History, Ethnology, and Geography*. London: Macmillan, 1864.

Thévet, André. *Cosmographie universelle*. Paris: Guillaume Chaudière, 1575.

————. *Les Singularitez de la France antarctique*. Edited by Paul Gaffarel. Paris: Maisonneuve, 1878.

Tooley, R. V. *History of Cartography*. London: Thames & Hudson, 1968.

Tremearne, A. J. N. *The Tailed Head-Hunters of Nigeria*. London: Seeley, Service, 1912.

Villault de Bellefond, Nicolas. *Relation des costes d'Afrique, appellées Guinée, avec des remarques historiques sur ces costes*. Paris: Denys Thierry, 1669. [Reproduced in Yusuf Kamal, *Monumenta cartographica*.]

Yusuf Kamal, Prince. *Monumenta Cartographica Africae et Aegypti*. Cairo: n.p., 1927–37.

Zahan, Dominique. *Religion, spiritualité et pensées africaines*. Paris: Payot, 1970.

Zurara, Gomes Eanes de. *The Chronicle of the Discovery and Conquest of Guinea*. Trans. B. Miall. London: Allen & Unwin, 1936.

Chapter 2. Baudelaire

Baudelaire, Charles. *Oeuvres complètes*. Bibliothèque de la Pléiade. Vol. 1. Edited by C. Pichois. Paris: Gallimard, 1975.

————. *Curiosités esthétiques: L'Art romantique*. Paris: Garnier Frères, 1962.

————. *Les Fleurs du mal*. Edited by Jacques Crépet and Georges Blin. Paris: José Corti, 1942.

Secondary Sources

Ahearn, Edward. "Black Woman, White Poet: Exile and Exploitation in Baudelaire's Jeanne Duval Poems." *French Review* 51 (December 1977): 212–20.

Apollinaire, Guillaume. *Sculptures d'Afrique, d'Amérique, d'Océanie.* New York: Hacker Art Books, 1972.

Arrom, José Juan. *Certidumbre de America.* Madrid: Gredos, 1971.

Blachère, J. C. "Apollinaire et l'antériorité de l'art nègre." *Afrique littéraire et artistique* 43 (1977): 64–70.

Bodin, Jean. *The Six Bookes of a Commonweale.* Edited by K. D. MacCrae. Cambridge: Harvard University Press, 1962.

Brombert, Victor. "Le Cygne de Baudelaire: Douleur, Souvenir, Travail." *Etudes baudelairiennes* 3 (1973): 254–61.

Clark, Beatrice Smith. "Elements of Black Exoticism in the 'Jeanne Duval' Poems of *Les Fleurs du mal.*" *CLA Journal* 14, no. 1 (September 1970): 62–74.

Crépet, Jacques. "Charles Baudelaire et Jeanne Duval." *La Plume* 10 (April 15, 1898): 242–44.

Debbasch, Yvan. "Poésie et traite: L'Opinion française sur le commerce négrier au début du XIXᵉ siècle." *Revue française d'histoire d'outre-mer* 48 (1961): 311–52.

Deguy, Michel. "Le Corps de Jeanne (Remarques sur le corps poétique des *Fleurs du mal*)." *Poétique* 3 (1970): 334–47.

Delille, Jacques. *Oeuvres complètes.* Paris: Furne, 1833.

De Man, Paul. "The Rhetoric of Temporality." Pp. 173–209 in *On Interpretation,* edited by Charles S. Singleton. Baltimore: Johns Hopkins University Press, 1969.

Duchet, Michèle, "Du Noir au blanc ou la cinquième génération." Pp. 177–90 in *Le Couple interdit: entretiens sur le racisme,* edited by Léon Poliakov. Paris: Mouton, 1980.

Eichtal, Gustave, and Ismayl Urbain. *Lettres sur la race noire et la race blanche.* Paris: Paulin, 1839.

Eigeldinger, M. "La symbolique solaire dans la poésie de Baudelaire." *Revue d'histoire littéraire de la France* 67, no. 2 (April–June, 1967): 357–74.

Freud, Sigmund. "The Sexual Aberrations." In *Three Essays on Sexuality.* Trans. James Strachey. New York: Basic Books, 1962.

Freycinet, Madame Rose de Saulces de. *Journal (1817–1820).* Paris: Société d'Editions géographiques, maritimes et coloniales, 1927.

Hollander, John. *The Figure of Echo.* Berkeley: University of California Press, 1981.

Humphries, Jefferson. "Haunted Words, or Deconstruction Echoed," *Diacritics* 13, no. 2 (Summer, 1983): 29–38.

Isambert, François-André, *Recueil général des anciennes lois de France.* Paris: Plon, n.d.

Johnson, Barbara. *Défigurations du langage poétique: La seconde révolution baudelairienne.* Paris: Flammarion, 1979.

Levaillant, François, *Voyage dans l'intérieur de l'Afrique, par le cap de Bonne-espérance dans les années 1780–1785.* 2 vols. Paris: Desray, 1791.

McClaren, J. C. "The Imagery of Light and Darkness in *Les Fleurs du mal.*" *Nineteenth-Century French Studies* 7 (1978–79): 32–49.

Nelson, Lowry. "Baudelaire and Virgil: A Reading of 'Le Cygne.'" *Comparative Literature* 13, no. 4 (1961): 332–45.

Nnadi, Joseph E. *Visions de l'Afrique dans l'oeuvre de Baudelaire.* Yaoudé: Editions CLE, 1980.

Pasinetti, P. M. "The 'Jeanne Duval' Poems in *Les Fleurs du mal.*" Pp. 86–93 in *Baudelaire, A Collection of Critical Essays,* edited by Henri Peyre. Englewood Cliffs, NJ: Prentice-Hall, 1962.

Portal, Frédéric. *Des Couleurs symboliques dans l'antiquité, le moyen-âge et les temps modernes.* Paris: Niclaus, 1938.

Receuil général des anciennes lois de France. Edited by François-André Isambert. Paris: Plon, n.d.

Virgil. *The Aeneid of Virgil.* Edited by R. D. Williams. Basingstoke and London: Macmillan, 1972.

———. *L'Enéide.* French trans. by André Bellessort. Paris: Société d'Editions Les Belles Lettres, 1962.

———. *L'Enéide.* French trans. by Jacques Delille. Paris: Chez Giguet et Michaud, 1804.

———. *Le Troisième livre de l'Enéide.* French trans. by A. Desportes. Paris: Hachette, 1862.

Chapter 3. Rimbaud

Rimbaud, Arthur. *Oeuvres complètes.* Bibliothèque de la Pléiade. Edited by Antoine Adam. Paris: Gallimard, 1972.

———. *Oeuvres.* Edited by S. Bernard. Paris: Garnier Frères, 1960.

———. *Les Illuminations et Une Saison en enfer.* Edited by Ernest Delahaye. Paris: Albert Messein, 1927.

Secondary Sources

Bonnefis, Philippe. "Onze notes pour fragmenter un texte de Rimbaud." *Littérature* 11 (October 1973): 46–67.

Bonnefoy, Yves. *Rimbaud par lui-même.* Paris: Seuil, 1961.

Briet, Suzanne. *Rimbaud notre prochain.* Paris: Nouvelles Editions Latines, 1956.

Brosses, Jacques. "Le Silence de Rimbaud." Pp. 206-27 in *Rimbaud.* Paris: Hachette, 1968.

Carré, Jean-Marie. *La Vie aventureuse de Jean-Arthur Rimbaud.* Paris: Plon, 1926.

———. "Un article inconnu de Rimbaud sur son voyage en Abyssinie." *Mercure de France.* New ser. 200 (November–December, 1927): 558–74.

Charles, Pierre. "Les Noirs, fils de Cham le maudit." *Nouvelle Revue théologique* 55 (1928): 721–39.

Chaulet-Achour, Christiane. "Langue française et colonialisme en Algérie: De l'abécédaire à la production littéraire." Diss., University of Paris III, 1982.

Concordance to the "Oeuvres complètes" of Arthur Rimbaud. Edited by William C. Carter and Robert F. Vines. Athens, Ohio: Ohio University Press, 1978.

Coulon, Marcel. *La Vie de Rimbaud et de son oeuvre.* Paris: Mercure de France, 1929.

———. "Les vraies lettres de Rimbaud, arabo-éthiopien." *Mercure de France,* March 15, 1930.

Courtois, Michel. "Le Mythe du nègre chez Rimbaud." *Littérature* 11 (October 1973): 85–101.

Dehérain, Henri. "La Carrière africaine d'Arthur Rimbaud." *Revue de l'histoire des colonies* 4 (1916): 419–50.

Dumas, O. "La race noire dans l'oeuvre de Jules Verne." In *Jules Verne: Colloque de Cérisy.* Paris: Union Générale d'Edition, 1979.

Eigeldinger, Marc. *Rimbaud et le mythe solaire.* Neuchâtel: La Baconnière, 1964.

Etiemble, René *Le Mythe de Rimbaud: Structure du mythe.* Paris: Gallimard, 1952.

Forbes, Duncan. *Rimbaud in Ethiopia.* Hythe, Eng.: Volturna Press, 1979.

Jalabert, Louis. "Rimbaud en Abyssinie: Aventurier, mercanti, et contrabandier." *Etudes* 76, no. 238 (January–March 1939): 165–88.

Kittang, Atle. *Discours et jeu: Essai d'analyse des textes d'Arthur Rimbaud.* Grenoble: Presses Universitaires de Grenoble, 1975.

Loepfe, Willi. *Alfred Ilg und die äthiopische Eisenbahn.* Zurich: Atlantis, 1974.

Mattuci, Mario. *Le Dernier visage de Rimbaud en Afrique d'après les documents inédits.* Paris: Marcel Didier, 1962.

Maurois, André. *A History of France.* Trans. Henry L. Binsse. N.p.: Minerva Press, 1960.

Mézeray, François Eudes de. *Abrégé chronologique ou extrait de l'histoire de France.* Paris: Chez Louis Billaine, 1668.

Ngate, Jonathan. "'Mauvais sang' de Rimbaud et *Cahier d'un retour au pays natal* de Césaire: La poésie au service de la révolution." *Cahiers césairiens* 3 (Spring, 1971): 25–32.

Rivière, Jacques. *Rimbaud.* Paris: Kra, 1930.

Ségalen, Victor. *Le Double Rimbaud.* (1906) N.p.: Fata Morgana, 1979.

Starkie, Enid. *Rimbaud en Abyssinie.* Paris: Payot, 1938.

Verne, Jules. *Five Weeks in a Balloon.* Trans. W. G. Bebbington. London: Allen & Unwin, 1958.

Chapter 4. Conrad

Conrad, Joseph. *"Heart of Darkness" and "The Secret Sharer."* New York: New American Library, 1950.

———. *Heart of Darkness.* Edited by Robert Kimbrough. New York: Norton, 1971.

———. *Heart of Darkness.* Autograph manuscript. Beinecke Rare Book Library.

———. *A Personal Record.* New York: Harper & Bros., 1912.

Secondary Sources

Brooks, Peter. "Un rapport illisible: *Coeur des ténèbres.*" *Poétique* 44 (November 1980): 472–89.

Buls, Charles. *Croquis congolais.* Brussels: G. Balat, 1899.

Chevrillon, André. Article in *La Revue de Paris,* March–April, 1899.

Commission of Enquiry. *Report of the Commission of Enquiry in the Congo Free State.* Trans. E. A. Huybers. Brussels: Hayez, 1905.

Hawkins, Hunt. "Joseph Conrad and Mark Twain on the Congo Free State." Ph.D. diss., Stanford University, 1976.

Jean-Aubry, Gérard. *Joseph Conrad in the Congo*. Boston: Little, Brown, 1926.

———. *The Sea-Dreamer: A Definitive Biography of Joseph Conrad*. Trans. Helen Sebba. Garden City, NY: Doubleday, 1957.

Karl, Frederick. *Joseph Conrad: The Three Lives*. New York: Farrar, Straus & Giroux, 1979.

Leavis, Frank Raymond. *The Great Tradition: George Eliot, Henry James, Joseph Conrad*. London: Chatto & Windus, 1948.

Morel, Edmund D. *King Leopold's Rule in Africa*. London: Heinemann, 1904.

———. *Red Rubber: The Story of the Rubber Slave Trade, Which Flourished on the Congo for Twenty Years, 1890–1910*. Manchester, Eng.: National Labour Press, 1920.

Najder, Zdzisław. *Joseph Conrad: A Chronicle*. New Brunswick, NJ: Rutgers University Press, 1983.

Said, Edward. *Joseph Conrad and the Fiction of Autobiography*. Cambridge: Harvard University Press, 1966.

Sherry, Norman. *Conrad's Western World*. Cambridge: Cambridge University Press, 1971.

Singh, Frances. "The Colonialistic Bias of *Heart of Darkness*." *Conradiana* 10, no. 1 (1978): 41–54.

Slade, Ruth. *King Leopold's Congo*. New York: Oxford University Press, 1962.

Todorov, Tzvetan. "Connaissance du vide." *Nouvelle Revue de psychanalyse* 11 (Spring, 1975): 145–54.

Vidan, Ivo. "*Heart of Darkness* in French Literature." *Cahiers d'Etudes et de recherches victoriennes et édouardiennes* 2 (1975): 167–204.

Watt, Ian. *Conrad in the Nineteenth Century*. Berkeley: University of California Press, 1979.

Chapter 5. Sade

Sade, Donatien-Alphonse-François. *Oeuvres complètes du Marquis de Sade: Edition définitive*. 15 vols. Paris: Cercle du Livre Précieux, 1962.

Secondary Sources

Bakhtine, Mikhail. *Rabelais and His World*. Trans. Hélène Iswolsky. Cambridge: M.I.T. Press, 1968.

Banier, Abbé Antoine. *Cérémonies et coutumes religieuses de tous les peuples de monde*. 7 vols. Paris: Chez Rollin fils, 1741.

Biou, Jean. "Lumières et anthropophagie." *Revue des sciences humaines* 37, no. 146 (1972): 223–33.

Blanchot, Maurice. *Lautréamont et Sade*. Paris: Minuit, 1963.

Démeunier, Jean-Nicolas. *L'Esprit des usages et coutumes des differens peuples ou Observations tirées des Voyageurs et des Historiens*. 3 vols. London: Chez Pissot, 1776.

Favre, Pierre. *Sade utopiste*. Paris: PUF, 1967.

Fink, Beatrice C. "Sade and Cannibalism." *Esprit créateur* 15, no. 4 (Winter, 1975): 403–12.

Gallop, Jane. "The Immoral Teachers." *Yale French Studies* 63 (1982): 117–28.

———. *Intersections: A Reading of Sade with Bataille, Blanchot, and Klowssowski.* Lincoln: University of Nebraska Press, 1982.

Goulemot, Jean-Marie. "Lecture politique d'*Aline et Valcour*." In *Le Marquis de Sade*. Paris: Colin, 1968.

Laborde, Alice M. *Sade romancier*. Neuchâtel: La Baconnière, 1974.

Lacombe, Roger C. *Sade et ses masques*. Paris: Payot, 1974.

Laroche, Philippe. *Petits-maîtres et roués: L'Evolution de la notion de libertinage dans le roman français du XVIIIᵉ siècle.* Québec: Presses Universitaires de Laval, 1979.

Lemay, Edna. "Naissance de l'anthropologie en France: Jean-Nicolas Démeunier et l'étude des usages et coutumes au XVIIIᵉ siècle." In *Au Siècle des lumières*. Paris-Moscou: Ecole Pratique de Hautes Etudes, 1970.

Mercier, Roger. "Sade et le thème des voyages dans *Aline et Valcour*." *Dix-Huitième Siècle* 1 (1969): 337–52.

Miller, Joseph. "Requiem for the 'Jaga.' " *Cahier d'Etudes Africaines* 13, no. 1 (1973): 121–49.

Pauw, Cornelius de. *Recherches philosophiques sur les Américains, ou Mémoires intéressans pour servir à l'histoire de l'espèce humaine.* 2 vols. Berlin: Decker, 1768–69.

Randles, W. G. L. *The Empire of Monomotapa from the Fifteenth to the Nineteenth Century.* Trans. R. S. Roberts. Gwelo, Rhodesia: Mambo Press, 1981.

Raynal, Abbé Guillaume-Thomas-François. *Histoire philosophique et politique de l'établissement et du commerce des Européens dans les deux Indes.* 10 vols. Neuchâtel and Geneva: Libraires associés, 1783.

Chapter 6. Céline

Céline, Louis-Ferdinand [Destouches]. *Oeuvres de Louis-Ferdinand Céline.* 5 vols. Edited by Jean A. Ducourneau. Paris: André Balland, 1966.

———. *Cahiers Céline 4: Lettres et premiers écrits d'Afrique, 1916–1917.* Paris: Gallimard, 1978.

Secondary Sources

Blanchot, Maurice. *L'Espace littéraire*. Paris: Gallimard, 1955.

Cahiers Céline 1: Céline et l'actualité littéraire. Edited by Jean-Pierre Dauphin and Henri Godard. Paris: Gallimard, 1976.

Day, Philip Stephen. *Le Miroir allégorique de Louis-Ferdinand Céline.* Paris: Klincksieck, 1974.

Gibaut, Francois. *Céline*. Paris: Mercure de France, 1977.

Jaloux, Edmond. Article in *Les Nouvelles littéraires*, December 10, 1932.

Lavoinne, Yves. *"Voyage au bout de la nuit" de Céline.* Paris: Hachette, 1974.

Lévi-Strauss, Claude. Article in *L'Etudiant socialiste*, January, 1933.

Mitterand, Henri. "Le Discours colonial dans *Le Voyage au bout de la nuit*." *La Pensée* 184 (December 1975): 80–88.

Morand, Jacqueline. *Les Idées politiques de Louis-Ferdinand Céline*. Paris: R. Pichon et R. Durand-Auzias, 1972.

Chapter 7. Yambo Ouologuem

Ouologuem, Yambo. *Le Devoir de violence*. Paris: Seuil, 1968.
———. "Le Devoir de violence." *Figaro littéraire*, June 10, 1972.
———. *Lettre à la France nègre*. Paris: Edmond Nalis, 1968.
———. *Les Mille et une bibles du sexe*. Paris: Editions du Dauphin, 1969.

Secondary Sources

Ananou, David. *Le Fils du fétiche*. Paris: Nouvelles Editions Latines, 1955.
Benot, Yves. "*Le Devoir de violence* est-il un chef d'oeuvre ou une mystification?" *La Pensée* 149 (January–February, 1970): 127–31.
Bu-Buakei, Jabbi. "Influence and Originality in African Writing." *African Literature Today* 10 (1979): 106–23.
Decraene, Philippe. "Un Nègre à part entière." *Le Monde,* October 12, 1968.
Elaho, Raymond O. "Le Devoir d'amour dans le devoir de violence de Yambo Ouologuem." *L'Afrique littéraire et artistique* 56 (1979): 65-69.
Erickson, John. *Nommo: African Fiction in French South of the Sahara*. York, SC: French Literature Publications, 1979.
Françon, André. *La Propriété littéraire et artistique*. Paris: PUF, 1970.
Galey, Mattieu. "Un grand roman africain." *Le Monde,* October 12, 1968.
Greene, Graham. *It's a Battlefield*. New York: Viking, 1934.
Kane, Mohamadou. "Roman africain et traditions." Diss., University of Lille, 1978.
———. "Sur les 'formes traditionnelles' du roman africain." *Revue de littérature comparée* 3–4 (July-December, 1974): 536–68.
Kuehl, Linda. "Yambo Ouologuem on Violence, Truth, and Black History." *Commonweal* June 11, 1971, pp. 311–14.
K. W. "In Defence of Yambo Ouologuem." *West Africa,* July 21, 1972.
Mbelolo ya Mpiku, J. "From One Mystification to Another: 'Négritude' and 'Négraille' in *Le Devoir de violence*." *Review of National Literatures* 2, no. 2 (Fall, 1971): 124–47.
Nwoga, Donatus I. "Plagiarism and Authentic Creativity in West Africa." *Research in African Literature* 6, no. 1 (1975): 32–39.
Olney, James. *Tell Me Africa: An Approach to African Literature*. Princeton: Princeton University Press, 1973.
Rutimirwa, Alec. "A Case of Plagiarism." *Transition* 42 (1973): 8–9.
Schwartz-Bart, André. *Le Dernier des justes*. Paris: Seuil, 1959.
Sellin, Eric. "Ouologuem's Blueprint for *Le Devoir de violence*." *Research in African Literature* 2, no. 2 (1971): 117–20.
———. "The Unknown Voice of Yambo Ouologuem." *Yale French Studies* 53 (1976): 151–57.
"Something *New* Out of Africa?" *Times Literary Supplement* [London], May 5, 1972, p. 525.

Soyinka, Wole. *Myth, Literature and the African World*. Cambridge: Cambridge University Press, 1976.

Wolitz, Seth. ''L'Art du plagiat, ou une brève défense de Ouologuem.'' *Research in African Literature* 4, no. 1 (Spring, 1973): 130–34.

INDEX